ISBN: 9781314450408

Published by:
HardPress Publishing
8345 NW 66TH ST #2561
MIAMI FL 33166-2626

Email: info@hardpress.net
Web: http://www.hardpress.net

GIFT OF

Class of 1900.

SIGILLVM · VNIVERSITATIS · CALIFORNIENSIS

LVX

FIAT

MDCCCLXVIII

EX LIBRIS

Port Resolution, Tana

The Skipper, "After Suva"

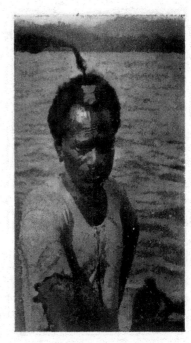

The Puzzled Monkey-Brow

Jack and Charmian London

THE
LOG OF THE SNARK

BY

CHARMIAN KITTREDGE LONDON

New York
THE MACMILLAN COMPANY
1915

To
MY HUSBAND
who made possible these happiest and most
wonderful pages of my life.

LIST OF ILLUSTRATIONS

LIST OF ILLUSTRATIONS

THE BEGINNING

It was all due to Captain Joshua Slocum and his *Spray*, plus our own wayward tendencies. We read him aloud to the 1905 camp children at Wake Robin Lodge, in the Valley of the Moon, as we sat in the hot sun resting between water fights and games of tag in the deep swimming pool. *Sailing Alone Around the World* was the name of the book, and when Jack closed the cover on the last chapter, there was a new idea looking out of his eyes. Joshua Slocum did it all alone, in a thirty-seven-foot sloop. Why could not we do it, in a somewhat larger boat, with a little more sociable crew? Jack and I loved the water, and a long voyage was our dream. He and Roscoe fell at once to discussing the scheme, the rest of us listening fascinated.

This was a few months before we were married. "Say we start five years from now," figured Jack, who always seems to be making plans for a tangible eternity. "We'll build our house on the ranch and get the place started with orchard and vines and livestock, at the same time going ahead with boat-drawings and building a yacht to suit. Five years will not be too much time."

Then, privily, he asked what I thought of it. Too good to be true, was what I thought; but why wait so long? We'd never be younger than we were, and, besides, what was the good of putting up a home and leaving it for seven years?—seven years being the time roughly calculated to carry out our far-reaching plan. I won the day.

And the boat. She should be ketch-rigged, like the English fishing boats on the Dogger Bank. We had never seen a ketch, but knew that for our purpose it combined the virtues of both schooner and yawl. There should be six feet of head-room, under flush decks unbroken save by companionway, skylights, and hatches. The roomy cockpit should be sunk deep beneath the deck, high-railed and self-bailing. There should be no hold, all space being occupied by accoutrement, and engines—one a seventy horse-power auxiliary, and one five horse-power to spin out electric lights and fans. Forty-five feet should be her water-line, with a length over all of fifty-seven feet. She should draw six feet, with no inside ballast, but with fifty tons of iron on the keel. There should be used only the strongest and best materials of every kind—a solid, serviceable deep-sea craft, the strongest of her size ever constructed.

But we counted without the Great Earthquake of April 18, 1906. The vessel was already begun, and the iron keel was actually to have been cast the night of April 18. Following that date, what we did not suffer from damage to other property, was inflicted by post-earthquake conditions which made our shipbuilding triply expensive and incomprehensibly protracted. Everybody and everything went mad; and it was nearly a year after the delayed laying of her doughty keel that the yacht, unfinished, unclean, her seventy horse-power engine a heap of scrap-iron from the ignorant tinkering that had been done to it, sailed from California for Hawaii, manned, or unmanned, by a more or less discouraged crew, whose original adventurous spirits and efficiency had been sorely dampened by the weary postponement of departure dates. The final one was set behind an extra week-end by a ship chandler who libelled the yacht because he was afraid he would not get his last bill paid, the while Jack was settling accounts right and left aboard the boat, one pocket full of gold and silver, the other containing check-book and fountain pen.

However, Jack and I were undaunted, if sad and puzzled, and all those months of waiting worked hard to meet the expenses of incredible mismanagement, going about drowning our disgust in libations of poetry, such, for instance, as:

> "We must go, go, go away from here;
> On the other side the world we're overdue."

Or,

> "You have heard the beat of the off-shore wind,
> And the thresh of the deep-sea rain;
> You have heard the song—how long? how long?
> Pull out on the trail again!"

I am sure we ought to thank Mr. Kipling for contributing largely to our undauntedness.

The naming of the yacht was not the least of our difficulties. Friends were prolific with *Petrels* and *Sea Birds;* they even dared *White Wings* and *Sea Wolves,* not to mention *Calls of the Wild.* Jack recalled Mr. Lewis Carroll's *The Hunting of the Snark,* and held that name up as a warning inducement for better suggestions. Such were not forthcoming, and when we sailed for Hawaii, the elliptic American stern bore the gilded inscription:

SNARK
San Francisco

Now the way my Log came to be written was mostly due to Jack. Be it known that he detests letter-writing, although a more enthusiastic recipient of correspondence never slit an envelope. His friends consider him sheerly selfish, but I can vouch that he is very busy. At any rate, when I decided to keep a typewritten diary, to be circulated in lieu of individual letters, my husband hailed the scheme with acclaim.

And here it is, my journal—the one accurate, continuous story of the adventures of the *Snark,* from San Francisco Bay to the Cannibal Isles.

CHARMIAN KITTREDGE LONDON.

Aboard Yacht *Roamer,*
   Sacramento River, January, 1915.

". . . To burst all links of habit—there to wander far away,
On from island unto island at the gateways of the day."

THE LOG OF THE SNARK

THE LOG OF THE SNARK

Aboard the *Snark*, Pacific Ocean,
Thursday, April 25, 1907.

IT is too good to keep any longer, this joy of living that is beginning to make itself felt aboard the *Snark*. For an hour I've been dangling my feet over the edge of the life-boat lashed on the deck to windward, watching the purple water swash in and out of the lee scuppers. Our midday meal is finished, concocted by Martin and myself (Martin has been and still is a little worse off from sea-sickness than I), and we are all comfortably lazy. And speaking of the joy of living as felt aboard the *Snark*, it is a matter of degree. Martin has not yet come to feel it; and Tochigi, our alleged cabin-boy, has succumbed to the effects of *mal de mer* with the characteristic abandon of the Asiatic. He can't or thinks he can't lift a finger, and as there are many fingers necessarily to be lifted in the management of the ship, he is very much needed in our midst.

But the water is purple, and I am recovering from my seasickness, which seemed quite violent to me, but was in reality a mild attack. Roscoe and Bert have had no nausea, but a heavy lassitude has taken the place of ordinary seasickness. The five-horse-power engine is pumping "juice" into the storage batteries, our dinner is settling in the most encouraging manner, the life-boat is being packed with staples of diet, for emergency, the deck has been hosed down—although Jack was the only one with energy enough to make a start at it; and, joy of joys, the *Snark*, under mainsail, staysail, jib, and flying-jib, is steering herself night and day. This is a great relief, because several hours at the wheel, keeping the course (south by east), is very monotonous, as

3

well as tiring to the untried spine. But we keep a wary
eye upon the compass, and of course set regular watches at
night.

We have been out only three days from Oakland wharf
and all the souls who waved us farewell and fair weather;
but there is so much to tell. To begin with, the water is
purple, and such purple! Jack and I took a trip out to the
end of the bowsprit this afternoon, and sat for a long time
watching our little white ship cleave the amethyst flood.
Afterward we lay over the stern-rail, looking at the red-
gold rudder dragging through the purple. Do you remember that gorgeous picture by Maxfield Parrish, ''Sinbad the
Sailor''? The colours we have seen to-day rival its oriental
splendour of indigo and gold and purple.

Just this moment, reminiscent of our sally out on the bowsprit, I glanced that way. Behold Jack! arrayed in Jimmie
Hopper's famous blue-and-gold sweater, gazing again at the
purple water under the bow; Jimmie Hopper's first 'Varsity
sweater, which we flew at our mast-head when we left Oakland.

This morning Jack called to me, ''Hurry on deck—the
ocean is alive with Portuguese men-o'-war!'' My first
thought was one of alarm; next I wished Jack would say
''water'' instead of ''ocean''—the latter sounded so remote.
(You see, in my inner consciousness I am still on land.)
Then I oriented myself, took a good look at the ''mighty
wet,'' the ''prodigious damp'' that encompassed us, and began to shake the land-dust out of my brain. The fearsome
Portuguese men-o'-war turned out to be pretty, jelly-like
bits of life—turquoise-blue, transparent organisms, each with
a milky, finny sail hoisted to the breeze. The sea was floating countless myriads of them, and we hauled one or two
aboard in a canvas bucket, finding them no less beautiful at
close range.

Then the gunies. (I said there was much to tell.) First
day, one guny; second day, two gunies; to-day, four gunies.
And they will eat anything but orange-peel. A human be-

ing is the only animal that has sense enough to make use of orange-peel—though he disguises it pretty thoroughly before he finds it palatable. A guny—in case you don't happen to know—looks like a dark-grey, overgrown seagull, until he essays to fold his wings upon the water. Then there is a difference. I say "tries" to fold his wings, because each attempt appears to be a brand-new experiment, each experiment rivalling the last in awkwardness. Once folded down, the three-jointed pinions do not always seem to sit comfortably, whereupon the bird fusses around and re-settles them until, possibly, another bird has eaten what he was after. These are the birds that get seasick when they are captured. I'd like to see something seasick besides a human being. And I'd like to see Tochigi make even a feeble attempt to be something else than a corpse. It cannot be possible that he *enjoys* seasickness! He was ever a willing worker. —

But do not think for a moment that watching gunies and Portuguese men-o'-war and purple seas have been my only occupations. I have cleaned up the greasy, filthy, littered floors of the engine room, the bathroom, two staterooms, and, with poor sick Martin's help, the cabin. I did not think I could stay so long below; but the mess was unbearable, although it did not seem to bother any one but Jack and me. You should have seen my hands these three days. But I have made merry with much soap, strong ammonia, and as little precious fresh water as was practicable. Now I feel more like a white woman.

Have I said anything about the weather? It would not do to leave the weather out of a Log. We anchored off the Alameda Pier the day we bade Oakland good-bye, Monday, and spent the night there under starry skies. The next day was overcast; Wednesday was overcast; Thursday, to-day, is overcast, and we have had no observation. Our patent log registers about seventy-five miles for the past twenty-four hours and now, at five o'clock P. M., we are swinging along in a fresh breeze, still overcast, a faint silver sunset on the grey horizon.

Later.—They are rigging up a topsail to put speed on the yacht, and Bert has climbed the mainmast to straighten out something. He is a goodly sight, clinging high, his bare, powerful arms working at the swaying masthead. The extra sail is making the boat drive faster, but something is wrong with it, and although adding to our speed, it is so horribly ill-setting that Roscoe is promptly taking it down. And oh! it's great, this rush of wind and wave—a wonderful new life, all the working of this little world of plank and iron and brass and canvas. And if I can feel enthusiasm while my stomach is still wavering between belt and throat, fancy the enjoyment to come.

At sea, Friday, April 26, 1907.

This has been a very exciting day. Listen: Jack shaved, and I washed my face and hands. If you are inclined to smile at our simple pleasures and excitements, stop and consider if it is really funny for a water-loving crowd to go without washing for forty-eight hours or so. I love to wash my hands. Ordinarily I wash them a thousand times a day, more or less. So imagine the black filth and oil and grease *and* the seasickness that could make me more contented to sleep and wake in grime than to make a fight for cleanliness. I hope that I may never again be so soiled and unkempt. However, there's nothing like being adaptable. It is what makes a trip around the world.

I further celebrated to-day by manicuring Jack's and my own nails. It took me all of three hours. If I move too rapidly, I'm liable to lose my latest meal. I am having my turn at the prevalent lassitude, lying in the life-boat for hours without ambition enough to open my eyes. The crew seems to be demoralised. Work doesn't go on. There is no system about anything, and this spirit is contagious. Jack is growing restive, but has not yet interfered. Some piece of work on deck is begun, and never finished, and the general lack of interest is astounding.

The sky is overcast, for a change, and winds are variable.

Eighty miles have been left behind since yesterday noon. We are beginning to wonder about all the fish Jack promised us, for we have not seen a single one. Jack trolls, but has no luck. There is not even a flying-fish, the herald of the king, which is the dolphin. The Portuguese men-o'-war still escort us, and an occasional guny casts a shadow on the deck. Oh! for a sunny day. These cloudy skies are indescribably depressing. They are not heavy clouds—every now and then the blue breaks through or a bit of sunlight straggles down, only to withdraw again behind the pall. I can see my first stormy petrels, Mother Cary's chickens. (NOTE. If I make any mistakes, please remember that I am calling things by the names that are given me by those aboard who have either sailed the seas before, or have read extensively about the sea. Now, I don't know whether yon sable scavengers are yclept gunies or gonies. No one, upon being pressed, can help me out. I can only go my phonetic way— even the dictionary fails me. Jack and Roscoe pronounce it goo-ny, and "guny" is as near as I care to come to that. There is nothing so valuable as a husband upon whom a woman can shirk her responsibilities.)

Tochigi came to life to-night while the rest of us were trying to consume a shifting dinner (except Martin, who peered jealously down from his bunk-shelf at the table he had furnished and of which he could not partake)—Tochigi, I say, came to life and feebly piped over the edge of his bunk: "Mr. London, I think I could take my watch to-night." Of course we knew he couldn't—he was weak as a whisper; but it was encouraging to hear him offer, he had so utterly succumbed up to then. While the rest of us who are seasick are alternately working and sloughing off our nourishment, he refuses to leave his bunk except for the last-named exigency (which has become rather attenuated by now), and meanwhile his cabin-work lapses and conditions below are unspeakable. If I looked at it all with land-eyes, I know I could not stand it. But I brought an extra pair of eyes with me, for it doesn't always pay to observe too closely. I have earnestly tried to ease the disorder below, but cannot keep abreast of the accumulation; besides, it makes Jack indignant to see me do it. The aforesaid joy of living is considerably dampened by the demoralisation aboard.

We had a three-handed game of Hearts before eight, this evening, after which I took my watch, from eight until ten. The moon showed occasionally, in a sickly, unwilling sort of way, and the sunset ought to have been ashamed of itself.

At sea, Saturday, April 27, 1907.

This also has been an exciting day, but in a different way. There was a steady increase in wind, with the accustomed overcast sky, until it was blowing what the men called "half a summer gale," although to me it seemed far more than that. In the morning we sat in and around the cockpit for a while, very jolly, talking about the colour of the water and the size of the swells and the sailing qualities of the yacht. A boat is as absorbing a topic as a horse, for lengthy discussion. Little did we dream what we were to learn about her before the day and night were gone. You see, when a boat is built, no matter upon what lines or by what rules, no man knows what peculiarities may show up. Boats are as uncertain as babies. It is too dreadful. Let me take my time.

As the wind kept on freshening, sail was shortened and two reefs were put in the mainsail; and finally Jack and Roscoe decided that it would be best to heave to for the night so that all hands could have some sleep, rather than set long watches for the wise ones or to trust the steering to the green hands—as it was a case of running before the wind with a little rag of a flying-jib if we sailed at all.

Toward night the weather looked very nasty indeed (I knew I'd have a chance to report some weather), the waves seemed enormous to me, the *Snark* rolled and pitched, water running deep across her deck, water sloshing around below and squirting up through the floors, water squeezing in through the buried side and into the galley stores and all over the dishes and stove. But the boat acted well in the heavy seas, until it came to putting her through the paces of heaving to. *Heaving to* means bringing a vessel's head up into the wind, the sails being trimmed to hold her that way any length of time. This means safety so long as a sail stays on a boat.

Now, listen well; the *Snark* refused to heave to. Not all the efforts of three men for hours and hours could make her heave to. She simply wallowed—and most creditably wallowed, it must be confessed—in the trough of the sea, but would come no farther into the wind. Fortunately the gale did not increase, nor was it cold. But oh, the hills and valleys of the ocean! There may be real storms for the *Snark* somewhere on the wide ocean of our adventure; but the waves this day loomed quite large enough on my new horizon. If they had been really big waves, we, rolling there in the trough, might have been turned over and over, with only a stray life-preserver left floating upon the boundless briny to tell that the *Snark* had been lost with all on board. And, of course, the wind *might* have blown harder, and the worst *might* have happened, with the yacht acting as she did. The final thing to be done, in a case like this, or in any extreme case, is to put out a sea anchor, a contrivance of canvas and half-hoops that is warranted to hold to the wind the head of 'most anything that floats. So our sea-anchor was rigged up. And it failed. Then Jack and Roscoe stood by the mizzen and talked it over with serious faces. They had tried everything, every possible combination of sails that they could think of, and failed to bring the yacht up nearer than eight points into the wind, which means that we were rolling in the trough, as I have said. The men talked it over, wondered at the incredible fact of the failure, and could solve nothing of the wonder. I wish I had a picture of the three, in the pale grey moonlight that drifted through the flying clouds, leaning over the forward weather rail watching the sea-anchor. It will be with me always, that grey scene, the three darker grey forms in oilskins, the heads in sou'westers, leaning at the same angle, hanging upon the success of that sea-anchor.

There is no explaining these things that happened this day. I can only tell the facts and leave folk to wonder as we wonder.

All these hours I stood in the cockpit hovering over the compass, wheel hard down, watching vainly, oh! how vainly, for the yacht to round up into the wind, and at the same time marvelling that some of the grey seas which brimmed to the very lip of the rail did not come aboard and whelm us. I remember, some years ago, figuring out that I was too old to die young; but this grey night, especially after I went to bed in my rubber boots, I caught myself dwelling on the conclusion that I was too young to die!

The other day I was bending over the stern watching the rudder trail golden through the purple water, when the mizzen boom unexpectedly jibed over. (This purple water will be the death of me yet.) I was in imminent danger, but knew nothing about it until Jack cried "Mate! come back! Come back! Quick!" At the same time he grabbed me and jerked me over a coil of rope and the rail into the cockpit. I might have been badly injured by the swift-swinging tackle. I can see Jack's face as he pulled me in. One sees many things in faces at such moments. The wheel needed his undivided attention to avert a possible smash-up of everything on deck; but the man left the ship to save the woman. "There are many boats, but only one woman," he briefly summed it up.

At sea, April 28, 1907, Sunday.

It is not physically restful to sleep in one's sea-boots— nor mentally restful, what of one's reasons for so sleeping. There is a sense of responsibility every moment of every night, let alone a night like last night. And little of a sailor though I am, I cannot help sharing this sense of responsibility. Jack bears the heaviest share, of course; and it is not to be wondered at, when you consider that outside of himself our only sailor is a bay-yachtsman.

We ran before the wind all last night, and learned another thing about the *Snark*—that she can run beautifully, even if she can't—or won't—heave to. (Certain sage acquaintances of ours in San Francisco, for some unexplained reason wagged their heads over the lines of the *Snark* and said that in the very nature of things she would never be able to run. Why they thought so, or why they thought they thought so, they seemed unable to say. But I wish they could have seen her race that breeze last night.)

Jack, Roscoe and Bert divided the hours into three watches, for I was not expected to steer in such a sea, nor did I care to attempt it. Four-hour watches are anxious stretches for a tyro in an ugly wind and sea.

Coming on deck this morning, I stopped in the companion-way to watch my man at the wheel. His face, framed in the sou'wester, was toward me; but his big sad eyes were turned aside to the bitter sea. Four hours and more he had stood there guiding his boat of disappointment, his boat that will not heave to in a storm, that will not even mind that last resort, the sea-anchor—a boat that would be a death-trap on a lee-shore.

But as the day wore on and the wind blew more gently, and the waves went down a bit, and the sun came out and made the water purple, every one grew more cheerful. Devices, to be worked out in Honolulu for correcting the terrible fault of the boat, were thought out and discussed, and we were able to make jokes at one another's expense, and to mourn over Aunt Villa's Christmas fruit-cake, made months before the voyage, and upon which somebody put a heavy box in the engine-room the night before. I remember going down into the dark and swash and saving a huge chunk of the shattered goody, and trying to feed it to the hungry, toiling, heart-sick men on deck. There had been no dinner, no hot coffee, nothing but disappointment and a damp bed.

Martin was very ill, and gazed down from his bunk with lack-lustre eyes. I don't know what is the matter with him. It is not all seasickness; but the seasickness is so blended with other things that one cannot name his trouble. Prob-ably he has the grippe in conjunction with the seasickness. During the trouble in the night, Martin heard Jack mutter something about "Twenty-five thousand dollars gone to blazes," or words to that effect, and somehow gathered that the *Snark* was about to go down with all hands. But even this dismal prospect did not in the least jog his apathy.

Tochigi continues bunk-ridden, and the pig-pen situation below abates no jot. Jack has an accession of disgust and discouragement whenever I try to ameliorate the awfulness —says it's a little too much to have his wife doing the work of two men. So I do things surreptitiously, although it is rather hard to be surreptitious in such close quarters; and then I wax philosophical again about the filth, and the futility of one small woman trying to keep abreast of the accumulation. At this point I climb the greasy, sooty, slip-pery companionway of beautiful but disguised teak, and seek surcease from sordidness in the cockpit where Jack, Roscoe, and Bert are discussing the weather. (Jack can be found at the wheel, steering and reading, any hour of the day after his morning work is finished. No one ever sug-gests relieving him.) Then I forget the desperate dirt in the exhilaration of the speed we are making, reeling off the knots at the rate of ten an hour and sometimes eleven. A knot is eight hundred feet longer than a land-mile. So figure out our speed when the *Snark* is walking along in a fair wind. Other times three knots will be the tale of the gay little patent log over the stern; but even so, that is seventy-two knots in the twenty-four hours.

We sailed beautifully to-day. We must do justice to the yacht's fine points, even if she is treacherous and may drown us all. Jack says he never heard of a sailing vessel that would not heave to, although some steamers are so con-structed that they are obliged to heave to stern-first. Her failure to do what was expected of her last night was a fitting culmination to all the distress of the building—the unaccountable delays, the frightful waste of money in material and worthless labour, down to the attachment on our sailing day, for $242.86, put on the boat by that wretched old ship chandler, Sellers, who did not even first send over his bill. And Jack had paid him thousands of dollars in the preceding months, and was waiting for all final bills to come in for settlement before he sailed, waiting with pen and check book in one pocket, and another pocket full of gold. And now think of his feelings, after all his troubles, to find that his own boat is the only one he ever heard of that refused to perform the important and necessary function of heaving to. He declares it is enough to make a man turn to wine and actresses and race horses, to be so thwarted in his clean and wholesome scheme to gain pleasure. I shall try to persuade him to stay by the ship!

The sea is not a lovable monster. And monster it is. I thought a great many thoughts about it last night, those hours I studied the binnacle or watched the men make their fight. It is beautiful, the sea, always beautiful in one way or another; but it is cruel, and unmindful of the life that is in it and upon it. It was cruel last evening, in the lurid low sunset that made it glow dully, to the cold, mocking, ragged moonrise that made it look like death. The waves positively beckoned when they rose and pitched toward our bit boat labouring in the trough. And all the long night it seemed to me that I heard voices through the planking, talking, talking, endlessly, monotonously, querulously; and I couldn't make out whether it was the ocean calling from the outside or the ship herself muttering gropingly, finding herself. If the voices are the voices of the ship, they will soon cease, for she must find herself. But if they are the voices of the sea, they must be sad sirens that cry, restless, questioning, unsatisfied—quaint homeless little sirens.

At sea, Thursday, May 2, 1907.

If something does not occur soon, my log's items will be reduced to: No fish, light breeze, large swells, growing warmer, Martin and Tochigi improving, also bill of fare, likewise appetites. We had a little variation, however, on Monday, the 29th, when Roscoe took his first observation. We found ourselves in 31° 15' 21" North Latitude, 126° 48' 8" West Longitude, with 120 knots to our credit in the preceding twenty-four hours, in a fresh northwest breeze. About sunset on the same day we sighted a full-rigged ship several miles off. She crossed our bows and disappeared in the twilight, sailing a west by south course. That night, Martin being very ill, I took his watch as well as my own—four hours on end. And when I did go below, I could not rest, for the wind was lively, and I had a sense of responsibility during the watches of the green hands. My worry is a reflection of Jack's, which is based on the fact that our crew seem to regard this voyage as a mere picnic on the breast of an unruffled lake. Jack has sailed deep water before; and while standing the same watches as the others, he has the entire responsibility as well. The other day he called all hands aft and gave them a very short and very mild lecture on system and discipline aboard ship. He had made no sign, but as no one had displayed any ambition to improve the appearance of the boat, above or below, he thought he would try a little talk. It will probably be resented in the long run; but things could not go on as they were.

My eight-to-ten night watches are a never-ending joy. Such gaudy fan-rays of sunset, and such distorted moonrises, the weird light mingling with the phosphorescence in the water; and I often lie over the stern rail looking down at the rudder leaving behind a "welt of light" like a comet's tail. The little waves break and crumple in wild-fire, and everything is a wonder. One thinks calmly and simply these hours alone at night upon the ocean. Artificialities and conventions and the strains of ordinary life are remote and trivial.

Jack is at work on a boat article, entitling it "The Inconceivable and Monstrous.'' It deals with the outrageous circumstances under which the *Snark* was built, following the earthquake and fire; and it deals with the worthless work and materials that were given us for our money. For instance, the "gooseneck" on the main gaff has broken short off. It took three men two hours to substitute another gooseneck, which had to be worked out of a spare gaff that belongs to another sail. Half an hour after it was tried, it snapped. This being the last one we had, the gaff was lashed to the mast with rope—and in this trig and seamanlike shape shall we enter the port of Honolulu, like a sea-bird paddling along with a broken wing. Now please take note that both of these wrought iron goosenecks were made to order. I wonder what the maker had against us!

And never for a moment do we forget that our staunch little ship will not heave to.

A year ago to-day, Jack and I set out upon a long horseback trip up the California coast. It just came over me, sitting here in the midst of the wide ocean—the feel of the sweet country, the perfume of mountain lilac, the warm summer-dusty air. What a life we live, and how we do live it while we live it!

At sea, Friday, May 3, 1907.

This is the northeast trade-wind with a vengeance. The *Snark* is sailing before it, with a regular but heavy roll that made me stuff a pillow between my body and the ship's side last night before I could get any sleep.

Bert has had a cold dip under the bowsprit, and now, in a red bathing suit and a scarlet Stanford rooter's hat, is helping Roscoe put to rights the "boatswain's locker." Our deck, what of desultory scrubbings and much sea-swashing, looks fairly respectable. Jack got Tochigi up and put him at the wheel, and the enforced exercise made a great improvement in his condition. Martin is able to cook an occasional meal, and in fancy's flights serves up many delicacies of the deep, such as sharks, whales, and dolphins. Because the vegetables that came aboard in Oakland were almost entirely worthless, our cuisine is mostly garnered from tins—and the bean-bag.

Saturday, May 4, 1907.

We are bowling fast into the Torrid Zone, into Hawaiian weather. I am sitting on the rudder-box, steering with my feet while I write. Oh, this water, and this brave trade wind. The big sapphire hills of water, transparent and sun-shot, are topped with dazzling white that blows from crest to crest in the compelling wind. Just now a huge swell picked us up and swung us high, and the merest little fling of salt spray was in our faces. The *Snark* is what sailors call a "dry" boat. And she sails easily, without jerks or bumps. Along comes a blue mountain that looks like disaster; and we slip over it and down into the blue abyss on the other side, without a jar—just a huge, rolling slide. And ever the strong sweet wind blows from behind, sending us forward to the isles of our desire.

The steering-compass has become a part of my consciousness, sleeping and waking; and I often go amidships and hover over the big Standard Compass. I think in terms of "south by west," and "south half west," and other expressions that were Greek to me a month ago. I can "luff her up," too, when the men are aloft fixing something. And I can box the compass. Jack calls me various jolly names, such as "The skipper's sweetheart," "The Crackerjack," "Jack's wife," and I swell with pride and feel very salty indeed. And I am reminded to mention that when we call each other "Mate," this has no connection with boats, but is an interchangeable nickname.

Monday, May 6, 1907.

To-day is the first time I have felt that we are actually bound for Polynesia, and all backward thoughts are swinging round to the goal. The boys have the big chart stretched over the book-case in the cabin, with our course, so far travelled, marked upon it. It looks a staggery course, for we let the yacht steer herself much of the time, under short canvas, to save being continually at the wheel; and we are not in the least hurry. If the mizzen were hoisted, and some one at the wheel all the time, there would be a different story, for the *Snark* can walk right along with half a chance. She shakes her heels pretty well even as things are, with a heavy load and crippled mainsail, her staysail and two jibs.

The sky has been clearing, and we are able to dry a little of the dampness below. I wonder if we shall ever get things running with any discipline. No one seems to care. Roscoe came on the voyage as sailing master, but he doesn't take charge; which laxness demoralises the rest. My fitful nightmarish sleep is troubled with trying to get the crew to do something, or of trying to get the *Snark* away from San Francisco. Waking, I put my hands to all sorts of strange tasks, to see if it will not encourage the others. Even Tochigi, now well on the mend, cannot seem to realise that this is home, and that the same round of duties obtains on a boat as in a house. But we shall get harmony out of it all yet.

Thursday, May 9, 1907.

Another item of the Inconceivable and Monstrous: Day before yesterday, when the men tried to set our spinnaker for the first time—the beautiful wing of speed that stretches overside—an important piece of wrought iron on the boom threatened to give way. So we shall have no spinnaker to shorten our time to Honolulu.

The deck has been washed!—I do not say scrubbed, or swabbed, because dripping a few pailfuls of water over the planking is neither scrubbing nor swabbing, nor will it remove the accumulated dirt. I should not have known the deck was being washed except that my decklight was open and I was slumbering thereunder when the deluge came.

Jack and I have decided that although we wish we were a little younger than we are, we are glad we are not too young. Extreme youth must be the trouble with the rest (barring the sailing master, who is sixty), for the spirit of adventure seems far from them. While Jack and I are on deck or out on the questing bowsprit, enjoying the glorious sun and flowing air, watching for the life of the deep and congratulating ourselves on the mere fact of living, the others stay in the dim and musty cabin, reading or talking or sleeping, or just sitting listlessly with idle hands. It must be that we knew what we wanted, Jack and I, and are getting what we knew we wanted.

We have sailed well in a fair wind to-day, with a big sea, and followed by some spike-tailed grey and white birds called "boatswain birds," because of their hoarse, exhorting cries, which are supposed to resemble those of the ordinary ship's boatswain—pronounced "bo's'n," of course.

Jack has begun a new article, to be entitled "Adventure." It deals with the numberless and varied individuals who applied for berths in the *Snark* for this world-voyage.

This day ended with a wild tropic sunset that lingered for a long while—a sunset of brilliant white and silver, with only faint suggestions of gold and red, and great broad rays flaring up from the horizon, fanwise. It was nothing like any land sunset we ever saw, and when the sun had dropped below the crinkly horizon, a copper streak persisted, for nearly an hour blending a ruddy tinge with the dull purple of the water.

At sea, Friday, May 10, 1907.

Ominous black clouds pressed down upon the seascape during my watch last evening, and there was such an accession of brave trade wind and so imminent a rainsquall that I called Roscoe to take the next watch instead of Tochigi. Nothing alarming happened, only an exasperating rolling of the sea. And they say to me, "Wait until you're in a gale, sometime, and see what real rolling is!" I am waiting, as I am waiting for the promised dolphins and bonitas. Tired out trying to get a morning nap, I joined Jack at the wheel before six. It was my first sunrise at sea, and the great morning sky was a whirl of tinted clouds poured over with melting sunshine, a glossy sapphire satin ocean reflecting the glory. And we saw a fish, we did, we did!—and it was a flying-fish. If you don't believe me, ask Jack. He saw TWO. He shouted, "Flying-fish! Flying-fish!" and went right up in the air. Now the fish-line is trolling for dolphin, for there should be dolphin where are flying-fish.

Later in the day Jack enticed me out to the tip-end of the bowsprit, with a heavy sea rolling. I must frankly admit that I felt shaky climbing out, my feet on a steel stay only a few inches above the crackling foam, and my hands clinging to the lunging spar itself. But the end was worth the pains, and it was wonderful to watch the yacht swing magnificently over the undulating blue hills, now one side buried in the rushing, dazzling smother, now the other, the sunshot turquoise water rolling back from the shining, cleaving white bows, and mixing with the milky froth pressed under. We gained such manifold impressions of the boat from our vantage at the end of the bowsprit. Now the man at the wheel would be far, far below us, a great slaty mountain rolled up behind him, and the uneven horizon high in air; now he was 'way above us, sliding down that same mountain. But he never overtook us, for about that time we were raising our feet from the wet into which they had been plunged, and were holding on for dear life as the *Snark's* doughty forefoot pawed another steep rise.

But this day has not been all gladness. I did the initial suffering, and Jack suffered vicariously. He knew nothing about it until, following me below to play a game of cribbage, he found me sitting on the floor at the foot of the companion-stairs, unable to speak a word. Before me sat Roscoe, watching me curiously. Above us, Martin eyed me suspiciously, and ventured tentatively, "Now, in Kansas, in my family, the women cry when they hurt themselves like that." *I couldn't* cry—it hurt too much. I am not very heavy, perhaps a hundred and fifteen pounds; but this weight behind one small elbow-joint, in a six-foot fall, is no light matter. My rubber soles were wet, slipped on the top step, and I touched nothing until I landed below, on that right elbow. No, I shed no tears—then. But when I was alone at the wheel, under the stars, I wailed right woman-like.

At sea, Monday, May 13, 1907.

The "Inconceivable and Monstrous" has cropped up again. The bottom dropped out of the bean-pot, right in the oven, when said pot was simmering a delectable mass of *frijoles,* tomatoes, onions, garlic, Chile peppers, and olive oil. My great earthen bean-pot, my noble bean-pot, my much-vaunted bean-pot, has gone to pot! Whoever heard of a bean-pot cutting such capers? I leave it to anybody. But nothing commonplace ever happens aboard the *Snark.* Why, the very particular universe in which she moves is of an uncommon variety—a dual universe, in short. You may not have heard: but Roscoe is making the voyage on the inside of the earth's crust, while the rest of us (barring Bert, who is on the cosmographical fence) have a strong belief that we are progressing upon the outer surface of the globe, with an ascertained astronomical system surrounding us. Either Roscoe will have to find a hole through which to climb to our stratum, or we shall be obliged to crawl through to his warm kennel; and I don't know which event is the more unlikely. No, there is nothing commonplace about the *Snark* or her voyage. It wouldn't surprise me to see the water canary-yellow and the sky bright green. I forgot to tell about the dolphins. There aren't any. But there are plenty of flying-fish.

This is a fine sunny day, and I have been steering for an hour and a half while I write, to give the others a chance to do the deck-work. Everybody is in good health, but without animation or ambition or pride in the yacht. When they are not making listless bluffs at working on deck, they continue to sit below, dully wondering when we will reach Honolulu. I believe Jack and I are the only ones who do not care how long the trip lasts. We are happy in the sailing and the health and life and beauty of everything about us, and one hour is as another for pleasantness. I rejoice to observe that Jack has unconsciously resumed his wonted light-foot gait, which I call his "merry walk," and his smile is like a sunbeam.

Yesterday I had a little lark all by myself, sitting on the lee rail and dabbling my feet in the warm gurgling water overside. Next time I'll wear a bathing-suit. Jack declined to join my refreshing gambols, saying that he would go in all over when he chose to get wet; but he trained a cautious eye upon me, for it would be decidedly inconvenient to pick up a "man overboard," especially if that man were a woman who knows little about keeping afloat in restless water. At three o'clock we went below and answered a huge bunch of mail, Jack dictating to me through the narrow doorway that separates our rooms. We got the work done quite comfortably.

The sunset last evening claimed us for an hour, as we lay on the fore-peak hatch, heaving upon the mighty lungs of the ocean. It was the first time the sun had sunk into the sea instead of into banks of clouds. It dropped slowly through rainbow mists, a dull orange ball that we could gaze upon to the last without straining our eyes. The big night-purple waves rose and broke against it, turning slowly to ashen-rose in the shell-rose light that followed the setting. But no matter how pale the tints of the tropic world, they are very simple and crude. With the loveliness of the day-ending still in my soul, I took the wheel at eight o'clock, and was thoroughly enjoying the rhythmic solitude when I was jarred rudely from off my blissful plane by the appearance of a bald head in the engine-room hatch-way and a querulous and accusing voice demanding,

"How on earth do you expect anybody to sleep when you're making that noise?" I was singing! And it is not out of place to mention that only those near to us by marriage or blood are privileged so to break in upon our raptures!

Wednesday, May 15, 1907.

This is the most perfect morning yet. And it isn't so merely because I have had two good nights of sleep; the sea disk is of deepest sapphire, the trade-wind clouds, lying low and puffy on the horizon and straggling up here and there into the blue, are the real trade-wind clouds we have been looking for so long, while a not-too-dense white cloud follows the face of the sun and tempers the heat. We are sailing along well on a comparatively smooth sea, in the gentle but steady trade-wind. At nine the course was changed to "W.N.W. true, to clear Maui by 25 miles."

Jack looks like a picture of a sailor, at the wheel, in a suit of white sailor-togs, against a classic watery background. Bert is going over everything on deck with a brush, and the deck itself is being washed. (I am glad there is some activity on deck, for last night, leaving the wheel in a sudden rainsquall to put the cover on the boatswain's locker which had been carelessly left open, I nearly broke my neck over a sack of coal that has been lying for days across the one available gangway on deck.) Martin is planning a big platter of spaghetti and mushrooms, Italian style, and Tochigi is cleaning up below. My flannel sailor-clothes are towing overside (this is the way we launder), and when they come up, clean, and have hung in the shrouds until dry, they shall be wrapped carefully and packed away until such time, how long hence, and where, who knows? as they may be needed in a cooler clime. Yesterday, although only 88°, we suffered from the heat. We are well over half way to Hawaii.

A few scaly scales were found on the deck this morning, attesting to our having been boarded by one or more flying-fish, but nothing was on our hook. But yesterday, while Jack and I were working hard below, there arose a great yelling on deck for us to come up. Which we wasted no time in doing, for news is scarce these days; and there, to leeward, we saw a goodly school of fin-back whale.

I am reading Isabella Bird Bishop's *Hawaii*. It was written long ago, but is splendid live stuff, being her letters written to England from the Islands. I am also studying our Planispheres, in order to familiarise myself a little with the changing skies. Jack told me to watch for the Southern Cross, and last evening when I came on deck to take my watch, there it was, just as it looked on the Planisphere, and I realised I had been looking at the constellation for several nights, without knowing. I must confess that I had expected something larger and more bejewelled. But it is a very good, bright little cross, and is going to mean much to me.

Later. Bert has blossomed resplendent in white trousers and a blue shirt. He washed his face and shaved yesterday, saying in extenuation (!) that he had not looked in the glass for a week, and didn't realise how unkempt he was. Martin is almost well, and furbished up his camera this afternoon. Jack wrote in the morning, and dug at navigation later on. I wrote letters, did some typewriting, and actually got out my sewing. I did not realise how dark the backs of my hands were from sunburn until I saw them against the fine white linen. But for a wonder my face and neck are not much tanned.

The setting of the sun, the blossoming of the new moon in a bright rose afterglow, and the coming of the stars, are a feast of beauty each evening. That growing silver of a young moon was so brilliant last night that it bewildered my sight, and I could not avoid seeing two crescents. Jack brought up his sextant and took some observations, during which he remarked icily that he *did* wish I could manage to call that fine and beautiful instrument something besides a *hydrant*.

Lat.   20° 56′ North,
Lon. 152° 52′ West.
At sea, Thursday, May 16, 1907.

Our trade-wind died down to the faintest breathings in the morning, and this afternoon it is so calm that we have little better than steerage-way. At this rate we shall not see land to-day as we had hoped. I worked below for hours in my stateroom, writing letters, typewriting, and reading, for once finding it cooler than on deck. With decklights and skylights open, it is nearly always cool below—a very encouraging thing to look forward to in the tropics. And if our electric plant ever works satisfactorily, we shall be in clover. This coolness of the *Snark's* interior is one of the few things about that much-sinned-against craft that are not Inconceivable and Monstrous. So much luck may be Inconceivable, but I don't like to call it Monstrous. It might be tempting fate.

But we faced it again this afternoon, the Inconceivable and Monstrous, all done up in a blue and green package seven or eight feet long in the shape of a shark, attended by his fleet of black and white striped pilot-fish. Bert saw it first. He had been bathing from the stays under the bowsprit, and no sooner had he regained the deck than he saw the dorsal fin of the shark cutting the surface a short distance away. Jack immediately baited a hook of the proper size with a goodly chunk of fat from our best boiled ham, from which Martin happened to be carving slices for supper. And that tempting bait, that superfine—for sharks—morsel of salt pork was smelled by that shark, and that Inconceivable, Monstrous, Epicurean shark even jauntily scratched his back upon the light rope that trailed the hook!

Now, who ever heard of a shark that would not rise to salt pork, or sink to salt pork, or, at any rate, be interested in salt pork one way or another? It's in all the books and on the tongues of all the sailors, that salt pork is the unfailing bait for shark. Perhaps it isn't exactly Inconceivable that this particular fish may have been gorging himself to repletion before he sighted us; but it is certainly Monstrous that the first fish we have seen on this strange, uneventful voyage (barring flying-fish and whales), should be a shark, and that this particular one should refuse super-fine salt pork. It is on a par with the *Snark* refusing to heave to. That still rankles; I cannot forgive her. It would rankle worse still if this calm should prove to be the forerunner of a real gale.

We even had a cold supper served aft, that we might keep an eye on that disagreeable, ungrateful scavenger that wouldn't scav.—I've got it! I've got it! That shark was a scavenger, of course, and a mere scavenger would not know first-table ham if he saw it; and he would therefore be suspicious of it, of its smell and its taste. I know there ought to be some explanation, and perhaps I have found it.

A lovely, colourful sunsetting, a shining silver sickle in the afterglow, a little studying of the constellations, and my watch began, a beautiful watch except for the fact that the tops of the brass binnacle lamps are hot, and I laid the tender palm of my left hand on the port one. Then I called for some kitchen soap and plastered the palm with it. How I do hurt myself! Why, I have to go around with my right elbow bandaged in a salt-wet towel, and cannot use the arm. Therefore I am black and blue from violent contact with various articles on the crowded boat. It is more difficult than one would dream to adjust, physically, to this moving base.

There is a new feel about everything, with this closeness to land. We seem suddenly to have a place in the universe, a character of our own. We have had nothing all these weeks with which to compare ourselves, ourselves as a boat. We have been alone of our kind, with no one to see that we existed. This is almost as good as annihilation, isn't it? But now we seem about to take our place once more in a known world. On a big ship, carrying hundreds of persons, it is different; the many souls form a community, and the unrelated character of the vessel is not so conspicuous.

We are so very, very little; the daily surprise is that we know where we are at all, that we can do aught but drift, a mote in a sunbeam.

Lat. 21° 23′ North,
Lon. 154° 13′ 45″ West.
At sea, Friday, May 17, 1907.

In a thin kimono I joined Jack at the wheel to enjoy the sunrise with him. It is delightful to be so safely careless about warmth of clothes, in this blowing air. We sneeze occasionally, for old-time's sake, but there is no cold in the head to follow. There were some showers in the early hours, with calm afterwards, but we are picking up a little breeze, enough to steer by. Nothing but clouds on the horizon; no land. There is a familiar high fog overhead that makes me homesick; but I think I am homesick for the Islands.

While Jack and the boys were taking a bath to-day under the bow, clinging to the bob-stay, Roscoe and I poured brine over each other's heads, aft by the cockpit. This was after we had soaped our hair. I haven't been able to do up mine since; and now, while I write, I am steering and drying my locks after a fresh-water rinse.

Tochigi made some candy yesterday, rice boiled in molasses. The rice remains brittle, as do the brown beans that are added. Tochigi's success made Martin ambitious, and we are waiting for the molasses confectionery he is making while he bakes. His bread is very good, by the way; and he has easily learned to make the simple yet difficult graham bread. I don't know who is going to pull that molasses candy. Martin thinks he should be exempt, having made it; besides, he is too busy. Roscoe also says he is busy. Jack is writing, and can.'t; and the nice, round, burned circle in my palm prevents me from volunteering. Bert has announced that he can, but that he doesn't want to—sunburned hands being his excuse. I think I can see Tochigi pulling the candy for the crowd.

Later. At last, our first land! After supper, Jack and I were playing cribbage on the fore-peak hatch, before going

The Oaken Frame of the *Snark*

into the bows to watch the sunset, when he shouted "Land!" at the same time pointing over the starboard bow. Oh, it was exciting! Our first island, faint and-far, hardly distinguishable from the clouds around it. And the best about it is, that it is just where it ought to be (if it is the Island of Maui), ten thousand feet high and a hundred miles away, which would prove our observations to have been correct. Everybody began to climb. "Martin-Johnson-Discovering-Hawaii" hung in the shrouds, while Bert, having attained the head of the mainmast, came sliding precipitately down the jib-stay—rather a risky undertaking, we thought, until he explained to us that he had practised it in California. Tochigi deemed it unnecessary to climb a few feet the better to observe a 10,000 foot mountain. Tochigi has the wisdom of the East in his gentle head.

I remember what a paradise Jamaica looked, one New Year's morn when we saw it rising out of the Caribbean Sea. But this is different; now we are adventuring in a little boat of our own, and one could almost wish no charts had ever been made of the region in which we now are, and that we were discovering it for ourselves.

Aboard the *Snark*, off Island of Maui,
Hawaiian Islands, Saturday, May 18, 1907.

Coming on deck at six for my sun-bath, I could not even say good morning to my Mate at the wheel, so exquisite was the greeting. I looked south right at the snow-hooded summit of mighty Mauna Kea on the Island of Hawaii, rising 14,000 feet out of the sea. The clouds must have lifted only that moment, for Jack, scanning the horizon, had missed seeing the island; so we enjoyed it together, a dream of white and blue opalescence. It was very thick to the southwest, but soon Maui broke through, and the navigators were able to verify their calculations. Haleakala is on Maui—the greatest extinct volcano in the world, with a crater measuring over twenty miles around. It is impossible to describe my sensation when I look at those bulking blue shapes cleaving up through the summer sea, as we sail. It is all wonder, a mystery of beauty and delight.

Double watches were kept on deck all last night. If this were Maui, we were of course too far away to lose sleep worrying about running into anything. But a sailor cannot be too careful. There is always the chance for a mistake, and there was much studying of charts in the grimy little cabin of the *Snark*.

Everybody has been strenuously occupied this morning in keeping the ship afloat. We want variety of experience; but when our cook pokes his head up the companionway and protests that the floors below are all awash, the owner of the vessel strives without delay to reduce the order of the day to the ordinary commonplaceness of existence. Bert had forgotten to close a seacock in the engine room, and the water was rushing in. The five-horse power engine was immediately switched off to more important work than the deck-washing that was going on when Martin gave the alarm, and Bert felt around for that seacock and closed it. How amusing it would have been to go down with all on board, in sight of our first land. And as likely as not the life-boat could not be got overside in case of need, as Roscoe has had no drills.

The flying-fish are large and fat to-day; but still no dolphin. Tochigi, cleaning deck-lights and skylights, found in a nook on deck one small, very much over-ripe flying-fish. This is a rather deferred (!) item, but it isn't my fault. It shadows another item, however, that certain portions of the deck have not been investigated in the deck-washing.

Later. A busy afternoon typing this Log, rendered difficult by the rough sea, which has increased to the biggest swell we have had on the whole voyage—probably the result of some gale to the northward. There is plenty of wind now. Jack has changed the course to N.W. by W., to clear Molokai, lying low and sad among heavy clouds, under a drowning moon. Roscoe's optimistic brain does not consider the change of course necessary, but Jack's brass-tack judgment says we could not clear Molokai on the other course, with this wind holding all night, and for the first time since San Francisco he, as captain, has over-ridden the sailing master with a positive command.

Aboard the Snark, off Oahu, Hawaiian Islands,
Sunday, May 19, 1907.

Jack set double watches again last night, Tochigi and I taking the first, from eight until twelve. It was eerie, watching forward in the grey light of the moon struggling through the murk, and ever and again I would seem to see land looming close ahead, only to find it was the huddling dark clouds on the horizon. I would stay there for an hour, then relieve Tochigi at the wheel and send him forward to watch. At 5:30 this morning, Jack jibed the boat over, and I came on deck, to find the Island of Oahu, upon which is the city of Honolulu, right ahead. As we sailed nearer, the land looked very familiar, accustomed as we have been to pictures of it. The waters are deserted; it does seem as if we ought to sight some sort of a vessel, so near to Honolulu. Such an incidentless voyage—although I forgot to tell that I found one flea the other day. Where he had been hibernating I do not know. And this morning a horsefly came aboard.

The sea is transparent; one can see into illimitable depths of sun-shot blue. And of all the Inconceivable and Monstrous things yet, here we are drifting toward the reef of Oahu in a dead calm. The trades are supposed to blow here almost the year around, especially at this season. But we have had unusual variable weather all the way. Oh! for the big engine now—we could be in landlocked Pearl Harbor in a couple of hours. Of course, if the engine were in commission, there would be plenty of wind. It could not be otherwise. Don't try to convince me that anything reasonable

could attend the workings of our venture. Last night it was
blowing briskly, and then the wind cut off short, and here
we are turning round and round under cloudless sky and
blazing tropic sun, wondering why it is not hotter. It is
only comfortably warm, and this does not seem reasonable,
either. Perhaps I am crazy.

Still off Oahu, Hawaii,
Monday, May 20, 1907.

We drifted past the growling reef, inside of which we
saw little fishing-boats sailing at sunset; past Makapuu
Head, and past Diamond Head, that beautiful sentinel of
Honolulu; and now, while we slip smoothly along toward
port, I will tell the rest of yesterday's experiences. The
horsefly, I think, is the only special excitement I have mentioned. After the midday meal we succeeded in hooking a
guny—don't doubt me, I saw it with my own eyes, and the
others will bear me witness. He knew salt pork a mile
away. It was a funny sight, that guny with the hook caught
in the downward curve of his upper beak, coming toward us
against his will. He measured six feet from wing-tip to
wing-tip, and was a thing of great beauty, with marvel-
lously feathered, triple-jointed pinions of cloudy warm-
brownish grey. His brown eyes were large and sagacious,
more like a dog's than a bird's, and he used them, too. He
was angry rather than frightened, and not especially vicious,
although he did manage to get hold of Bert's trousers and
a small pinch of Bert. But when we tethered him on deck,
the Inconceivable Monster would not be seasick as is the
wont of captured gunies. We finally cut him loose, un-
hurt, and when he went over the side he awkwardly sub-
merged, something to which he was evidently not accustomed, for he could not raise his wet wings high enough to
fly. Just then we picked up a fan of wind and the distance between the stern of the *Snark* and the stern of the
guny lengthened rapidly, the bird paddling for dear life,
head-over-shoulder like a coyote. While we had him on deck

we noticed an old break in one of his legs, and two birdshot holes in his web-feet. He must be a regular old war-horse, and deserving of his liberty. —

Then we glimpsed a big freight steamer going southwest; and there was quite a sociable time in the late afternoon, with numerous things to discuss—the flea, the horsefly, the guny, the steamer, a flickering breeze, and one lone Portuguese man-o'-war. And then there was the summer isle before us with promise of rest from perpetual movement, and lure of velvet green mountains and valleys.

Jack slept beside the cockpit during my watch, indeed all night until his own watch. The reef with its white-toothed breakers could not have been more than a mile and a half away, and the calm was absolute, the current fortunately setting us on past danger. At ten o'clock, I told Tochigi, who was sitting in the cabin studying, to go to bed. I felt anxious and knew I should not sleep if I went below. Twice the *Snark*, with her wheel hard down, turned completely around. I was disgusted, and remembered when a smaller yacht did the same thing with me in the bay of San Francisco, in the Doldrums off Angel Island.

How I watched that line of reef in the misty, elusive moonlight. Imagine four hours at the wheel, eyes riveted on the round, small, vital compass, heart aching for it to indicate some control of the boat. The only rest for the eyes was to strain them on the dark shore until it blurred, or try to pierce the mysterious gloom of the horizon for lights. It was tense business; but in the midst of it, worried and lonely as I felt, I caught myself thinking how happy I was.

. . . .

And now, a word aside.

In shaping up the *Log of the Snark* for publication, I am forced to see that the enthusiastic book I have written, covering five months' land travel and experience in the Hawaiian Isles, has no place in a ship's log. Labour of love though it has been, the recounting of all those happy days of glamour in our first landfall must find itself between

other covers than those of a sea diary. I must pass by the
month in Pearl Harbor—Dream Harbor, Jack called it; the
subsequent blissful tent-and-surf life at Waikiki; our days
in saddle and camp through the crater of mighty Haleakala; that amazing week spent in the Molokai·Leper Settlement; the trip on horseback through the Nahiku Ditch
country on Windward Maui, with its hair-raising old chief-
trails and hair-breadth swinging bridges over great waterfalls—all those vivid hours of living shall have a place to
themselves elsewhere, together with tribute to our friends,
the Thurstons, and their friends, who helped us to know
Hawaii off the much exploited "tourist route."

Aboard the *Snark* once more, after months of work on her
engines in Honolulu, and repairs in Hilo on that same work,
we set our faces to the sea again, answering its clear call as
we answered it in California in April; as we shall want to
answer it, I am sure, in all the months of all the years.

.   .   .   .

Lat. 15° 8′ North,
Lon. 151° 30′ West.
Aboard the *Snark* at sea,
Hilo, Hawaii, to Marquesas Islands,
Monday, October 14, 1907.

A week ago to-day we sailed away from Hilo, Hawaii, on
our voyage to the Marquesas Islands. So began the second
chapter of our boat-adventure. It is six months since we
left San Francisco Bay for our voyage around the world, and
what of the many delays connected with completing the
yacht and repairing her wrecked engines (wrecked by in-
competent workmen), we have spent far more time in Hawaii Nei than originally planned. We cannot be sorry,
however, for we had a glorious time all through. But here
we are at sea again, with our first port of call, Honolulu,
hundreds of miles behind us, and our next, the Marquesas,
thousands ahead of us—unless this head-wind and sea shift
and let us get on our proper course. South 28° East it is,

while we sag south, due south, and at times even west of south.

Everything is dove-grey, sky and sea, and there are occasional warm showers. I am tucked snugly away in a corner of the deep cockpit, while the little *Snark* steers herself by-the-wind as successfully as ever she did before it. Herrmann de Visser, the Dutch sailor, is sitting near by sewing canvas, pushing the huge sail-needle with a "palm" on his hand. And Herrmann is singing "The Last Rose of Summer" in Dutch, in a wonderful light baritone that makes me feel selfish in being the only listener. Incidentally, Herrmann, a small black rain-hat on one side of his head, looks as if he had just fallen out of 'a Rembrandt canvas. But Rembrandt van Ryn never designed that tattooed ballet-girl on Herrmann's short and powerful right forearm— a figure that any muscular movement of the arm makes dance amorously.

Martin Johnson, sole survivor, so to speak, of the original crew that sailed from California on the *Snark*, has come into the cockpit, and is rigging up an electric light extension for me to see by when I read to Jack on watch. There's a brown-skinned cook in the galley now, and Martin is flourishing in our midst as engineer and electrician. Martin has made good, and he is the only man who was aboard the *Snark* when we left the States, who was not chosen from the ranks of our intimates.

Captain James Langhorne Warren, our Virginia master, is sitting to leeward of me for the purpose of smoking a cigar—and bless us all if it isn't the first he's smoked' since we left Hilo! You see, the captain hasn't been feeling equal to anything stronger than cigarettes during the past week. We have lost all false pride about seasickness, we of the *Snark*. We have been hopelessly, disgracefully sick, all of us, except Herrmann, who seems to enjoy remarking at irregular, inconsiderate intervals, "I do not know vot seasick iss."

It is comforting to a captain-discouraged yachtsman like

Jack to see the way Captain Warren runs things. The boat has never looked so orderly; never were commands obeyed so promptly; never was such forethought shown in keeping everything ready for emergency—for the expected unexpected. For instance, last Wednesday night, the 9th, looked squally and strange, after a most remarkable sunset which made our sensitive barometer oscillate; and before dusk Captain Warren and Herrmann had everything on deck in readiness for possible trouble during the dark hours —movable articles lashed securely, ropes in perfect working order. After all there was no blow; but if there had been we would not have been caught napping.

That great sunset was a miracle of colour. Who ever heard of vivid peacock blue in the sky? But it was there; and such turquoise and green and gold, in an Oriental riot of gorgeousness. Then the air became so flooded with living rose that we all looked as if we had been feasting on roses and the elixir of youth.

To-day Jack has done his first writing since we left Hilo. A six-days' vacation is an unusual thing for him. Also, he has inaugurated a general setting-to-rights below, as to contents of drawers and lockers, clothes, and so forth. I am unable to join in the perfumed revel, as a very few minutes below are enough to convince me that I am not yet quite myself.

Our new cabin-boy, Nakata, shipped at Hilo, is very different from the æsthetic and poetic-looking Tochigi of the first voyage. Nakata's hair far more resembles a roughly-used shoebrush than the glossy "football bang" that crowned Tochigi. But Nakata, little plebeian that he is, has the body of a brown cherub and a smile that is inextinguishable. He seems to have more teeth than the rest of us, and shows them on all occasions except when he is asleep. Also, he brushes them sedulously for just fifteen minutes every morning. When he slumbers, his funny little face is tired and drawn, for he has been and still is quite seasick. But he never gives over. No matter what his qualms, whenever he is spoken to he bobs up with his everlasting jack-o'-lantern grin and benevolent interrogative "Yes-s?"

Wada, the Japanese cook, is more Indian than Japanese in appearance, and so far has proved just an ordinary, greasy sea-cook, his dishes a sad contrast to Martin's imaginative cuisine. But Martin and I are slowly getting him into our ways.

Our prolonged stay in Hilo was a trial to us all. This was not the fault of Hilo, nor of the very dear people who entertained us there. The irk and strain was from enforced delay—the dreadful condition of our 70-horse-power engine, which had to be gone all over again in Hilo, at an expense equal to the outlay in Honolulu, although our "friend" 'Gene (sent for from San Francisco), while knowing better, assured us that the engine was in good condition at that time. But that is of the vanished yesterday; and now Martin, in 'Gene's place, is devoting himself to preventing a recurrence of the conditions brought about by the latter's neglect.

And so we go sailing along this grey-and-gold late afternoon, involuntarily looking up now and again for a return of the splendid dolphins that played with our hook around the stern this morning. You will remember how utterly dead was the ocean those four weeks from California to Hawaii, except for one school of hump-backed whale, and a few, a very few flying-fish, and one small shark off Maui, that had not sense enough to bite at boiled ham. Why, this morning there was *kaku* for breakfast—that's the Hawaiian for it—a fish with long eel-like body and sharp head and a jaw fitted with rows of fine white teeth. But don't let me deceive you. This was the first fish ever caught aboard the *Snark* at sea.

Dolphins—they are like all the living rainbows of the aquarium at Honolulu wrapped in azure. They are all the colours of all the skies that ever were, with touches of solid green as green as solid earth. Brilliant as peacocks, and a thousand times—

—Oh, this is too much excitement for seven persons! A thousand porpoises are about us, the captain is on the bowsprit wielding a harpoon, while Martin tugs at the line set for dolphin, over-stern, and—there! the fish has carried away the hook. The fabulous blue dolphins are swimming alongside; sunny-green porpoises are darting with incredible swiftness all around and under the white yacht, leaping clear out of the water, singly and in twos and threes, like colts over hurdles. Our ocean is alive at last with the beauty and motion of the people of the sea.

There's a white and gold sunset now, like a flight of angels in the western sky; and before the stars come out I am going to sit and dream for a little space of the beautiful world and of the swift sleek forms of vibrant colour I have seen this day.

Lat. 14° 53′ North,
Lon. 152° 7′ West.
At sea, Tuesday, October 15, 1907.

There's a subtle change in the atmosphere aboard ship this morning. Nakata, showing an unusual number of teeth, even for him, summed it up in two words: "Seasick *pau!*" which last word, translated from the original Hawaiian, means *finished, done away with, gone, past, eliminated*—all the blessed meanings that should predicate that dread subject. Fortunately, Nakata was not only voicing his own ecstatic state, but that of the company in general. I proved my own recovery by making the regulation four at the breakfast table below, for the initial time this voyage.

When I came on deck after breakfast, the captain and Herrmann dropped their work (the sewing of canvas into ventilators, or "windsails"), to rig up a little awning over the cockpit, so that I might write in comfort, out of the glare.

It is nine o'clock, and Jack has just gone below to write his thousand words of the novel under way. (I cannot call the novel by name because the author hasn't been inspired as promptly as usual in his choice of title.) The hero, Martin Eden, has been waiting to make his first love to Ruth all this week the author has been under the weather.

Jack slept on deck last night and looks a happy, healthy, blue-eyed young sailor this morning, in white ducks, the broad-collared shirt open at his tanned throat. Before we sailed from Hawaii he threatened to have his hair clipped very close for the voyage; but my pleading "Oh, not *too* short, *please, please!*" at the door of the barber-shop in Hilo, saved perhaps an inch. The present neat closeness is rather becoming than otherwise.

I am so happy. All the rough edges of the first week at sea are smoothing down, and the spirit of our surroundings is getting into our blood. The wave-tops are silvered with flying-fish. One leaped out just now, cutting the air like a steel sickle, all of a foot long—the largest I have seen. And where there are many flying-fish, one may look for dolphin. Herrmann didn't catch the fish for breakfast this morning that he prophesied last night in the second dog-watch, and for which Jack promised him a bag of "Bull Durham."

The 5-horse-power engine (which we call the "sewing-machine" because it runs so easily since it was broken and mended in Hilo), is pumping electric "juice" for lights and fans, and Martin's six feet of height are under deck, which means that he is going over the big engine and putting his engine-room to rights. Herrmann is relating some choice bit of personal history to the captain, of which I just now caught the information that somebody lived "four miles off the bay from." The cook, coming on deck from the perspiring galley to dry his shirt, is commenting to the world at large upon the moustache he has raised during the past week; and Nakata is making up for lost time by washing and polishing everything in the cabin, occasionally bobbing up to smile happily at the universe.

Jack whispered to me this morning what he has not yet

suggested to the others: that if this adverse wind and sea continue, he may decide to cut the Marquesas Islands from our route and head direct for Tahiti. We sail and sail and get nowhere on the present course.

Who has said "miracle hours after sunset"? Last night, quitting the talkative group around the cockpit during the second dog-watch (six to eight), I went for'ard alone into the bows, curled myself up in a big coil of sun-bleached hawser on a water-tank, and took a little trip to the moon. The sky had cleared of all but fleecy wisps of cloud, and a gleaming half-moon and a few rare stars hung in the shining rigging. "What dreams may come" when one is all alone on a flying prow, among the moon and stars, with the sweet wind filling the wings of speed! But the dreams cannot be told, for they are thought in a language that was whispered to us when we were very young, while listening to tales of Karl in Queerland—and to only the very young is it given to translate the language. I slid back down a moonbeam to the deck very quickly when a dolphin at least three feet long leaped his length out of the water on the lee bow; but I couldn't get any anglers' enthusiasm out of the crowd aft. They were too filled with comfort and moonlight. Jack joined me after a while, and we sat on a tank to leeward, close to the water, holding to the fore-jib-sheet, watching the pearly full-rounded canvas, while glistening spray swished over the weather bow above us and wet our faces. It was the loveliest night I have ever seen at sea. The memory of it belongs between the pictured covers of a book of fairy-tales.

Then came nine hours below, of which I slept eight; and now the wholesome reality of the day is as beautiful as the fitful unreality of the night. Herrmann has drifted into "The Last Rose of Summer" again, and I cannot work while he sings. To do so would be to scorn one of the good things that bless my life. There is a really Caruso-like quality in some of his middle tones. And while I am thinking about the ease with which he handles his untrained voice, he airily switches off into a spirited rendition of "La Paloma" in Dutch, with an appropriate catch and swing that make me wonder if the tattooed lady on his forearm is dancing to match the music while he plies his needle.

Alternating with bouts of cribbage we read up a few sheaves of late San Francisco papers, jerking ourselves rudely from this Pacific solitude, this desert of oceans, back into the crowded world of cities from which we have fled. Why, if we were cast away in this part of the Pacific, we should stand practically no chance of being picked up. It is out of the travelled way. It was something to think of, as I lay on a strip of duck on the deck, too ill to do anything but watch the veils of cloud drawing across the sky. The world was a round blue ball swathed in clouds like a jewel in white floss, covered by a blue bowl. Not a thing in sight but blue water and blue and white sky; and through the silent picture our white-speck boat moved upon her quest for palm and coral and mountain-isle and pearls and strange simple peoples. We are all the world, we of the *Snark*, so far as the rest of the world is concerned—unless a sail should break the line of the horizon, when we would become only a hemisphere; but no sail pushes up out of the blue of this painted solitude.

But accidents will happen. On Friday morning, the 11th, in the early hours some bolts worked loose in the steering-gear, and when I came on deck the captain and Herrmann were arms-down-to-shoulders in the casing around the rudder-head, heaping maledictions in several languages upon the man or men who planned and executed this casing so that it could not be got into except from the top. The teak cover, upon which the steersman sits, is the only movable part of the box enclosing the steering-gear; whereas the entire upper half of the box should be made so that it could be lifted. Just another instance of the outrageous mistakes that were perpetrated on the poor little *Snark*. There had been a stiff squall the night before, too, and it was fortunate the bolts did not come loose then. It would have been cheaper in the long run if Jack had given up his regular work during the building of the yacht, and done the overseeing himself.

Our winds have been fairly fresh, but not steady, the best part of the week. The days have been pretty warm, and I find the coolest spot to be on the cockpit floor, where I spend hours trying to read or write, or merely watching the colours under closed eyelids. That amusement is always left, when one hasn't energy enough for other exertion. Some days the wind blew harder and the seas piled high, hissing hungrily toward us, usually missing and going astern, but sometimes striking ponderously and snapping their white teeth over the rail. The rougher nights were hard on me, as my bunk, on the starboard side, came in for all the jarring weighty blows of water when the hull rose and fell in the trough.

One languid diversion during the days of our uselessness, was the discussion of who would gather the first quart of pearls in the South Seas. It rather lames the controversy, however, when I insist that the rest shall give all their quarts to me.

Lat. 14° 4′ North,
Lon. 152° 56′ West.
At sea, Wednesday, October 16, 1907.

There was dolphin for breakfast this morning—a heavy, steak-like sort of meat. Herrmann got it last night with the granes, an awful devil's-pitchfork sort of implement. And just as Herrmann landed his dolphin—Jack meanwhile shouting for me to come and see its wondrous tints in the moonlight—I landed my cockroach, the second horror of its kind caught aboard the *Snark*. The dolphin was about two and a half feet long. The cockroach about one inch. It was a good night's catch we made—mine, I thought, being the more important. Another and larger dolphin was struck with the granes, but tore itself loose; and this morning the poor pretty creature is swimming faithfully if rather indiscreetly alongside, its wounds gaping snow-white under the brine. We are not sailing fast enough to catch dolphins on the hook. They are too clever to bite at anything they have time to observe is not the real flying-fish.

"Who hath desired the sea, the sight of salt water unbounded"—oh! we had a feast of Kipling last evening in the cockpit, until half past nine, when Jack and I went forward to enjoy the moonlit bow again. The water was unusually placid, with a fair breeze, and we were making some headway, E.S.E. by the compass. Shadowy forms of dolphins slipped luminously past in the dark flood and like a whisper of the Far East came the voices of the two Japanese tucked away in the life-boat for the night. Perhaps the unearthly charm of our bow may grow commonplace some day; but not yet awhile.

Slowly we're getting everything into working order. Yesterday I started putting to rights my stateroom lockers, carelessly packed on leaving port. Writing is going forward, the captain pursues his unostentatious navigation, the wonder of the ocean-world is becoming incorporated into our every-day consciousness, and the *Snark* sails on, the *Snark* sails on.

Herrmann is like to burst with pride, for he has caught all the fish so far. This morning he displayed a small flying-fish that he found on deck, one of an unusual variety with four finny wings instead of two. These fish dash blindly over the rail in the darkness and fall to deck stunned. Just now, stitching away at a jib that was dragged and torn under the forefoot the other night, Herrmann is relating how he skated one hundred and ten miles in a day, from one town to another, on the canals in Holland. One day he explained to Jack why he never saves money. There was a time when he had three hundred dollars in bank in New York. Off the Horn the main hatch of the ship he was in was smashed in a storm, the ocean poured in, and for a while it looked as if the vessel would sink. But in all the smother of darkness and water, obeying orders from the desperate captain and mate, Herrmann's ruling thought in the very face of death was one of regret that he had not drunk up that three hundred dollars in the last port! Upon reaching Seattle he had his money telegraphed to him from New York, and wasted no time in spending it. As Captain Warren has it, "Money's no good except for the fun you can buy with it."

Lat. 13° 36' North,
Lon. 152° West.
Thursday, October 17, 1907.

There are two factors in sea-voyages that I cannot reconcile to advantage, namely, lack of exercise, and three meals a day. To be sure, there is a sort of passive exercise in the mere motion of the boat—continuous, and tiring until one gets used to it, but not sufficient, in my case at least, to offset a hearty diet. I have always bewailed the absence of some sort of exercising-bar on the boat; and all the time one has been staring me in the face and eyes every time I descended the companion-stairs, in the shape of the brass handle-bar at right angles to the side-bars. So now when I go below I usually "chin" that bar thrice.

Last evening, while having a cup of bouillon in the cockpit in lieu of supper below, I listened to Herrmann's story, as he polished away at Jack's set of surgical instruments, of how he left Holland in wrath ten years ago, to return no more to the bosom of his family. It appears that he was skipper of his father's boat (a ketch-rigged vessel, by the way, like the *Snark*), carrying small cargoes in the North Sea and on the coasts of England and Denmark. One Christmas Eve, Herrmann came from Rotterdam, where his vessel happened to be, upon urgent invitation from his family. He arrived at dinner-time and found his parents and his brothers and sisters with their guests around the table. Some relative, a clerk in an office, commented disagreeably upon Herrmann's clothes. "He told me as I shouldn't come mit my father's house to dinner in the clothes as I was. My clothes ben all right, blue English sweater and good pants. So I got awful mad for him, and I told him I could buy all his clothes a t'ousand times ofer, as I ben getting much money.'' More words passed, and Herrmann, who I gathered had been feeling somewhat convivial when he arrived, finally "got too mad" and landed across the festive board on his antagonist's countenance. Herr de Visser reprimanded his son for this breach of etiquette and peace. This proved too much for Herrmann's "mad." He rose in outraged dignity and left the parental roof forever. "And I told my father he would nefer see me more," Herrmann concluded, in a tone of mixed pathos and defiance.

"But your mother?" I asked.

"Oh—she cried much; she felt very bad."

Then I: "Why don't you write to her, Herrmann, some day? It wasn't her fault."

His delft-blue eyes looked past me across the sea.

"It iss too late," he said, softly. "She iss dead two years."

Lat. 12° North,
Lon. 151° West.
Saturday, October 19, 1907.

It was bathing-suits and bucketfuls of salt water this morning before breakfast. I assuaged some of my yearning for exercise by hauling in the canvas bucket, after which I replenished wasted tissue with a fairly stout breakfast. Wada is doing nobly with the cooking. He goes on his independent way, to the best of his ability, until some suggestion is made, whereupon he devotes himself to learning a different way.

We feel so very husky, drying our bathing-suits on us in fresh breeze and sun. The particular northerly wind our skipper has been whistling for, sprang up last evening in the dog-watch, after a day of calm that looked suspiciously like the Doldrums (far north of the Equator as we are), and during which we ran our crippled big engine for an hour or so. But the crank-bearings heated badly, and we flapped on the rest of the day by sail, but didn't flap far. With the wind came a smart shower, and we hung out some of our clothes to wash.

Sitting around the cockpit afternoons, reading Melville's fascinating *Typee* and Robert Louis Stevenson's and his mother's books on the Marquesas and Tahiti, we long more than ever to get forward into the South Sea. And it is a wonderful thing we are doing—full of romance and colour. Even while we are being held back from the Line by this calm, we have with us beauty rare and unforgettable. The calm ocean is a disc of sapphire encircled by a rim of clouds. Once, watching that wounded dolphin which still follows us, we noticed that the smooth blue water, through a trick of light, seemed to be dotted with bluer pools—something like the effect of oil on water.

But the calm is gone, and now we are travelling on our course, east by north; and it is cool and fresh in the shade of the cockpit awning.

Jack called to me the other day and said he had something to ask of me—that, every time I came on deck, I should look around over the water. "This is a lonely sea, Mate, and there might be some poor devil in distress." I told him I rather thought I already had the habit of looking around the horizon a great deal. "Yes; but make it your *duty* to do it every time you come on deck." Well, men have been lost for the lack of a dutiful eye in this regard, and I'm going to be very watchful.

I'm afraid Herrmann isn't quite equal to some of Jack's jokes. The latter announced lately that he wanted Martin and Herrmann to do two things for him on this trip around the world—Martin at some time to get a baby monkey for roasting, and Herrmann, for the same purpose, a baby cannibal. Martin reports that Herrmann said to him with an aggrieved expression, "*I* couldn't shoot a little baby!"

Lat. 11° 7′ North,
Lon. 150° 33′ West.
Sunday, October 20, 1907.

This was a morning to put the fear of Nature into the heart of a tyro at sea-going. I came on deck at seven, after what had seemed to me a rough night, and found the captain at the wheel, closely watching a black sky ahead, Herrmann shortening sail, and all preparations being made for trouble. Then one of the teak top-doors of the companionway descended upon my head and I went below for a few minutes to nurse my wrongs. There are plenty of ways to get hurt in squally weather on a small vessel. Yesterday accidents were rife, a cut finger apiece for Martin and Herrmann, and for me a thumb jammed in a heavy water-tight-compartment door.

Next, the mizzen was taken in, and the motion gentled down a little. After breakfast we ran well into the squalls of rain, and the men soaped their bodies and washed their clothes in the rain-water that stood in the slack of the canvas boat-covers; while Jack and I had a novel bath in the curtained cockpit, rain coming down on us and dripping from the mizzen boom also. The only complaint just now is that after our thorough soaping the rain stopped and we had to put on our clothes without rinsing off the lather! Dry bathing-suits are the clothes, however, and when it rains again we'll take another wetting. The captain said he guessed a bucket of fresh water could be spared for completing my shampoo. He holds every one else down close when it comes to using our water store. I am very economical, though—for I try to realise what it would mean to be out of water at sea, and this promises to be a long voyage. A very little water, with a drop or so of strong ammonia, goes a long way toward keeping one clean.

It was great fun bathing in the rain—you haven't any idea how something unusual like this varies the monotony of seafaring, however pleasant that monotony may be.

Now, at ten o'clock, the weather has moderated and the

sun is trying to come out. There is a great amount of movement, however, and none of us feels any too well. Persons who are going to be seasick ought to be broken in with a gale immediately upon sailing. The best I can do this morning in the way of work, with any degree of comfort, is to lie in my bunk and use a pencil. I had hoped to get at Jack's typewriting, but the very thought makes my narrow walls revolve. I am so glad they are even approximately white walls,—though even now, after two thorough coats of white enamel paint, old Captain Rosehill's salmon-pink coating shows through. Captain Rosehill was Roscoe's successor, and served as harbour captain while the *Snark* was in Hawaii.

We have learned something startling. Yesterday Jack was reading in the South Sea Directory the report of an old-time mariner concerning the difficulty of fetching the Marquesas and Society Islands, from Hawaii, on account of adverse wind and sea. He went so far as to hint at its being practically an impossible traverse. So we are on the way to doing something impossible, are we? Well, we have started, and it is easier to think of the impossibility of the trip for other people than for ourselves. We have just *got* to make the Marquesas.

Lat. 11° North,
Lon. 149° 50′ West.
Monday, October 21, 1907.

Two weeks ago to-day we left Hilo, figuring on three or four weeks for our passage to the Marquesas. Yesterday Captain Warren remarked that it might be fifty days yet before we see them. A Hilo friend's anxious questions, at parting, as to whether we really expected to reach our destination, will probably recur to her mind several times before our arrival is listed. Most persons seem unable to comprehend that we are not deliberately suicidal.

It's hard sailing this morning, in a big sea with steady wind. Yesterday we *seemed* to be sailing; there was abundance of movement, but it was mostly up and down—a troubled cross-sea and strong head-wind.

Just after the stormy sunset and sudden twilight yester-night, the moon showed dead ahead, a burning copper disc melting its way through a wall of lead. Then happened one of the amazes of the sea. Out of the turmoil of wind and mounting waves, out of the whirling chaos of the low overtaking sky, we sailed right through the leaden wall into a night of perfect tranquillity, lit by an incredible burst of moon and stars. It was a revelation, this peaceful ocean and dry north breeze and sparkling firmament. It was like the shifting of colossal scenery in some marvellous spectacle. The stars were too large and bright to be anything but tinsel and electric light; the sky was far too purple for a real night-sky, and the billows of woolly clouds too massy and tangible to be mere vapours of sea-water.

> Lat.   9° 45′ North,
> Lon. 136° 17′ West.
> Monday, November 4, 1907.

Death is farthest from one's thoughts these pleasant, busy days of semi-calm, when there is just breeze enough to slip us along slowly over the smoothly rolling flood. We are complete in our little working-world; the domestic machinery cogs along much the same as in a land-home. There is little danger of any one falling overboard unless he is attacked by vertigo, and we are in a live world in which death, I say, does not occur to our minds. But when, after such days, and placid evenings spent in the starlight with music and singing and poesy, one is startled into conscious-ness at midnight by being let down suddenly against the bunk-rail, and the further sensation of going on over, end-lessly, endlessly—then death is the first flashing thought. It might not be so to one in the open, on deck; but a closed forward stateroom, in a small yacht, is a trap. It may mean death by drowning, or, what is worse, *sharks*. Sharks are no myth in this populous Pacific—as the jaw of a young six-footer, drying its twelve rows of fine saw-teeth on the mizzen pin-rail, grimly attests. It all darted through my brain when the squall smote, and I went over the rail of my high bunk and landed on the five-by-two floor with an agility I would not have thought possible. Theretofore I had always taken off the rail before climbing carefully down. I turned on the electric bulb, cleared up fallen things as best I could, got on my clothes somehow or other, all the while wondering if the boat would ever right. My heart was beating in my throat with the suddenness and manner of my awakening; while my head told me I was not needed on deck, in spite of an urgent desire to get out from under, for I knew that every man was up and doing. A woman may be a very small item in the way of usefulness in stress at sea; but there is always something to be done, and after our careless days of placid weather things below had not been wedged in as tightly as usual.

I was glad to get out and up on deck in the driving smother. I "tooted" to Jack, while groping my clinging way to the wheel, and tried to satisfy my curiosity as to what was happening—which is asking too much with regard to a tropical gale in the dead of night. A sailor cannot see, he can only feel; and what he feels is a powerful gust that puts the vessel over and keeps her down, while he takes in sail and wonders what is behind the awful blackness to windward. So when I said to Jack at the wheel, "What is it?" he could merely answer, "I don't know." No one knows. It is black, it is blowing like a gale but it may be only a rain-squall, over in ten minutes.

One thing gratifies me: Jack and the skipper never try to reassure me at the expense of their own veracity. I begged this of them at the start. So I get the best there is to be had of their frank opinions. I want to know, and I ought to know; and they treat me in this respect as "one of the boys."

So Jack "didn't know"; all he was sure of was that with the sudden onslaught of the wind he awoke in the life-boat, aware of Captain Warren streaking past him to the main-boom tackle, for the squall had burst in the opposite quarter from a light breeze that had been filling the sails. The celerity with which Jack must have landed from his bed on the canvas cover of the boat amidship, into the cockpit and to the wheel, is partially told by a huge rent in the nether garment which adorned his person at the time, and which I have just finished repairing.

Nakata was steering when the squall smote, and immediately spoke to the captain, asleep on deck alongside. The captain is quick as lightning, and had things straightened out in no time. Fortunately the *Snark* is stiff, and shows no signs of turning turtle; so that while the man at the wheel eases her along in the violent puffs of wind, the others have time to handle the sails without fear of capsizing. When I came up, Martin and Herrmann were taking in the flying-jib and sails and Jack was succeeding in keeping the yacht before the wind. How I love men, and the work men do! Jack, keen at his task of steering in the squall—the sturdy little wheel flying under his hands; the men forward holding on by their eyebrows while they took in the jib; the captain everywhere; Nakata, cheerily fastening down the weather-skylight and taking bedding below—men, men, all brave men, doing their fighting work in the world.

And death receded into dim distance with the interest and excitement of our little battle with the forces of out-doors, as the small *Snark* buckled down to carrying every thread of her working canvas, which was re-set shortly when the wind grew no worse. The captain's voice broke warmly as he spoke of the way she did it, and the way she minded the helm. He is very emotional. Why, the other day when he had that shark on the hook over the stern, I thought he would weep with excitement and disappointment for very fear that Herrmann would not slip the bowline over the creature's tail in time. He was afraid the hook alone would not hold it.

The squall blew itself out shortly, leaving us a good sailing-breeze, and we went below and finished our sleep. But such an experience clinched what old sailors tell of the treachery of these latitudes, where the wind slaps out of unexpected quarters at unexpected times, and in the night at least no man knows what lurks behind the darker dark to windward. . . . Captain Warren, sitting at the wheel, nods appreciatively at what I have written.

Although personal death does not press upon us in pleasant weather, there is doom all around for the lesser things, swift and pursuing. For four days countless myriads of small fish resembling mackerel have been leaping and glinting around the ship, driven by tireless enemies below, and meeting pain and disaster at the surface from the ravenous young gunies scanning the deep from above. It is something like the tragedy of the flying-fish caught between dolphin and frigate-birds. Of this an old chronicler of the sixteenth century writes:

"There is another kind of fish (the flying-fish) as big almost as a herring, which hath wings and flieth, and they are together in great number. These have two enemies; the one in the sea, the other in the air. In the sea, the fish which is called the Albacore, as big as a salmon, followeth them with great swiftness to take them. This poor fish not being able to swim fast, for he hath no fins, but swimmeth with the moving his tail, shutting his wings, lifteth himself above the water, and flieth not very high. The Albacore seeing this, although he have no wings, yet giveth a great leap out of the water, and sometimes catcheth him; or else he keepeth himself under the water, going that way as fast as the other flieth. And when the fish, being weary of the air, or thinking himself out of danger, returneth into the water, the Albacore meeteth with him; but sometimes his other enemy, the sea-crow, catcheth him before he falleth."

Jack has been taking a hand this morning in the carnage, or trying to, getting out some of the pretty tackle we used to unpack so gleefully at Glen Ellen when the orders were

Her Trick at the Wheel

Jack Harpooning

Wada's Dolphin

filled from the East. But the fish were too busy with the other form of death to be caught by this lure of bright steel and colour.

We have fared better in the matter of wind during the past two weeks. On the 22d, at 4:30 P. M., a squall came up that sent us spinning along at six knots during the following hour, in the right direction; and the second day following, good winds started that kept us well on our course for several days. Everybody aboard is happier when the *Snark* is holding her own, especially the captain, upon whom a dead calm has a very bad effect, and during which his temper is short and his language, on the side, when I am not supposed to be within hearing, is hardly elegant.

It is a splendid sight, a rain-squall coming over the water in the daylight. It resembles a dust-storm or low rolling hills—fairly smoking along; and when the dust of the rain arrives you do not run for shelter, but just stand and enjoy the warm drenching. This morning Jack and I stood by the weather shrouds forward, watching it come from the northeast, the nearer waters broken by leaping fish.

We are in the Doldrums now, variable winds and frequent showers, whereas in the Variables there was more wind and less rain.

The horizons are dreams of cloud-beauty on the still days; or, toward late afternoon when a light breeze sends us smoothly ahead, we may see low-lying clouds of blue, the clouds themselves blue, and out of the low pillowy clouds on the horizon will puff up bursts of white that tint through with rose and gold as the sun goes down, while we sit with faces glorified by the rose of the west and the wine of the sunset sea.

Lat.   9° 37′ North,
Lon. 135° 18′ West.
Tuesday, November 5, 1907.

It has surprised me, as we have drawn nearer to the Equator, that it has not been warmer. "Stark calm on the lap of the line'' as we are, the heat is not distressing. Of course, one would not choose to be in the sun for long at midday; but there has been nothing unusual about the temperature. To-day, however, is quite hot enough for an introduction to the Line. A hat and green visor scarce shade one's eyes. I was fairly blinded just now when I took up some linen things to bleach on the launch-cover. Head and eyes ache from the brassy glare, and I am going to take better care of them and wear a hat oftener, although I love the warm colour of the sun-burn on my hair.

Keeping clothes from mildewing and yellow-spotting is a ceaseless responsibility, and deterioration of silk is appalling. A large portion of Nakata's time is employed in taking on deck and returning below our bedding and wearing apparel. Just now I am burning an electric extension in my crowded closet-locker, to offset the dampness, while a mass of *holokus* and other summery garments is on my bed benefiting by sunshine that filters through the decklight. There is one compensation, however, for the trouble of overhauling, and that is the pleasure of handling pretty things. My every-day garb on the boat is of a kind that, while comfortable and even picturesque (according to Jack), makes me appreciate the sight of more feminine and dainty possessions. You see, the grime of San Francisco has not yet quite worn from our ropes and tackle; and after completely ruining one silken bloomer-suit I said ''Never again,'' and adopted pajamas, rolled up at knee and elbow, as Jack wears them. In such a suit of white, black-figured, with a piratical touch of red at waist and neck, I go my free and barefoot way. As for the crew, they seem to take everything I do as a matter of course, without comment of eye or lip.

I am not the first observer in the world who has noted that most persons long to be something for which they are not fitted by nature. Nakata is no exception. His desire is to be a blond, and he waxes ecstatic over my burned locks. ''Bee-*yu*-ti-ful, Missisn!'' he cries innocently, his gaze lingering on my hair as I brush it in the sun. Now he is wild with a bird-like delight over my suggestion that we bleach his stiff black poll. I am equally keen for the lark, but there is no peroxide aboard. Martin, I think, has leanings toward brigandage, judging by the desperately evil look he attains by wearing a blue-and-white bandana around his head in lieu of a hat. He has lost overboard some eight hats and caps since we left San Francisco, and is now reduced to a bandana, and his precious Baden-Powell, and he is afraid of losing that. I do not know in what character Jack would be scintillating, if he could find the scarlet bathing-suit he is hunting for—a new one bought in Hilo; but it has disappeared, either tucked away as things aboard the *Snark* are too often tucked away and lost to all intents and purposes, or else stolen before we sailed. Our shelf-copy of *The Sea Wolf* is gone, too, and a book-proof copy of *The Iron Heel*. And neither Jack nor I has a sou'wester—both stolen, as far as we can judge. I wear the captain's, at his urgent solicitation, although it is not fair to him, and Jack goes around in his old rummage-sale Tam o' Shanter, the age of which is beyond guessing. As for me, I am posing as the happiest and luckiest girl in the world, and it is an easy rôle.

Now let me tell about that six-foot-five shark we caught— the first ever landed on the *Snark*. The captain got it with a salt-pork-baited hook over the stern; Herrmann slipped a bowline under it, and then shot it in the head several times. But it died hard, thrashing on the deck a long time after the men got it inboard. Of course, it was hung up and photographed—strange, vicious monster, with eyes like a cat, yellowish, slit-pupiled, and with a cat's disinclination to give up the fight for life. It still thrashed about even after most of its internal economy had gone overboard. I never have heard a description of the eye of a shark, and its resemblance to the feline optic struck me instantly. "The tiger of the sea," to be sure—why, it *ought* to have cat's eyes. This shark of ours was a specimen of the man-eating variety, with twelve fearsome rows of saw-edged teeth. The meat of the shark is good and sweet, and not dry; but sailors do not care for it—probably because of their hatred of its propensity for human meat.

But sharks have annoyances of their own, one of these being a black sucker—*remora*—that clings to it as a sea-anemone clings to a rock, a marine vermin that can hardly be soothing to the shark. The longest we pulled off was about ten inches. The clinging-muscles of the slippery pest are under its head, under the jaw, if it can be called a jaw. At first we thought these parasites were young sharks. So tightly did they stick, that it was almost impossible to pull them loose while they lived. And now all that is left of our first shark are the jaws, drying on the pin-rail, and the vertebra, strung at the mizzen-masthead.

There were many dolphins swimming around us the morning we got the shark, Saturday, the 2nd—an orgy of colour in the sun-shot azure of the water. It was one of the days when the water is pale sapphire through which the sun-rays focus deep down in long slanting funnels of quivering golden light. The shark was attended by dozens of its black-and-white striped pilot-fish, and there were several bonitos around also.

Later. A small shark is following us this afternoon, but in a listless fashion that indicates a full stomach. It chased a big dolphin out of the water, and the pursued fish took a shoot of at least seven feet over the surface—a curving blade of flashing blue.

The first Portuguese men-o'-war that we have seen since we left Hilo, have shown up lately—one day a solitary little silver sail, and the next day myriads. Just here I am reminded of the "nature-fake" discussion that is raging in the United States. It appears that Mr. John Burroughs has incurred the displeasure of a correspondent of the *Outlook*, by stating that "the Physalia, or Portuguese man-o'-war, has a kind of sail in its air-sack that helps it sail to windward." The irritated correspondent jumps back with: "It does nothing of the kind; it cannot sail to windward, and it never did; it drifts to leeward." But another critic out-Burroughs Mr. Burroughs, as follows:

"The physalia has three masts, all square-rigged, and in windward work easily lies within three points of the wind. Going large he runs under bare poles. In the Bay of Barataria I have often seen a squadron of these Portuguese men-o'-war with stunsails set, beating to windward to get the weather gauge on a Spanish omelet, then furling everything and running down the wind to their less active victim. The nautilus has sails too, only it is barkentine-rigged, and in running sometimes sets a lower foretopsail."

One day, when the men were overhauling the fore-peak, eight infant rats, with their mother, were killed. We hoped they were all settled, but since then traces of another have been found. Probably it comes into the galley at night for water, as there is none handy anywhere else, all tanks being of galvanized iron, with no seepage. Captain Warren says that aboard ships a rat will gnaw almost through a water-cask, contenting itself with the moisture oozing through, rather than letting the water out freely and losing it all.

We have been practising with our rifles this afternoon—the first time I've had a gun in my hands since the heavy rifle on Molokai, when I hit the target at two hundred yards. To-day we were trying at pieces of wood and cans on the water. Perhaps, before the day is over, Jack will have a chance at the shark.

Try as we may to forget the inexcusable blunders in the building of the *Snark*, and the persons who are inexcusably responsible, things hitherto unknown keep creeping out to make us more than ever sick of commercial civilisation. The men who sailed with us from San Francisco insisted upon the honesty of those who betrayed us in the building of our boat—even insisted in the face of evidence to the contrary as strong as what came to light yesterday morning, when Captain Warren found the deck-beams forward of our staterooms, where they were not likely to be discovered, to be pine instead of the fine oak beams that were ordered and paid for in the east and delivered at the shipyard. To be sure, many a good ship's deck-beams are pine; but that is not the point: the shipbuilders substituted beams that cost about $2.50 apiece, for beams that cost us about $7.50 apiece. What became of the oak? But this is not the worst. The bitts forward, upon the strength of which depends our safety when at anchor, is a ghastly bluff. About one quarter of it reaches as it should down to the bottom of the boat; the other three quarters are supposed to go down to the bottom of the boat—*but do not*. A magnificent great beam of oak to look upon—it stops short at the deck, a farce, another heart-breaking reminder of the way the "honest" men treated us in the States. The rotten wrought iron—it still goes back on us, here and there; the deck-planking full of butts, ordered without butts and paid for accordingly; the pitiful futile engine. But I haven't told about the engine. After paying out five hundred dollars more in Hilo on repairs to it, now, after working it at half-speed (it would go no faster) for perhaps a couple of hours altogether since we sailed a month ago, the engine is *pau*, and cannot be used again until another machine-shop is handy, which will not be until we reach Papeete, Tahiti. Even the engineer in Hilo, our last hope, let us go out to sea with an engine he knew for a joke, and with some new faults of which he did not tell us, although he knew them, according to Martin. Why Martin did not give us the benefit of his information, I do not know.

From the engine room at intervals comes a heavy sigh. It is certainly appropriate, and quite affecting, even if it is produced by a metal valve! It is an expensive valve, by the way, installed in Hilo, doubly expensive because it is a failure. Ah, well—cold world and warm friend, it has been all one to Jack and me where the building of the *Snark* is concerned. But we have each other and the fair sky and water all about us, and we are alive and living in spite of them all.

Lat. 9° 4' North,
Lon. 134° 15' West.
Wednesday, November 6, 1907.

Have I said before that we are over half-way to the Marquesas?—and already a month at sea. There are potatoes for four more days; and with the potatoless prospect. arise vague longings for fresh *taro,* and *poi,* cocoanuts, and breadfruit! We shall be glad enough to welcome land and trees and growing things. But Jack and I are not in the slightest sense bored by the long passage—we haven't time to do the things we want to do. The captain frets and chafes sorely, however, although after a particularly crusty spell, he usually laughs at himself and explains again what it means to a captain to have a vessel held back.

We thought we had made an important discovery. It seems that the mackerel fishing-grounds of the world have been practically deserted of late years, and no one knows where the fish have migrated. Here, in this lonely part of the Pacific, we began to think we had solved the problem. But the books tell us that mackerel are not to be found far from land, so this boiling sea of fish through which we have been sailing cannot well be mackerel, but is more likely to be the skipjack and young bonita —both related to the mackerel, however. Also, the extreme shyness of the supposed mackerel toward our hooks, tallies with that exasperating characteristic of the skipjack, as noted in the book of reference that we dug up. Our little library is of unending use and joy to us.

It being too wet to box after breakfast this morning, Jack read aloud to us all,—Joseph Conrad's *Youth,* a masterpiece of which he and I never tire, many times though we have read it. I, at least, can appreciate it much better than I could before my acquaintance with the sea. Books and stories about the sea and sea-going bring the world closer than ever about me, as I touch more intimately, day after day, the life of the sea. Captain Warren swears by Conrad—a sailor vouching for the capable work of another sailor. And speaking of the captain reminds me of an incident that occurred yesterday which made a great impression upon me. Our little arsenal has rusted in spite of present care-taking, having got a bad start during 'Gene's régime, and the guns jammed yesterday, after the first few shots. Jack was firing his Colt's automatic pistol, and it jammed. The empty shell would not eject, nor would the loaded magazine come out. I was watching his efforts to straighten out the thing, and the captain could see I was nervous lest there be an explosion in Jack's precious hands, although I declare I made little fuss. So the captain begged Jack to let him experiment, adding something about its not being so important a matter if anything happened to his own hands. It was said quite as a matter of course—the captain of a boat taking as a matter of course the first risks in all things. Jack did not relinquish the pistol, and I was immensely relieved when the magazine finally yielded and came out. But I shall not soon forget the captain's words and intention, and told him so later on. He looked pleased, and said simply, "Mr. London's hands are worth more than mine."

Everybody had a good time to-day, for there was plenty of incident. The captain hooked our first bonita, a small specimen about fourteen inches long, dark changeable blue on top and all delicate mother-of-pearl and rose underneath. Being a dry fish, it was relegated to a chowder for supper. Jack did not finish his chapter of the novel this forenoon, because, soon after he had gone below to write, after inspecting the bonita, we spied a turtle not far off. Captain Warren wore ship and made for the bowsprit, dropped down upon the martingale back-rope, calling meanwhile for a line to put around his body, while he should fasten another rope around the turtle, after which we were to haul them both in. He did that once before, he says, and shows a scar from the turtle's bite. But he did not go overboard this time, for we drifted to the left of the creature. Waking from sleep, it paddled astern, bobbing

against the starboard side of the boat, heavy with a meal
off a dozen small-fry. Over the stern the captain hung
on to the granes that Herrmann put into the turtle's
shell just back of its head, while Jack shot his automatic
rifle into the head. Herrmann and Martin were frantically
hunting for the harpoon, which was not where it belonged,
strange to say! Only one barb of the granes had caught
in the shell, and the captain had his hands full to keep from
losing the catch. Herrmann could not manage to stick the
harpoon where he wanted it, so he put a rope around himself
and dropped overboard, passed the turtle up and was himself hauled in. One doesn't feel quite happy with a fellow
voyager overboard in these waters, I can tell you. One
never knows when a shark may be loafing just under the
keel, dozing lightly and alert for anything that looks like a
meal. Like our shark, the turtle was attended by pilot-fish.

Handling a sea-turtle is a thing to be done gingerly; for
besides the vicious mouth with its sharp beak inside in lieu
of teeth, he has a thick strong claw on each flipper. And
when a turtle is dead, he isn't dead; you can't trust him—
he is worse than a shark. A story is told of a turtle-shell
hung on a tree, with only tail and head left attached. A
sailor put two fingers into the mouth, and the "abysmal
brute" beak closed and the sailor left his two fingers therein.

The dissection of this creature, which is "neither flesh,
nor fish, nor fowl," but resembles all three, was worth seeing. I wonder sometimes how I can watch these bloody
operations. But I want to see, I want to know; and these
good reasons brace me up. The most remarkable thing I
saw in the interior of this turtle was the canal leading to
the stomach, which canal was lined with yellow spikes
like those of a sea-anemone. Nothing that is swallowed can
return to the light unless the swallower wills. Captain
Warren is drying this curiosity in the sun, and says it is
going to make me a purse! Our turtle measured three feet
from nose to rear end of shell, the shell itself being twenty-
six inches long. The tail alone was about ten inches.

During the catching, there happened a thing of wonderful beauty. Twice, a brilliantly coloured dolphin, at least six feet in length, leaped high and shot out over the water, twisting and turning in the air before falling on its side with a loud splash—just having a good time enjoying its life and strength. There were many dolphins swimming close around us at the time, as if curious about the turtle, and we saw a four-foot albacore, resembling the bonita, only many times larger than any bonita we have come across. Schools of tiny skipjacks swam under the yacht, and a small flying-fish came aboard. Jack's old promises are being abundantly surpassed.

It is an unending happy dream of youth and romance, this idling over the face of the waters, taking anything and everything that comes along, as a matter of course, rain or sunshine, cloud or wind, pleasure and danger; and it is all pleasure.

Lat. 6° 45′ North,
Lon. 134° West.
Friday, November 8, 1907.

Captain Warren is trying hard not to be short and glum in this near-calm, in which the only fan of air that blows takes us more to the south than we care to go as yet—easting being what we must make in order to gain the Marquesas. But Jack and I are most cheerful, with our work and reading, sparring, playing intense games of cribbage and "admirin' how the world is made."

The turtle has been served up in various forms, each better than the last—broiled, fried, soup-wise, and in chowder; and the end is not yet.

. . . Last night a slim new moon came out above heavy slate-blue clouds after sunset, and under the clouds glowed a dull-gold horizon, while the sea was all a pale purple flushed with rose. If my sunsets grow tiresome, forgive me. They are so lovely that it seems I must speak of them. This morning the ocean reminds me of a great round aquarium, the rim wrought with frosted filagree of clouds—a bowl of blue water wherein the fish leap clear as if trying to escape. But the bowl has a cover of palest blue, and there is no escape.

Monday, November 11, 1907.

To-day a new element entered into our romance—the element of raw, red, brutal sailor-life that lands- men and -women read about in books. And it has left me sad and sick and with a cruel sense of disillusionment. I have already hinted at the emotional disposition of the *Snark's* present skipper; but I did not dream that I was preparing my readers for the horrid thing that happened this afternoon. It is like a nightmare; only, when I look at the ugly cut on poor Wada's blanched face, with the purple-bruised eyes swollen almost shut, I know again the sickening reality of this new page in the *Snark's Log*.

The captain's moroseness had been increasing steadily and probably he had reached the stage when he had to take it out on somebody. He chose the smallest man on board. Warren has a cleft in the top of his skull that he says was dealt him by a crazy ship's-cook; but after to-day's experience I don't mind hazarding that maybe that cook was not crazy.

And here's what occurred: This morning at breakfast the captain suddenly remembered a box of honey some one had given him at Hilo. He also remembered having subsequently seen this box in the galley, and now asked Wada sharply why he had not served the honey with our hot-cakes these many mornings. Wada, very flustered and small in the voice, answered haltingly that he had never seen the box. He was commanded to produce it immediately, but failed to locate it. Then the captain, half rising from the table, cried in a voice shaking with rage, "You find that honey, *or I'll show you how to find it!*" His fury was out of all proportion to the occasion, and much out of place at table, to say the least.

After breakfast, Wada, with drawn face, and assisted

by a silent but sympathetic Nakata, searched through locker after locker, in galley and in cabin; but, presumably through the very forgetfulness of fear, he did not happen on the right locker. After lunch, which passed off rather constrainedly under the lowering looks of the captain, there was a general air of uncomfortable expectancy aboard ship. In the afternoon, while Jack was steering and reading aloud to me in the cockpit, there came through the galley decklight the sound of a one-sided conversation in the trembling, uncontrolled tones of Captain Warren. Nakata was hovering on deck with the longest face we had ever seen on him. Few words reached us; but there followed a thudding pause that turned me faint. Then the captain came on deck, and his hands were bloody—I know I can never look at them again without thinking of it; and he was followed by a shrunken, blinded little brown man whose entire face was a red smudge. I did not look again, for I felt somehow that along with the pain Wada was suffering, there was pride and a shrinking from observation. So I looked at Jack instead, and something in his eyes told me the happening would never be repeated.

The captain came aft with his brutal hands; and would you believe it?—he had so relieved himself that he was now all apology for making a scene, and further, his voice broke sympathetically over the "punishment" he had been obliged to give Wada. The cook had ordered him out of the galley, and of course it was a captain's right to go anywhere he pleased aboard his command.

Martin had heard and seen everything through the glass window in the wall between galley and engine-room. The captain, Martin told us afterward, who is twice as large as Wada, had blocked the galley door with his person, and demanded "that honey." Wada, scared out of his wits, said it was not on the boat. The captain started to enter, threateningly, and Wada, in the last extremity of terror, said, "Don't you come in my galley." Which is where he made his big mistake, for it was just what Warren had tried to frighten him into, so he would have an excuse to take the boy by the throat with one hand and smash in with the other. There was no escape in the confined space, with the stove behind.

Wada was stupid, granted—for the honey was found later —but he was terrified, and not intentionally mutinous or impudent; and his punishment was entirely disproportionate to his offence. This is not a merchant ship nor a tramp steamer; it is a pleasure-boat, and such extremes are uncalled for.

Poor little Wada! That evening I was alone in the lifeboat, when he crept on deck. I called him to me and asked him if the cut on his forehead was painful. He answered in a dead, level voice that it was not, but that his throat ached. I noticed that he was hoarse. He seemed to grieve most over the possibility of a scar, for he said he had never been in trouble like this before. He thought a scar would be a sort of disgrace.

"Cap'n big man—just like hit little baby when he hit me," he said with a sigh.

> Lat.   8° 30′ North,
> Lon. 131° West.
> Wednesday, November 13, 1907.

I am sitting on a new corner seat in the cockpit, at seven bells in the evening; Jack, Captain Warren and Martin, are perspiring over a game of poker in the cabin; Herrmann is on the rudder-box holding the boat to her course, southeast one-half south, in a fair wind that has been blowing since three o'clock, to our delight. Upon my assurance that it will not bother me in the least, Herrmann is singing "The Last Rose of Summer," although I have discovered that the tale he carries to our familiar air is not the one we know, being a recital of a Dutch Maud Muller who scorned the rich suitor, preferring her poor but honest yokel.

To the northeast, in an otherwise clear and moonlit sky, a low black thunder-cloud is spitting intermittent flashes of steely lightning that make my electric light yellow by contrast. It is too lovely a night for me to be stuck in an artificially lighted corner; but this has already been a day full of neglected work, and if I wait too long to write what I see, the freshness and colour will go out—like the life and colour that went out of a dying dolphin Herrmann landed yesterday. I was sleeping late, and Jack tiptoed in at 8:30, not wanting me to miss this first dolphin caught in daylight. It took me just about two minutes to get on deck, and even then the living peacock-blue was gone, all but speckles of it dotting an iridescent green. This in turn shaded out of a dark blue line underneath, which soon faded to glossy white. Most of the dolphins we see in the water are of all shades of bright blue, passing into emerald green; and to-day, through some light and shade effect, they appeared to be broadly striped with black and green and blue. They are the chameleons of the deep—except that their colours are not protective; they shame everything else in air and sea.

This fish measured over three feet. Although we have seen them twice this length, the captain says this three-footer is the largest he ever caught. As with the sunsets, I must be pardoned for recurring to the dolphin, so beautiful a thing he is. We have been surrrounded by enormous ones these days of calm. Imagine a vision of luminous azure deep down in transparent dark sapphire water—why, we drop everything to watch. The turtle shell, towed close astern, brings various sorts of inquisitive fish around us when the water is calm.

To-day Jack and the captain classified our charts—some already used, some unnecessary ones, to be returned to California, and the ones for the future put into the order in which we now expect to need them. After these days of turning around and around in calms, or fighting head winds and currents and getting nowhere, we are fired with fresh ambition to follow the islands shown by the charts.

Big drops of warm rain are blobbing all over the page as

I write; but they cannot put out my covered light, so I don't mind them.

Poor Martin has been wrestling with defective plumbing in the bath-room; also with certain faults in the engine-room electrical apparatus. His opinions as to the integrity of the people dealing in ship chandlery are undergoing a transformation, now that he must keep in order these faulty things. "The darn things were only made to play with," he complained, looking ruefully at an inefficient pump-handle that had been defying all efforts to make it do its work, and that had finally broken short off.

> Lat.   8° North,
> Lon. 129° 42′ West.
> Thursday, November 14, 1907.

Not much sleep these hot nights, for the "juice" that runs the cooling fans gave out a few nights ago. About 4:30 this morning the wind freshened to a strong squall that called for all hands on deck to take in flying-jib and mizzen. How it does pour in these squalls! The big stinging drops seem to shoot from the clouds rather than fall, with a drive that sends them through oilskin. But it is such cleansing rain. The ropes grow whiter after each deluging; and I love to feel the water run off my slicker and drench my bare feet.

It is so cheering to hear the brave bright voices of the men through rain and dark, reassuring us as to their safety. One could go overboard so easily at night in a big sea and not be missed for a time; and even if he were missed immediately, how pick him up in the gloom and noise and confusion?

I am more or less painfully aware of the many places aboard a small craft upon which one can "bark" his anatomy. I would better say "her" anatomy, since I have a more than ordinarily brilliant faculty for decorating myself with bruises that vie with the lunar rainbow in smothered tones of violet and orange. I am particularly conscious of such abrasions after a rough night. I recoil in sleep from a wicked encounter of my temple with a sharp-cornered pigeon-hole on a locker-door by my head, only to receive the full weight of my descending body on the flattened end of my poor sun-tender nose against the bunk-rail, as I turn, assisted by a violent roll of the boat, for consolation to the other side of the bed. Oh, it is not at all funny—until I come to tell about it, when I have to laugh even if it hurts to laugh. I am minded of the solicitous old sea-dog who warned Jack by letter that it was not safe to take a woman outside the Golden Gate in a boat of the *Snark's* size; that we would be bruised over our "entire persons, unless the boat be padded, which is not usual." I'll give him the satisfaction of knowing that I am pretty much bruised over my "entire person," but that I am growing hardened both in spirit and muscle. Every one aboard knows when I hurt myself; but I really think I make less outcry than of yore. I would be willing to wager a good round sum that more than one reader of my tale of bumps and humps will say that my husband is a brute to risk me on such a voyage—unless he wants to lose me. But to all such I make reply that they should just see me if he tried to leave me behind. However, I think I must have been inspired when I suggested, in America, that we take the trip before we were any older!

No woman but an idiot would embark on a round-world voyage in our fashion without sundry flutters and misgivings. I did not worry very much about trouble or danger; but at first I could not help being a little nervous sometimes in the sizable seas through which the little *Snark* would thread her way with that impudent adventuring nose of hers. But now, except when shocked awake from a dead sleep, I take the pawing and clawing, lurching and bounding over the bucking seas, quite as part of the day's work. This is not to minimise the possibility of the awful things that could happen to us and may yet happen to us, for the sea is a cruel, unlovable monster of caprice and might; but now my accustomed nerves are beginning to dread nothing less than the worst.

We are all becoming more and more a part of the boat. We take less conscious care of ourselves near the rail—but we are actually more cautious than ever, in a finer and more intelligent, if more subconscious way.

. . . Think of the mails that must be waiting for us at Papeete, Tahiti. It will be six weeks next Monday since we sailed from Hilo; and it struck me with a pang the other day, that before long, dear ones at home may be saddening their days with apprehensions for our fate—and life is so short, and terrors of this kind shorten it, if life be measured by heartbeats of happiness. It is bad enough for people to think of us out in this cockle-shell, without the agony being piled up by "overdue" press reports. Our obituaries may even now be in preparation in newspaper offices where news is scarce!

Jack says this is probably the longest single stretch we shall ever have. Where we should be logging one hundred miles a day at the least, we are only doing a few. Take yesterday: we made thirty knots on our course, and I don't know how many off our course; and this morning after the squall, which kept us on the course, the wind broke off and we are now fighting slowly northeast with plunge and splurge, in a big short sea, making very little headway. It is a comfortless movement, too. We are past getting sea-sick now; but I for one am not quite at rest in the region of my solar plexus.

After making the acquaintance of the tropic cockroach, the centipede, and other unsympathetic co-dwellers in this vale of tears, a woman's heartfelt desire is to keep them from possessing the household. My household is a boat, with all sorts of attractive nooks and damp lockers and dark corners for insect or reptile. No centipedes have shown up; plenty of time yet for them to come aboard with island fruits. But after several days' vague curiosity about certain black husks in the graham bread, it was discovered that the flour was alive with weevils and black bugs. Well, there's no use being *too* squeamish; but Jack, horrid thing! said he had noticed a distinct change for the better in his physical well-being, as if, forsooth, he had been living on a fresh-meat diet!—Ugh! the flour was carefully sifted and sunned on the skylight to-day—don't think for a moment that we wasted it overboard. We are too far from land to do anything so unwise.

It is an even chance, now, which port we fetch first, Nuka-Hiva in the Marquesas, or Papeete in Tahiti. When the wind is contrary, which, when there is any wind at all, is usually the case, there is talk of our being unable to make the required slant to the Marquesas, the chance being that we shall be lucky if we can lay a course that will not miss Tahiti. I rather wish it would be Tahiti first, in order that we might pick up our mail sooner; then, granting a fair wind east, to run back to the Marquesas, taking in Tahiti again and later mails on our westward way. There is certainly nothing cut-and-dried in our calendar—we do not even know where we are bound!

But we'll let go our anchor in some lovely haven this side of the "Port of Missing Men."

Sometimes I think of the women of my New England family, scattered from their home-Maine throughout the South, in New York, and Philadelphia, and Boston, who in their time have gone abroad in ships with their master-mariner husbands, travelling for years, until some swift disaster widowed them, stranded and desolate. In the town of Searsport, Maine, where some years ago I visited a beautiful white-haired cousin with the look of loss in her eyes—in Searsport there are some eight hundred inhabitants, the majority of whom are widows of sea captains. And it seems strange that I, born and reared in the opposite corner of the Union, should be out adventuring to strange lands myself with a man who loves to sail the sea. How much closer I shall ever be to those women of my father's family.

. . . The other morning, lying late, I heard the captain

say he had never seen so many fish in his life. During the day I learned what he meant. They were mostly bonitas, cresting the waves with their flashing silver bodies, the water boiling and seething with them as they darted and leaped—countless thousands of them.

. . . Nakata is learning much English; but once in a while he shows preferences for words of his own coining above those taught him. For example, yesterday I told him to clean the blades of my electric fan, which pick up all sorts of fluff out of the atmosphere. The small heathen (who is a Christian, by the way!) told Herrmann that he was going below to clean the *wind!*

> Lat.   7° 52' North,
> Lon. 126° 36' West.
> Monday, November 18, 1907.

I gave up trying to sleep below without the electric fan, and have spent my third night on deck, forward, under the bow of the life-boat. Sailing softly along before light airs, the nights have been lovely, moonlit, with no squalls.

Herrmann cannot be brought to see that it is quite the right thing for a woman to sleep on a hard deck with no mattress; but I am entirely satisfied with my yielding spread of many-folded, clean canvas, a duck coverlet and a comfortable pillow; and if my feet grow chilly, there's a poncho to pull over. It is a novel picnic to turn in under the moon, face and body softly swept by the palpable, flowing wind—air that one drinks rather than breathes. And when I rouse and lift my head to look in the waking eye of dawn, I truly wonder where I am, and glance momentarily into the airy rigging above with a sense of lacking weight and substance, of being part and parcel of myth and mystery. The face of morning is very beautiful, bending over the flushing sea.—Think of our little white boat, floating loneliest of all boats, in this desert of celestial colour. It is adventure, pure and simple; it is enrichment of one's most precious store of imagination. . . . We stood last night

after supper, Jack and I, leaning over the launch and gazing
spellbound at a sunset of forms and hues so grotesque and
crude, contrasts of rawness and garishness so rude, that our
senses were shocked. The simplest pigments were used to
limn the picture, greens and blues and pinks; and from the
basic flaunting gold there shout out great spreading rays
of rose and blue. A cloud-genii, inky black, developed
in the centre, and as the colours deepened around, long
cloud-capes on the horizon sent up strange forms like insane, toppling mountains. It was exciting, tonic, jarring
blood and brain like an electric bath or a burst of cannonad-
ing or anything unusual and shocking. Something made me
face to the east as if to seek peace for the eye. The op-
posing vision was untouched by the spirit of the first. A
cold silver moon hung in a sky of dove, over a sea of silver-
grey, all softly luminous but as wanting in colour as grey
can ever be. To change to this calm desolation of grey and
silver was as if to turn from a gaud-tricked, painted woman
to see a grey nun standing.

November 19, 1907.

Whenever there is any good fishing over our rail a sort of
tacit holiday obtains, affecting all hands but the cook. Yet
our brown chef revels in the sort of work entailed upon
him by our catch. Three hundred pounds of sea-meat happened on our deck the other day. "Fish market," Nakata
unctuously commented; while Wada, squatting on his bare
heels, dexterously carved a seven-foot shark, sharpening the
knife on its hide now and again. In addition to the shark
there were some dolphins varying from three to four feet in
length, and several bonitas larger than any we had yet seen.
The sport began with Martin hooking his first fish—a ten-
pound bonita that put up a game fight and came aboard
glowing with angry colours as bizarre as our sunsets—a
painted fish if there ever was one. Raining and blowing
though it was, Martin hied him to the end of the bowsprit
and promptly caught a five-pounder of the same species,

that looked for all the world like an elongated soap-bubble, blown from Paradise, if Paradise can fling off anything so exquisite. Martin hooked one smaller bonita, which exactly fitted Wada's eye for a baked stuffed fish.

Jack knocked off work for a while and came up to try his luck, but his success was reserved for larger game. The bonitas shot along near the top of the water, straight and true and brightly gleaming, like steel shuttles weaving a prodigious fabric of grey and white. Jack had no sooner returned to his work again, when "Shark!" was the shout on deck, and I reached the stern in time to see the tiger of the sea with his yellow cat-eyes turn leisurely on his side and swallow bait and hook, the captain yelling meanwhile for Jack to come and have the fun of pulling it in. But Jack was not going to spoil a sentence for any second shark, and came up a moment later to empty his shot-gun into the head of the furiously struggling monster. It was not so game as our first shark, giving up both the conscious and the unconscious fight much sooner.

Jack offset all his hitherto unsuccessful sport when the dolphins began to bite that same afternoon. For several days the birds that hunt flying-fish had been scarce, and we had noticed an absence of the latter. For this or some other reason the dolphins were hungry, and we hung over the rail and watched the orgy of colour they made in the calm blue underneath as they would sniff at the bait several times, suspiciously, and finally, reassured, catch it up next time they shot by. Every one but Nakata and I pulled in a dolphin. I didn't try, and Nakata failed. Jack caught two, and Martin two, and Jack's larger one turned out to be an inch longer than any other, measuring four feet seven inches, and weighing twenty-six pounds. He played it for three quarters of an hour with rod and reel, and a small hook baited with flying fish. It passed through indigo and turquoise to the most brilliant luminous gaslight-green, and, when finally landed with the help of the granes, faded into fairest gold all over, then quickly spotted with electric-blue.

Some dolphins came aboard a hard, bright white, immediately changing to other tints; others arrived in pale blue, or pale green, or both, and no two went through the same succession of colours. They are unbelievably beautiful.

Since this big catch, different ways of putting fish on the table have kept Wada's ingenuity busy. They have been baked and stuffed, with tomato dressing; boiled; broiled with a rasher of bacon; have made excellent chowder; and this morning dolphin fritters made their bow, nicely light and done in olive oil. And the roe is a great delicacy. Wada is beginning to look like himself again, but for a nasty healing scar between the eyes. The captain keeps a wary eye on the cook, as if fearing treachery; but Wada goes his way unconcernedly.

One big dolphin swallowed four expensive hooks from off a white wooden lure in the form of a fish, but gulped another baited hook presently, and when Wada came to clean the fish he discovered the lost hooks.

We do not want for incident these days. What of the weather, the sunrises and sunsets, the extreme loveliness of the reflecting liquid expanse round about, the squalls, calms, winds fair and foul, there is endless novelty; but it is life-incident, or the scarcity of it, that pitches excitement high when anything new in this line turns up. We are all like children at a circus parade. Herrmann, with the murderous granes poised for a cast at dolphin or turtle, his face alive with earnest attention, is a model for a sculptor of old-country types—to be wrought in bronze; the captain, breathless and with quivering voice, hanging to a line around a shark, the Japanese emitting little barbaric squeals and cries of delight, Jack talking fast, with his eyes shining, and I tumbling over the main-sheet to a place of vantage—oh, I can assure everybody that it is exhilarating! One day lately we sighted a small white sea-porcupine about eight inches long, bobbing calmly on the long swell, head and tail extended, like those of a turtle. Its arched white back glistened with wicked spikes. We tacked and tacked in order to pick it up, straining our eyes to keep track of it; but the wind was too light, and we failed. We saw another turtle last night, but missed it. These turtles are unusually far from land, I have learned.

To offset our very unstimulating record for speed on this traverse, we contemplate the fact that, so far as we know, no other yacht has ever travelled the course at all.

Jack has resumed his navigation again in earnest; and on the 15th, Friday last, took his first chronometer sight on this cruise. Herrmann is much impressed, and wonders why we employ a captain!

We have taken up Saleeby's fascinating work, *The Cycle of Life,* which Jack found he could not be selfish enough to read by himself; so, several times a day, while I stitch away on summer lingerie, or embroider, he reads aloud to me of the sufficient wonder of the ascertained fact and the relativity of all knowledge, worked out in beautiful clear style in chapters under such headings as "Swimming," "Cricket," "The Living Cell," "Song," "Fratricide," "The Destiny of the Horse," "The Green Leaf," "Atoms and Evolution"—all related in a way that makes one glow with enthusiasm over the universe that is and the particular brain-cells of the man who can present the conclusions of science in such enchanting form.

. . . Our course staggers tipsily over the chart, but we are going to get in cahoots with the southeast trades some day, and now, having accomplished the requisite easting, we are sure of the Marquesas if we can be sure of anything in this capricious ocean. As the *Snark* buckles down each day to her work, we discuss our future plans for that region indefinitely termed the South Seas, and have about made up our minds to try for the Paumotus, of "infamous reputation" for danger, as Robert Louis Stevenson says— the Dangerous Archipelago of old-time navigators.

Jack has spent to-day's holiday in overhauling all his fishing-tackle—coils of line, coarse and fine, shining reels of different makes and sizes, hooks of roughly murderous or of

finely cruel aspect, elegant rods of varying degrees of slen-
derness and polish, dainty nets of white or yellow; and the
spoons of steel and mother-of-pearl and gay pigments are
fit to make an angler's fingers twitch. One lure represents
a curving silver minnow, cunningly armed with wicked
hooks.

After boxing this morning we had to borrow a pail
from the galley for our bucketing, for on Saturday Martin,
open-mouthed over the stern while the captain held the
shark, deliberately let go the canvas pail he happened to be
holding; and later in the day, hauling up a galvanized iron
pail full of water, the rope parted and a second container
was lost. Herrmann is now manufacturing a new canvas
bucket, having finished my windsail, which even as I write
is conveying cool draughts of air down through an open
deck-light.

Lat.   6° 45′ North,
Lon. 125° 36′ West.
Monday, November 25, 1907.

There is something wholly exasperating about the weather
this morning; and as it was the same all of yesterday and
last night, our nerves are a bit on edge. The wind blows
briskly from the wrong direction, sending us east by north,
when we want to go southeast; and we are bucking the head-
sea that has certainly been no novelty on this long passage—
forty-nine days to-day. You cannot move without bumping something, in this contrary motion; and when a big
swift roll comes, things slide and fall in all directions. Just
now, among a shower of articles set loose by a vicious surge
of the yacht, one book struck the floor with such force that
it slid right out of its binding, and it was not flimsily-bound
either. My pocket-diary took a trip across the deck, poised
in the very teeth of the scupper, and the instant after Jack
rescued it a wave washed in where it had been. There has
been little sunshine for several days, and, on account of
wet weather, less opportunity for open decklights; so our
staterooms and lockers have a disagreeable odour of stale-

ness and mouldiness. The air is sultry, and I had a surprising attack of prickly heat this morning. This is the first day I have felt as if I would rather sight land than not; then I appreciate that if it were not for my work with which I never catch up, and my desire to make the most of my uninterrupted time, I might be tainted with Captain Warren's impatience. Altogether, I feel very much like breaking my cheer and being real cross for a spell! But what's the use? I know, when I come right down to "brass tacks," as Jack says, that I would rather be here, on this buffeted boat, in this up-ending head-sea, than in lots of other states I can think of—say on an abused and stumbling horse, riding over a bad road, in another person's ill-adjusted saddle, under a hot sun; or, to come nearer home, I'd rather be in present circumstances than in those of last Wednesday, the 20th, when we found ourselves short of water, with no prospect of rain and with only twenty days' rations left. But the unpleasantness of that prospect, which I am using to offset to-day's irk, was mitigated somewhat by the interesting touch of danger. A taste of sea-peril of this kind has a thrill in it—something new to go through and to think of afterwards, provided, of course, that there be any afterwards. There was an element of romance, somewhat dimmed by humour, in the spectacle of the galley-pump, shackled with steel handcuffs against the possibility of the cook drawing more than his allotment of water for cooking purposes. We experienced a hitherto unknown sense of miserly vigilance over our quart-bottles filled to last twenty-four hours, and hung up in shady places.

The threatened water-famine affected us according to our several natures. Martin was seized with an aggravated thirst and consumed his quart in the forenoon. To bring home to him the consequences of his unbridled license, we compared our plenty with his want by trickling our own supply loudly and ostentatiously from varying heights into our glasses. As for Jack, he drank moderately, and had a little of his allowance left the following morning. I was not driven into excess by imaginings of a future parched throat; indeed, I was less thirsty than usual—although I am not prepared to say how much of my lack of desire was affected by the discovery that there was a flavour of kerosene in my bottle. At night, however, Jack let me have some of his hoarded store in exchange for some of mine for his morning shave. Naturally, no provision for washing entered into the régime, each scheming the disposal of his single quart as he saw fit. I tried ammonia in salt water, and it was an improvement over salt water plain; but I did not put any of this mixture on my face. I cleansed that mirror of my soul with cold cream, and judged my countenance to be the cleanest of the ship's company, as I saw no one else making any sort of shift to wash.

The cook was given seven quarts of water for general use in cooking only, and employed this so discreetly as to put chocolate or coffee on the table at all three meals, whereas we had expected none for at least one of the three. Herrmann was inclined to survey the whole proceeding as a joke, which called forth a few serious remarks from Captain Warren, who is the only one of us who really knows the terrors of thirst.

. . . Jack and I added a great picture to our brain-gallery on Thursday. Alone in the cockpit, we watched our men rig up the large deck awning, tilted up at the sides, the centre breadths lowered at the forward end over a tub set on the skylight, while a funnel was stuck into the opening of the 'midship tank to catch all gleanings from the awning in event of rain. For the sky had clouded and the wind freshened from N.N.E., and squalls, white squalls and black, curtained the horizon. The awning rigged, our men rested; and the picture we saw was of three of them leaning at about the same angle on a boat, watching for rain—unconsciously straining forward toward the thing desired, one mastering thought bringing them together in one bodily expression of that thought. They leaned a long time, motionless, absorbed, unaware of our scrutiny or our appreciation. And those eluding squalls lifted and fell and glided like marionettes on a revolving stage, leaving us dry, until about midnight. Between then and daylight about one hundred gallons were poured into the 'midship tank. And by Saturday, for it rained on and off till then, as much water was stored as before the shortage was detected.

You have been wondering at our sudden discovery of this shortage of water? (Bang, rattle, snap! the flying-jib has just carried away. The only advantage of this is that the boat doesn't paw quite so wildly with her headsail off.) But as I was saying. In a sudden squall Tuesday night, during the hoisting of the spinnaker-boom, in some way the faucet on the port bow tank was turned, and not before morning did we discover our loss. Investigating the other tanks, on deck and below, it was also found that somebody had miscalculated in a former inspection, and we found ourselves facing a serious predicament. We might have drifted around in these doldrums for an indefinite time without rain.

To-day we are still three hundred and seventy-nine miles north of the Equator, with a current setting us eastward. The barometer is normal. I often think of the Stevensons in the *Casco*, sailing from San Francisco to the Marquesas in the eighties.

. . . 3 P. M. Jack is popping away at some snowy pink-billed bo's'n birds that are flying very close, crying sharply to one another. A rummaging for lost possessions has been going on in the cabin, and Jack's red bathing-suit came to light along with other missing articles. And speaking of losing things: when one loses them on land, there is always the possibility of recovering them; but at sea, when a thing is overboard, there is a finality about it that is positively startling. That canvas bucket, for instance—the new one can never take its place, and we know we shall never see the old one again. It is oscillating somewhere in the deep, pressed equally from above and below, there to stay until dissolution disposes of it into the primordial ooze. And the granes broke away the other day; also a white silk neckerchief with a red border, that floated astern for a time, then suddenly disappeared—probably into the maw of a dolphin. Evidently it did not please his palate, for it came up promptly.

. . . Nakata is a thing of joy to all hands—except to Herrmann, who cannot understand the boy's amused incomprehension of his queer Dutch-English. Herrmann carefully explains technicalities of steering to Nakata, who bends his oriental brows in strict attention to language he wots not of (although he is learning *our* English fast) and then promptly brings the vessel say up into the wind. This sometimes perilous experiment fetches the long-suffering and exasperated Hollander aft on the jump, to explain with augmented ambiguity of speech, that that was what he had expressly explained to him not to do.

I myself have failed in one glaring particular, to elucidate something to the cabin-boy, namely, that "sir" is not the accepted manner of addressing a lady. Perhaps my pajama knee-breeches are to blame; but when, to my call, he cheerily responds, "Yes, sir!" I know, by his correction to "Yes, *man*," that all my care in pointing out the contraction of *madam* has gone over his bristly black head, and that he is still puzzled as to why he should say "Yes, *man!*" to a woman. He also insists gently but firmly upon calling the cockpit the cockroom. There is something fascinating about him, his ready smile, his cheerfulness, his temperamental happiness—like some wild thing of docile instincts. His frank expectance of kindness, as expressed in his winning bearing, bring him goodwill all round. The captain has to hide his face repeatedly, for the sake of dignity and discipline, at some evidence of frisky humour on the part of the little brown mannikin with the homely face that his smile makes beautiful.

. . . Sometimes down through the open skylight, as we

The Beach at Taiohae

Marquesan Tattooing

sit at work in our cubby-holes, come fragments of conversation that hint of a different state of affairs on board the *Snark* from that of old—hint of discipline, and continued discipline. One doesn't hear all; but the other day the captain's voice cut out: "Do I *mean* it? Wha' d'you suppose I give an order for, if I don't mean it?" But there's plenty of friendliness among the men, although it doesn't do for a minute to allow a sailor, who has lived on law and order aboard ship all his life, to become lax on a boat as small as ours. Herrmann is so extraordinarily susceptible to praise or notice that he quite loses his head if we approve any little act of his, and begins to suggest improvements in everything around with an originality and fearlessness that is rather discomfiting. After he has been called down by the master, he is perfectly lovely.

. . . A week ago we began economising on fuel by having cold suppers; but there is a small burner aboard, used for melting solder, upon which Wada manages hot drinks and occasionally rice and curry, or soup. Our table is a raised skylight, and thus we have a chance to see all of the sunset.

On Tuesday, the 19th, in some cider we unearthed aboard, we celebrated the second anniversary of our marriage. I wish we knew who sent it to us so we could return thanks. Jack waxed reminiscent and regaled the others with anecdotes of our honeymoon in Cuba and Jamaica. And—well, here we are, out together hunting the thrills of new experiences with as much vigour and enthusiasm as ever, and no abatement in sight.

Jack has the delightful characteristic of always wanting to share everything in which he is interested—his amusements, his books, or the thing he is studying. He explains to me his advancing steps in navigation; he reads aloud to me; he wants me to feel the tug of his fish on the line; and he draws all of us together to re-read, aloud, some book he knows will give pleasure. Sunday forenoon, having done more than his usual "stint" of writing the previous day, he took a holiday and read Conrad's *Typhoon* aloud, to the delight of the sailormen. And so, a unity of good spirit is preserved aboard, because one man is fond of sharing knowledge, the acquirement of which is the business of his life.

There is one of Jack's pleasures, however, that I cannot share with him, what of a congenital lack. This is his beard. He is "letting his face rest" for a week, and as I cannot appreciate the rest it gives *him* to let his whiskers grow, it makes me restless to contemplate his rough chin and jaw. And I take less delight in any sudden and unforeseen juxtaposition. But I consented to let him raise this mat, upon his promise that I may take his picture just before he shaves.

. . . On Wednesday last, Jack landed a thirty-pound dolphin, one of the finest we have seen—all exquisite variations of abalone and gold and blue, green and rose. We tried to capture a big skate that bothered around for hours, attended by two white baby sharks and a lot of pilot fish. But the monster flopped away finally with its black wing-like propellers. Wada hooked one of the infant sharks, less than two feet long, which cooked up into the best baked fish we have had.

The bonitas are easily fooled these days with a small white rag on the hook, which is jerked ahead to simulate a flying-fish. Friday, the 22d, the boys had eighteen bonitas on deck at one time. Jack added a good-sized dolphin, and the collection was hung on a pole reaching clear across the deck amidship, from shroud to shroud, a flying-fish dangling at one end, the bonitas grading up to the big dolphin at the other end. Since then bonitas are caught for the keen sport only, and thrown immediately back. They are a hunger-cruel spawn. The instant one is hooked, his mates make a rush for him. Many a fish, even dolphin, brought aboard, shows healing wounds from great mouthfuls that have been taken out by its enemies, many of them among its own kind.

The stomach of a fish usually tells the story of this continual fight for existence.

It is a wonderful sight, in a squall at night when the vessel is racing over the water, to behold in the depths shoals of bonitas slipping along whitely in the phosphorescence, their flight in perfect relation to the speed of the boat, so that they look like pale stones seen in the bed of a stream. By day, their backs show like swift olive-brown shadows, until they turn their gleaming sides up to the light. Two of the latest catches weighed twenty-five and twenty-four pounds respectively—chunky, fat fish.

Lat. 6° 2′ North,
Lon. 125° 30′ West.
Tuesday, November 26, 1908.

Referring again to our fishy satellites, last evening while we were listening to *Typhoon* in a flood of rosy light, the water pink, the clouds bright pink, and the sky of startling blue, an enormous dolphin was playing about, leaping clear and falling loudly on his side, over and over again, adding to the evening radiance his flash of blue-white—his colour-mood for the moment. When a dolphin has felt the tear of the hook, and got away, or when he has carried the hook off, he leaps and flashes through the air, recklessly shaking himself, landing on his side or his back with a crash, with all the mad abandon of a colt in the breaking yard.

. . . The wind has gone nearly into the southeast and it now looks probable that we may be picking up the trades. There is a good-sized sea and swell running, and it is hard to adjust one's movements to the lunges of the boat when she takes a header into the abyss or is flung from the crest of one big wave only to fetch up smack against the next. But the little *Snark* noses her way pretty wisely in the labyrinth of heaving hills, and no small vessel could ride more easily than she.

. . . Something very reassuring and encouraging occurred just now. The flying-jib was not replaced after carrying away, and we sailed all night without it. This morning the jib-sheet was unhooked, and the jib also hauled in, after which the mainsail was lowered, to put in a new lace-line—the rope that laces the head of the sail to the gaff, and which had worn through during the night. Jack was bringing the yacht up into the wind to ease things for the men working on the mainsail, and all at once the good thing happened. The *Snark* was right up in the wind, practically hove to, under staysail and mizzen, in light wind, and with a moderately heavy sea kicked up by the blow that had preceded that light wind. And she would not heave to that night coming from San Francisco to Hawaii! But why? Why? That is our everlasting query. The captain says it is ridiculous to think she would not heave to; we agree with him, perfectly. But she did refuse, just the same. As Jack says, "I don't believe it—I only saw it."—How one learns to love a boat. I am beginning to appreciate how sailors feel about ships, no matter what happens, never quite admitting even to themselves that the vessel is at fault. Captain Warren swears more and more heartily by the *Snark* the more he sees of her performances.

. . . And now, at 9:50 A. M., every visible sign points to our being in the southeast trades—the blue, white-capped sea running with the wind, the wind itself, the "wool-pack" clouds. All at once I am willing and even anxious to reach the islands—to see land again, mountains, bays and safe anchorages; to eat fruit, and fruit, and more fruit—bananas, guavas, oranges and lemons and limes, yams, breadfruit, taro. . . .

We have all bet a dollar each with Jack, who wagers that we shall see the Marquesas by December 12; but it begins to look as if he may win.

. . . Martin developed a roll of film for me yesterday, and spilt his hypo on the bathroom floor; but he went right on developing where the fluid deepened in the leeward corner. This morning, asked the cause of the peculiar odour, Nakata enlightened us with: "Mr. Johnson . . . he . . . yester-

day . . . make come kodak-medicine!'' ''Nakata's latest''
is a sort of daily newspaper. I verily believe that if the
Snark went down with all hands, our last conscious picture
would be of Nakata's toothy smile, and the last sound in
our ears would be the pæan of sheer exultation of being that
this child of Japan lets out whenever anything happens,
whether of good or ill.

. . . During these weeks under the tropic sun I am surprised at my lack of deep sunburn. To be sure, I am less
white; but considering that I seldom wear a hat, only shad-
ing my eyes with a green visor, this freedom from tan is remarkable. Herrmann remarked quite innocently one day
that the only man aboard who was not burned was Mrs.
London. But my hair is burning—a gorgeous red and yellow, without apparent loss of gloss or moisture. It is
''Oh-h-h-h *beau*tiful nice!'' according to the exuberant
cabin-boy.

> Lat.   5° 41′ North,
> Lon. 126°   2′ West.
> Wednesday, November 27, 1908.

My birthday—and we are celebrating with a true southeast trade. We have logged one hundred and two knots
in the twenty-four hours, and now, at 4:30 P. M., are smoking along on a course of south by west. Jack and the
captain are grinning and chuckling like schoolboys over a
chart of the Marquesas and Paumotus, spread between them
on the rudder-box, while the captain reads aloud ''Hostyle
Inhabitants'' over and over, printed against tiny dots of
islands in the Paumotu cluster. Jack has just looked up,
in answer to my question, with ''It's a hundred to one now
that we'll make Nuka-Hiva all right. We're on the home-
stretch—'' ''—And a short home-stretch—excuse me, sir!''
interrupts the captain, with shining face. They both agree
that eight or ten days ''at this lick'' ought to bring us to
port. Martin popped a land-famished face over the boatswain's locker a moment ago, and asked what I was smiling
about. And I am willing to admit that I am now frankly

satisfied to exchange these longed-for days of all work and no fresh fruit, for a different programme. Also, I want a level place to sleep on for a spell, where I can present the unwinking eye of sleep to "Policeman Day" for about ten hours at a stretch. I have had but one uninterrupted night in fifty-two.

I inaugurated my birthday's entrance by catching two large bonitas, landing one of them unaided; also I hooked a good-sized dolphin, but lost my head and forgot to "play" him, so he broke the hook and streaked for parts unknown. Jack was hugely elated over my catch—the first time I have tried. Once, I caught six mackerel in Penobscot Bay; and, unmentionable years before, I bent-pin-hooked thirty-five minnows, without bait! This is the extent of my fishing experience.

Dolphins and bonitas are with us in gleaming hordes to-day. The *Snark* is flushing the flying-fish for them, most of which seem to be four-winged, like dragon-flies— dragon-flies of the deep, sailing down the wind.—It is continual slaughter, and they are a cruel lot, these big fish; but by what manner of reasoning cruel? What other food than their own kind is provided for them by beneficent nature? And when they are haled aboard by their unwilling mouths, straining and resisting, staring horribly with lidless eyes of fright, it all lines up in one's mind as a game— a game wherein men and fishes and beasts destroy to live. And war of man or war of fish or beast, it is all of a piece with the game.

Jack harpooned three dolphins to-day, using the harpoon in lieu of the lost granes; but it is not the proper weapon for them, does not go easily into their firm bodies, and they get away. But they doggedly stay with us, recognisable by their scratches, as intent as ever upon damaging smaller and weaker ones.

Last evening at supper time there was the worst rain squall we have ever weathered. It came from two directions—or rather *they* did, for two squalls struck at about the same time, one from the weather quarter, one from the weather bow. Below, holding the dishes from spilling into our laps, we knew only that the *Snark* stayed down a long time; but the captain, coming to supper—it was over quickly—said it was our stiffest squall yet. Earlier in the day I had my most disagreeable experience on the voyage. I had settled before the typewriter in my state-room. Everything was lovely—the windsail pumping cool-ness down through the open skylight, the decklight open, with a poncho spread on my bunk to catch any chance spray that might come down; I had just typed "Chapter XXX" at the head of a page with four carbon copies under it—and then the deluge. My newly cleaned and oiled machine was drenched with salt water, inside and out; the water ran down my draw-tables into the packed lockers beneath the bunk; a gallon or so fell through the decklight on to the poncho, and I was quite forlorn with water. I felt like a quenched candle, and went about dispiritedly soaking up the brine with cloth and sponge, while it took Martin the best part of two hours to get the devastating salt water off the typewriter and the works carefully oiled. Just to show how quickly rust forms in this climate: Jack had shaved in the morning (and I did not get that photograph, after all!); and being called on deck suddenly, asked me to lay the soapy safety-razor on his bunk. Within two hours red rust was on the blade.

Lat.   1° 18′ North,
Lon. 127° 30′ West.
Friday, November 29, 1907.

The only thing that roused me at seven this morning, after a disturbed night, was a dash of cold water that sent me shooting feet-first out of my canvas covert alongside the cockpit—the dryest place I had been able to select this breezy weather. It was a second dose, the first having caught me just after I went to sleep, about ten, when the lee-quarter failed to dodge the edge of a wave going obliquely astern. That time I got it on the head, and slept damp. Herrmann has hung me a canvas stretcher between cockpit rail and weather rail, with a tent-like protection from the spray. It was very rough, angling across the big seas; and the jaws on the mizzen-gaff, which are chewing away at the mast till the chewed section is in splinters, rubbed skreakily all night, the bell in the cockpit keeping up a doleful rhythm like a fog-bell. For all our bobbed-off little craft with her barnacled copper and her small sails wrought for ease of handling and comfortable sailing, we logged seven knots during the night, and this morning, at ten, we have covered one hundred and twenty knots since noon yesterday—and still humming. Captain Warren is keeping the vessel off a little, for the comfort of Jack writing below, so that he can have the weather skylight open and the windsail working. But think how wonderfully "dry" the *Snark* is. The few instances I have cited of water coming aboard, are all I can remember—a pretty good record for these many weeks in squalls and rough seas. Oh, yes—one other instance: last evening Jack and I were perched up forward on the windy weather bow of the launch, dodging flying spray and drinking deep the flowing trade, while watching the everlasting miracle of bright fishes darting so effortlessly and swiftly. Finally came a monster swell that the *Snark* decided to have a little fun with at our expense. She rose like a hunter at a fence and then descended, the wave curving back and down from her bow, but the wind flinging the heavy spray upward. Jack's feet preceded his body up the rigging, while I, farthest from the rigging, hanging to a horizontal steel stay back of my head, raised my own feet and escaped some of the drenching. I wish I had a picture of the pair of us. The bulk of the water went below, all over the set dinner table, on the leeward seat in the cabin, on my bunk, a gallon or so piling up in the floor-corners. But these infrequent splashings are nothing compared with the sweeping a "wet" fast yacht endures, where there is no comfort on deck, because of water, and none below for closeness of air. Why, the Stevensons were, kept in the cabin for days at a time when the *Casco* was doing her best paces.

We are about one hundred and fifty miles from the Line, as we go—about ninety as the bird flies; and to-morrow we hope to cross—into the South Sea at last. The weather is actually cool. The books tell us that the southeast trades are cooler than the northeast. Fancy the charm of verifying this and that item in the old books—especially in such a little travelled section of the globe.

The fishes are unusually beautiful this morning—to the leeward the bonitas showing red like autumn leaves in a torrent. Sometimes they display a streak of this glowing crimson underneath when they are brought to deck, but never before have I seen them so red in the water. It is something to live for, once to behold, near the close of day, an upstanding wave between you and the sun, transparent blue, green-topped, white-tipped, sun-shot, and glinted through with rainbow shapes of the sea.

. . . Inconceivable and Monstrous, again! Yesterday Captain Warren ordered the topsail set. So far on the voyage it had never been set. It was promptly dragged forth from where I had been sleeping on its folds for many a night. Herrmann was aloft in the hot sun for quite a while, making an unsuccessful effort to get it set. Finally the captain took a climb, for something was radically wrong. Then the trouble was made plain. When it was discovered, in California, that the mizzen-mast had been stepped too far forward to allow for the mainsail, instead of re-stepping the mizzen-stick (which should, by all that is right and honest, have been done), the mainsail had been cut down and the topsail left as it was—to match a mainsail that no longer existed so far as its original size was concerned. This is the second time on the voyage it has been set, and we now realise why Roscoe took it in so hastily the first time.

(Right here, a bonita close by leaped his length into the air, got his flying-fish, and we saw him with the rainbow half swallowed, as he tumbled ingloriously back into the water tail-first.)

Lat.   8° 11′ South,
Lon. 138° West.
Aboard the Snark, South Seas,
Thursday, December 5, 1907.

There is one incident in human affairs that it is safe to say never fails of interest, never palls. Perhaps it is the only one—but I will not go that far. The raising of land on the horizon is the one thing that induces a thrill even in the most experienced—from the very connoisseur of travellers to the oldest sailor afloat. It seems to me that I have centred in my soul all the fascinated, illusioned expectation of all peoples in all days under similar conditions; for to-morrow is the day when we confidently hope to see land, the first in nine weeks, come Monday next. It seems as if I can hardly wait for the loom of it ahead. How will it look? Will it be floating in the blue and gold of sunset, or will it show hazily in the blazing afternoon?—or mayhap in the pearl and rose of dawn? "The first love, the first sunrise, the first South Sea Island, are memories apart and touch a virginity of sense." Thus Robert Louis Stevenson.

We crossed the Line last Saturday, November 30, in longitude 128° 45′—which was even a little better than Captain Warren expected; and immediately we fell in with such cool temperature that I promptly caught cold. It doesn't sound probable, I know, that right below the Equator I caught my first cold in months; but I'm the one that caught it, and I ought to know.

We had planned to do some weird stunts to celebrate crossing the Line; but it turned out a very busy day in one way and another, in which there seemed no place for pranks. I copied ninety pages of Jack's manuscript, for one thing—work I had neglected for other work. We must have tripped up against Neptune somewhere, however, for I found yellow whiskers that looked very much like rope-ravellings, on the stays under the bowsprit.

While I write, lying under the life-boat for shade, the men are trying to lure a big shark that is sniffing around. He is of a size to make one glad of a few planks between. The waves are a-hiss with leaping bonitas fighting for some food they have run into, any unlucky one that happens to get bitten being immediately devoured by the rest. We have not seen a single dolphin since the day before we crossed the Equator. "They dropped us cold!" said Martin. The bonitas and flying-fishes alone have been sliding with us down the bulge of the earth since we topped the rise, at the rate of one hundred and forty miles a day. Night and day, night and day, everywhere we turn, the countless purplish-coppery bodies of the blood-mad destroyers keep us in sight while we thresh out the flying-fishes for them.

Ah, but I forgot the Wiggler! He lives and moves and has his being under our keel, wriggling out occasionally to take a snap at a passing bonita, like an irascible little backyard terrier. He is about a foot and a half long, and of a whitish green—a sort of suppressed hue, showing like a cellar-plant among gay flowers when he lines up against the sun-blazoned bonitas. On Sunday, the spinnaker was set, and as we begin gliding ahead at a seven-knot clip, in the wake we saw our Wiggler, left a little astern on one of his expeditions out from under. He was making the run of his life to catch up. We yelled and hooted affectionate encouragement—he was doing such a plucky and manful sprint, nearly wagging his tail off. "Go it, you son-of-a-seacook!" "Come on, *now*, once more! That's it!" "You'll make it, keep up the fight!" were heard from various quarters of the stern rail. Presently it seemed as if the chase were lost. The only way we might have helped him was by throwing him a line—with a hook on it. Martin saw him next day, however, as much at home as ever; but he surely had his fins full to make up the speed handicap caused by that spinnaker.

. . . We are betting heavily as to who will first see land. I am pledged for all of forty cents among my shipmates. It cannot be more than a hundred miles dead ahead; but the sun is in our eyes, and it is not a 14,000 foot Sandwich Island mountain we are looking for—only one of 2800 feet. We are going to lose our dollar bets to Jack, for the date we wagered on fetches up to the 12th, one week from to-day.

Jack is sitting on the weather rail, with his feet in a pail of fresh water—unwonted extravagance. He has not had a shoe on these two months, and is trying to coax his feet into shape for the trial that awaits them, who knows?—maybe to-morrow. In order not to waste his golden hour, he is reading, and also, at intervals, shooting bonitas with his 22-Winchester automatic rifle. I wish I had known him better before I married him!—just listen to this: Yesterday I said, "I don't feel like typing to-day." "Don't do it on the boat then," urged Jack kindly. "Don't type until you get to TYPE-E!!!"

. . . There have been many heralds of the land about us the past two days—various kinds of birds, with gunies and boobies among them; bo's'ns, and smaller white birds, fluttering by twos, like love letters in the wind against the blue sky. There are small black birds, too, and brownish grey ones, neither of which we know.

The South Seas—think of it, we are sailing, beautifully sailing, over the very waves of that storied region of islands of strange form and composition, peopled by strange men of unspeakable customs. But we are not in time—the devastating civilising years have preceded the *Snark* venture, and we can only see the islands themselves with little trace of the people who roamed them of old. What of Melville's Valley of Typee now? But listen: When I wander through Typee, a few days hence, I am going to people it to suit my fancy; I am going to see the chiefly Mohiva and kind Kory-Kory, and the matchless Fayaway, and all their beauteous straight-featured tribe. I alone may see them, but see them I will!

The other day I read a book by Edwin Somebody-or-other,

in which he tells with casual cleverness of his meanderings among the islands of the South Seas, and in his chapter on the Marquesas, especially devoted to the Island of Nuka-Hiva, he does not once mention Typee. Can it incredibly be that he never heard of it?

It is all very well to romance about the fantasy of the South Sea Islands; but my imagination persists in rioting in fields of cabbages and onions, potatoes, cauliflowers, and luscious tomatoes; in taro patches and fabulous banana- and cocoanut- and breadfruit-groves. Captain Warren's desire carries him closer, into the chicken-coop; while Martin is content to dream merely of the nests—one dozen variously prepared eggs being his first order. ⌣

. . . There are no more spectacular twilights; the days have grown much longer than they were on the other side of the hill. And the sunsets do not compare with those of the Variables and the Doldrums. But the sailing is wonderfully lovely—the boat rocking, rocking, on waves that pursue from astern and overtake and propel us, spinnaker and mainsail winging us straight toward the setting sun.

. Nor are the water and skies so gorgeous as we found them above the Equator; but any lacks of this sort are offset by the "silver-winged breeze" that blows from the right direction, and every hour of the day I am thankful for the change from past exasperating, bone-racking, flesh-bruising head-seas and -winds. Here everything is with us—wind and billow, fair days and nights.

. . . I am curled comfortably in a hollow of the life-boat cover, shaded by the mainsail, and the swinging of the boat is so restful—not a jar, nothing but soothing curves and undulations of movement, ever rocking forward and sidewise, but imperceptibly making five knots an hour in the light but steady wind. We are in the sun's highway, a broad and glittering stretch directly before. We must be absorbing the gold as well as the miles, for there is none of it in our wake. . . .

We often try to picture different friends, suddenly transported into our midst aboard the *Snark,* and wonder how they would comport themselves. With no experience of the sea it would be remarkable if they saw anything beautiful in earth or heaven. The roll would attend to that. The smallness of the boat, the nearness of the water, and particularly the size of the waves, would about wreck a nervous woman for the time being. The very middle of the yacht would be the only livable place for her, as being farthest removed from certain destruction over the awful rail. Now, I am not making sport of anybody. I can project my viewpoint far enough to put myself in the other fellow's mind under such a strain. I have been here a long time and it is only comparatively lately that I have felt quite secure, free from nervousness and sickness.

. . . We have finished Saleeby's book, and are now reading Ball's *The World's Beginning.* Astronomy helps me to new appreciation of this world we are circumnavigating, and of the whole universe of worlds and suns. At night, before turning in, we lie in the lifeboat a while, Jack and I, and study the Southern skies, sometimes dropping below to scan our planispheres; and last evening we had a feast of meteors, that streaked long trains of light across the sky.

Nightly a poker game obtains in the second dog watch, and the only monotony in it that seems to strike Jack and Martin is the way the captain wins and continues to win. He usually does it with a royal flush in his face and say a pair of sixes in his hand. He has had a run of luck that deserves greater scope.

There is always one perfectly contented soul in our party, no matter what happens, and that is our inimitable cabin boy. At dinner to-day I asked him, "Are you happy, Nakata?" "I, happy? —oh-h-h, Missisn, *v-e-r-r-y* happy—yes, ma'am." (He has mastered the "ma'am" at last.) "But why happy, Nakata?" I pursued. He threw back his head to look up at the sunlight through the companionway, smiled seraphically and said with pure sweetness: "Oh, *ev-e-r-r-y*-thing, Missisn!"

. . . The only thing with which I can compare my state to-night, is my Christmas Eve sensations of old time. I am sure there must be a stocking of mine hanging up somewhere on the boat, and that there is going to be something nice in it when I wake.

Lat. 8° 47′ South,
Lon. 139° 44′ West.
Aboard the *Snark*, in channel between Ua-Huka and
Nuka-Hiva, Marquesas Islands, 3:30 P. M.,
Friday, December 6, 1907.

Can't you see it?—can't you see it, Cape Martin right ahead there in the west, and Comptroller Bay just around the point? —Comptroller Bay, into which the Valley of Typee opens, where Melville escaped from the cannibals. Then another and dimmer headland, beyond which is Taiohae, where we shall anchor at sunset if the fair wind holds.

Captain Warren picked up Ua-huka (Washington Island) at daylight, and the first I heard, awakening under the lifeboat, was Herrmann up the mainmast calling down. But so sure was I of my full stocking, and so very sleepy, that after rising half-way and seeing nothing, I subsided for another nap. I had been up at a little past three, looking at the Southern Cross—the first time below the Line.

When I did finally turn out, I saw a volcanic island of beautiful form and proportion, grey-green and shimmering in the morning radiance. We sailed toward it, passed it, and now it lies astern, touched with the sunset. The island looks as if it has had a drouth, for its steeps are as yellow with dried grass as California's in the autumn, with here and there a hint of dull green.

. . . This has been a full day. I was bound and determined that I should not be caught arriving at Taiohae with a lot of back work on hand on the typewriter—in spite of Jack's vile pun on Typee; so I copied a chapter of his novel, sacrificing our daily reading; closed up a lot of letters with the advice that we were coming into port (against the possible sailing of some vessel from Taiohae immediately after our arrival), and did a thousand little things for shore-going. After lunch Jack and I went forward with our rifles, and shot at the numerous birds fishing in the olive current of the channel. It was my first shooting at moving objects, and, considering that the aiming was from a plunging boat, I didn't do so badly, for I got three boobies on the wing, two or three more that were just rising, and ruffled the feathers of others. Also, I struck a bonita, which instantly up-bellied, and as instantly disappeared among its ravening brothers. I tried porpoises, and they immediately grew shy and came seldom to the surface. And we fired at a small whale, but it quickly sank out of danger.

. . . Now we are nine miles from Taiohae Bay, and with the glasses can just pick out the two Sentinel Rocks guarding either side of the entrance. The headland features I have already mentioned are on the southern side of the island, the northern coast stretching far to our right. Cape Martin reminds me of the castled outlines of Wyoming, with a natural tower standing atop the abrupt black head of the promontory. The face of the island toward us, the east side, seems ruggedly bluffed; and above, fold on fold of volcanic green mountains range back and up to the highest point of the island, 3890 feet. Perhaps that is the farther wall of Typee Valley that we can just glimpse beyond those first bluffs. It seems to me I never wanted to see a place as I want to see Typee.

All sorts of business is going forward, while the yacht slides steadily nearer. The captain studies the coast with his binoculars; Martin is putting finishing touches of green paint and aluminum paint on the rejuvenated launch-engine. (It had been about given up by Martin until Jack got out the books and made a suggestion that, when applied, set the machinery going merrily.) Herrmann, the while trying to explain how it happened that in Honolulu he had bought both his sea-boots for the same foot, is scraping wood— teak, pine, oak, on yacht, launch, and life-boat; Wada steers; the spinnaker has just been taken in, and, the wind hauling,

we have jibed over. The sturdy anchors are in readiness to
let go when we come to our resting-place, and I'll warrant
the skipper knows exactly where the red-marked lead-line is.
Jack is stretched out beside me on the life-boat cover, reading,
and, I think, dreaming a little. When he was a small boy he
happened on Melville's *Typee,* and promptly thirsted for
Marquesan exploration. Years later, after one trip to sea,
he tried to ship as cabin boy on a sailing vessel bound for
these islands, but failed to secure the berth, for he thinks
the captain must have seen desertion in his eye. But here
he is, and here am I, lucky enough to be the partner of his
realised adventure; although for his sake I wish he could
have fulfilled his desire when the dream was young.

. . . The little *Snark!* She seems to be reaching out
eagerly, after sixty days of unremitting motion, for her
shelter under the land. Consider—for six times ten days we
have never been still one moment. I am afraid the imminent
level repose that threatens will disquiet more than soothe,
until we readjust.

5 P. M. The captain is now thinking of putting in at
Comptroller Bay for the night, for squalls are closing in
around us and dimming the sunset light that we depended
upon for conning into Taiohae harbour. I rather hope we
do go into Comptroller. It would be enchanting to wake in
the morning with Typee Vai spread out before us.

We are surrounded by untold myriads of sooty little sea-
swallows with white heads and sweet piping voices. As we
curtsy past Cape Martin, its striking profiles change from
moment to moment, and we can see green trees that look like
Hawaiian *kukui,* trooping up the shallow erosions.

Aboard the *Snark,* Taiohae Bay,
Nuka-Hiva, Marquesas Islands,
Saturday, December 7, 1907. 10 A. M.

It is a cyclorama of painted cardboard, done by an artist
whose knowledge of perspective was limited. The walls in-

closing the green, still water in which we ride at anchor, the pinnacles and bastions half-way to the rugged scissored sky-line, the canyons and gorges, sun-tanned beaches, grass-huts under luxuriant plumy palms, and the rich universal verdure —it is all painted boldly on upright cardboard. There is a rift in the amphitheatre, toward the sea, and on either side the entrance, booming surf breaks upon the feet of the two Sentinels of tilted strata, crowned with feathery trees. It is an astounding scene, and cannot be compared with any place I ever saw. The mirrored effect of the atmosphere on the perpendicular mountains is not unlike that on Winward Oahu in Hawaii; but the form and lines of the landscape round about this bay surpass anything in my book of memory pic-tures.

The entrance looks very innocent this morning in a sunny calm; but it did not appear so harmless last evening, our waning daylight shut off by a blinding rain-squall, just when it seemed indispensable that we should see clearly in order to make our way around the eastern Sentinel. The captain had finally decided to try for Taiohae. The distance across the mouth of the bay is only seven cable-lengths, and it is necessary to hug the eastern side, because the equatorial cur-rent sets over toward the west shore of the bay, and with only light fans of air, there is liability of going on the rocks.

It was tense and delicate work. Every one was on deck, Jack at the wheel, Herrmann standing by the three headsails, Martin and Wada obeying general orders, and Nakata haul-ing in the lead-line for the captain after each cast. And over it all was the trained intelligence of the captain, whose was the responsibility of the *Snark* and the lives on board. He stood in the bow, before we entered the harbour, with straining eyes on the fading outlines of the East Sentinel, close by which lay safety, and praying that the wind would hold. But it held only until we rounded the rock, then swept on seaward past the entrance, leaving us to fare as best we might with current and tide, rocks and surf. The spinnaker was taken in and the mizzen set, and each man returned to his post, ready for prompt obedience. I longed to be a man, to take some active part; but they don't let me do much—and besides, there are plenty of men to handle the boat. (Why, the picturesque 500-ton bark lying yonder carries only eleven men, while our ten-ton yacht has six all told.)

I was fascinated with the working of the *Snark*. The captain's questions, "How is she now?" or "How is she heading?" were rapid and frequent; and Jack, eye on binnacle, busy with instant replies and instant compliance, had no chance for extraneous observation. Muffled in oilskins, I sat on the cockpit rail, and posted him on what I saw—the looming rocks close at hand, the white-toothed breakers snapping hungrily and loudly, and the vague suggestion of the dreaded western shore. Captain Warren commanded my respect. His head was clear, and he seemed high-strung in a way that only refined his certitude of judgment and action. Much though I have absorbed of knowledge of the sea, in relation, at least, to our particular craft, I was open-mouthed at his quickness of perception. I knew, of course, how carefully he had "crammed" the sailing-directions, and how sharply the chart was reproduced on his brain; and these things, coupled with his practical experience, were sufficient to satisfy my reason; but it was wonderful just the same—as man is wonderful in everything that raises him to primacy over the brute earth-forces.

By and bye we picked up the "fixed red light," hung at ninety feet, described in the Directions, and had something tangible to steer by. We fanned in, tack upon tack, with the mere breathing of the mountains to give us steerage-way. The *Snark* responded faithfully to the hand on her helm when there was the faintest air to make it possible. The near water was very still, and sometimes the only way we could tell that we were inching ahead was by the slight passing riffle against the boat. The bay is very deep along its sides, so we had no especial worry except for the current. Once or twice we seemed to be drifting toward the west, for the sound of the surf from that direction came clearly. Then suddenly a big light flared out in the murk ahead, although try as we would with our glasses we could not make out whether it was on land or vessel.

But as we approached our anchorage, there were other and less disquieting sounds in our ears than breakers. Down from obscure heights drifted the querulous bleating of kids, which I bewildered into more distressful tones by answering them in kind. And then a cock crew cheerily, and another, while the venerable *blat* of a patriarchal goat hushed the timorous young. The breath from the darksome steeps came down fragranced with spice of flowers—the yellow *cassi* loved of wasps, which distils perfume far and wide.

At quarter before ten we dropped anchor in nine fathoms, having passed the entrance at about 7:30. You cannot imagine what a feeling of utter rest followed the rush of the anchor chain through the hawsepipe—the sea-song of adventure. We found ourselves unexpectedly tired, and although we slept in the warm below on account of rain, we slept profoundly. I know I did not turn over in seven hours. I was awakened by voices on deck, and coming up found that Mr. Kreiech, the German trader who has charge of the Taiohae Branch of the Société Commerciale de l'Oceanie, had called. I could see him going shoreward, a big figure standing in an outrigger canoe paddled by scarlet-breeched Marquesans.

. . . It seems rather odd, as the morning wears on, that no one else comes out—only one indolent native has had curiosity enough to approach—a well-featured brown fellow. We sent him in search of bananas, and he wanted five francs for one bunch. He accepted half of that with perfect contentment; and then we all fell to and stuffed inordinately on this first fresh fruit in two months, and agreed that we had never eaten bananas before, so luscious were these.

As we have seemed to be in no danger of interruption from the beach, we have gone ahead with our work as usual—in the cockpit, shaded by the awning. Little flaws of wind, pollen-scented, flurry down upon us from the pictured walls of the amphitheatre, that are slowly taking on a less artificial aspect—losing nothing of their exquisite beauty, but becoming more earthly and approachable. The water is not clear—rather a dull olive-green, deepening into rich blue toward the mouth of the bay. Outside, we can see the channel white-caps racing past the Sentinels.

. . . After lunch we climbed reluctantly into our "store clothes," shoes being particularly odious. I had in my mind's eye pictures of several provincial white women, wives of the traders, and arrayed myself with care in brown linen with a touch of red scarf and corals—a "neat but not gaudy" effect that was destined to be appreciated solely by our own crowd and Mr. Kreiech and his assistant Mr. Rahling, to say nothing of the silver-laced old French Marechal who looked over our ship's papers; and to be wondered at by the natives. There were apparently no white women on the beach. But later on, when we inquired if there was any one in the place who would board Jack and me, Mr. Kreiech recommended a Mrs. Fisher, and we learned that besides herself there were her daughter and a niece, a French school teacher, and the Sisters at the Mission. We were also informed that fruit, eggs, fowls, vegetables, and nearly everything else that we have been hungering and thirsting for, are extremely scarce —almost out of the question, in fact. However, when making arrangements with Mrs. Fisher for two meals a day, she assured us that good limes and oranges are plentiful; that fowls can be had occasionally, for a reasonable price; that the mangoes are beginning to ripen, although the breadfruit season is not yet; and that cocoanuts are abundant. There were also hints of fresh-water prawns, fish, wild goat, water cress, and tomatoes, but no potatoes—the last importation from California being exhausted. Mr. Edwin Some-body-or-Other misled us by his glowing description of the lavish and automatic supply of everything edible in Nuka-Hiva. There is a French bakery, glory be, where crusted loaves are made at frequent intervals. This is a welcome surprise—an excellent cross between French and Italian bread.

But let no toddy-thirsting mariner be deceived as to this chaste strand. Whiskey is *taboo* in the Marquesas, although rum and wines and absinthe can be purchased at the Société store.

This afternoon we decided to rent the only available cottage. Imagine our gratification when we learned that it was the old club-house where Robert Louis Stevenson frequently dropped in during his call at Taiohae. In one corner of the large main room is a sort of stationary stand, where drinks used to be mixed. The house is now owned by the Société; and before promising it to us on any terms, Mr. Kreiech had to negotiate with exceeding deliberation with the native couple who live there as caretakers. No one here ever makes the mistake of doing anything on time or in haste, and the man who tries to rush the natives is the man lacking foresight. But Mr. Kreiech is evidently destined for success with the kanakas, for the elderly pair are to move into the detached kitchen, and we shall take possession of the cottage tomorrow. Jack and I could easily in ten minutes move all their belongings—a bedstead and bedding and a few garments hanging on nails; but twenty-four hours is not considered too much notice to allow. We saw these two old persons at the store at five o'clock, at which gala hour the workmen gather on Saturday afternoons to be paid off. Practically the entire population of the village drops in socially—a pitifully dwindled community in these latter years. The woman from our cottage is constantly attended by an enormous *puarka* (hog), given her by the captain of the Norwegian bark. She fondles it as if it were a beloved dog—although I could not help wondering if her affections were not slightly gustatory in character. And we saw her pitch viciously into a Norwegian sailor who waxed too familiar with her pet.

Jack and I sat on a big drygoods box on the veranda of the little store, dangling our happy heels against the sides,

and stared and were stared at by the natives, while we
munched and sucked some villainous striped candy that
Martin bought. Here were our first Marquesans—and hardly
a pure-breed among them! The blend is baffling in many
cases—Spanish, Portuguese, German, French, Corsican,
Italian, English, American. One little girl with snapping
black eyes and curly hair was pointed out as a true Marquesan specimen; but some one contradicted the assertion
with the statement that her mother was half Irish. She had
been ''given away'' as Hawaiian children are passed along,
and lives in terror of the short temper and long arm of
her adoptive sire.

When these people are displeased or contemptuous, they
express their feelings mainly by writhing their mouths into
the most astonishing contortions; and whenever our female
caretaker emerged from the crowd, facing our way, her
shapely lips wore an expression that led us to believe she
was not altogether enthusiastic about our impending occu-
pancy of the cottage. She moved restlessly here and there,
attended by the enormous pink *puarka*, reminding us of
some one trying to force an objectionable relative into society.
She has been a beauty, this old aristocrat of Nuka-Hiva, and
most persons might envy her straight features and beautiful
eyes. She wears the old-time tattooing on face and hands,
the latter looking as if blue-lace mitted. The Marquesans
were famed for the fineness of their tattooing.

The language of smiles is efficacious here as in Hawaii—
more so, in fact, for these Marquesans are far less sophisticated folk than the Hawaiians.

Walking from the little wharf to the store to-day
on first landing, we passed a building where half-naked
natives and Scandinavian sailors from the bark were chopping copra (the dried meat of the cocoanut) with spades,
preparatory to sacking it for export. Other natives, brawny
fellows wearing only a red and white loin-cloth *(paréu)*,
carried the filled bags out through the surf to a lighter which
was towed to the bark by her small boat. The men, chopping

on the floor of the dark room piled high behind them with the copra, composed a striking picture. Fair sailors and dark natives, all shining with sweat, they bent to the work, and we would catch curious tattooed faces with savage features, peering from out the gloom at the strangers. We fell in with the captain of the bark while we were looking on, and he explained the work.

We were immediately struck, upon landing, with an ominous narrowness of chest and stoop of shoulders among the natives, only a few showing any robustness. And the explanation came from moment to moment in a dreadful coughing that racks the doomed wretches. The little that is left of the race is perishing and it is not a pretty process. The men and women are victims of asthma, phthisis, and the sad "galloping" consumption that lays a man in two months or less—to say nothing of other and unnameable curses of disease that "civilisation" has brought. And as for children—there are very few born any more. A handful of years have made a fearful change in the Marquesas, the islanders going down before disease so rapidly that to-day, for instance, only nineteen able-bodied men can be mustered in Taiohae for ship-loading. It is only the infusion of outlander blood that holds the fading population at all.

The women wear the *holoku* of Hawaii—in Marquesan *éuéu*, in English Mother-Hubbard—the men being variously habited in overalls with bright striped net shirts, or merely in the *paréu*, a large square of red, or blue, blotched with bizarre designs in white or yellow—an English importation. Everybody, of all ages and both sexes, smokes cigarettes of strong native tobacco rolled in a spiral of dried leaf, or bamboo strip, or cane. The women are disappointing as to looks; but we have to remember that it is a far cry to the days of Herman Melville, who spoke of the Marquesan race as being the handsomest and fairest of the South Sea islanders—that the women would compare favourably with "the beauties of Europe." We had a glimpse of the husband of the old care-taker, and he, too, has the fine straight

Marquesans Dancing a Tahitian *hula* to Hawaiian music on an American phonograph

nose, well-sculptured mouth, with large and well-set eyes, and the marvellous tattooing.   Mr. Kreiech vouches for the pair as being of the purest Marquesan aristocracy.

Taiohae, Sunday, December 8, 1907.

Owing to the requisite delicacy in handling the old couple, we were obliged to sleep aboard again last night, and with our men returning from the shore at all hours there was not much sleep.   It was quite novel, for once, for Jack and me to be alone together on the *Snark*.   We spread a mattress on deck and lay on our backs looking up at the sparkling stars and a thin new moon that trembled on the edge of the sky.   The warm tide rippled along the sides of the boat, the surf droned soothingly in the distance, and the balmy air was filled with drifting scents of flowers and cocoanuts.   My thrumming *ukulélé* fretted the wild kids, and their drowsy plaints came down from the steeps.   Then the whole firmament was blotted out with sudden clouds and the face of the tropic night completely changed.   I went below; but Jack chanced it in the life-boat cover, and later on I found him fast asleep in a pool of rainwater.

Once up this morning and the cobwebs brushed out of my brain, I was glad of another morning afloat in the incomparable harbour.   We were lucky enough to arrive in time for a very important event in Marquesan circles.   One Taiara Tamarii, a part-Hawaiian part-Marquesan familiarly called Tomi, was to hold a great feast commemorating the first anniversary of his mother's death.   On such occasion, an important ceremony is to erect a cross upon the grave. But over against this pious symbol, the feature of rarest interest is a procession of the natives bringing in roasted pigs for the feast, imitating the days not so far gone when successful warriors returned with the bodies of their vanquished foes.

The host himself, the huge and burly Tomi, was waiting when we went ashore, together with Mr. Kreiech and Mr.

Rahling and the captain of the bark. We strolled along the wide green beach road (if road it can be called where never rolls a wheel), past Mrs. Fisher's picturesque tumble-down cottage, on up a gently rising stony trail, over brooks and by scattered grass houses built on ancient *pae-paes* described by Melville—high platforms of stones laid by dead and gone Marquesans. The natives of to-day have neither the ambition nor strength to pile such masonry, and so they squat upon the stages of their forefathers.

Now and again we were overtaken by hurrying natives who had some part to perform in the festivities or who were carrying articles for the feast. One wild-eyed, strapping young woman, reckless with drink that she had obtained somehow, attracted our attention by her exasperated attempts to pick up a battered accordion that kept dropping out of her bundle. Although she fell repeatedly, any offer of help was fiercely resisted.

We passed one hut before which lay spread a half-dozen roasted porkers, done to a turn and awaiting transportation to the house of Tomi. Finally we came within hearing of a barbaric rhythmic harangue in a woman's high strong voice, and were told it was a chant of welcome, the burden being that the occasion was made perfect by our presence. Following the wild sound, we turned, full of tingling curiosity, into an enclosure containing a spic and span new cottage built above a high open basement. To the right, through the trees, we could see the welcoming chantress—a swarthy, elderly creature with a certain lean, savage beauty, ham-wise upon a corner of a noble *pae-pae* that supported a grass hut. We were made very much at home by Tomi and his family, who received us in a half-shy, affectionate way. His wife had a refined, well-featured face, while his youngest daughter, a girl of twelve or thirteen, was a veritable beauty of any time or place.

We were soon out of doors again, seeing what we could see. Martin and I worked our cameras energetically, for never was there such incentive. Behind the house was a

long arbour of freshly plaited palms, under which, upon the
ground spread with leaves, the natives were to eat their
puarka and *poi-poi*. There were mighty wooden bowls of
this *poi-poi*, which is a thick and nutritive paste made from
breadfruit, instead of from *taro* as in Hawaii. Breadfruit
poi-poi is buried in the ground for an indefinite period, that
used on this occasion having been entombed for years. I
surreptitiously poked my finger into one grey mess in a huge
hand-hewn calabash, but I did not like the taste so well as
the taro poi.

Scores of merrymakers moved or sat about the grounds,
women gossiping in groups and inhaling endless numbers of
cigarettes of the acrid native tobacco, naked pickaninnies
tumbling in the grass or sucking sections of fresh young
cocoanut, while to and fro stalked Tomi's brothers carrying
more calabashes of *kao-kao* (food) on their polished shoulders
—magnificent brown savages girdled in scarlet, and over
these bright cinctures ordinary leather belts in the backs of
which were stuck murderous knives.

Altogether fourteen huge cocoanut-fed hogs had been
roasted whole in the ground among hot stones. These hogs
were laid, four or five at a time, in a savoury row near the
arbour. Tomi's brethren drew their long knives with a
flourish and fell to carving the steaming meat, meanwhile
surrounded by yearning, sniffing dogs of all mongrel breeds
under heaven. As soon as one lot was carved, another lot
was brought. The two biggest brothers willingly posed for
us, once bearing a greasy pig on a pole between them, and
again with the great wooden bowls of calabashes upon their
glistening shoulders.

There was a sudden alarming change in the music. We
ran to the front of the house, not to miss anything, where an
old woman was loudly mouthing a rude and protracted cry
that was much too sinister and menacing to be pretty, and
made creepy sensations down one's spine. There were
answering warlike cries in men's voices from a distance
among the trees. The exchanging calls, like tom-toms and

war-drums, split the calm air; weird and ghastly questionings
seemed to be in the voices of the women, and incommunicable
horrors of suggestion in the resounding replies from unseen
bearers of victorious burdens.

It was not a long procession that wound into view through
the palms and twisted *burao* trees and past us to the rear of
the house; but it was led by a king's son, and as the slow,
ominous double-file came on, he repeatedly turned to it with
exhorting vociferations that called forth a howling clamour
of assent to some ungodly proposition. The men carried
long leaf-swathed bundles, each bundle slung high on bamboo
poles between two bearers. It was comforting to be assured
that the packages were only pig wrapped to resemble *long-pig*
—which term is too mortuarily obvious to need explanation.
But the actors in the tragedy entered with such zest and lack
of shame into the spirit of the seeming, that we were led to
speculate upon how many years, if left to themselves, it would
take them to lapse into their old habits of appetite. I hate
to spoil the vivid, savage picture; but the anachronisms were
too funny to leave out. For instance, one man sported a top
hat above a tattered rag of a calico shirt; several wore ludicrous derbys of the low-crowned "Weary Willie" variety,
and the king's son (who, by the way, was none other than
the man who wanted a dollar a bunch for bananas the day
before), shone in decent ducks and a native straw hat. But
we had to be satisfied, our willing imaginations eliminating
the comedy and grasping the beauty of the entirety of the
scene, while Tomi's brawny half-nude brothers, carrying the
biggest bundle of leaf-wrapped flesh, made up for any dis-
crepancies. In spite of the anachronisms in costume, there
was a tremendous sense of unreality about the whole proceedings.

Upon the instant the procession appeared, several old
vahines began jumping stiffly up and down like electrified
mummies, their arms held rigidly to their shrivelled sides—
after the manner of the "jumping widows" described by
Melville—and emitting the most remarkable noises that ever

came from human throats. This they kept up during the
passing of the procession, and it seemed that their function
was to announce the readiness of the feast—not to spoil the
appetites of the guests, as a fastidious diner might have
suspected.

But no epicure, however outraged, could have quarrelled
with the collation to which we were bidden. There was but
one disappointment—to our sorrow we were specially
honoured by eating in the house, at a table, with all the im-
plements of an effete civilisation. We bowed to the inevitable, but with secret rebellion in view of that palmy banquet
outside on the ground.

Our dinner was course-served by the cook himself, a slim
Marquesan, and he certainly was a chef to remember. We
had fresh-water shrimps, big fellows tasting like New England lobster; wild chicken (descended from the domestic
ones brought by old-time ships) boiled in milk squeezed from
the meat of cocoanuts, and delicately flavoured with native
curry and other spices; roast sucking-pig, as fine and white as
spring fowl; for salad, they gave us water-cress, crisp and
succulent; and there were potatoes, real Irish potatoes, come
all the way from San Francisco via Tahiti, French-fried and
with a flavour of homesickness. We were not served with
poi-poi, but our old favourite the *taro* was there, to my utter
gratification. Absinthe was passed around before eating, and
California wine, white and red, flowed during the meal, followed by a sweet French champagne.

Mrs. Fisher and I were the only women at the board;
while outside on the veranda, in fine white *éuéus*, with their
black locks flower-crowned, the more pampered of the native
women had their goodies, unavoidably reminding one of a
dusky harem. Now that I am having a chance to observe, I
think one might discover more beauty among the women
here were it not for the shocking manner in which they wear
their hair, white women as well as natives—brushed straight
back from the forehead and hanging in a braid behind.
Such a fashion is trying to the most lovely face.

We were a long time at table, during which there was opportunity to study the heterogeneous company from the head of the board. On my right, next to Jack, came Mrs. Fisher, then Captain Warren and Martin, by whom sat the ship-carpenter from the bark, a huge grizzled Scandinavian with bearded mouth and dull and introspective eye—a Viking in size and form, but with all the fire gone out. At the foot of the table was the captain of the bark, a man with nose and mouth that deserved better eyes for company, a nose severely Greek, a mouth sensuously so, but the eyes just ordinary Scandinavian blue eyes, set too near together and remarkable for nothing but their insignificance. On my left, next Mr. Kreiech, our diffident host, Tomi, sat beside one of his eight brothers, and next following was old Mr. Goeltz, father of Mrs. Fisher. The mate of the bark, a medium sized young fellow with a homely, amorous face, came next to Mr. Rahling, who completed the circle.

Dinner was diversified by considerable exercise, for we must run to the windows to see the *hula-hulas* of the natives, who would nearly kill themselves laughing at the untranslatable sentiments of the songs. These were accompanied, of all things, by an accordion, that had a habit of sighing profoundly at the end of each stanza. Then there was much mirth and banter over the swift sneakings for home of certain men carrying large portions of *puarka*. It is the custom that each guest may take home whatever of his allotment of meat he does not consume on the spot. One furtive kanaka trying to get away unobserved with what looked to be a whole hog in two sections slung each on the end of a bamboo pole, was detected and hooted out of sight. We were told that this man always departed early with all he could lay his hands on.

It was a wild afternoon that followed, dance upon dance, until it became an orgy. The *hula-hula* here is largely Tahitian, and is faster and briefer and less graceful than the Hawaiian *hula,* while the music has not the charm of the Hawaiian. In fact, we heard only one air to-day, played on the accordion; and the only virtue it had was that it made the men and women dance. Everybody danced, everybody applauded. Even I had to join in a waltz with the two captains, much to the amusement of the natives. Sailors from the bark shook a leg or so to keep the fun boiling. At the height of the prevalent madness, the old bow-shouldered Viking, who had been gazing heavy-lidded and vacuously at the scene with an idiotic expression on his pendant lip, without warning sprang up like a monster marionette, and crashed into the middle of the suffering floor in a mighty hornpipe. Pandemonium broke loose, everybody yelled and screeched with delight, until the giant was suddenly smitten self-conscious and dropped foolishly into his chair; but later, when Martin, who was having the time of his life, took a whirl in the *hula-hula* (with great credit to himself), the old man could not hold still any longer. After wiggling his great feet for a little while, he essayed another hornpipe, and wound up in an angular *hula-hula* that brought tears to our eyes. I know I never laughed so in my life. The clutter of dogs in the house greatly enhanced the orgaic spirit of things. Jack and I sat dangling our feet from the high window-sill, and wondered if we knew where we were this time!

The windows opening on the porches were crowded with shining dark heads wreathed in white flowers, and when I begged for a wreath I was soon crowned with a fragrant circlet of tube-roses, or such they most nearly resembled, twined with glossy green leaves.

But to the natives the most deeply significant event was the photographing of Tomi and his family before the imposing white-painted, black-decorated wooden vault entombing the dead mother, with the new cross planted in front. It is nothing out of the way here to inter the dead in the house-enclosure. Martin posed the group and took the picture, but there was difficulty in getting all the subjects to look serious at the same time. Tomi wore not the ghost of a smile, not he; he knew what was what. But the majority of the long line of relatives signally failed in gravity, with disastrous results.

While this was going on, the old ship-carpenter awoke once more from his lethargy and tried to dance with the women; but he was evidently not accustomed to handling anything so fragile, and they refused to dance more than once with an uncouth giant who stupidly bruised their wrists.

We were somewhat delayed in our farewells by Martin, who at the last moment engaged in a particularly brilliant *hula-hula* with half a dozen of the men. At length he was torn unwillingly away and preceded us down the rocky pathway, a Bacchanalian tilt to his leafy coronet, a shoe in either hand to rest his feet, and a worshipful *vahine* on each arm. Jack also carried his shoes, which he had taken off as soon as he reached Tomi's. I kept mine on, although I was not entirely happy; but the stones were many and sharp and I considered I was choosing the lesser torture. The homeward walk included many stops and rests, and it was an intense relief to strike the soft green turf of the main road. This lovely thoroughfare is called the Broom Road, after the driveway so-named in Tahiti. Mrs. Fisher says "Broom Road" means a road which many feet have brushed in passing. That woman bids fair to be a mine of interest and information, and we are congratulating ourselves upon having her take us to board, especially as she is the only one here who can or will do this.

We are going to be very happy in our independent fashion in this clean little house with its big living-room and closet, an ample veranda for sleeping and working, and best of all a concrete bathing place out-of-doors under a shed connected with our side door. There is room in the house for the Victor and all its records, and word of the talking machine has already gone forth so that there are many peepers through our vine-clad fence.

Monday, December 9, 1907.

We slept eight unbroken, dreamless hours last night in makeshift beds on the porch—at least I did; Jack never sleeps without fantastic dreaming. The quiet did not disturb us in the least. We were lulled by the musical purr of the little surf only a few rods away, and the patter of warm raindrops on the banana leaves in our garden. But just as we were losing consciousness, the soft night-sounds were rent by a chorus of Gargantuan laughter—horrible, raucous, as from the throats of insane Titans. The splintered turrets of the mountains fairly reverberated to the astonishing orgy of noise. This morning we learned that the goblin chorus had issued unaided from the throat of a diminutive and entirely amiable jackass that grazes untethered about the village.

The air of Nuka-Hiva is pure and sweet, with frequent showers that cool it deliciously—and it is certainly warm; but perspire as one may, there is no great discomfort if one dresses sensibly. I am going to wear kimonos and my Hawaiian *holokus*, without strictures of any sort in the way of belt or sash.

It's early to bed and up early in this tropic Elysium, with *déjeuner* about ten and dinner somewhere around five. There are no stated hours for any functions of living. So before seven this matchless morning I sat me down in the long grass under a giant-leaved banana tree, with a pan of golden-rosy mangoes and a sharp knife, and plunged into the preparation of a luscious breakfast. *Plunged* is an excellent word, although *dived* might be better, for one cannot dally with the gracious mango without getting pretty well up to the elbows in its squashy ambrosia. I shall not tell how many mangoes Jack ate, nor how many oranges, nor how much lemonade he drank in addition. Such oranges! Except for seedlessness, the finest California oranges are no better.

While Jack wrote at a table in the middle of the big room, I fussed about making the cottage homelike with our belongings, Nakata watching me out of the corners of his eyes to learn points about housekeeping, the while he unpacked and furbished our saddlery; and the sight of the comfortable pigskin Australian models made me smile at the memory of Mr. Rahling's pained look when I declined his kind offer of a

side-saddle on a ride that Mr. Kreiech suggested for the afternoon.   No comment was made; but methinks I am about to
learn that the dusky women of this green isle are still in the
clutch of the feudal ages.

At ten, Jack and I, both in kimonos, under a pongee parasol, strolled up the green boulevard, and the cut of our
garments caused much whispering and giggling among the
loafers as we passed.   Whatever Mrs. Fisher may have
thought, she kept it to herself, and went cosily about the
laying of a small table in her cool front room.   But we pro-
tested vigorously when we found she had not planned to sit
with us, for we were looking forward to talking with her.
We had our way in the end; and while we stowed away a
meal that was an earnest of our being well looked after by her,
Mrs. Fisher told us vividly of her life.   She has been in the
South Seas for thirty years, although born in San Francisco
of German and English parents.   She married in Tahiti at
fifteen, and, besides most of her eleven children, she has
buried husband and mother.   Being a keen observer, with
strange things to observe, she is ripe with knowledge of the
islands and their inhabitants, both white and brown.   Weird
were some of her tales of both colours.   In spite of a life
of unusual trouble and hardship, she is wonderfully young
looking.   She has a striking profile and carriage, her rather
austere expression relieved by a pair of irresistible dimples
when she smiles.

By noon we were in the saddle.   Our horses were small
black stallions, full of mischief from lack of exercise combined with natural cussedness.   I was unwarned, and mine
began by variously rearing and kicking all over the road, with
sudden shying slides down the banks to the beach, and wild
leaping runs over precarious foot-bridges that spanned nasty
gullies.   Thank goodness he did not know how to buck.   It
was about the only thing he did not do, however, to get me
off; but I managed to stick, and at length he decided that he
wanted to follow the party.   We fell into line, a small but

turbulent cavalcade, horses snorting, neighing, kicking, fighting, but sure-footed as goats, and gentle of gait when they
chose to have any gait.   I have read of the surety of these
Marquesan ponies, but the writers neglected to mention their
beauty.   The original stock came over from Chili, and has
bred true in form and spirit, though not in size.   They are
firm bodied, shapely beasts, with slender legs, small trim
hoofs, fine coats, and beautiful heads.   They are also hardy,
although they do not know hay and grain, and are merely
turned out to forage in the jungle.

The object of our ride was to inspect an ancient god that
is doomed to voyage over-seas in the black hold of the Norwegian bark, provided a way can be devised to transport it
through the intricate jungle.   Our trail lay northeast, and
imagine my delight when they said this was the way to
Typee, and that to-morrow we should start out on the same
path to the fabulous valley.   I was too busy at first with my
India-rubber steed to appreciate our surroundings; but
presently he grew weary of tearing up the landscape to overtake that merciless rider, the Norwegian captain, and I was
able to look about.   On either side of the trail, as far as eye
could penetrate, were the splendid ruins of ancient *pae-paes*
terraced up the hillsides in tangled jungle of blossoming
burao that strewed the earth with brown and golden bells.
(This is the same tree as the *hau* of Hawaii.)   Some of the
nearer stone platforms carried most picturesque little grass
huts; but we saw very few natives, probably because there are
very few left to see.   It is mournful, all this grandeur of
wasted masonry, left in solitude by a wasted race.

But it was a lightsome forest, for all its old associations.
Sometimes we rode in a mist of golden silk-cotton growing on
a tree that is like a delicate drawing of straight lines and
right angles, with scant and lacy foliage and bursting pods
of cotton depending from its cane-like branches.   Among the
burao trees we also saw the *lauhala* of Hawaii, which is likewise used here for hat-plaiting and basketry.   There is a

lack of wild-flowers in Nuka-Hiva; indeed, almost the only flowers we saw were those of the *burao,* and the flame-coloured flags of the *flamboyante* tree.

We tied our now submissive horses a mile or so up the trail, and plunged on foot into the denser woods and up among a world of moss-grown *pae-paes.* The stillness was intense, a waiting solitude that made one listen and look for the unexpected. You could fancy faces and contorted limbs in every gnarled *burao,* or shadowy forms crouched along fallen mossy trunks; and it seemed sacrilege to tread the springy undergrowth, for surely it had risen from the dust of forgotten Druids. There was a mute sacredness in the forest that was in no wise destroyed when, after a panting climb, we came in sight of the ungodly idol that we sought, leaning moss-clothed and isolate against an old and broken tree. And the god was a goddess, after all—Tataura, the rotund deity of fecundity, to whom childless brown women prayed in the long ago.

Our dream was broken when the German trader and the soulless Norwegian captain fell to wrangling over ways and means for transporting the quaint image to the beach, and stuck their iconoclastic knives into the soft red stone to see whether it might not be of a consistency for sawing to advantage. We glimpsed a stealthy brown figure, almost naked, lurking near, watching the intruders into his ancestral wood, in his eyes a blending of modern agnosticism and the superstition of yesterday, with a tinge of suspicion and regret. Jack and I left the two white men haggling over the fallen immortal, its almost obliterated heathen face seeming to grin sarcastically. We wandered down through the twisted temple of out-doors, touched by the romantic hillside where once lived a laughing, careless people, beautiful to look upon and dwelling in amity and abundance—when they were not out besieging or being besieged by the dwellers of other hill-sides and valleys.

The two men overtook us down the trail, and on the way

home we turned off to visit a mineral spring that supplies irreproachable drinking water to the fastidious in Taiohae. Our caretakers are to keep us with full jars at the cottage. The captain forged ahead and tore through the trees, I close after, supposing he knew what he was doing—and he did, but it was not the right thing to do. I followed him over a place that I would have disliked to attempt on foot. He forced his poor horse down the boulders with savage unscrupulousness, and it was too late for me to withdraw, although my doughty little stallion tried to recover on the brink. I was angry, and took pains to explain the situation to Mr. Kreiech when he came up on foot, having tied his horse somewhere like a sane man. Jack had been drawn over that boulder as I had been, and neither of us wanted Mr. Kreiech to think we were accustomed to abusing horses. Of course we had to claw out the way we descended, for there was no other way.

At the spring, the water of which had a pleasant mineral tang, we were treated also to a draught from cocoanuts which a native opened with his long knife. These Marquesan cocoanuts are much superior to the Hawaiian ones in sweetness and richness of water and meat. They are picked young and full of the delicate-flavoured water, and the delicious meat is soft enough to eat with a spoon.

On the home stretch the irrepressible Norwegian raised general havoc in our ranks by wickedly whooping by downhill, and Jack's small stallion promptly bolted. Mine took after him in turn, and I could only trust to his tiny nimble feet, for there was no checking him. So I made the most of the mad descent, which was exhilarating if risky. By the time we drew up at Mrs. Fisher's at the foot of the hill, Jack's saddle was on his horse's neck, and it was a mercy the horse was not overbalanced to a fall.

. . . Such an appetite! And what a dinner! Mrs. Fisher has engaged as cook the man who set the feast at Tomi's yesterday, and he seasons his dishes most toothsomely. There is a combination of fine French cuisine and native cookery that keeps us hungry to the end and looking forward to the next meal.

We asked Mrs. Fisher and her household down to hear the phonograph in the evening, and passed the word along to others as we leisured on foot back to the old clubhouse. They turned out in force, flocking to our garden with smiles and bashful laughter, then disposing themselves here and there, sitting or standing around on the grass inside the gate, as well as on the broad green beyond, while some crowded on the porch where Jack was working the Victor. The women were nearly all in white, the men in ordinary suits of white duck or blue drilling, or in brilliant paréus. I wore a holoku, which pleased the women; and I went among them and tried to make them feel at ease, for they were very diffident with me at first. I, too, sat in the grass, laughing with them and trying to learn their words—one, in particular, *maitai*, meaning good, being worked most successfully in a hundred connotations. And they in turn put fragrant wreaths of rich white flowers about my neck and upon my head, patting my hands and smiling appreciatively like lovable children.— Poor things! Over and under and all about their mirth-making is the coughing, coughing, a running accompaniment to everything they do; and they continually soothe their racked lungs with the strong native tobacco.

Roaming among our guests outside the gate, I found lying under a *flamboyante* tree in the moonlight an old Corsican beachcomber with white hair and beard. He would not come inside, indicating that he could enjoy the music better where he was. How did he happen to come to this place, and, more remarkable, why did he stay on? I wonder what his thoughts were, listening to music from the outer world, there in the short grass under the *flamboyante* tree in the moonshine. Some one has whispered *leprosy*. This may explain him.

The men proved better listeners than the women, who, after their first curiosity about the "man in the box" had worn off, fell to chattering, chattering, till even Sousa's *baton* could not command clamour enough to drown them. Once in a while some kanaka, interrupted in his own racket by the superior clatter of the *vahines,* by hissing loudly restored a brief general silence.

And all the time, out on the bay, fairy-like in the moon-shine floated the quaint old grey bark with her painted ports, and the tiny white-speck boat that brought us to this lovely isle—four thousand miles to cover a twenty-one hundred mile course. But she did it! she did it! And there she lies these pleasant days, resting until she is called upon to bear us on over the purple seas, through the pearl lagoons of the Dangerous Archipelago, to Tahiti—Papeete, the "Paris of the Pacific," on, on, endlessly, the receding horizon our goal. It is all wonderful and unreal, here in the midst of it; and my heart is full of marvel at the beauty of life, my life, although at my pitying feet in the grass the poor fading creatures of this fair land lie coughing their lives away, pathetic aliens of no true race, waifs of the drift of many and incongruous bloods.

Against our door-post an old tattooed savage leans, squatting on the floor, his eyes dumbly agog at the talking-machine; in front of him, chin in hands, sits a degenerate of French-Marquesan stock, with a fine and delicate face marred by a look of concentrated foolishness in the great brown eyes. Mrs. Fisher sits straight and white and still, eyes fixed and far-dreaming, while on her long-tried knees sleeps a grandchild. And woven into the picture is a score or so of dogs, more oddly-bred than the people who tolerate them and cuff them by turns. Some departed Great Dane has left his gold-striped coat stretched upon many a strange frame, and the lineaments of a pug-dog mock at one from the shoulders of a hound sans pedigree.

. . . At a little after ten we told our friends *"pau,"* which is current here as in Hawaii to express the end, the finish, and, to the blare of *La Marseillaise,* the men and women trooped away singing.

Then a great black cloud rose from behind the mountain

and covered the moon; and in the darkness we found the way under our lacy canopies of mosquito netting, and drowsed off to the staccato of big rain-drops on giant banana-leaves, to dream of Typee Vai on the morrow.

December 10, 1907.

The plan had been to get away at five for Typee, but when that birdlike hour dawned it seemed that Jack and I were the only ones who had taken it seriously. No one else had made any preparation. We got away at half-past ten. But it did not matter—nothing matters in this leisure-land.

There were six besides ourselves—Captain Warren, Martin, and the Norwegian skipper with two native girls he had asked to bring. And last, and very important, was Nikko, an Easter Islander whom Jack had engaged as guide. The Norwegian had offered, as he had once before made the trip; but we preferred a resident of Nuka-Hiva, and Nikko knows his adoptive island thoroughly.

With my husband's entire approval I had concluded, in view of a hard ride through all sorts of country on a skittish horse, to discard skirts altogether; so I sallied forth booted and spurred and in khaki riding breeks—of course to find the native girls, arrayed in voluminous *éuéus,* lounging in roomy side-saddles. Take my word for it that they betrayed more surprise and disapproval than I did.

The bark captain had the ride very much to himself, because he was the only one who had no consideration for a horse, albeit his was a fine animal, borrowed at that, from one of the women. The rest of us struck a humane pace and stuck to it, while he raced over the rocks regardless of rise or declivity, his poor brute dripping rivers and quivering with exhaustion.

I rode my little stallion Jacques, and Jack's mount was a sure-footed "buckskin" gelding. Martin, had he but thought of it, might have assisted his tiny bay mare with his own long legs, for they could easily touch the ground. But Captain Warren's close-knit figure just suited the stocky, wicked little stallion that had been allotted him. It set its will against his at the start, but the stern-jawed mariner prevailed through a course of cajolery, heeling, and thrashing. Jack and I laughed ourselves weak during the first half hour.

The morning was fresh and sparkling, but the sun, touching the purple peak-tips with gilt, soon let loose its whole golden flood into the valley, and we were glad of a cool breeze to the summit. Such a gallery of incomparable pictures! First, the beach with its frilly surf, the vessels rocking in the wind-crisped water beyond, and yet beyond the blue flashing sea. Then the coloured palisades about the bay, sprayed with rainbows from little waterfalls born of a night's rain. On the landward side we were greeted by palm-vignetted sketches —here a warm-brown grass hut with its warm-brown dwellers smiling *kaoha* to us as we swept by; or the old grey-white mission with its peaceful garden where a cowled priest tended his flowers; and we passed the *ha'e* (house) of the dead Queen Vaeheku, spacious and imposing by contrast with the dwellings along the Broom Road. Then we plunged into the wooded trail where opened ferny vistas and the golden cotton brushed our faces with morning dew. It was familiar going for a time, with a memory of the forsaken red goddess in the enchanted forest; but presently we were beyond our ken and following our guide up-mountain—a mile behind the flying Norseman and his unfortunate charger.

We crossed shady streams and drank deep while the horses breathed, and ever we fought our way up, until we came out upon a rocky ridge and turned to look back upon one of the loveliest visions in the world. Such green, such unbroken emerald verdure—the valley a great round green-lined nest, dotted with feather of cocoanut; with little white birds, two by two, floating dreamily in the void. The sides of the nest, the wonderful mountains, shimmered in a tinted mist, and far down in the silver horse-shoe of the bay the boats lay tiny and toy-like. As in a chart spread out before us, we saw the twin Sentinels, and lying mistily on the horizon the violet islands of Uapo and Hiva-oa—"Yonder Far." We could even glimpse the ragged edges of the western wall of Comptroller Bay. This reminded us of our objective, and we turned once more to the ascent. Just as the encircling walls of the valley below looked too diaphanous to be real in the blowing blue vapours, so even the perpendicular cliffs close at hand looked unreal. This magic atmosphere idealises everything, far and near.

Our last pull out of Taiohae Valley was on a zigzag trail, some sections of which were narrow and steep enough to recall the Molokai *pali*, and we rested the horses frequently and enjoyed the ever-widening panorama growing beneath. Much of the trail was smothered in a slender though sturdy cane-growth, and we were warned not to cut ourselves on the green blades. This must be the cane that so discouraged Melville and Toby in their flight from the *Dolly*. The bank on the upper side was mossy and a-wave with familiar ferns, one variety resembling the stag-horn of Maui in Hawaii, although without its vicious thorny attributes. We saw a ripe guava, just one, and that was hollowed out by bird or rat. There was an abundance of guava-scrub, but the fruit season is young. On the top of a bank level with our eyes, we found a Liliputian wild passion vine bearing the most fragile lavender blossoms, miniatures of those we know at home.

The whole land was solidly green, valleys and glens, mountainsides and summits, broken only by chance scarry cliffs upon the bald faces of which clung desperate contorted palms.

We peered ghoulishly at a huge rocky funeral-crag near the divide, where corpses, embalmed so that even the eyeballs remain intact, are said to be hidden. Shall I *ever* be able to explore such a place? I let my opportunity slip at Kealakekua Bay, Hawaii (where Captain Cook died), because they said the sun was too hot for me to climb the face of the tomb-honeycombed cliff. And there's not the ghost of a chance on Nuka-Hiva. It has been tried, with most unsatisfactory results, by some of the white residents here in times gone by. They could not get even a whiff, so to say, of their loathsome quarry. The native carrying their camping things became

suspicious, found some significant tools in the outfit, and refused flatly to have anything to do with the expedition. And
of course he didn't keep still about his find; so that ever
since it has been considered unhealthful by the whites to
make any attempt to scale the frowning monument.

We now emerged upon more or less of a table-land, and
galloped along high breezy ridges from which fell away on
either hand a world of hills and wild fruitful valleys; while
ahead, beyond the last ridge, rose the farther wall of Typee.
A little way on we discovered that we were at the very head
of Hapaa Valley, whose inhabitants were the fiercest enemies
of the Typeans in Melville's time. To-day the green gloom
of the deep pocket is unbroken by hut or smoke or human
form. Not one man is left to point out past glory of conquest nor triumphant feast of pale, grim long-pig. Melville
spelled it Happar, and the spelling of Typee should rightly
be *Taipi;* but Typee it will always remain for the wander-
luster.

To make our travelling more perfect, the sky had somewhat overcast, and just enough sun broke through at intervals to throw lavish swaths of light and shadow across the
tremendous landscape, while we went in cool comfort.

When Nikko pointed out the head of Typee Vai far to our
left, my sensations were all I could wish. There in the midst
of stern mountain bulks, black in the shadow, just where the
deserters sixty years ago perilously let themselves down into
the valley, was the waterfall described by Melville—a distant shaft of purest white, still as a pillar of marble. And
very likely the long, embowered pathway down which we
gained the floor of the valley is the very one by which Toby
escaped from the man-eating tribe.

Near the head of the valley we could see the white welt of
the trail to Hatiheu angling up ravines and erosions. One
of our native girls came from Hatiheu, granddaughter of a
chief, and part French. She is an indolent, insolent-eyed
creature, and as neither she nor the other girl seemed inclined to be sociable, we soon left them to themselves.

The only other striking feature on the opposite wall of Typee was a sloping enclosure of several acres, overcrowded to bursting with breadfruit and cocoanut. The walls looked to be of piled stone, and we could not doubt that this was one of the walled groves made so much of by Melville.

And the valley itself—one cannot be surprised that its olden visitor thought it extraordinary and had no words to tell of its extreme loveliness. Deep in the heart of the mountains it rests, an inexpressible wilderness of greenest green, threaded by a beautiful river fed by cataracts at its magnificent scowling head. The mountains of Nuka-Hiva are not very high, but have all the character of greater mountains and make grand effects among the shifting, tumbling cloud-masses. The length of Typee I should judge to be about seven or eight miles by two broad, and the valley opens into nothing less lovely than the bay of its own name, the midmost of the three arms of Comptroller Bay.

Melville saw much of Typee blossoming and fruiting abundantly under savage cultivation; but I cannot think the general view is any less overwhelming in our day, with its mad riot of vegetation. It is when one walks in the old paths and comes close to Typee that the change hurts. It is as if a curse had fallen upon it—spreading over it a choked jungle of *burao,* damp and unwholesome, on the edges of which, near the river, unkempt grass houses stand upon the lordly *pae-paes* of decayed affluence.

And the people! Where are the beautiful women and the splendid men who loved so sweetly in their happy land? Look for them you must—for Fayaway and her maidens, clad in white *tapa* cloth; but what you see is a wretched thing dragging toward you in bedraggled calico, her face discoloured and blotched with leprosy, her very existence a shame to mankind and the sun.

Melville estimated some two thousand warriors in Typee Vai; now there are perhaps a dozen vilely-bred men and women whose cross-strains alone have kept them alive, declining as they are in disease and misery.

Human Hair Dancing Dress, Turtle Crown, and Old Men's Beards

The Nature Man in Street Costume

We unsaddled and tied our horses by an ancient stone enclosure, and Nikko carried the lunch down by the river. We came to our first case of elephantiasis in a hideously deformed young native with a face smacking strongly of Chinese. He brought us cocoanuts for our lunch, and for which we paid him. His feet were literally elephantine— the leg swelled until the toes were no more conspicuous than those of an elephant. The man wore a deprecatory expression, as if he would apologise for his unlovely existence.

We were extremely annoyed, as we sat under the trees by the stream, by myriads of the diminutive black flies, called *nau-nau* (pronounced now-now), that have bothered us somewhat in Taiohae. Mrs. Fisher had warned us against allowing them to sting us, as the bites, after lying dormant for days, almost invariably fester and continue to fester. She urged me to wear long sleeves and gloves. To-day the pests settled in clouds, getting into the food and robbing us of peace. Later on, when Jack and I took a swim in a pool of the river, which we tried to think was "Fayaway's lake," we were obliged to keep under water to escape the flies; and when poor Jack, going out first, essayed to dress on the bank, he was beset by such numbers that he was beside himself, and his language not at all pretty. I placidly treaded water and chaffed up at him from my comfortable seclusion. But he got back at me. When *I* tried to clothe myself, omitting all towelling for the sake of speed, the vengeful man stood by and made remarks when I went quite, quite mad in my efforts to get things on without imprisoning the clinging tormentors. Perhaps I deserved my punishment; but he needn't have been *quite* so mean!

After lunch I remembered my promise to myself that, once I was on the spot, I was going to people Typee Vai to suit my imagination. So I stole away up the hillside, past an immense *pae-pae* bearing a filthy hut, and struck a damp pathway that led into the *burao* thicket. I walked on and on, but the trail seemed to lead nowhere, so I gave up and retraced. This moist, unholy jungle has possessed the land. I saw nothing of special human interest except a big mossy stone that gazed dimly sphinx-like out of what may have once upon a time been pictured eyes.

Baffled, I tried the up-river path. This was better—really exquisite in fact. The way was smothered in sunny trees and shrubbery and the most alluring little pathlets tempted away from the riverside into a happy tangle of growing things. One could easily imagine a phantom Fayaway playing there at hide-and-seek. I saw a ripe warm orange lying under its tree, and pounced upon it, catching at the idea of having one golden apple out of the lost Eden. It was a capital orange, too, even if hot. There was another ruddy ball on the slender tree, but I let it hang. I wandered on in the steaming tropic air, under the blue flame of the noonday sky, and found the going fair and my dream good. The valley rang with bird-calls, although Melville made a point of the absence of birds, and they must have been imported later on—along with the *nau-nau!*

Jack was asleep under a tree upon my return. Before long we were in the saddle again, with only one horse-fight to mark our departure. After I had mounted, my coal-black steed rose to his full height per hind legs, and descended upon the mounted Scandinavian, raising a considerable lump on the man's knee. Then we started back the way we had come, but, instead of crossing the river to the home-trail, kept to the left, galloping through a grove of the biggest banana trees we have ever seen. A scant handful of natives peeped apishly at us from under the giant leaves. Climbing to a pass leading out of Typee, we gazed down upon the tan beach where Melville escaped to the ship's boat. Two men were fishing in the river where it met the bay, and we caught the gleam of their silver quarry lying on the sand.

Now came a joyful surprise. Typee had depressed us with its desolation; but here, the other side of a low hill, we dropped into a little vale that looked more as Typee must have in her hey-day. This was Hooumi Valley (pronounced Ho-o-oo-me). Melville never mentioned it in his book, and, since he was zealously guarded from approaching the mouth of his own valley, undoubtedly knew nothing of it. Still, judging from the accessibility and smallness of Hooumi, its people must have been counted among the Typeans, for such a small contingent could not have held out against the powerful valley proper. Melville probably saw the people of Hooumi among the others, and included them in his two-thousand estimate, while ignorant of their actual headquarters.

It is a bit of aboriginal fairyland, this Hooumi. We raced along, following the windings of its blue stream, many a turn taking our breath away with the beauty it unrolled. The prospect was one of plenty, the "profitable trees," breadfruit, bananas, cocoanuts and the like, growing profusely on every hand. The breadfruit is magnificent, reminding one of the jewelled trees in the story of Aladdin, for the very leaves, broad and indented, glisten like polished gems, while the large fruit, sometimes round, sometimes oval, is studded with emerald knobs.

Once we rounded a broad bend, where a healthy, hearty savage, gleaming like copper in the westering flames, fished ankle-deep in pebbly shallows; again, we came upon a still elbow of the stream in which a perfect grass hut, with all its trees and background of wooded hill, was reflected; or there flashed upon us a straight stretch of road, striped with tree-shadows, and opening up the lofty shoulder of a jagged crag, tipped with sungold; and once I drew up abruptly, having almost missed, in sheer enjoyment of my horse, one of the prettiest sights in the valley—a particularly well preserved *pae-pae* by the roadside, supporting a ruined grass house shaded by three plumy palms of varying heights and angles, and one justly proportioned breadfruit tree that laid its purple shadow distinctly upon the tessellated platform. A grass hut is the very quintessence of savage picturesqueness.

We fetched up at the mouth of the valley in a little village of native huts and one small frame house built on a modern *pae-pae* in a grassy enclosure. It might have been more romantic for us to put up in native fashion; but we were quite willing to forego that pleasure and accept Nikko's arrangements, what of our aversion to centipedes and such things—although, if grass house it had been, well and good. One's lust for the outlandish chills somewhat in face of sharing bed and board with unpleasant crawling vermin of elongated aspect and with bites up their sleeves.

Upon riding into the yard, Jack and I were entirely absorbed in a young man who moved about as one in possession, without affectation, and with a dazzling smile in mouth and eyes whenever he met our gaze. His face was not handsome, except as his ready smile made it so; it was the body of him that stayed the eye with its complete symmetry of line and proportion. And more than beauty of form was the carriage of it—never did a Prince Charming bear himself with more regal grace. With all his thewy masculinity there was a flowing softness of line and motion that led away from any thought of iron muscle; but later on, when he jack-knived himself up a cocoanut palm that our sailor-eyed men pronounced all of a hundred and twenty-five feet high, we saw the steel sinews of him, the deep lungs, and the control. It was an astonishing thing he did: merely walked up that swaying column on all-fours, and descended similarly, backward; and when he reached the ground and walked past us with his inimitable port, he was only breathing quickly, as a man after a short run might do. Now I come to think of it, he was the only being in the village whom we did not hear cough.

It seemed ill fitting to offer a young god from Olympus a franc for braving a mere cocoanut palm; for one grows used to such irregularities of circumstance, although I must not forget that this royal-bodied youth did not even look toward us for approval or for the money that had been promised. He approached only when bidden, naked in his perfection

save for a scarlet cloth, and received double the prize with
the manner of a victor in the athletic field taking his reward as his due and no more, pleasantly without servility.
Indeed, he did not even look at the coins in his hand until
he had swung with leisurely dignity across the green to
where the cooks were busy, and there we saw him laugh like
a pleased boy while the men congratulated. Later on, this
Marquesan Adonis was fairly commonplace in blue overalls
and a net shirt; but he could not disguise walk or smile,
and whenever he appeared, Jack and I followed with our
eyes. You see, he meant old *Typee* to us, for he was neither
half-caste, nor sick. Excepting the fisherman in the stream,
he was the only specimen we saw who approximated the
Typean of Melville and the other old chroniclers.

Everything in the neighbourhood was in a bustle over
our feasting and lodgment. A dozen men were preparing
kao-kao in a large half-open shed in which we saw a reminiscent wooden trencher the length of a man, and wondered if
there was a resident in the village old enough to remember
its grisly use; while other men dug a shallow pit in which
the sucking *puarka* was to be roasted whole, and Adonis went
about the preparing of that goodly item. —

We sat on the ground leaning against a plaited side of
the shed, enjoying the yielding turf under our tired limbs
and long draughts of the incomparable cocoanut. Every
living thing eats cocoanut meat in Nuka-Hiva—fowls, pigs,
men, dogs, women, horses, cats and birds. So we amused
ourselves seeing how near the domestic livestock would come
to take our cocoanut from us. The horses nearly drove us
out by their voracity—and speaking of horses: although it
is not much above fifteen miles to Hooumi from Taiohae,
they are hard miles, and one would have thought our animals would enjoy a rest; but from the instant the saddles
were removed there was a continuous vicious engagement
among the stallions that kept every one on the lookout lest
he be run down. My Jacques' first offence was to walk up
to Jack's innocent horse and deliberately bite a generous

mouthful out of the soft part of the back, which cannibal outrage he twice repeated before nightfall. And Jack does so hate to ride an animal that has the slightest scratch under the saddle!

It would take too long to go into the details of how a pit is prepared, so that when the pig is wrapped in leaves and laid among hot stones it becomes roasted as the natives like it. Suffice it that our *puarka* was thus buried, piled with leaves, and the whole covered with earth; whereupon a long, lean dog that had missed no jot of the proceedings, composed himself to sleep on the warm grave.

It takes these people endless times as long to do anything as it does white men. Most white men, I should qualify, for the Norwegian captain never knows his mind two minutes and backs and fills with staggering rapidity when any kind of decision has to be made. I cannot see how he commands a ship. He had been vociferating sixteen times in every fifteen minutes during the latter part of the journey and while we were getting settled in camp, that he would not stay over night; he had stated positively the day before that he could not go at all, and this in reply to no special urging; he had been largely to blame for our tardy start, and whenever any hitch occurred, he would roundly abuse Nikko—Nikko, who was our guide, not his.

But to get back. The dilatory methods of the native cooks made it quite imperative to assuage our appetites with fruit and cocoanuts; and, strange to say, so great a void was there that we were in no way daunted when we dropped cross-legged on the cottage porch and surveyed the banquet. We leaned against our saddles and saddle-bags and partook of boiled breadfruit that we knew was the real thing at last. I cannot name the flavour of this substantial comestible; but I can say that the man who described it as tasting like sour potatoes and cheese and turpentine and kerosene must have had accidents in his kitchen. Lake the taro, which it resembles in excellence only, it is a noble vegetable—or fruit we must call it, I suppose, since it grows on a tree; and I am quite sure that if I had to live entirely on breadfruit or taro, or both, I should not miss bread or potatoes.

They set breadfruit *poi-poi* before us, and very good it was, with its tart flavour; but I think we shall never like it as we do the taro poi. There was a big bowl of fowl deliciously boiled in the pressed milk from the meat of cocoanuts, and we added Taiohae bakery bread that we had brought in a sack. There were eggs, nicely soft-boiled, and the Hatiheu princess and her friend, who had warmed toward us by now, affably demonstrated how to eat certain small chunks of fish from the fingers, first dipping into a slightly fermented cocoanut sauce. For wine, we quaffed from fresh cocoanut flagons. Home is sweet, to be sure; but I wish Marquesan cocoanuts and breadfruit grew in my kitchen garden!

The women of the place were very shy with me for a while. I do not think they have seen many white women, for all the European blood that pales their own faces. Besides, there was the difficulty of my trousers to be got over, and I cannot wonder at their corner-comments and embarrassed smiles.

After dinner we were invited into the main apartment of the two-roomed house, where we sat in a circle on a spotless, polished wooden floor, and were offered absinthe for a *liqueur*. A bit of French helped us along, and the Scandinavian, besides his English, knew a little Marquesan from the Hatiheu girl, so we did very well. I noticed the sewing machine that books all mention as the invariable *pièce de résistance* of South Sea Island well-to-do homes—indeed there were two, and the fresh red calico *éuéu* worn by our hostess showed that the machines were not allowed to rust. This lady had kept in the background until now, and we found her very handsome, of a big, sumptuous, Hawaiian type.

One thing I was determined to find out—if there was any of the old *tapa* cloth left in this forsaken country. The mistress of the house looked a likely person to ask; and she went into the other room, nodding her head. After an anxious time for me, out she came with a nine-foot roll of pure white fabric, undoubtedly made many years ago from the breadfruit bark, for no tapa of any description is made by the Marquesans now. This piece exactly answered Melville's description of the clothing worn by the maidens, and it was in good condition. It was the only good white piece we were able to obtain, all the rest being deep cream and of coarser fibre. Dear me—if Fayaway came to Typee now she would have to array her loveliness in a red calico wrapper. But the daughters of Nuka-Hiva are quick to emulate a new style. Already, in Taiohae, I have noticed the luxuriant locks of several swarthy damsels going topward in imitation of my modest chignon. Perhaps, who can tell? one visiting Hooumi a few years hence may find the leaders of fashion promenading in khaki riding breeks!

But I cannot allow myself any kind of a joke at the expense of these dying Hooumians. Although this little community was more prosperous and sanitary than what we saw in Typee, it is not saying much, as we soon found when the news of our tapa purchase went out and the women began to bring in the sheaves of their foremothers. The lame, the halt, and the blind, the asthmatic, the consumptive—shyly and painfully they came and laid their faded bundles at our feet, eagerly watching our discriminating eyes, some gasping for breath, their sunken chests rattling. One woman in particular, a half-breed, had the prettiest French face imaginable, "pale as the milk of cocoanuts," with big soft brown eyes that lighted up when she saw our approval of her creamy fathoms and the money Jack held out to her. And all the time the poor soul was fighting for breath, her hands often clutching the air. When she went from us, Jack and I looked at each other silently, for we could hear a long way off the involuntary groans from her ruined lungs. And her father—where is he? Who might he be? For a thoughtful moment the universe was "jangled, out of tune."

We collected quite a bale of rare old tapa, accepting only the best. I suppose we saw about all there was left in the valley, and it was not much. As far as I can discover, this white and cream tapa was the only kind made by the Marquesans. The patterns and warm colours of the Hawaiian and Samoan sorts were unknown here.

Before bedtime, we two stole off for a little look-see about the beach. There was an air of happy excitement even in the moonlit woods, for foreign visitors are very infrequent and the village was out and a-whisper with our coming.   •

Aside from the witchery of shining strand and the shadowy woods, we saw nothing of special interest except a long, graceful whaleboat that lay wrecked and rotting in the rank grass.

The rest of the party had decided to return to Taiohae at six next morning, for our captain had work aboard the *Snark*, and the other skipper was near the end of his lâding and must get back. Jack and I planned to take our time in order, if possible, to pick up some wooden bowls and other curios. We secured one small but beautifully-grained bowl, or calabash, this evening.

We were allotted the one small room off the large one, and found on the immaculate floor three spotless white pillows, stuffed with silk-cotton, and a white bedspread. It would be interesting to know where the lady of the house learned her civilised cleanliness. We laid our heavy oilskin saddle-slickers, for mattress, and turned in under the white counterpane. Outside on the porch a string of natives of both sexes and all conditions slept side by side, heads to the wall. I say slept, but it is only a manner of speaking. There was a clamour of coughs, wheezings, expectorations, and conversation more or less desultory—principally less, for just as I would decide they were at last dead-o, and compose myself for that coveted end, somebody would break out again, the whole chain catching like a pack of firecrackers. Our invasion being their latest topic, we knew we were the

subject of debate. At last they quieted, and we succumbed
to the liquid lullaby of the little surf.

Wednesday, December 11, 1907.

I opened my eyes at seven this morning. Jack was standing inside the porch window. He seemed to be disagreeing
with a native outside who held up a dark, oscillating object
in both hands. Jack turned away as if he had lost interest,
whereupon the thing was flung on the window sill in a curly
heap.

"Goatskin?" I inquired.

For reply, Jack gathered up the dusky fleece and dropped
it into my lap. Involuntarily I shrank from it. Goatskin!
It was human hair—long, thick, wavy, the seal-brown matted
strands curling tawny at the ends. The eerie locks were
deftly gathered on a band of woven cocoanut fibre, and the
dancing-skirt, the hula-hula fringe, stood confessed. All
very beautiful; but when one was assured that undoubtedly
this garnered wealth of hair had been shorn from the heads
of human sacrifices that had been cooked and eaten by their
captors, the lightsomeness of romance dimmed somewhat.
I handled the ghastly trophy gingerly, but with a determina-
tion that it should not escape the "Snark room" we mean to
build at home; and a little later a bargain was struck. The
curio would have been cheap at any cost, for it is a priceless
memento of a vanishing race.

The lethargic Hooumians were aroused at last. Acquisi-
tiveness was the order of the day. Their hoarded ancestral
treasures were snatched from mouldy seclusion and showered
on the sunlit pae-pae. While the bartering was on, much
counsel was offered to each seller by his companions. Children mixed with the chattering, coughing crowd, and an occasional yelp attested to some skinny dog having been landed
by a flipper-like savage foot.

A pair of armlets to match the hirsute hula-hula skirt
came to light, and the eager villagers all tried to explain at

once that there should also be anklets, but that none were to be found. We felt like paleontologists reconstructing an antediluvian monster—but instead of bones we had only *hairs* to go by. And speaking of hairs, we made another lucky find in several of the "old men's beards" that Stevenson describes as so precious to the Marquesan heart. These are thin grey fringes about a foot long, stiff and grim, and are worn on the forehead, held by a brow-band and thrust starkly upward.

The asthmatic French-faced girl glided toward us with seraphic smile and shining upraised gaze, bearing in her two hands a crown of carved yellow turtle-shell, thick and beautifully spotted, the curving sections held together by delicately plaited threads of cocoanut fibre. King or priest, we could not find out whose had been the head or heads that once bore this rare ornament. Each piece is carved differently, with fine workmanship, and we shall probably never know the meaning of the figures wrought into the shell. Perhaps to the present generation they are meaningless. That the crown is old, is shown by the condition of the cocoanut sennit, as well as the firm dirt-incrustations in the shell. We were shown how to fasten the "old men's beards" inside the circlet, and the effect was startling enough.

The pretty crown-bearer proved a good business woman, and did not cheapen her wares by showing them all at once. Once the curio had become ours, she brought out another, a brow-band of porpoise-teeth and beads. This did not appeal so strongly, although in the eyes of the natives the porpoise-teeth rendered it far more valuable than the turtle-shell crown. They pressed close in their efforts to explain the distinction. But it was the woman who won. She was so sweetly wistful, that we bought it mainly to see her smile again.

Then we turned to the calabashes (*kokas*) that had been collected for our inspection—bowls, great and small, of heavy *mio* wood, hard as stone. Nothing we had seen in Hawaii could excel these old Marquesan vessels. To be sure, they were not polished; but it was easy to discern, through the grime of many years, the splendid graining of the wood and its possibilities for a shining surface. Our only difficulty was how to carry them, and we wanted them all; but our quandary was simplified by finding that most of the biggest were undesirable on account of cracks; so we compromised on three that were perfect, and a lot of small ones, some round, some oval. We gave our hostess all the bread that remained—a coveted delicacy—and Nikko used the gunny sacks for packing the calabashes on his horse, while Jack and I carefully stowed in our saddle-bags the smaller and more fragile things. I shall never cease to regret that we could not manage that long-pig trencher from the cook-shed.

By now it was time for breakfast, and we fortified ourselves with eggs, bread, bananas and cocoanuts. After which we strolled about with the kodak for a last look at the village. At half past nine we were mounted and bidding farewell, and oh! it was a joyous jaunt across the island. Hooumi thrilled with bird-voices and river-songs in the green-and-gold forenoon, while Typee lay sleeping her long, long sleep, her sombre head wrapped in a grey cloud-pall. We sat a little space looking our last on the great, silent picture, before leaving it forever.

"Don't try to take it," Jack advised, as I trained my tiny camera on the splendour of Typee Vai. "You will be disappointed—it will be only a blur."

But I snapped it all the same, thinking that even a blur of Typee would be better than no record.

When we reached Mrs. Fisher's about noon, our horses fresh and lively, we found that the others, who left Hooumi three hours ahead, had beaten us in by only fifteen minutes. At first we could not understand. But it turned out that the captain of the bark had forced the pace until his horse gave out in an hour, and the others, nearly as badly off, were held up waiting for it to recover. Martin was indignant, because try as he would to hold the rest, he was obliged to overdo his own horse to some extent.

. . . While we were faring to Typee, the nineteen labourers of Taiohae were bringing the red goddess down the mountain. It is a significant fact that no *Marquesan* would touch it, which leads one to conclude that of the total of able-bodied workmen of Taiohae, not one is a real Marquesan. And there were murmurings on the beach that day—impotent and spiritless protests of the old blood against this desecration of its hoary wood. So the maternal Tataura was toted down out of the jungle and deposited whole and unharmed in the rickety old bark's hold.

. . . This evening we dropped in to see Mr. Rahling in his pretty cottage smothered with vines and flowers—one yellow bell-shaped blossom, called by the natives *épuua*, rioting everywhere. He came out from a little workshop next his bedroom, and at our request took us in to see what he had been doing. Among other cleverly wrought articles, he had carved several saddle-trees out of the hard *mio* wood—excellent models of the McClellan type. There were also two side-saddles. "Nothing to it!" declared Jack. "You must sell me a saddle-tree." And we added this to the rest of our Marquesan curios. But never fear but this saddle, although of the nature of a curio, will be rigged up some day and see good use on the home ranch.

Mr. Rahling also parted with a little red god of stone and two small calabashes; then to our delight we found a pair of human hair anklets which he was willing to forego, although he had no idea where he could duplicate them. Indeed, both he and Mr. Kreiech are astonished at the number of valuable things we have secured, insisting that they did not know they still remained on the island.

Returning home, we walked in upon the two old thoroughbreds, sitting a-ham before the collection of heirlooms we had haled from Hooumi. They Oh'd and Ah'd lugubriously when we added the red god and calabashes and anklets to the mound, then rose sighing and went to their own quarters. Poor things—it is a wrench for them to see the last of their relics going into the hands of pale interlopers, although we, at least, are not unmindful of their sentiment.

But of all the outlandish trophies from our Typean quest, none holds the grisly allure of the hair skirt and its accompaniments. More than one head must have fallen to furnish such abounding tresses. Those of the skirt are all of two feet in length, and piled thick, layer upon layer, so that the least movement produces that oscillation I had noticed on the window-sill. We try to vision the unholy rites wherein this ghastly garmenture was worn.

Thursday, December 12, 1907.

This is the day upon which the *Snark's* company had wagered it would see Nuka-Hiva. So we have been paying Jack his ill-gotten dollars. His judgment was six days better than ours; and thinking over the happenings of the past six days, we are mightily glad of it.

Taiohae may be a quiet place; but we somehow find ourselves beset with engagements of one sort or another. Jack wrote all this morning on his novel, which he will name *Success,* while I typed in another corner of the porch. When we went to Mrs. Fisher's *déjeuner* at eleven, she showed us a pair of beautifully carved dark-brown calabashes which her father, Herr Goeltz, had sent over for our approval. We "approved" promptly, and they were ours in no time, as they were the handsomest things of their kind we had ever seen. Herr Goeltz also sent word that he had more of these, as well as other curiosities, if we cared to pay him a visit across the way, which we shall do to-morrow.

We had promised to go aboard the bark this afternoon; and, after a siesta on our shady veranda, went out in the ship's boat with the captain. That man is so good looking, and has such charming moods, that we could like him wholly were it not for his inhumanity to horses.

There is strong romance to me in old ships, especially in such a setting. We climbed up the side ladder and found ourselves in the rickiest vessel imaginable. The topmasts had a raffish cant that made one think apprehensively of Paumotan hurricanes. Decks were unkempt, ropes looked risky; even the "absinthe-minded crew" had a gaunt, uncanny, unfed appearance. Our movements on deck were impeded by frightened and fragrant goats running at large, together with the vociferations of an unseen litter of lusty puppies added to the weird din. We moused around the mouldy quarters of the vessel, peering into bilgy holes and weevily stores, and then went below, where I sat in a cushioned nook of the really cosy little cabin of Norwegian pine, the walls of which the captain had himself decorated with *fleur de lis* picked out in aluminum paint. We drank smooth French beer and swapped yarns for an hour or more—at least the men did, and I listened. Captain Warren was somewhat gloomy, for this very morning he fell down the bark's companionway and all but broke his ribs, and a bigger baby than an injured sailor is hard to find.

Jack got some Norwegian pine and several Asiatic pilot books in exchange for superfluous manila hawser from the *Snark*. This skipper runs his ship very easily, it would seem. Parting with a pilot book or a volume of sailing directions means nothing to him. Short a 1908 Almanac, he is too careless to copy a few pages from ours. Why, he has actually allowed his chronometer to run down, and it looks as if he intends to go to sea day after to-morrow without setting it by ours! But he's a man for a' that, for who but he flared the big light for us the night we crept feeling our way into the harbour!

We took him over to the *Snark*. Our men were holystoning the deck—the first it had ever received. Herrmann met us with his Mona Lisa smirk, and almost burst with pride over the new whiteness of the deck. He seemed much impressed with the change my "shore clothes" made in me, and commented respectfully, not for the first time, on the lack of tan on my complexion. But on this occasion he quite eclipsed himself. He broke out heartily:

"I tell you, there is of only one white man aboard the *Snark*, and that's Mrs. London!"

And the goose did not know why we laughed.

Herrmann had permission to take Jack's Mauser out for goats yesterday. He made a day of it, and has been busy ever since explaining in detail the various reasons why he did not bring home any game.

Mr. Rahling was on the wharf when we landed, swimming Jacques in the deep water alongside. Seeing the horse in the water reminded me that our men noticed a shark near the yacht the other day. I had thought of taking a swim every morning off the pier, but this changed my mind.

Friday, December 13, 1907.

No matter how hard we work, it is rest to live in this tranquil house. In one corner of the viny porch a chapter of the novel is being finished, in another my eternal typewriter clicks; while at the fence awed voices murmur, as Tomi's daughter Tahia explains the writing-machine. *Tahia* means "above the rest," and this little brown-eyed girl of fourteen is certainly the superior of her playmates in beauty and intelligence. She has been allowed to come close to the wonderful machine that manufactures books (more amazing, I do believe, than the talking-box), and feels very important. I go on typing while they stand a few feet away whispering under a whisper, fearful of disturbing. Then they steal away on their bare, fan-like feet, with a soft *kaoha* in thanks and good morning. The natives are very considerate of our privacy, never making themselves nuisances in any way.

While we are busy with our end of the work, refreshing ourselves ever and anon from our pitcher of orange-nectar (we have thirty-five oranges squeezed every morning), Nakata goes about learning the ways of a white man's house, although the makeshift manner in which we are living is not the best of training. Aside from the routine of the *Snark*, the little man is innocent of European habits—with the exception of one, fine washing and ironing. What a boon in the South Seas! Jack's white crêpe shirts and my sheer lawns and linens—they're all one to Nakata.

The seaward aspect of our Elysium showed a trifle ruffled this morning, a heavy swell sending an unusual surf on our brown shingle, where the men loading lighters with the last of the bark's copra cargo were having a lively time. The southeast trade, the *tua-to-ha,* is blowing briskly, with the same twist to the north'ard that gave us fair wind here from above the Line.

We added to our knowledge of South Sea *kao-kao* at break-fast to-day, in the shape of roasted *fei*—pronounced fay-ee. It resembles a plantain in appearance and tastes like a hardy, substantial banana, though less sweet. The natives are especially fond of it.

From Mrs. Fisher's, accompanied by her purring, tailless cat, we crossed over to Herr Goeltz's. He met us on the tottering, trellised veranda, on his grey head a faded black velvet cap trimmed with yellowed lace, on his sunken frame a nondescript suit, trousers tied in at the ankles to keep out sandflies—the *nau-naus.* (Jack and I are already wishing we had been more careful.) The old man led us into the dim and dusty twilight of his cobwebby castle—a fairly commodious house of five rooms. I at once became lost, poking around in the musty corners, into spidery cabinets brought in old ships from Germany; old albums; baskets of shells and green cat-eyes from Samoa, and cupboards of beautiful china and heavy old French porcelain. Our eagle-faced host, sharp and keen of wit for all his eighty-two years, while showing us about talked upon a score of topics. One of these was his cruise through the Paumotus on the *Casco* as Stevenson's pilot; another was his noble Polish family, for estray though he be, he has a title all his own. He brought out several more of those fascinating carven bowls of wood, concerning one of which, a symmetrical oval laced with intricate traceries, he told us a creepy tale. Without going into the sanguinary particulars, you may take it that the blood of two white skippers has been drunk from this ornate receptacle; and, if history be true, their fate was far too good for them. For instance, one of these captains, among other atrocities in return for the goodwill and royal hospitality of the natives on one of the islands in the group, presented the chief with a wholly rotten whaleboat that had all the seeming of staunch newness, what of shining paint and gay trimmings. That captain had the bad luck to be wrecked at the self-same place a few years later. If you don't believe it, we'll show you the bowl!

Herr Goeltz had disposed of the bulk of his possessions long before we touched at Taiohae, which made us wish we had been earlier. However, it took half a dozen to carry away the spoils of our forage. I had often noticed the green-trimmed porcelain with which Mrs. Fisher set the table, and it turned out that she had borrowed it from her father, who had the remainder of the set. Such tureens! Such platters, and such great plates! Said Jack, with a small amused smile at the "pictured corners" of his mouth:

"I think we could use the whole set, couldn't we?"

It is very nice to be treated like a small daughter occasionally, and thereupon we fell to counting the pieces to see what was missing. The dishes had been often borrowed and some of them broken; but there was a goodly array left. Mrs. Fisher came over during our despoiling, and, while glad to see her father making a little money, she could not hide the sadness in her eyes at the last family treasures going the way of the rest.

I added some delicate teacups; then there were a couple of old ivory fans, and a pair of fine conches. We also found some thick round *héis* (wreaths) of small yellow-and-white landshells, and a true (?) piece of the elm, or whatever the tree was, that grew over Napoleon's grave at St. Helena.

We were tired and warm upon reaching home, and, piling our burden in a corner of the big room, retired to the concrete bath and sat reading for an hour, the water up to our chins. It would be hard to eclipse our schemes for comfort. Stevenson doesn't mention this rude tub. Think what he missed. His description of the club is: "A billiard-board, a map of the world on Mercator's projection, and one of the most agreeable verandas in the tropics." We are heartily ready to indorse this last, even in advance of any other experience in verandas under the Equator.

The Norwegian came in to bid us farewell, as he expected to sail at daylight, and incidentally he trimmed Jack's hair according to a promise made yesterday.

The day ended with music, and we had the novel entertainment of merry Marquesans dancing the energetic hula-hula of their Tahitian cousins, to Hawaiian music on an American phonograph—under a tree with a French name!

Saturday, December 14, 1907.

Up and out at half past five this morning, we watched the old grey bark with painted ports square away for the Azores her chronometer dead and no 1908 Almanac aboard. A fair vision she was for all that, dipping her flag to the *Snark*, where Wada was running up the colours. A gun saluted from the shore, and dusky women, sitting beneath the trees and on the pier, raised a mournful wailing for the men who had been so briefly theirs. "For men must work, and women must weep"—it is the sea-song for white women, brown women, black women, wives and sweethearts, the world over—the old, old game.

We lingered to see the last of the bark, as she passed through the portals of Taiohae and took the rocking swell. Soon her last royal was out of sight behind a headland, and we wondered if we should ever see her again. Then we watched the painting of the morn upon a shell-pink sky above the sculptured heads of the Eastern range, and drank deep of the cool sweet breath of waking day. We were too full of peace to stir, resting there at the grassy edge of the sand. One by one the tear-stained women picked them-

selves up and went disconsolately along the green road to
their lonely homes. When we, too, finally rose and walked
toward the old club-house, Nakata was starting to hunt for
us. He paused when he saw us—a quaint and smiling
Japanese figure in grey kimono, standing under a small
broad tree laden with flowers like pink tiger-lilies.

"Breakfast ready, Missis-n," quoth the cheerful picture;
and ye of the cities with your steaks and chops, ham-and-
eggs, and fried potatoes, have nothing on us, with our mangoes, butter-yellow, rich and spicy, our wild pineapple,
sweet as sugar-cane, and our pitcher of orange juice. —

. . . There were two arrivals to-day—one, a canoe from
Hooumi bringing two big calabashes for us, in the pink of
condition, and the other the beautiful schooner *Gauloise*,
spic and span as a gentleman's yacht, carrying mails every
several months between here and Tahiti. Captain Chabret,
a striking, swarthy man, born of French and Paumotan
parents, and educated in Europe, called with his mate, who
interpreted, as the captain speaks little English and our
French is very lame. The Hooumian made the sleepy afternoon vibrate with solemn blasts on our war conches. Once
heard, one could never forget the barbaric mournfulness
of their long, resonant, bell-like call. It conjured up night-
mares of stealthy tattooed savages gathering for the fray
and secret orgy of long-pig.

At five o'clock we went to the store to see for the last time
the social gathering of pay-day—for Jack says we shall get
away Wednesday. I cannot say enough for the kindness of
Mr. Kreiech and Mr. Rahling. They have never been too
busy to give their undivided attention to our slightest want
When Mr. Kreiech discovered that I was interested in the
old French silver which is current here, he had me into the
inner office free to rummage in the money-bags. I found
several five-franc pieces bearing the head of Napoleon over
the dates of 1809, 1811, and 1813, for which, of course, Jack
paid the equivalent.

Captain Chabret dropped in, and Mr. Kreiech opened

bottles of sweet French champagne on a counter, and brought a couple of watermelons from his garden. How Martin Johnson's Kansan eyes did shine!

After a while Jack and I gravitated out to the big box on the porch to dangle our heels once more under the yellow spilth of the sketchy cotton-tree. The grief-stricken girls of the early hours were arm-in-arm and eye-to-eye with the men of their own kind, who looked well content. We saw our two aristocrats of the cottage, the woman, whose name I have discovered to be Mauani ("Sky is covered"), as usual on such occasions making herself and her *puarka* very much at home. The jolly workmen, in the big white cook-caps they often wear, jostled one another in the store as they spent their earnings in gaudy paréus and tobacco. Among the dark skins, Mrs. Fisher's daughter shone white as a lily, moving about with her plump pink baby. She is a veritable Madonna, and Leonardo would find himself in his element here, for this girl, like Herrmann, has a Mona Lisa smile and the inscrutable gaze that goes with it. Mrs. Fisher, a head above the crowd, trod her stately way into the store, with a grandchild hanging to her skirt.

Everybody was invited down to hear the phonograph at half past seven. They turned out en masse, less shy than before, dancing the hula-hula with fervour, Tahitian sailors from the *Gauloise* swelling the fun. Simeon, a bright native boy who clerks in the store, was the envy of all when we showed him how to run the Victor. This left Jack and me free to mingle with our guests.

The captain of the *Gauloise* was familiar with the operas, and enjoyed the music immensely, murmuring little expressions of appreciation in French. But I had to bother him to tell me about pearls in the Paumotus. Then Jack and Captain Warren plied both him and his mate with questions concerning the Paumotan atolls. The weather in their vicinity seems to be a joke in the South Seas, although a serious one, as the name Dangerous Archipelago would imply. We have decided not to risk the *Snark* any length of time among these treacherous coral-rings. One of them, Rangiroa, in one side of the broken circle and out the other, will do for us on our way to Tahiti.

During all the merrymaking of an evening like this, Mauani and her old mate, Taituheu ("Burned-out cinders") sit in the living room, proud to show that they are part of our household—quite a change from their original attitude. What is in their minds behind those wide-set eyes as they watch the gambols of the decadent remnants of their purple blood?

It is impossible to form any true estimate of what was the moral status of the original Marquesans. The Sailing Directions of 1884 give them a black reputation for licentiousness, and warn shipmasters against putting in at thése islands. Persons here with whom we have talked say that a widow is grievously insulted if a new admirer fails to appear on the day of her husband's funeral. We are assured that the people have little love and absolutely no gratitude. That polyandry exists, we have evidence; but it is an institution of old standing and high repute.

But from Melville one does not get the impression that the Typeans were unusually lax in their social relations, and Stevenson, in 1889–90, gives the Nuka-Hivans a good character for modesty, pride and friendliness, as well as endless courteous observances. At any rate, whatever they once were, they are passing; and those who are left are so altered that one's conclusions are worth little.

We asked Mrs. Fisher if she had known Robert Louis Stevenson. She said she had met him at Anaho, on the other side of the island, where the *Casco* first touched, and she added:

"He used to go about barefoot, with his trousers and singlet-sleeves turned up, and never wore a hat; and 'most every one thought he was a little crazy."

Dear Robert Louis!—he was "crazy" because he was saving his own good life in his own good way. I wonder what is the general opinion of Jack and me in our kimonos as we trail over the landscape bareheaded under a pongee parasol, our bare feet thrust into Japanese sandals.

December 15, 1907.

Strange Christmas holiday weather this, our first tropic winter. We look forward to eating our Christmas fowl aboard the *Snark,* provided she hasn't become fatally involved in the Paumotus. They tell us that until very recently the insurance companies refused all risks on vessels in this vicinity, and now, while they will insure, the rate is twenty per cent. The owners, however, take out no policies. They estimate the life of a schooner in the Paumotus to be five years, and merely write off twenty per cent. a year.

I could almost find it in my heart to wish for a week of California climate. The warmth here, while not oppressive, keeps my north temperate cuticle in a ferment of invisible prickly-heat and visible bunches of exasperating hives; and by now the *nau-nau* bites are becoming more than exasperating; and Jack's are worse than mine.

But do not think that these trifling annoyances interfere in the least with our plans. Jack asked Mr. Rahling to arrange a goat hunt, and to-day, with two mounted kanakas to carry guns and game, we three started. For the first time our ride took us off to the left of the Typee trail. We saw more of the beach, and, once out of the valley, had an entirely new aspect of the island. Nuka-Hiva is only fourteen miles long by ten broad; but every foot of it is worth seeing, from sea-brim to mountain-rim and all the verdant laps of the valleys between. The changes that are wrought in such small space stir one's blood from moment to moment. From dreaming over sweet vales of repose, the eyes, startled by some sudden gloom, rise to the black trouble of stormy peaks where thunder-clouds are rolling. Oh! to have seen the volcanic chaos of the making of this isle of the Southern Sea, with her sister isles lifting their heads round about to keep her company.

Once across Taiohae's western bastions, we rode through fragrant lanes of yellow *cassi* at the head of another and smaller valley almost as beautiful, that ended in a wonderful blue bay, bounded by lofty perpendicular rocks to the west, and on the other side by the wild eastern declivity of Taiohae's wall. I dislike to mention that the name of this lovely anchorage is Port Tschitschagoff, although it will soften your anguish to know that the natives mercifully call it Hakaui, and, even more gently, Tai-oa. It may further interest to learn that it took a master mariner born a Krusenstern to outrage such a heavenly port by a name like Tschitschagoff.

The entrance is twenty fathoms deep, with fine sandy bottom, while the azure basin itself is two hundred fathoms in depth and one hundred wide. In it the greatest man-o'-war yet built could anchor in safety from the worst hurricane that ever blew; and to careen her on the even, sandy beach, would be child's play.

The valley is luxuriant with palm and breadfruit and banana, and well watered by streams; and we startled from cover many a reverted chicken, which swept with strong pinions over the tree-tops on the incline. But not a human being makes home in this ideal spot—and it can be bought for $1000 Chile, less than $500 in American gold. Think of the smothering cities of the world, and this exquisite haven gone to waste. That it was not always thus, is shown by Captain Krusenstern:

"Behind the beach was a green flat resembling a most beautiful bowling-green. Streams of water flowed in various places from the mountains, and in a very picturesque and inhabited vale. . . . A ship in need of repairs could not wish for a finer harbour for such a purpose. The depth is exceedingly convenient. Bananas, cocoanuts, and breadfruit, are superabundant. The chief advantage is that you can anchor about 100 fathoms from the land, thus having the king's house and all the village under the guns of the ship, in case of an attack."

That was a hundred years ago, and now wild fowl, goats, birds, wasps, and the ubiquitous *nau-nau* have sole possession. The wasps warned us menacingly off their premises, and we went; but this wasn't a circumstance to what they did to us coming home. But more of that later. —

Looking back as we climbed into yet another valley, we saw a big boulder that they call the Rocking Stone; but we did not take time to prove whether it really "rocked" or not.

The valley in which we did our shooting is a very fast-ness of natural disorder, as if the primeval forces had stopped midway in setting it to rights and let grass grow over the wreckage to see what the effect would be. No gradual slopes and placid beaches lead into this goat-scented retreat. It would be a dreadful misfortune to run a ship's nose into its snarling, frothing lip.

Tying the horses, we took our rifles and proceeded on foot. I have never done such rough climbing. It took all my wind to accomplish the rocky pulls, and all my confidence to descend their other sides. Once—and for the second time in my life—my nerve deserted me. I had to cross the bare face of a horribly-sloping rock, and midway, in spite of hands reaching close to me, I suddenly saw myself on an icy incline in Switzerland where once I felt I must cast myself in the abyss. But I gathered my wits, and before long we were sitting on the knife-edge of a windy ridge, with a world of green hills behind, and the chaotic goat-haunt before us. We kept very still, and breathed our panting lungs full of the flowing air while cooling off from the hot scramble. Then a dotted line strung out far below our toppling perch, and one of the men fired. The dotted line lost a dot, and the rest swerved across the green lawns into the brush, where another dot that had been struck, fell just at the edge. One altruis-tic goat came back out of safety to sniff at the fallen one.

The two kanakas, with two others who had appeared out of the woods, went back into the hills, and Mr. Rahling, Jack and I worked seaward along the ridge. I found I was hold-ing their stride back a little, and begged them to go ahead.

I followed in their tracks, and overtook them down a long sweep of grassy hill after they had killed several goats. We sat a long time at the edge of a chasm, picking off stray victims—virile little billy-goats that wagged their wiry beards in dismay at the invasion of their stronghold. But the distressed cries that rose from the stricken were not sweet in my ears, and I about made up my mind that now I had proved I could bring down distant game, I would leave killing to others in future, and do my practising as before, on twigs and grasses and targets.

A sudden shower blew up, and we sheltered under the brow of a crag in a small red lava cave, odorous of goat, meanwhile watching rain-squalls drift like brown veils across the stern features of the mountains.

While our men were packing the game to the horses, we rode on up the mountain for a further view of Nuka-Hiva. And it was all a piece of the same beauty—the castled rocks, the hills shrugging their round shoulders against the blue mantle of the sky, the unearthly atmosphere and colouring of the little world of island. Is there anything lovelier waiting for us further on in our voyage?

Out of sight from where we stood, is a long slope of country that lacks the rugged character we know so well, and the natives call it the "desert land"—*Henua-Ataha.* I wish we could visit Anaho, on the northern coast. From what Stevenson and his mother have written, it must be very beautiful, although I cannot imagine anything to surpass Taiohae. I wonder if the discoverers, those "careless captains," had the imagination really to be shaken by the beauty of the Marquesas—Mendaña, and Marchand, and Ingraham.

There was quite a row going on when we rejoined the others. The horses had seen fit to take fright at the familiar sight of dead goats, and were literally kicking up a rumpus. Jack's diminutive stallion—the one Captain Warren rode to Typee—joined in the fracas. He was looking for trouble. And he got it. When we came to the yellow *cassi* thicket the wasps got him, and unfortunately that meant poor Jack as well. He rode in the rear, Mr. Rahling leading, I in between. Jack yelled: "Get out of my way *quick!*" How could I? The only way was ahead, for the trail was exceedingly narrow, to say nothing of steep and stony. So we got ahead, and I'll never forget the way we "got," dropping down that perilous path to Taiohae. Mr. Rahling's horse broke into a headlong scramble as the insects stung him, at the same time kicking my horse, who, stung behind, let the rear horse have it, and caught Jack's foot, while I was nearly pitched off. Jack's horse, frantic with pain and fear, tried to pass me, plentifully urged by his rider, who was holding the side of his face. Aside from one or two stings Mr. Rahling's horse and mine went free, and we were untouched. Jack was the scapegoat. The wasps were the largest we have ever seen—canary-yellow, with bunches of long yellow legs hanging out behind. Jack says they were as large as canaries. I don't know. I wasn't quite so close to them as that!

Friday, December 20, 1907.

We were a lame pair to-day, from the unusual climbing. Then Jack had a painful lump on his neck where a wasp had pierced a cord, and other lesser lumps. The *nau-nau* bites did not add to our comfort, and we decided that as a place of permanent residence Nuka-Hiva could be improved by exterminating canaries—I mean wasps—and sandflies. There are divers reasons why the Marquesas are not at present entirely desirable for white immigrants. One of these is the high duty on everything one would want to import, and another is the incredible fact that the French government imposes an *export* duty on copra, which is about the only remunerative article of commerce.

This forenoon Jack had his first chance to use his dental instruments. A shrivelled little old Chinaman whom we had often seen about the copra sheds, came shambling up the steps. In a tinny voice and the most birdlike of pigeon-

English he volunteered that he once worked in San Francisco as a cook, and then asked Jack if he would pull a tooth. Jack laid aside his manuscript of an article on Typee, and hunted up the dentistry book to refresh his memory on the experience he had had with a skull in a dentist's office in Honolulu. He then examined the Chinaman's suffering jaw, and selected the requisite forceps. Martin and I induced him to perform the valiant act behind the house under a banana tree, that we might photograph it. And a curious picture it was, the broad-shouldered white man in Japanese garb, bending over the withered, shrinking Chinaman. The ancient fang came easily; but just as Jack brought it loose and triumphantly held it up, Martin cried:

"Oh, Mr. London, *please* put it back—I wasn't quite ready!"

Shortly afterward, a sensitive-faced Tahitian youth, with big, scared eyes, came on to the porch. He pointed to his mouth and made unmistakable gestures. Jack rolled up his sleeves and went at it again, looking almost as important as when he worked out his first chronometer sight. The victim stood it like a man, albeit he quaked and breathed hard with the strain. He seemed very grateful, and went away laughing nervously with the tooth in his hand.

While we were talking over the morning's professional doings, a shadow fell upon us. It was cast by Tomi, who had quietly approached and stood regarding us with lugubrious eyes and crooked mouth. He had had a toothache all night, he said, and only just now had met the jubilant Tahitian. (I have not told the latest about Tomi. Unless he has been maligned, it looks very much as if he is responsible for the untimely end of two successive wives—which may account for a certain worried look worn by his present consort.)

He sat his mighty frame upon a protesting chair and opened his mouth warily, keeping a suspicious eye on Jack as if he might purposely seize upon the wrong tooth. The correct one was laid upon by the shining forceps, but the

instant they began lifting, the giant clapped his jaws together and grasped Jack's arm in both hands, emitting the
most blood curdling groans. Captain Warren and I took
a hand at holding him down, but it was no use—although it
was already loosened, Tomi would not allow that tooth to be
extracted. He was finally coaxed into having another drawn,
which he said had been aching also.

"More power to your elbow, Mr. London," giggled Captain Warren, as Jack began to pull. This time Tomi did
not get away. We held on, and so did the dentist; and the
big hulking fellow went away as aggrieved as if we had
enticed him in to rob him of his teeth.

"The great baby!" Jack said disgustedly, as he passed the
forceps to Nakata to cleanse. "I didn't believe about the
wife-killing until I tried to pull his teeth."

. . . This afternoon we were in the most typical Marquesan *ha'e* we have seen. Strolling about in a final search
for curios, we were accosted by an eager young woman who
explained brokenly that she would like to show us some *kokas*.
She led to a high-roofed wooden cottage that we had seen
many times; but immediately behind, on rising ground
and connected with the cottage porch by a plank, was
another house, a grass one, not visible from the road. We
bent our heads to enter, and emerged into a long room the
floor of which was of the broad polished stones of a pae-pae.
Against the farther wall, full length, were spread beds of
clean native matting, folded and thick-piled just as Herman
Melville had them in Typee. Everything was spotlessly
clean. Apparently the family that lived in this ha'e took
pride in keeping up its traditions.

In a dark corner we made out a number of large bowls.
The woman dragged them out feverishly, and with the help
of Tahia, who had followed in, made us understand that they
belonged to her husband, Tomi's brother, and that she could
not sell without consulting him. There were other and
smaller calabashes on the wall, all in good condition. They
like their big poi-poi kokas, these people, although not seri-

ously enough to go to the labour of making new ones; so the well-to-do hang on pretty closely to the ancestral vessels, at least in Taiohae. We were lucky in finding a few persons who were not so well-to-do, and when the results of our hunt were nested on our floor, they totaled sixteen bowls. While Tomi's brother was not anxious, he parted with two or three.

On the way home we bought some paréus of gorgeous designs and hues, to use for the double purpose of souvenirs and of packing fragile articles. Our boxes will go to San Francisco by a barkentine that is expected in about three weeks. Before we left the store, Captain Chabret came to bid us good-bye, and then went aboard, for the big mainsail of the *Gauloise* was already being hoisted. Shortly we noticed the boat returning. The captain hurried to the store, and with the Frenchiest of bows and most gallant compliments presented "Madame" with a Paumotan pearl—a lustrous oval with a slight crease around the centre as if it had tried to be two pearls. My first Paumotan pearl—and a gift at that. And think—when I showed it to Mrs. Fisher at dinner, she cried:

"Why, do you like those things? Come in here a minute!"

I followed her into a little room where the Madonna sat at a machine stitching hand-plaited bamboo sennit into a hat for Jack. Mrs. Fisher delved into an old wood mosaic case on a mahogany dresser, and at length brought to light a tiny box. In it was a miniature of herself which she asked me to accept, and then she unrolled a wisp of tissue-paper in which lay five pearls—all a good match for the one I had.

"You take them, and welcome," Mrs. Fisher urged. "I've had them a long time, and my girl takes no stock in them."

It did not seem right, somehow, to rob her of her last pearls, but nothing would do but that I take them.

"I wish you could see the big ones I used to have in Tahiti," she mused. "But they went the way of everything else. I had to sell them.

"See," she went on, turning to the bed. "Here's a hat we've been making for you."

It was such a pretty thing—a ''sailor'' of glossy white bamboo plaiting, and about the crown a hei of pale brown-and-white bird-feathers, soft and fluffy. It is hard to keep even with these kindly folk. The Madonna makes hats to sell, so Jack and I had put in an order for one; but any advantage to her was promptly offset by this gift to me.

We asked everybody to a final musicale, and, as before, Simeon squatted on the porch with a bare brown foot on each side the machine and tried not to look too superior as he reeled off disk after disk of opera, hymn, and sea-chantey.

The old Corsican reclined in his place under the flaming tree beyond the gate. I wonder if he misses the Tattooed Man. They must have known each other well as rival celebrities. Did you ever hear about the Tattooed Man of Taiohae?—although it would be hard to pick up a book on the South Seas that does not mention his curious tragedy. He was white, and, as I understand it, fell hopelessly in love with a high chiefess in the neighbouring island of Uapu. To propitiate her, he resorted to the extreme measure of being tattooed—a matter of fine torture and ineradicable consequences. The tattooing of the Marquesans was the finest in Polynesia, and the suffering from the process so keen that great chiefs have been known to back out before their decoration was completed. But their incentives must have been less powerful and their nerves less firm than this white man's—he was red-headed, too, they say. He was covered from head to foot with lacy designs, not omitting the fashionable broad bars across the face. And what was his reward? The high-born damsel went into violent hysteria at sight of him, frightening her relatives so that they ordered him off the premises. She could never behold him without laughing, and at last, discouraged, he returned to Taiohae, where he died an old man.

Tuesday, December 17, 1907.

While the music was going on last evening, an attenuated grey figure angled through the festive gathering and whispered to Jack. It was Herr Goeltz; and great was the surprise, for no one could remember ever having seen him out after dark. He took Jack away, and I wondered what was up. Jack returned in a little while, accompanied by a native, the pair of them bearing two wonderfully carved, full-sized paddles, and a model of an old-time Marquesan war canoe. No one knows exactly where or when the canoe was made, but it is thought to be all of a hundred years old. It is the handsomest thing we have, the hard wood dark with age, and the deep-cut devices on its sides and full figures at each end demonstrate that the Marquesans were wood carvers of no mean talent. Model though it is, the canoe looks almost big enough to use; but while it is several feet in length, it represents the proportions of the exceedingly long war canoes, and its narrow sides would pinch a child. These things were part of the furniture of a little cottage next the store, belonging to an old captain who was absent, and we saw them one day when the Norwegian, who was sleeping there, took us to look at some of the curiosities in the place. The owner came in on the *Gauloise* and remained over. Herr Goletz heard that he was feeling convivial, took a look in and found him in a mellow mood, and then came after Jack, who in some way wheedled the old sailor into selling.

So Martin has been hard put to-day to make a case to fit the barbaric battleship; but it is done now, and stands with five other boxes as big, one way or another. We all worked. Wada came to help Martin, and Jack schemed to stow safely the thirty-five-odd weighty bowls we have gleaned from Nuka-Hiva. As late as this morning, two more came in.

While the men did the heavy work, I sat on the floor and carefully wrapped the more delicate articles. On the back porch, his chair placed so he could watch us, old "Burned-out-Cinders" sat muffled in a blanket, for his asthma was bad—poor old Taituheu, with his perfect Greek face, banded across with the wide bars that were once blue but have now

turned green, as a turquoise turns. And Mauani—the dear
old thing hovered about me all day, sometimes passing her
slender hands, mittened with their fine tattoo, over the treasures we were looting from her land; sometimes crooning,
vowel-throated, in the "evading syllables" of her tongue,
above some carven koka; and once, going out of the room, she
came back with hands full of the flowers I call tuberoses,
fastening them, one by one, through my hanging hair and
over my ears. Would that I could pack her in a box, too,
that she might greet us along with her appropriate furniture
when we go home again.

It is said that the nether limbs of the late Queen Vaeheku
were noted for the most marvellous tattooing in all the Marquesas. And I imagine our friend Mauani could show some
traceries worth studying, if one may judge by her feet and
ankles, which are covered with "lace." But she hasn't given
me a chance to see any more, either through modesty or mere
shyness. It is easy to see she is very proud of her tattooing,
nodding her head in appreciation of its excellence whenever one points to it. I notice that she also uses the word
"tattoo" in reference to wood-carving, turtle-shell-carving—
any sort of ornamental scratching.

The only excitements of special moment to-day were the
disappearance of a young and exceedingly agile centipede
(probably brought into the house with the dry banana-leaves
used in padding) into a full packing-case; and the arrival of
the schooner *Roberta* from Tahiti. She is much larger than
the *Gauloise,* and looks quite a ship alongside the *Snark.*
It *is* a little world, this! Why, years ago, when Jack was
seal-hunting off the coast of Japan on the *Sophie Sutherland,*
the *Roberta,* then the *Herman,* was working in the same
waters; and Jack used to go "gamming" aboard of her,
pleasant evenings on the sealing-grounds. This particular
vessel, of all others, is now in the hands of the French Company, away down here in the South Seas, and anchored
smack alongside Jack's own boat. What next?

December 18, 1907.

We hated to get up this our last morning in the Marquesas. I wish we were going to "Yonder Far" (Hiva-Oa) and others of the group; but Jack is anxious to receive his mail at Tahiti, and we must hurry hence. It is going on three months since we saw home letters or newspapers.

We lay in our netted beds, conscious of the sweet-scented air, and looking up the eastern battlement of the bay, with the old fort on tiny "Calaboose Hill" in the foreground, all woven into marvellous tapestry by the straight lines of a heavy tropic shower. The rain turned from diamond to rose-tourmaline and lastly into opal and gold as the sun spilled rainbows into it, and then the downfall stopped as quickly as it had begun, startling us with the sudden cessation of bombardment on our iron roof. I heard Jack quoting:

"You have heard the beat of the off-shore wind,
  And the thresh of the deep-sea rain;
You have heard the song—how long? how long?
  Pull out on the trail again!"

I saw his mottled face and hands as he emerged from the mosquito-netting, and felt the burning irritation of my own outraged skin, and was glad, after all, of the prospect of getting to sea once more, away from the wretched nau-naus. Well are they named—not *yet-yet*, nor *then-then*, but *right-now-now*, with past and future all welded into the insistent, existent moment. If Nuka-Hiva never sees us again, it may be put down to the nau-naus.

It did not take very long to make the *Snark* habitable once more. A trip or so of our lifeboat (the launch engine has never worked since the morning we arrived) returned all belongings, and Jack and I went aboard and stowed our personal things.

In settling up accounts at the Société store, Mr. Kreiech left out the item of house-rent, saying that he was only too glad to do this for our entertainment. And he had two men raining cocoanuts all morning from the big palms next the

Snark at Tahiti

Double Canoe, Bora-Bora

"Porpoises!"

store, and others bringing in oranges and limes, that we might have our favourite drinks all the way to Tahiti.

It was hard to big Mrs. Fisher good-bye. There is something infinitely lonely about her patient life. Our final sight of her was on her low-eaved veranda, smiling sadly, with that wistful grandchild clinging to her skirts and weeping heart-brokenly at he knew not what.

Tide would not serve until about ten in the evening, and there was no need of going aboard early. So we sat on the porch of the empty club-house that once echoed to Robert Louis' voice, and for the last time watched the sun go down behind the twilight crags, in the foreground the fruit of our mango trees and the acacia fronds of the *flamboyante* silhouetted against a palpitant sky.

Tahia came and sat at my feet, laying on my knees an armful of roses and a circlet of white blossoms on my hair; and a Tahitian girl brought more roses and a wondrous hat she had made, even the flower-trimming of which was of glistening white bamboo.

We spoke low in the dusky quiet, and from the water heard with a thrill the shadowy *Snark* heaving her anchor short. Sitting safely in this peaceful land, among the whispering of cocoanut palms and great banana leaves, I felt vaguely averse to embarking again on the unrestful ocean, and visions of the infamous Paumotus would creep in between my eyes and the storied shores of Taiohae. Then I remembered that fear is only a word to us of the *Snark*—a word without meaning. And I also remembered the nau-naus. So I was all-too-glad when Jack rose and said it was time to start—adventure leaping afresh in my heart.

The going out was lovely as a dream. We slipped along in the smooth dark tide with a fair light wind, while plaintive little night-voices from the hills stirred the stillness. The moon literally burst from an inky cloud at the edge of a cliff, and the misty ridges round about the bay lay like garlands looped upon the mountainsides.

Our German friends saluted with a shot from shore, and "Hoist that spanker!" Captain Warren cried from forward, while Jack, at the wheel, let go the single stop that held the willing mizzen wing.

How different this, from that dark night we entered. Then we could only feel our way; to-night we were lit by moon and stars and snowy reflecting clouds, fans of moonrays upon the mountains, and growing patches of light upon the water—all the paint and tinsel of night under the Southern Cross.

Never was I so happy, I do believe, as on this dazzling night, when the rush and muffled roar of the outside breakers came to our hearing and we felt the *Snark* taking the first swells. At last I know it—the lure of the sea, the real glamour of it, a thing that can no more be explained than Love, or the beginning and end of the universe.

And with the happiness came a sense of homesickness; but that often comes in my fairest hour of this wild free life that is mine, with its great spaces and flowing wind and rolling waters.

To the nestling night-pipings of sea-birds above the breakers, we passed out the sea-gate of Taiohae and lost the "fixed red light" on Calaboose Hill. The spinnaker was set, and blossomed and swelled like a great white petal in the moonlight.

"The old girl!" Jack said affectionately, giving her a spoke as she foamed ahead in the jewelled flood.

"O happy! Happy! Happy!" joyed Nakata, executing a queer little Japanese pirouette, with his hands full of glasses of lemonade.

"Good-bye, Typee," we saluted, as we drank and looked back on the capes, showing grey in the moonlight like grim heroic statues of monster mastiffs. .

The ghostly flowers piled on the bosun's locker sent out unearthly sweetness, and the off-shore wind came laden with breath of cocoanut and cassi. I know I am growing to be like the man who so loved the tropics that he feared his blood was purple.

Good-bye, Typee, and incredible Nuka-Hiva, the first fairy port of our southern dreams. And low lie the atolls before us, and that mystic lagoon of tinted coral and rainbow life.

At sea, Marquesas to Society Islands,
Thursday, December 19, 1907.

This has been one of our ideal days at sea, after a restful night during which the *Snark* logged sixty knots. It is good once more to feel the ocean crooking its sleek back under our iron keel. As yet there are no warnings of Paumotan vicissitudes, although Herrmann has been looking for a change, and talked so much about it that the captain told him testily not to count his squalls before they were hatched. The wind is fair, the waves most comfortable, and a spirit of industrious prosperity pervades the yacht.

While Jack and I read our astronomy, the deck is being gone over with clean sand from Taiohae beach, and painted stanchions under the rail scraped and oiled to show the natural oak. Chickens in a coop for'ard keep up a querulous clatter, and the captain and Herrmann have interminable discussions concerning obvious trifles. It seems to me from my slight experience with sailors, that their minds are very immature. They become utterly absorbed in harangues about unimportant details that could be disposed of in two sentences by the average adult. These differences between Captain Warren and Herrmann afford us much secret amusement. The skipper is irascible, Herrmann obstinate; and when they have parted in the wrath and despair of continued misunderstanding (the captain muttering ''The bally squarehead!'') Herrmann can be heard complaining (while the lady on his arm oscillates sympathetically), ''The captain is of too excited. He gets as too excited already.''

We used up our last daylight by reading from Conrad's

The End of the Tether, Jack with the book, while the rest of us lay or sat around the cockpit watching the burning of a golden city on the sunset horizon, beyond the rose and amethyst swell of the sea.

Monday, December 23, 1907.

Before I proceed further, here is a quotation from Robert Louis Stevenson's *In the South Seas,* as an earnest of what one may expect in this region of lagoons:

". . . the atoll; a thing of problematic origin and history, the reputed creature of an insect apparently unidentified; rudely annular in shape; enclosing a lagoon; rarely extending beyond a quarter of a mile at its chief width; often rising at its highest point to less than the stature of a man—man himself, the rat and the land crab, its chief inhabitants; not more variously supplied with plants; and offering to the eye, even when perfect, only a ring of glittering beach and verdant foliage, enclosing and enclosed by the blue sea.

"In no quarter are the atolls so thickly congregated, in none are they so varied in size from the greatest to the least, and in none is navigation so beset with perils, as in that archipelago that we were now to thread. The huge system of the trades is, for some reason, quite confounded by this multiplicity of reefs; the wind intermits, squalls are frequent from the west and southwest, hurricanes are known. The currents are, besides, inextricably intermixed; dead reckoning becomes a farce; the charts are not to be trusted; and such is the number and similarity of these islands that, even when you have picked one up, you may be none the wiser. The reputation of the place is consequently infamous; insurance officers exclude it from their field, and it was not without misgiving that my captain risked the *Casco* in such waters. I believe, indeed, it is almost understood that yachts are to avoid this baffling archipelago; and it required all my instances—and all Mr. Otis's (the captain) private taste for adventure—to deflect our course across its midst.

"For a few days we sailed with a steady trade, and a

steady westerly current setting us to leeward; and toward sundown of the 7th it was supposed we should have sighted Takaroa, one of Cook's so-called King George Islands. The sun sets; yet a while longer the old moon—semi-brilliant herself, and with a silver belly, which was her successor— sailed among gathering clouds; she, too, deserted us; stars of every degree of sheen, and clouds of every variety of form disputed the sub-lustrous night; and still we gazed in vain for Takaroa. The mate stood on the bowsprit, his grey figure slashing up and down against the stars. . . . At length the mate himself despaired, scrambled on board again . . . and announced that we had missed our destination. He was the only man of practice in these waters, our sole pilot, shipped for that end at Taiohae. If he declared we had missed Takaroa, it was not for us to quarrel with the fact, and, if we could, to explain it. We had certainly run down our southing. Our canted wake upon the sea and our . . . course upon the chart both testified with no less certainty to an impetuous westward current. We had no choice but to conclude we were again set down to lee- ward . . .''

They sighted an island in the morning, not the one they were looking for, but Tikei, "one of Roggewein's so-called Pernicious Islands." This seemed entirely out of the question, and "at that rate, instead of drifting to the west, we must have fetched up thirty miles to windward. And how about the current? It had been setting us down, by observation all these days: by the deflection of our wake, it should be setting us down that moment. When had it stopped? When had it begun? And what kind of torrent was that which had swept us eastward in the interval? To these questions, so typical of navigation in that range of isles, I have no answer. Such were at least our facts; Tikei our island turned out to be; and it was our first experience of the dangerous archipelago, to make our landfall *thirty miles out*."

Mine are the italics. And ours is the expected. On

Friday it began to squall and continued off and on all day, with a lively blow once during the night. We were obliged to work sweltering in our staterooms with skylights screwed down. In a lull toward evening, Jack was lying on the life-boat cover, reading, when the main-boom jibed over, the sheet catching his head and giving it a wrench that luckily did not break his neck. He is still lame in neck and shoulders. That night, when the drowning moon struggled out of the watery vapours astern, there appeared before us a perfect lunar rainbow, the first Jack and I have ever seen. It only differed from a sun-bow in its subdued tones. Next, a flying-fish came right down into the cabin, looking like an offshoot of the rainbow.

Oh, it is classic Paumotan weather! Saturday the fair wind broke off, and it blew from the southwest, with a big swell, and we had no rest for rolling. The captain took off the jib toward evening, and at midnight, in a nasty squall, lowered the mizzen. We have been averaging over a hundred knots daily, and on Sunday night, in a tremendous black thunder-squall that spit forked fire, we drove through the water at ten knots. We sighted a bark that afternoon, miles ahead, going the same way with the *Snark,* but soon lost her.

No chronometer nor latitude sights have been possible for two days, and we are wondering how near we shall find ourselves to Rangiroa to-morrow, when we should be picking it up. To-day has been squally and overcast. At 9 A. M., we should have been abreast of the small atoll Ahii to the southwest, but were unable to pick it up. Heavy squall at noon—so heavy that the rain drove through raincoats, and even got below in spite of us. Followed a dead lull, in which the galley-stove smoked for want of draught. Next the wind slapped out of the north for a change. In the afternoon there was a much stiffer blow that kept on so steadily that the captain thought it might be the beginning of a gale, although the glass was normal. Never did I see such a downfall of water. The flat-beaten sea smoked with its violence, and every line of rain left a white streak on the grey water.

We ate our fried fowl and taro in the cabin, without removing our seaboots, and solaced the muggy hours of work below with many drinks of cocoanut water and orange juice.

Nakata was laid up with a headache in the afternoon— the first time we have ever seen him indisposed—and when he awoke after an hour's nap, we had great sport trying to convince him that he had slept the clock around.

Off the Dangerous Archipelago,
Tuesday, December 24, 1907.

At half past four I came on deck in the wan moonlight. Jack was forward, on watch for Rangiroa. It was an anxious time, for these elusive atolls are but a few feet high, and Rangiroa being sixty miles long, we might, with light wind and strong current, drift too close. We thought of Takaroa, not far away, where the wreck of the British ship *County of Roxburgh* still holds to the reef.

I notice in the Sailing Directions that when Le Maire and Schouten discovered Rangiroa in 1616, they were actually driven from the lagoon by ''small black flies''—the nau-naus, of course. They named the atoll Fly (Vliegen) Island. As no one now mentions these sandflies as a feature of Rangiroa, we must conclude they were all blown off to Nuka-Hiva!

Every one will agree that I started this day wrong. In the first place, I rose too early, thereby losing sleep; and when I went below to wash for breakfast, I took down the wrong bottle, deluged my toothbrush with strong ammonia, and somehow missed the warning fumes until I started brushing my teeth with the fiery stuff.

All morning the captain tried to get a chronometer sight, but the sun gave him no chance. A little after nine the sky lifted to the southeast and we saw a line of cocoanut palms. ''Pincushion,'' observed Nakata; and at that distance they did look for all the world like pins.

But what island could it be? It did not seem to tally with the description of Rangiroa—there wasn't enough of it. Captain Warren made up his mind that an easterly current had swept us so far east that these trees were on the next atoll eastward of Rangiroa. So he altered the course to about southwest to pick up Rangiroa. He was rewarded a little later by another pin-cushion just where he wanted his island to be, and great was the general relief.

It was a marvellous thing to see that atoll rise from the sea as we approached, and from moment to moment develop in intensity like a plate in the dark-room. The feathered palms were stepped in a strand of pale-pink sand, against which combed a surf of every vivid shade of blue and green. It burst high and white against the rosy barrier, for there was a considerable swell and what Jack insisted was a westerly current, in spite of Captain Warren's contention.

Still, we were almost convinced it was Rangiroa, and it remained only for us to find Avatoru, the northwest passage indicated on the chart, con our way in, and anchor in the still, sunny waters of the fairy lagoon with its harlequin fishes. It seemed as if the sun shone only within that charmed circle.

The captain himself climbed to the masthead and presently called down that he saw the entrance. Fifteen minutes later he descended with sour and anxious countenance. His entrance was after all only a low part of the reef, with the surf breaching clear across.

Again we sheered off and followed along that puzzling island. And the more we scrutinised, the less it tallied with the Sailing Directions and the chart. The captain fumed and fussed, but held to his opinion that it was Rangiroa. Then something showed on the edge of the reef that looked like the wreck of a ship, and we wondered if it could be the *County of Roxburgh,* and that we had inexplicably happened upon Takaroa. Coming closer, we saw only some blackened boulders of coral.

Jack began to look about with purpose. Day was wearing,

weather threatening, and something had to be done. He found that we were now due west of the island, and since we had skirted the entire northwest coast and found no passage, it could not be Rangiroa, which has two well-defined northern entrances. Therefore he reasoned that the land we had sighted in the morning to the southeast was Rangiroa, and this atoll we had coasted all day must be Tikahau, the next island northwest of Rangiroa. Jack himself got two afternoon sights, and asked the captain to work them up; but the man seemed to have gone completely to pieces, and would not even make an attempt. So Jack did it, charted a Sumner Line, and confirmed his opinion of our whereabouts; but Captain Warren refused to accept his conclusions. He simply would not admit that he had gone thirty miles wrong, even if Stevenson's captain and a special pilot, with days of successful sight-taking behind them, as well as countless other skippers, had been quite as unavoidably unfortunate. Also, he clung to that eastern current of his, although all signs pointed to the contrary.

We now steered north, for the sky was stormy and wind shifty, and it would not do to spend the night too near that reef. Jack said he thought he would go "butting around for a day or two" and find Rangiroa in spite of torrential tides and other adverse elements. But no one was enthusiastic, and he went below and studied the chart some more. When he came up, he walked aft to where the rest of us were sitting, looked back thoughtfully at the receding "pin-cushion," and said brightly:

"Well, Captain Warren, shall we put about for Tahiti?" —and to me, "What do you say, Mate?"

Everybody cheered, even I, for I was as tired as any one, hunting for needles—or pins—in this aqueous haystack, in such criminal weather.

So the course was laid to pass between Tikahau and a little island to the northwest of it, Matahiva, and peace descended upon the *Snark*. Next time Jack came on deck he made all hands a Christmas present—all but me. We had nothing for each other but each other; and, besides, we make our gifts at any and all times, instead of upon conventional occasions.

Jack had been suffering from an increasing headache, and before supper it sent him blind to his bunk. . . . And now, standing up and writing on my high bunk, I wonder if woman ever before spent exactly such a Christmas Eve. I have soothed my sick Mate to sleep, and feel very much alone, for the thunder and lightning are terrific, the water rough, the wind roaring—and the white-speck boat only forty-five feet long. The captain is on deck and so are the men, including the cook, for squalls are stiff and frequent and there cannot be too many nor too keen eyes to keep a lookout in a night and place like this, nor too many hands to obey orders.

Just now a heavy blow shook the bows. I was certain we had struck, for never had a wave dealt such a shock to the *Snark*. I rushed on deck, blinded by the blue sheets of lightning, and somehow managed to reach the cockpit where Captain Warren was sitting as calmly as if nothing had happened. No, he had neither felt nor heard anything. It made me appear rather foolish, and I crept below again. I am reminded of the dry and comforting lines:

> "The heavens roll above me; and the sea
> Swallows and licks its wet lips over me."

Christmas Day, 1907.

And it's "Merry Christmas" from stem to stern this day. The sun came up at the proper hour for a sun to rise, the natural phenomenon of the southeast trade set in, and there is a general aspect of restored poise in the universe, except that now, southwest of Rangiroa, the fickle Paumotan tide is running east! Well did Charles Warren Stoddard observe: "If you would have adventure, the real article and plenty of it, make your will, bid farewell to home and friends, and embark for the Paumotus."

When I opened my door this morning, Nakata, head cocked

on one side like a bird, contemplated me with that elfish sweetness of his, and, after giving me full and respectful time to spring my "Merry Christmas," himself proffered a timid "Missis-n—Merry Christmas!" Wada, wide of smile in the galley doorway, repeated the greeting. I went on deck determined not to be caught again, and nailed Martin and Herrmann; but Jack and the captain spied me from the cockpit while I was busy with the first pair, and shouted in unison.

Poor Jack encountered hard luck again this morning—and fortunately a hard head. At four, his headache slept off, he was coming up to take his watch, when Herrmann, not seeing him in the darkness, jammed down the heavy teak companionway covers and caught him squarely on the crown. It will never do for me, a sailor, not to be superstitious enough to wonder what Jack's third accident will be. He is having a holiday, however, and it will do him good. But he joined the captain in taking chronometer sights, both men working them out with assumed latitudes, and differing only a mile in their results. These proved Jack's correctness the day before, and the captain said Jack's observations this morning were perfect. A good noon observation dispelled all uncertainty about our position, and we should sight Tahiti day after to-morrow. It is very fascinating, this finding one's position on the world of waters, and I often wish I had time to study the science of it. I'd rather see my husband navigate and sail his boat than write the greatest book ever written. It is living life, whereas writing is but recording life, for the most part. Jack himself always insists that he wishes he had been a prizefighter!

All day the sunshine has scorched down from a broken sky, and I cannot express the comfort it spread throughout the little ship. Everything moulds so quickly when the sky is over-cast, and rainy days have made cabin and staterooms stale and unwholesome. It is hard enough to keep even with must and rust in good weather. I was caught on deck by rain the second night out from Taiohae, and my blankets sadly needed drying. The skylights have been raised straight up, and drawers and lockers below opened wide to sun and air.

The men have been tired and sleepy, after a wakeful night of squalls. In one especially ugly one, the mainsheet parted, worn by unpreventable friction in calms north of the Line when the boom slatted back and forth in defiance of tackles.

Wada's Christmas dinner was a brilliant success. There was tinned soup, followed by shrimp fritters, roast chicken, fried taro, tinned corn, salad of tinned French beans and mayonnaise; and for dessert a luscious dish of sliced oranges and bananas grated over with fresh cocoanut. Martin and the captain contributed a quart of champagne they had brought from Taiohae to surprise us.

Nakata emerged on deck about two o'clock, looking well-filled and contented, having banqueted on roast brown chicken and plump white kernels of rice. He walked to the fringe of bananas swinging above the port rail, contemplated it desirefully, selected two large ones, and went forward to eat them at leisure. Jack offered a dollar if he would eat twenty bananas in the space of half an hour. Nakata could not see why Jack wanted to lose money, but wasted no time in helping him do so. He took a half-dozen bananas, squatted on the deck, and began to assimilate them in judicious, well-masticated mouthfuls. The six disappeared, Nakata stood up and shook himself, took a further half-dozen from Jack, looked critically at their size, then at the fringe and back to Jack, and requested that he be allowed to select his own fruit. But Jack held him to that already picked, so he peeled the seventh and began on it, his eyes passing from one to another of us with calm, unblinking, Asiatic certitude. By the ninth he was sitting again, leaning against the rail and gurgling an occasional "O *my!*" or imploring smaller fruit, his eye no less calm, but wandering more frequently to the clock. Once in a while he would break off to laugh at himself, and lay a caressing hand upon his distended pod. "Allee same chicken-crop," he giggled stuffily.

By the eleventh banana his laugh was very wheezy and his eye less certain. He gazed long at the twelfth before tackling it, and half-way through rose stiffly and carefully and threw the remaining half overboard, declaring with amiable finality, "No can!" He explained in pantomime that he was like a cup into which he had been trying to force the contents of two cups, and no raising of stakes and lengthening of time, even to twenty dollars and another half-hour, could tempt him. He leaned painfully over, picked up the remaining eight bananas and ranged them across his body to show, by comparing them with his stomach, how unreasonable we were. As he went down the companionway, he flashed back at us one of his inextinguishable grins.

"He et so much as it can be," Herrmann commented, with his jocund smile.

Our way is now clear except for two islands. One of these, Makatea, lying in latitude 15° 48' South, longitude 148° 13' West, we should sight late to-day. It is an uplifted atoll two hundred and fifty feet high, revealing its coral formation distinctly and having an encircling reef of coral in turn, but no entrance for large vessels. It would be interesting to visit, for there is something alluring about the idea of such an isolated isle, inhabited by a few Polynesians. Visible for twenty miles, there is no danger of our running upon it unawares. The second island, Tetuaroa—or group of islets enclosed in a reef thirty miles in circuit—is farther on.

Thus, we have almost sunk the mysterious Dangerous Archipelago. While it means relief to have run around behind such weather, one can but regret not having entered just one coral sea-girt ring—not to have bartered for one "pale sea-tear," one pearl just risen from its coral bed. Their very names make one long to know them—these thousand miles of rosy coral wreaths flung northwest to southeast across the blue Pacific, with Pitcairn, high Pitcairn of *Bounty* fame, geographically if not geologically belonging to the group, bringing up the southernmost end. Are they not enticing, these names? Listen—Mangareva, Oeno, Mururea, Ahunui, Vahitahi, Negno-Nengo—and Fakarava, where Stevenson sailed in.

And the people of varied origin that live under the cocoanut palms and fish for pearls in the lovely lagoons—think of seeing those wonderful native divers. It is said the natives are very hospitable, most of them resembling the Tahitians, although formerly of a more warlike character than the Tahitians ever were, so that King Pomare I of Tahiti had his body-guard chosen from among them.

But Jack comes to me and says that many are the pearl atolls ahead of us in the southern seas, on to the west, and that my lap shall be filled with pearls if I will only wait!

Off Tahiti,
Thursday, December 26, 1907.

Makatea was passed in the night, but no one saw it, as there were squalls all around. We glimpsed Tetuaroa this morning. At ten we were about forty miles off Tahiti, and the captain will sail until he picks up Point Venus, the northernmost jut of the island, then hold back and forth all night and at daylight make for the Papeete entrance through Tahiti's coral cincture. Point Venus, according to our Sailing Directory, is the most important geographical site in the Pacific, as it has been the point most accurately determined, or at least has had more observations made from it than any other point. In 1769 Captain Cook, on his first expedition, went here in company with Green, the astronomer, to observe the transit of Venus. If I had a son, and he looked through this old South Pacific Ocean Directory, and then did not want to run away to sea, I should disown him! Such unbelievable romance is spilled through these pages of bare facts, such exploits of such brave gentlemen and gallant commanders! English, French, Dutch, and what not—theirs are names to conjure with, and we run upon them everywhere:

Captain Cook, Mendaña, Roggewein, Bougainville, Ingraham, Quiros, Bligh, Boenecheo, Wallis, Marchand, Schouten,
Cartaret, and so on down the blazing line of men who went
fearlessly to sea in all sorts of queer craft and drew charts on
this vast sheet of water. I wonder that any one ever grows
old in this storied region, this purple desert of the ocean,
littered with ''fragments of Paradise.'' As it is, people age
leisurely. Atrophy is stayed by the atmosphere, physical
and mental, of Polynesia. That they do die some time or
other we know, from the plaintive Tahitian proverb:

"The coral increases, the palm grows, but man departs."

''We have lived a little, you and I, Mate-Woman,'' Jack
said this morning, as we took our book under an awning out
of the glare. We had been talking over our travel experiences and the people we had met, from Cuba to Molokai, from
Paris to the Masquesas. A vivid life it is, and we hold it
and cherish it, every minute, every hour of to-day, and yesterday, and the fair thought of days that are coming.

. . . You should see Herrmann this afternoon. Probably
taking note of a camera on deck, he disappeared below for
a quarter of an hour. Then he came up, all in white sailor
ducks, the broad collar flaring back from his powerful neck,
long time free from any restraint of ''high-heeled collars''
as he innocently calls them. He was exceedingly debonaire
in a jaunty white hat, on his face the frankest possible smirk
of satisfaction and expectancy of admiration. He had
shaved a three-weeks' stubble, and the smirk was a whimsical
ghost of Mona Lisa's smile, lurking half-abashed behind the
mandarin-droop of a yellow moustache.

He has been irrepressibly talkative all day, has Herrmann,
and the captain correspondingly glum. ''The fool Dutchman,'' he growled, reminiscent of Herrmann's enthusiastic
efforts at being clerk of the weather in the Paumotus. His
moroseness passed lightly above the sailor's guileless head,
however, for presently, bending over a piece of canvas with
the statement that he was not so quick mit the needle as he

was more time before yet, Herrmann went on to tell of his last experience in an American ship, where, contrary to the usual custom on vessels from our country, the men were poorly fed. Their fare, he said, was but six slices daily of unrisen bread, with rusty, weevily pea-soup five times a week. The captain wanted to make him bo's'n, but Herrmann would not accept the promotion. "I cannot as drive the men of the way I must ought," he lucidly explained to us. "I cannot of swear a more o' many than *dom*, and like o' that, when I am as very mad." Then he recounted how one day a seventeen-year-old boy fell overboard, and the captain did not turn his head until one of the officers rushed past to the wheel. "Then the cap'n called him back, and came alongside the rail up, and nevermore did I as hear such a language as he of used. The youngster boy he vas as trying save himself mit the log-line, and like o' that, and the cap'n swearing at him of to let go. And that youngster boy he let go. But that was not any never mind to the cap'n. It vas awful to see that boy as of left behind. . . . No, I cannot as drive the men. I cannot as swear yet as like that already."

According to Herrmann, his association with the *Snark's* company has wrought great improvement in his English. "I have of learning more English as every day," he beams repeatedly (he is always afraid he will not be heard); but I vow he isn't learning it from me! His ambition is to own a farm in America. "It is the only country of what I like," he avers.

. . . The day had been sticky hot. Sky and water have vied in outshining each other and have met in a brassy glare. My head has ached, but my fuzzy utterance concerning it, produced by the ammonia ravages inside my mouth, has caused more mirth than becoming sympathy.

The bulk of Tahiti is plainly to be seen, but its eight thousand feet of volcanic upheaval is lost in leaden billows of cloud. Jack and Martin are laying plans for getting to work on engine repairing as soon as may be after arrival.

The captain pores charts, and, as twilight comes on, sweeps the nearing coast for the Point Venus Light, supposed to be visible at fifteen miles. The captain was in Papeete some twenty-five years ago in a training-ship, but remembers little about its approaches.

What are our dear ones at home thinking, all these weeks without report of the *Snark?* We had written before leaving Hawaii that we should not be more than three weeks going to the Marquesas—and we were over eight. There is no cable from Tahiti. There never was one, in spite of a certain English writer to the contrary. The first word we can send will be by the old steamer *Mariposa*, which Captain Chabret told us would leave Papeete on January 13, making a twelve days' voyage to San Francisco; and on this steamer will go all the mail we sent from Taiohae by the *Gauloise*. The *Mariposa* should be in Tahiti on the 9th, and we can hardly wait to get our hands on our letters.

. . . .

Again must I break into the Log, briefly to narrate months passed in Tahiti, a land which, although surpassingly beautiful from craggy mountain head to smoking surf, is very much on the "tourist route," and very much exploited in book and steamship circular.

. . . .

No one who has entered the harbour of Papeete, "Paris of the Pacific," is ever likely to forget the emotional impact of it. Outside the coral barrier, one sees to the south the smoke of reefs, rising, drifting over the rainbow-coloured channel between Tahiti and pinnacled Moorea, lying to the west; then follows the exciting fight through the swift outward current of the narrow reef-entrance into the harbour, with the wicked waters leaping, hissing, reaching, snapping, from the treacherous coral on either hand. Once safely inside and past the reefy wooded islet in the middle of the harbour, Motu-uta, the calm of the haven is like peace of prayer after deliverance from peril, and you lift your eyes to green palmy hills, on to the abrupt heights of solemn Orohena, Aorai, Piti-Hiti, and other stern mountain heads— The Diadem, a thorny tiara of spikèd peaks, like the Dent du Midi of Switzerland.

And then the town: never was anything sweeter to look upon than this garden spot of flowers and vines and trees of deepest green, the quaint French roofs peeping here and there from among the *flamboyante* and *fau* and mango foliage. The Quai de Commerce, Papeete's main thoroughfare, runs along the in-curving water front, embowered in magnificent *flamboyante* trees, with houses and shops on the shore-side only, while the seaward outlook of the broad avenue is unobstructed save for gnarled tree-trunks, and little white schooners and sloops backed up in deep water right to the sheer margin of the street, their graceful bows facing out toward the barrier reef.

Near the southern end of the crescent, a high white church, red-roofed, is reflected upon the glassy water inshore, and other buildings, long and white and many-windowed, are duplicated as clearly—like a fleeting glimpse of a Swiss city on a lake.

Along the street occasional slow forms in long gowns of white or pink, red or blue, move to and fro, or a duck-suited Tahitian, going just fast enough to keep from falling, wheels on a bicycle.

To north and south of the harbour lie idyllic points of low white beach, crowded with laden cocoanut palms; and as you gaze at them and between their pillared trunks to the intensely blue water of other bays beyond, over the whole lovely picture comes a change that is all in your own brain. In place of the houses of the French and their half-castes, you behold golden brown grass huts of the early Tahitians, scattered under trees that are not *flamboyante* trees. Moored in sheltered places, or drawn up on the beach, you see scores of enormous war canoes, perhaps the mighty fleet of nearly two thousand that was here in Cook's day. There are no streets, only haphazard pleasure-lanes among the pandanus-thatched dwellings; and no steamer-wharf and long unsightly sheds of commerce mar the perfect sweep of shore-rim. Under the palms pace stately figures of men and women, and a warm trade-wind rustles the great fronds above them.

Then you fancy a commotion in the happy village, and, following the stretched arms of the natives, turn to greet a wonderful sight—two painted galleons, questing along the outer edge of the barrier reef. They spy the passage and alter their course—fair vision of strangely fashioned hulls and gleaming canvas, as a favouring zephyr swells the fantastic sails. Perhaps it is morning, or maybe flush of sunset; or, again, it is the brazen noon that strikes upon land and sea. It does not matter—each phase of the day is more beautiful than another.

In the carven bows stand two Spanish adventurers, Luis Valdez de Torres and Pedro Fernandez de Quiros. Three hundred years ago, first of European *voyageurs*, they raised Tahiti; and secretly from all the world but Spain they carried home the name they gave to their discovery, *La Sagittaria*. So well did Spain guard her knowledge that when, more than a century and a half later, Captain Wallis came upon Tahiti in the *Dolphin*, he did not dream but what he was the first white man to set foot upon King George Island, as he christened it, in honour of George III who had equipped the expedition. A year later came Bougainville—1768—and called the land *Nouvelle Cythére*. In 1769, the ubiquitous Captain Cook dropped in. Don Domingo Bonecheo happened along in 1772, and changed *La Sagittaria* of Quiros and de Torres to *Tagiti*. And on his last voyage, Cook, with Furneaux, made his third visit to Papeete Harbor, August, 1777. Eleven years later the *Bounty* arrived in Matavai Bay, on the other side, commissioned by George III to transport breadfruit trees to British West Indies. Captain Edwards, in search of the *Bounty* and her mutineers, reached Tahiti in March of 1791, and Vancouver saw the island in the same year. The London Missionary Society sent out the *Duff* to carry missionaries and Bibles to this group and anchored at Tahiti on the fitting day of Sunday, March 5, 1797. Truly, we are late in this part of the world. Everything is altered, except the up-thrusting spires of the amazing mountains; so it is good once in a while to give rein to the imagination and restore as best one may the unspoiled paradise of past centuries.

. . . .

After standing off all night in the squalls, keeping Point Venus light in our eye, in a gorgeous sunrise Captain Warren steered for the entrance through a breaking reef, while the ship was made trig and trim and I added a duck skirt to my costume. Everything seemed in our favour as we dipped and slid in a pleasant sea toward the narrow channel. We had no cause for misgiving, and could devote ourselves to enjoying the beautiful picture of the island.

Alas—the breeze dropped us very near the entrance, and in a dangerous position, for even so chunky and sturdy a hull as ours could never survive a pounding on this iron coral. So it was up with signals, and promptly our friend Captain Chabret responded, coming out in a launch; and promptly broke down as soon as he had made fast to our side. Anxiety? Try it once—a small vessel like ours, drifting straight toward a toothed ledge of adamant roaring with bursting seas, her sails slatting uselessly with each lurch, and an impotent tug bobbing alongside.

It was not the tug that pulled us through, but the good old much abused wind, which picked us up at exactly the right point in our game of chance. And we made as pretty an arrival at Papeete as Jack's yachtsman heart could desire, beating lightly across the harbour, the yacht like a graceful skater on ice, her white sails filling now to this side, now to that, as Jack steered, his bright face all alive with achievement and pride in his dear little tub! "The old girl!" I heard him laugh.

The American cruiser *Annapolis* was in port from Tutuila, Samoa, and Captain Warren fairly strutted when she dipped her flag.

The port doctor, M. DuBruelle, came out and assured himself of our excellent health. He seemed especially interested in knowing if we had any live rats aboard, and we learned that the plague scare in San Francisco had not abated.

Before the port doctor's boat left, another came skimming out, this time a tiny familiar outrigger, paddled by a native and carrying a blood-red flag. Standing in the canoe was a startlingly Biblical figure—a tall, tawny blond man with russet gold beard and long hair, and great blue eyes as earnest as a child's or a seer's. His only garmenture was a sleeveless shirt of large-meshed fish-net and a loin cloth of red.

We were fairly spell-bound by the striking vision, and still more mystified when it broke the silence with a matter-of-fact friendly "Hello, Jack!" and "Hello, Charmian!"

Then Jack recognised him—"The Nature Man," Ernest Darling, whom he had met in California some years before, and greeted him cordially.

"But what's the red flag for, Darling?" Jack wanted to know.

"Why, Socialism, of course," he answered simply.

"Oh, I know that," Jack said, "but what are *you* doing with it?"

"Delivering the message," Ernest Darling declaimed, with a sweeping gesture of both tawny arms toward Papeete.

"To Tahiti?" Jack asked incredulously.

"Sure." And the Nature Man clambered aboard, shook our hands, and gazed into our faces with his sweet, mystical, unsmiling eyes, and then became suddenly and utterly absorbed in unpacking a little basket, setting on the cockpit seat a small jar of clear white honey, two bursting-ripe mangoes, a tiny jar of heavy cocoanut cream, and two small, perfectly ripe alligator pears, which latter Jack hailed with a hungry smack.

He is a picturesque creature, this Nature Man, and good, good clear through. Of course he is a little mad—patently because he lives differently from the generality of people; as Robert Louis Stevenson was a little mad in that he chose to walk barefoot; as I must also be mad, on that same score. In spite of his interest to us, however, Jack and I had the same thought about Darling—one look between us told it all —that he would be a disturber of our coveted solitude ashore, and that, as sure as doom, he would proselyte unceasingly in the sacred cause of nakedness, diet—or lack of it—cocoanut hair-oil, fish-net shirts in winter, and so on. . . . How could we dream of his delicacy, that kept him from intruding until, weeks later, we sent for him; nor his devotion in illness, nor his generosity with all he possessed?

. . . .

"Any old place I can hang my hat
Is home, sweet home, to me,"

one tramp sang; but with this glowing young tramp of mine, this peripatetic Jack London, any old place he can hang his writing elbow on any old table, is good enough for him. He is a wonder to me. My first responsibility in any new place is to find or devise a table for his work; and there have been some queer ones. No matter how alluring the situation, how novel, how exciting, at nine of the clock down he sits, peppers the plane before him with little note-pads, some already scribbled, some blank, squares his manuscript tablet—or diagonals it, rather, for that elbow rests well on the table— selects an ink-pencil from the half dozen that Nakata keeps filled, reads over the previous day's thousand words—usually aloud to me—and then, with a little swooping bob that seems to shake him free of all external bother, and a busy, wise little smile, he settles for two hours of creation—of bread and butter, he will have it. Sometimes he looks up, with a big smile in his eyes, and says to me:

"Funny way to make a living, isn't it, Mate-Woman?"

And I often wonder how many men can do it—carry their business around with them, and attend to it strictly, day after day, at stated hours, living romance and creating ro-

Off for Tahaa with Tehei

Pahia, Bora-Bora

mance at the same time. Now I can spill my thoughts over many pages at the end of the most thrilling day; but to restrain oneself to certain hours is another matter. Also, Jack practically never writes of experiences while he is in the thick of them. He waits; he gains perspective and atmosphere through time. He is the artist, the painter; I am mere photographer—with colour plates, true, at times, but still a photographer.

．　　．　　．　　．　　．　　．　　．　　．　　．

In Lavaina's famous hotel I left the artist to his painting, and went house hunting. I found a cottage embowered in roses and tiare and blumeria, shady with breadfruit and palm, and drowsy with honey bees. The ground sloped greenly up at the back to a mossy high wall over which drifted choral voices of men and boys in a Catholic school. The cottage was let to us by our good friend Alexandre Drollet, government interpreter. It was ours for three months, during which we made a month's round-trip to San Francisco on the steamer *Mariposa*, leaving the *Snark* engines to be repaired—for the third time. The history of these Papeete repairs is largely one of graft, in which our captain shared bountifully. We should have let him go, but for one thing. We had learned, from him, be it said to his credit, of his having served seven years of a life sentence for murder. He had been pardoned, and we, to give him this chance to rehabilitate himself, kept him on despite his known crookedness to us.

．　　．　　．　　．　　．　　．　　．　　．

We worked very hard in Tahiti—we had to work hard to keep even with the graft. Jack knew it long before he told me; but his way is always to let people hang themselves in their own way. Perhaps it is a good method by which to learn one's essential human relationships.

Although we enjoy work and the opportunity to work, I am not sure it is the best thing for us under this ardent sun. Our friend Dr. E. S. Goodhue, in Hawaii, warned us repeatedly that we were living too strenuously in an ener-

vating climate. I am tired beyond all apparent reason, much
of the time. But be this as it may, one thing is certain, as
Jack says—we shall never *rust*, in this or any other latitude.

The custom among the French in Tahiti requires a visitor
to make the initial call. Since we did not learn this until
near the end of our three months, and since we are ever
poor callers, we were practically uninterrupted; and Omar
himself might have benignly envied us our life in that idyllic
garden. A few delightful souls broke through the inhospi-
table habit of the country, and gave us some happy social
hours—the Meuels of the Steamship Company; the Tourjées
(his father was founder of the Boston Conservatory of
Music); Consul Dreher and his wife; and Mr. Young, a
wandering friend of the Nature Man's. Also, the famous
Tati Salmon bade us to his home at Papara for the New
Year's festival. There we met his daughters and sons—
splendid examples of the physical aristocracy of Polynesian
chief-stock mingled with English blood; all educated in
Paris, and now living their sumptuous tropical life. Husky
Jack London was a mere babe alongside these strapping
girls, who easily weighed three hundred. We attended
a fair and a feast at Papara, and, most remarkable of all,
in the narrow white French church heard the *himine* singing
of the native Christians, a beautiful production in which the
women carry the air, and the men produce an accompaniment of sound, the volume and tone of which is akin to a
pipe organ. This is familiarly known as "the Tahiti
Organ." The melodies are based upon old hymns, but have
become infused with an indescribable barbaric lilt that is
infinitely stirring.

We also came to know dear old man McCoy and his kind-
hearted daughter—of the McCoys of Pitcairn and the *Bounty*.
Our acquaintance with them was a rare bit of luck for us.

One especial blessing, when we could tear ourselves from
the completeness of our home life under the breadfruit and
palms, was our sunset swimming off the *Snark's* rail. We
were a mixed and exuberant company—Captain Warren,

our Japanese boys, Martin, M. and Mme. Drollet and their brood, the Nature Man and Mr. Young and others; and great was the splashing and laughter and defiance of sharks. Once, we arose before dawn, and, with the Nature Man, climbed the perpendicular heights to his tiny plantation. And often, of mornings, before Jack was awake, I sallied out in flowing native garb and bare feet for dewy walks in the foothills.

I believe our only really unpleasant experience in Papeete was Jack's bout with the dentist. His teeth had been threatening for some time, and finally "blew up," as he expressed it. His sufferings were such that the American dentist, Dr. Williams, finally begged Jack to take a vacation, as both of them were nervously exhausted. We acted upon this good advice and took a week's cruise to Moorea, which proved as beautiful as the sunset vision of it that we were accustomed to. . . . And here I shall shake off the temptation to speak more at length of Tahiti, and go aboard our little floating home once more.

Aboard the Snark, at sea,
Between Raiatea and Bora-Bora, Society Islands,
Thursday, April 9, 1908.

Five days ago, we bade farewell to Tahiti. All was packed and ready two days before; but the weather was outrageous, with a falling glass. Then, of course, something had to go wrong with the small engine so that we had no electric lights. The growing friction between Warren and Herrmann had ripened into a breach that lost us the sailor. A runaway seaman from a French ship took the Dutchman's place at the last moment of our departure—a rather good-looking but weak-faced youth from Bordeaux.

Having pulled up stakes at the Drollet house and sent our things aboard, we went to Lavaina's hotel. There were few guests, and our rest would have been good but for mosquitoes and the noisy revels of a couple of citizens of Papeete who were entertaining, in a near-by cottage, some of the officers of the Chilean training ship in port. Whatever may be the ship's discipline, these Chileans are a lawless lot off duty. So impudent are the dark-browned little rascals that a white woman feels uncomfortable alone in the streets. And they are such soiled, untidy creatures, both officers and men. However, they are more attractive than the general run of hoodlums at home, for, as with the Latin races generally, they are full of good music, and some have excellent voices.

First we heard the distant music of their band, which was giving a concert ashore; and after the home-going carriages of the Papeeteans had all rattled by, there came the ringing robust voices of the Chileans as they marched down street to the cottage across the way, the melting contraltos of their native girls blending in the rollicking chorus played by the band.

Once indoors, one convivial South American wrestled most musically with "La Paloma," evidently remembering it "by ear," with frequent assistance from his friends; but the spirit and go compensated for lapses and interruptions. Some one played his accompaniments on a piano and we lay and listened to the songs and cries of *"Bis! Bis!"* Then came dancing, hula-hula after hula-hula, to the strains (most strained) of an accordion, every one crazy with fun, while wild laughter and drinking songs broke out between whiles. In a lull, a man sang "Les Rameaux" in a glorious baritone to a splendid piano accompaniment; after which two others were inspired to make a triumphant duet out of the song. We could only compare the affair to some talented college fraternity turned loose—only there was something of true Bohemianism about these swarthy small foreigners that no cool-blooded Anglo-Saxon ever quite achieves—perhaps because he tries too hard. And also it is easier for those who have acquired music with their mothers' milk to infuse their fun with true abandon.

Evidently it makes a difference who breaks the peace of Papeete after 10 P. M. The line was promptly drawn by neighbours against our poor phonograph playing later than nine at Drollet's; and Lavaina's guests were called down for mere singing and piano playing shortly after the ultra-respectable hour. But these same guests are subject to annoyance from the immediate neighbourhood, and nothing is said. "Funny," as Nakata would remark. In this particular instance, however, Jack and I counted our sleep well lost.

Lavaina is one of the few honest business persons in Papeete. She is "all right," and there is no graft in her. It is even said that she often suffers by her lack of cupidity in dealings with less guileless ones in her bailiwick. Just as she had greeted us three months before, she now sped us with her famous cocktails, and we departed with a tall bottle of the same, and her good wishes.

We had M. and Mme. Drollet for our parting dinner at Lavaina's. He brought Jack a backgammon board, while Madame presented me with a roll of bamboo hat braid of her own make; and the twain sent aboard the yacht the last of their incomparable breadfruit. Mr. Young and the Nature Man loaded us with taro and feis and bananas, to say nothing of drinking cocoanuts.

And as we throbbed out through the breaking barrier reef, waving good-bye to our friends on the wharf, we knew that our last memory of Papeete Harbor, as it is our first, will always be the quaint Biblical figure in its scarlet waving loin-cloth, Ernest Darling, the Nature Man.

In spite of delay and graft, and Jack's terrible time with his teeth, our days in Papeete were very sweet, living on the fat of the land (blissfully garnished with garlic); but it was with a distinct joy of relief that we turned to the northwest and watched for our next island. Jack's spirits were somewhat dampened by a mild attack of seasickness. I had a violent headache all night, which may have been a form of the same malady. There was a distressing double sea, and not wind enough to steady us in it.

We carried three passengers from Tahiti, although not of

the description to cause us to forfeit our yacht license. One was an amiable yellow pup, en route to a native maiden on Raiatea; the other two passengers were served up brown just as we passed through Raiatea's reef entrance, and closely resembled one of Wada's masterly achievements of fried chicken. This was the first time on the run that we saw Jack interested in *kai-kai*—which is the Tahitian for food.

Skirting the reef for some distance, hunting for our entrance, we had a long vision of Raiatea—an elysium of green mountains and greener foothills. The highest is nearly four thousand feet, but the general outlines are less startling than Moorea's or even Tahiti's bluff shoulders. There is one mighty bastion, however, probably an ancient blowhole, to the right of the village—an important landmark for mariners.

Two miles north of Raiatea, and within the same reef (an unusual phenomenon), lies another large island, Tahaa, surrounded by its brood of islets.

As I sat up forward in the sunset, revelling in the fertile loveliness of Raiatea, Jack came behind, took my head in both his hands, set my face to the west, and pointed off between Raiatea and Tahaa to where a wondrous castled shape of earth was flung against the burning sky—and I knew it for that far-famed gem of Polynesia, Bora-Bora. Even now, days afterward, sailing closer and closer, this island loses none of its enchantment.

But to get back to our arrival at Raiatea:

The *Snark* passed between two emerald islets that guard either side of the reef entrance, into the Bay of Teavarua. There is another passage, but the water was breaking there and we chose the wider and smoother way—lively enough at best. Captain Warren remarked, as he did concerning Opunohu Bay at Moorea, that there was nothing the matter with the harbour except too much water, the depth being between eighteen and twenty-four fathoms, although with good holding-ground. We learn all we can beforehand about these anchorages. Our hook bit in at about eighteen fathoms, and the yacht swung to the puffy little willie-waws that ran down the hills. It was dark, except for a tender young moon and one lone light ashore. We could dimly make out a schooner lying close in by the land, and two or three long buildings that resembled factories.

We did not go ashore. The *Snark* is our home once more, and our own beds are the best we know.

The next morning, Monday, my head ached harder than ever, and I stayed below. About eleven Jack tentatively observed that if I felt able, we might take a short sail in a canoe with a most ingratiating native. I was not enthusiastic, but to please Jack I crawled out and up, to find a rusty outrigger alongside rocking to a snowy spritsail the size of which was comically out of proportion to the slender dugout. The owner, a bright-faced, alert-bodied islander with uncommercially honest eyes, was modestly blessing us with bundles of greens and a basket of knobby sweet potatoes, for all of which he would take no price. He was garbed in a paréu and a straw hat, and his name is Tehei (pronounced Tay-hay'-ee)—good Tehei, now at the *Snark's* wheel, piloting us to Bora-Bora; while Bihaura (Bee-hah-oo'-rah), his wife, sits near by and hemstitches like a Mexican needlewoman, after one lesson from me.

But I am anticipating—as I sometimes must when recapitulating.

Well, we dropped into the canoe, Jack in pajamas and I in bathing-suit (for I was absolutely sure that airy spritsail would capsize the outrigger), and Tehei lifted me down as carefully as if I were a baby. We sailed away toward the reef, Jack balancing on the outrigger, for any canoe is ticklish with a sail—and such a spread of cotton as this! Tehei was as fine and quick as could be in handling his boat, on each tack lifting a sun-bleached log over on the weather outrigger to offset the force of the wind, at the same time motioning Jack to shift his weight to wind'ard. I sat damply on a piece of board resting across the sides of the canoe, which sides were not more than a foot apart. A canoe under sail is little less than a keel in itself, its passengers mere ballast and disposed almost on a level with the water, their feet resting in the swash at the bottom of the narrow coffin-like thing.

We were children on a lark. I forgot that I ever had a headache. This merry adventure was more like the real thing than anything we had done yet. What mattered Papeete, with its degenerate civilisation and its business sharks? Or poor lovely Taiohae with its careless government that lets it go to rack and ruin, its sinned-against people dying without spirit to resist death!

Tehei's slim French and redundant motions finally convinced us he was serious in desiring to take us on to Tahaa, whence he had come; so we called on our own French and gestures to get him to take us back to the yacht for a few accessories such as cigarettes, a comb, a handkerchief. A tin cracker box was packed and wrapped in a rubber poncho, for a possible stay over night. While we had our midday meal below, Tehei sat contentedly on deck and ate *maitai kai-kai* (good food) according to his own pleased verdict.

By half past twelve we were careening dizzily off for a new island. Tehei seemed to know every fathom of the lagoon, and presently left the deeps, guiding swiftly over broad coral shallows. I found my breath coming quickly at the proximity of some of the large coral masses; but Tehei perched in the stern and serenely steered with a big paddle overside, winding in and out the little channels of the reef, familiar to him as our city streets to us. The smallness of the craft and its disproportionate canvas, together with our whizzing speed, recalled an ice-yachting experience I once had up in Maine, on a Mt. Desert lakelet.

Let no one imagine we arrived dry at Tahaa. We did not. Jack was drenched; as for me, the water had poured into my lap, and I had been kept busy, as my part of working the boat, bailing with a contrivance hollowed from a section of a small tree—a sort of scoop with two elongated parallel holes for the hand to grasp.

At the time we climbed out at Tahaa and waded ashore (Tehei first offering to carry me), we did not know of the olden fame of this island and Raiatea for hospitality. William Ellis, in his *Polynesian Researches,* published in 1829, while recounting some startling horrors of the natives of the Society Group, gives the Raiateans a reputation for gentleness and courtesy unequalled in any of the other communities. But we had no preparation for the wonder we were to know in the small thatched house before us. A dark, wiry little vahine, anything but a beauty but sparkling with intelligence, came running to Tehei's musical hail, and bustled us in. I am glad that an ancient custom of the natives has lapsed—that of greeting newcomers or friends with loud wailings and lacerations of the flesh with sharks' teeth!

The ground about the house had a damp, bare appearance as if it had lately been inundated. A few trees grew around, and a patch of sugar cane. We stepped on the flat bottom of an antiquated canoe-prow, mounted to a porch under long pandanus eaves, and were conducted into the one large room. Tehei followed, having first unshipped mast and sail and brought them ashore; and he and Bihaura brought us a foot tub of fresh water and a bath towel—think of it! a bath towel. Then, with delightful importance, they fished deep into a cedar chest in a corner for a dry shirt for Jack. I asked, *"Ahu?"* (which is Tahitian for éuéu), and the small vahine in limp black calico disappeared head and shoulders into the scented receptable, emerging with a clean white dotted muslin ahu and a chemise that was doubtless her Sunday best, for it was elaborate with cotton crochet. These luxuries were presented with little bows and ducks and smiles, and, finally satisfied that we had what we needed, the pair quietly withdrew outdoors—the very pink of unobtrusive consideration. Going to latch the door more securely, I found it had a quaint latchstring of cocoanut fibre, like one we once saw in Hawaii.

Invisible to those without, we could look through the breezy bamboo walls and see our friends bustling about a

thatched cookshed. Dried and dressed, we went to hang our
wet clothes in the sun. Bihaura materialised on the spot—
from empty air, I suppose, as we had seen her busy elsewhere an instant before, and took charge of things with
good-natured peremptoriness and capability.

It is not so much what Tehei and his mate do; it is the
way they do it, without apparent unusual effort. We have
been hospitably, gracefully, lovingly entertained before; but
never, in any land, by any people, white or black or brown,
have we received such absolute perfection of treatment as
from this simple kanaka and his simple vahine. The point
is, not that they placed their house, their raiment, their food,
and their personal service at our disposal, but that they did
it as if there were nothing unusual in the proceeding—as if
it were the most natural thing in the world to give their
comforts and their privacy to entire strangers from a strange
country, coming to them without scrip or purse. In fact,
they came out after us, as if they ached to devote their beautiful souls to some one. We had expected to find kindness
and hospitality; but we were overwhelmed not only with the
measure, but the delicacy and fineness of it. There was not
the shadow of curiosity in their demeanour—in spite of our
weird habiliments and our luggage of tin cracker box. We
were entertained with a solicitude that lacked servility, a
friendliness in which there was no obtrusiveness.

While Tehei did the main cooking (an excellent custom
in Polynesia that carries no onus with it), his wife worked
a transformation scene in the house. Their few personal
belongings were stowed in corners and covered neatly with
woven mats of lauhala. Other and finer mats were spread
double and triple on the floor beside a big high bedstead,
made up with clean sheets and pillow-cases, with a downy
red and white steamer-rug spread across the foot. The
bed-space they screened and canopied with ample quilts
that would put a New England county fair in the shade.
The bureau and inevitable sewing machine—which, with bed
and two chairs, was the entire European furniture—were

cleared for our use. A large packing box set in the middle of the room served as table, laid with a spotless hemmed cotton cloth, water bottle, two plates, two forks, one knife. Some of these were borrowed from a neighbour upon whom Bihaura seemed partially to depend for taste in setting and serving the meal. She was a well favoured woman, named Metua, not young, who had travelled to Raratonga and Hawaii, and spoke a few words of English. Later in the afternoon we were lounging on the porch, on a clean mat and a big white pillow stuffed with floss of cotton-tree, and once, hunting for change of position, I rested my head on the woman's knee. She caressed my head for a long time; and when she went home, Jack called my attention to her legs and feet as she pulled up her gown in a sudden shower. Then I saw she had elephantiasis *fée-fée*. It did not seem to embarrass her, nor did she attempt to hide the deformity. Fortunately for my peace of mind, this malady is not contagious, and the woman was as clean and neat as any one could be.

It takes these people hours to prepare a proper meal; so, a little before sunset, seeing no imminence of dinner, we took a walk through the village, which is composed of scattered dwellings, some native, some dilapidated European, stringing along both sides of a single thoroughfare built across a strip of the marshy lowland that forms the shores of Raiatea and Tahaa. There may originally have been some advantages in the introduction of "neat European houses," as they were dubbed by the old missionaries, into South Sea communities; but one cannot help wishing that a certain missionary of the early nineteenth century had not followed his bent. After repeated and discouraging trials to get the incredulous and unwilling natives to profit by his example and erect geometrical habitations of wood and stone and plaster after the manner of English cottages, this good man was struck with a glimmer of the fitness of things, for he plaintively admitted that sometimes he almost believed the rambling style of architecture and situations of the aborigines better suited the wild loveliness of the islands than the four-by-square atrocities he was painfully trying to substitute. The enormous glaring white meeting-house now falling into decay is a blot on the beauty of Tahaa, and as it does not seem to be used for any purpose, it will be a mercy if the next hurricane wipes it out of the picture.

Those whom we met accosted us with welcoming smiles and *Ia ora nas*, while numerous children trooped after, for few whites come to Tahaa, and there is but one white resident. The natives are very good looking, some quite handsome. One scarlet-girdled young wood god gladdened our eyes, swinging by with a long hunting spear over his shoulder, dog at heels, a chaplet of leaves on his curly head, and a laugh and song on his red lips.

But gone are the days when the people of Polynesia exerted themselves to any extent. They catch just enough fish for their own needs and a little over and above to sell when they want money; their cultivation of vegetables and fruits is sporadic, or, as some wit has put it, consists in not hindering the natural growth of things. The games and sports in which they once took pride seem unknown to the present generation. Where is Tahaa's doughty chieftain, Fenuapeho, champion wrestler of all Polynesia a hundred years ago—or one to take his place? Where are the lithe archers, the fleet foot-racers, the thewy boxers, the strong swimmers? These were all here once, but such ambitious pleasures lapsed along with customs less pleasant to muse upon —such as infanticide and older human sacrifice—until there is not even a cock fight left to remind one of the howling high times of yore. Most of the natives show little energy of purpose. Most endeavours are relegated to the *mañana* of the Spanish, the by and bye of the English, the *ariana* of the South Seas—it is all one; only, *ariana* means to-morrow or the next day, and maybe not then! On our return walk, a man came out of his yard and pre-

sented us with several chubby shells spotted like birds' eggs
and with an iridescent natural polish. Many of the neighbours dropped in to pass *Ia ora na* with us—with a more
pronounced accent on the last syllable than in Tahiti. Some
of the girls were exceedingly pretty; one, a Raratonga
maiden called Tunoa, was a decided beauty. I amused myself with fair success trying to spell the native names and
words Metua gave me, to our mutual delight, meanwhile
gnawing at a piece of sugar cane; Jack improved his time
reading his inevitable book (there was room for one even in
our tin cracker box), and took a nap. We ventured a peep
at the cooking of the delayed dinner, the devoted chefs actually making apology for the primitiveness of their method.
Upon steaming leaves laid over hot stones, Tehei piled sweet
potatoes to roast, taro, yam, feis, and a nicely prepared
young fowl. Also there was a dish with nice sticky banana
poi in it, along with the rest of the good things banked up
for roasting. Then Tehei spread large clean green leaves
over all, and again, on top of these, numberless round mats
made of leaves symmetrically tacked together with their own
stems. These leaf-mats had been used before, and were
therefore not allowed next to the fresh food. Every crevice
from which steam escaped was closed by these thick mats, tier
upon tier. In the end I think we managed to convince the
self-depreciating pair that their way was the best we ever
saw. It certainly was the prettiest cooking possible. And
they were so immaculate about it; I know Bihaura washed
her hands a dozen times.

In addition to the things put to roast, we were treated
to raw fish, coming on the table cut in small white squares
that had gone through the usual process of soaking in
lime-juice and salt. It was served in the delicious cocoa-
milk sauce flavoured with lime and salt, which we had learned
to like in Tahiti. There was excellent French bread, too,
from the native baker. While we ate from the packing case,
Bihaura and Tehei became invisible; but the *fée-fée* lady sat
on the floor and kept track of our wants. The seriousness of

all three in their anxiety that everything would not be quite right, was touching. Our well meant efforts to have them share our table so horrified them that we did not press.

Jack had been trying to explain to Tehei that we should like to go fishing, and he conveyed to us that he was arranging to take us in his canoe at eleven at night, to fish on the reef. That was more than satisfactory to Jack, who scented a novel experience.

In the early evening Tehei got ready hooks and lines. He and Bihaura made us a present of a wooden poi bowl of Tehei's manufacture, carved from one piece, oblong, with ends like a canoe and four squat legs. I am now less disappointed about the one I failed to get on Moorea. These legged bowls are more like the pictures of the Samoan kava bowls. Tehei seemed flattered that we should want his bowl!

While we talked, Bihaura, having discharged her duties of attending to our material wants, lost her expression of earnest practical solicitude, and broke into gracious little smiles as she and Metua sewed at their wonderful red and white quilts. With our few words of French and Tahitian, and their modicum of English, we managed conversation, and enjoyed the unique evening immensely. We learned, among other things, that Tehei and his wife once lived in Papeete; hence their acquisition of modern habits and possessions. These two work so harmoniously, and we have yet to hear a hasty word or a sharp command from either to the other. The woman is a small Martha, full of household affairs and the comfort of her guests. She sews, weaves mats and hats, and plaits fine cocoa-fibre ropes on which to hang things in the house. And she has made a basket of white and brown bamboo that is the only good basket I have seen in this part of the world where material and workmanship in hats and baskets generally seem to be flimsy. Across one corner of the room hung a gigantic fringe of lauhala strips, ready dried to split for strands from which to weave various useful articles.

My headache having tuned up, by eight o'clock I retired

behind the quilt partition and lay on the big bed gazing lazily at the colours and patterns of the hanging quilts, which, with the light beyond, resembled stained-glass windows. Jack came to say good night, and while we talked in subdued voices, we noticed a dimming of the lamplight. A few minutes later we realised that we were alone in the house. Thinking Jack had also gone to rest, our friends had faded away like quiet shadows into the darkness.

Jack went over and turned up the light, whereupon Tehei reappeared, as if to await the appointed hour for the fishing. But he fell asleep on a mat, and Jack, not wishing to wake him after all his labour for us, left him there.

And now let me warn you, that if ever you come to Tahaa to spend the night, bring along your mosquito netting. We did not, and there was little sleep, for it was too warm to pull the sheets over our heads, and we turned and tossed and flapped the air and slapped ourselves and each other until early morn. If I had known what inconspicuous bites these particular mosquitoes leave behind, I might have tried to go to sleep anyway.

After coffee and bananas in the morning, Metua, seeing me in my bathing suit again, thought I wanted to swim, and led westward down the road to a place where the bottom was sandy rather than prickly with loose coral. Mindful of Jack's warnings about sharks, I did not care to go in alone, so we sat on a log, watched the water, and soaked in the sunshine, while wee brown girls brought big yellow allamanda blossoms and stuck them in my hair and over my ears in their pretty fashion. It is sweet to be a guest in Tahaa.

I was just thinking about returning to Jack, when I heard his "Mate! Toot! Toot!" and discovered him and Tehei coming along in the canoe. They shot into a shallow, and took me aboard. Tehei's new tackle was in the canoe, and he paddled and steered at the stern, while Jack paddled in the bow. We skimmed over the broad shallow reef, past the wooded islets that lie upon it, and peered down into enchanted gardens of coral, yellow antlers and purple bunches, stretches of brown dotted with blue, and then there would softly gleam sheets of white sand bottom, wrinkled with black sea-slugs—*beche de mer*. Here was only enough water to float the canoe. We wondered what manner of fishing was to be ours, and after a while glided into deeper water, where Tehei called a halt, brought to light a squid, bit off portions of the live tentacles and baited all the hooks. He then handed me a line, so wound that it paid out from the inside, like a ball of twine, by the weight of hook and bait and sinker. When the sinker sounded bottom, Tehei took the line from me and attached it, where it left the water, to one end of a bamboo, then passed the unused line along the stick and tied it at the other end, and cast the whole contrivance loose, where it floated flat on the water, the fish-line sinking perpendicularly from one end. The idea is, that when a fish runs with the hook, the bamboo is forced end up in the water, the canoe puts after it and pulls in the catch. We must have set a dozen of these, in a crescent, before one of the sticks stood up, and we paddled vigorously to the shrill cries and shouts of Tehei. I should like to hear a lot of kanakas all going at once for their lines!

We hauled up a fish about eighteen inches long, the same kind we had had raw the night before—an iridescent wonder with long mouth and sharp teeth. Then another stick upended, and we flew screaming to the spot, making as much noise as twenty savages, and hauled in another beauty of a different kind, more like a dolphin. After that no more bamboos acted up; so after resting in the canoe for half an hour, absorbing the lovely colour of sky and land and water, we paddled ashore to a point covered with cocoa palms, where we were greeted heartily by an elderly half-caste woman of vivacious manner and rich-toned voice. In good English she regretted our short stay in Tahaa, as it would deprive her of the pleasure of giving us a native breakfast. They must all be large hearted, these islanders. She spoke French fluently, having been educated at the convent in

Papeete. Her Tahitian name is Terii Marama, and later on she mentioned Susan Bambridge as her English name. We gained some valuable information concerning the surrounding islands, particularly Bora-Bora, where she told us Bihaura, who came from there, owned a good house. And before we left, we had arranged, through her as interpreter, that Tehei should accompany us to Bora-Bora, where he would be able to bring about for us the stone-fishing we have heard so much about, and other amusements of the place.

While we sat talking in the tufted grass under a huge fau, Tehei spied a squid in the shallows on the edge of the water. Now, you would not have seen it, or at least all you would have seen would have been what we saw—a bunch of brown seaweed as big as an ordinary sponge. But Tehei knew, and Terii Marama knew; and first thing *we* knew, Tehei's teeth were tearing at the vitals of a desperate diminutive octopus that writhed its nauseous tentacles, strong with innumerable suckers, about the man's hand and arm. This was the way we were warned to do in Hawaii, if a squid caught us swimming!

On the final round of our lines, we found three fish drowned. The sky was lowering black to the east; so we pulled in all tackle and started for Tahaa village. The wind grew stronger in our teeth, and I knew Jack's unaccustomed arms and shoulders must be aching. But he kept up his rhythm with Tehei, and when we were in water shoal enough Tehei rose in the stern and poled the canoe along in leaps. However, the squall beat us out, and a heavy one it was. Tehei, ever keen for our comfort, insisted upon my wearing his hat—a brown felt this time, of indeterminate age and experience. I really much preferred wet hair; but no mortal but a prig could refuse such thoughtfulness on the chance of causing hurt, so the hat went on. I huddled down behind my drenched and weather-battered husband, for the wind made my wet clothes feel a trifle chilly. We were willing to go the whole way in the rain, but as it kept increasing, Tehei steered into a little indentation where stood his brother's house—a mere roof of thatch above a raised floor, built half over the water, and with no walls. Here the inmates, a fat and jolly native and his pretty young wife, lounged on mats and grasses in an abandon of the simple life, and with effortless cordiality welcomed us in all our bedragglement. I was an object of much friendly curiosity, for besides the fact that a white woman is not often seen in Tahaa, the fame of my swim across Opunohu Bay had gone before me. Jack had mentioned the incident to Tehei the previous day, and the intelligence had spread. I never dreamed that my feeble three-quarters-of-a-mile splashings would attract attention among the amphibious people I imagined in the South Sea; but times have changed in this respect as in others. A day or two ago two men in the bay off Raiatea were much alarmed by the presence of an enormous spotted shark which insisted upon following them. They said it hung perpendicularly about the canoe, opening and shutting its huge bristling jaws at them.

The rain pelted harder than ever, the sky grew blacker, and just as we were climbing into the canoe again to make a dash for it, we heard a call, and along the road came Bihaura at no mean gait, in her arms a small oval tub containing white chemise and ahu, covered with our rubber poncho. She promptly rescued me from the beached canoe and hurried me under the thatch once more, bearing the tub on one arm and half-carrying me with the other, her solicitude finding vent in a stream of vociferation against the heartless elements. Like a hen demanding the best for her chick, she shoo'd the inmates from under their own thatch, that I might change in privacy; and out they went, with no ill feeling. Probably they are used to Bihaura's energetic and uncompromising methods. When dressed, I gathered up my skirts, put on the poncho, overturned the little galvanised tub on my head, and climbed into the canoe. Bihaura had disappeared in her elfish way and when, after a stiff paddle, we beached once more at Tahaa village, she was waiting at the water's edge. Wading in, she took possession of me, and mothered me into her house, without a word placing me before an inviting heap on a mat—a fresh chemise and pretty blue ahu. And when I had donned these garments, I found to my hand a rose silk Chinese shawl, embroidered in lilac wistaria, and heavily fringed—probably a relic of her marriage day. Jack was furnished with dry things, and shortly afterward coffee and bread were brought. A couple of hours later we were feasted on choice roast sucking-pig. It was raining hard when we sat down to eat, and Tehei and Bihaura, leaving Metua to attend us, picked up the vessels in which they had brought our dinner, and made as if to return to the shed for their own kai-kai. But this was a little too much, and we refused to take a mouthful unless they ate in the house. Whereupon, well pleased, all three squatted on the floor and proceeded to enjoy themselves.

In the morning we had expressed our wish to return to Raiatea during the day, and now, on the porch, we found many baskets of limes, fruit, and bunches of taro and greens, leaning against the bamboo walls and covered with braided cocoanut fronds against the slanting "crystal rods" of rain that threatened to drive inside the house. These edibles we felt sure were intended for the *Snark*.

The weather increased, and presently, watching the hard squalls travelling toward the other island, we began to wonder a little about the yacht tugging at her long cable, and speculated whether or not another anchor had been bent, and if the captain would think to take a native pilot in case he had to move the yacht around the island to better shelter. It was a queer experience—away off on this island, separated from everything that was ours (even the cigarette prospect a dwindling one for Jack), sitting cosily in fine muslin and silken embroidery, peering through a windy wall of bamboo at the small gale that was blowing up we knew not what. We could see a cutter and a canoe weathering the wind and rain, out there in the smother on the reef. The cutter was running under bare poles, and the canoe had her spritsail lashed down into a little rag of a leg o' mutton, while her men weighed down the outrigger to keep her right side up.

Tired watching, we loafed on the big bed and talked, looking at the workmanship of this house not made with nails, the white rafters' naturally-arched crossbeams, and the shingle-like thatch. Jack fell napping, but I could not sleep for the loud strong wind and deluge of water on the grassy roof; but before an hour had passed, the blow eased. We got into our weather clothes and appeared on the porch, with an expectant look that raised consternation in Bihaura's maternal soul, for she did not want to trust her feminine paleface protégé on that water. But she obediently went in quest of Tehei, and a cutter was hired, the price for carrying us to Raiatea, $2.00 Chile, being carefully explained to Jack by Tehei.

We walked through the village, accompanied by Bihaura and the usual following of curious urchins, and halted at an old cottage that had once been painted white, where lives the one white resident of Tahaa, Mr. Lufkin, a native of Massachusetts. He has been in Tahaa over sixty years, off and on, and now, at the age of eighty-six, a victim of *fée-fée*, continues on in his chosen land, with a daughter of sixty. "She is all I have," he said plaintively, and the slim brown woman, with distinctive New England features, nodded and smiled. Tehei's arrival put an end to our visit, and we went on down the long quay of earth and coral and shell.

The sail in the staunch and fast little cutter was very exciting. I might have had a livelier time if Bihaura (who, with Tehei, went with us) had not kept me in the bottom of the boat, so well wrapped that I could see nothing, but only feel. There is no saying Bihaura nay when she chooses to exercise her motherly care. She herself helped in the sailing when we were in tight places, which were frequent, that dripping wrapper of hers clinging to her lithe little body like a sheath of skin. Thunder and lightning rolled and cracked, breakers growled and roared close by on the outer edge of the reef over which we were slanting, and we had to tack repeatedly to follow the channels known to our boatmen. At length the squalls came so fast and furious that the men took in all sail, leaving just a puff of canvas on the boom to insure headway, this puff being held and regulated by Bihaura's small brown hands. The men never had to tell her what to do. . . . "Do you know where you are?" was in our eyes this vivid night when Jack and I looked at each other in the lightning.

As we neared Uturoa we saw no light from the *Snark* for guidance, and we did not want to miss her in this ticklish weather, when the howling wind from seaward and any miscalculation in the darkness might cram us on the reef close to shore. We all united in calling this very careless on the part of the *Snark's* skipper. "Aita maitai," the natives said, shaking their heads gravely. And it certainly was "Not good."

Then we began dimly to discern the yacht at close range, saw a light going toward to the forestay, and as we swept astern our rope was thrown to a man who had climbed into the launch to receive it. That man proved to be a Japanese boy, one ever-faithful Nakata; but the weight our driven cutter put on the rope was too much for him, forcing him to let go. We heard a variety of foreign languages in distracted voices, a general furore and lack of head that led us to infer the captain was not aboard. We were lost to the yacht for the time, drifted to the wharf and got on the lee side of it, where the men alternately held the bounding cutter off and held on, to prevent her from being demolished.

The launch then came spluttering through the choppy sea, in charge of a voluble and excited Frenchman and an equally excited Japanese, namely Ernest and Nakata. Ernest landed from the weather side of the stone quay, leaving poor Nakata to hold the boat from breaking against it. Nakata, doing his small best, was terrified into wild ejaculations for fear he would fail—Nakata has ever a care for our property.

This was the first we knew that Ernest had learned to run the launch; but he had not learned it any too thoroughly, and now, when Jack got in to go to the *Snark* and fetch a line to the cutter, Ernest could get no spark from the engine. So they rowed through the smother, and poor Jack was again reminded that for a year he has been asking one captain after another to have more convenient rowlocks put into the launch. However, he brought the line, and the cutter was drawn safely to the yacht.

I never enjoyed anything so much in my life as I did trying to make our island friends comfortable. It would be hard to say which side knew the greater novelty. We had full measure of it with them; and to them our electric lights and fans were miracles. I led Bihaura into my tiny warm state-room and hunted up dry garments; but I could not get ahead of her—she had brought her own change! I then ransacked ribbons and trinkets for gifts, and she was very gleeful in her courteous and subdued way.

Wada cooked European food for them, opened tins of things that were new and desired, and delighted them with a heap of his beautifully cooked rice, of which they are inordinately fond and which they seldom see. We put them to bed in the cabin, the owner of the cutter included. I should be happier all my life if I thought we had given Tehei and his little vahine half the pleasure they afforded us.

After breakfast next morning, they returned home in the cutter, leaving us with the understanding that we were to pick them up on the morrow and take them to Bora-Bora on the *Snark*, Jack to arrange for a cutter to carry them back to Tahaa when we sailed for Samoa. Bihaura, as she bade us good-bye, said in the words of old King Pomare of Tahiti: "E mau ruru a vau!" ("I am so happy!")

When Tehei and Bihaura left us yesterday, we went to our work as usual, and after the midday meal Martin took us ashore where we called on Mr. and Mrs. Vonnegut, who had sent us an invitation to visit them. Martin tells us that when the *Snark* hove in sight on Monday outside the reef, they were out driving and immediately turned homeward to make ready to offer us quarters ashore. And we did not go near Raiatea, but ran off in a crazy canoe

From left to right: Vaega, Mrs. London, Mr. Morrison, Tuimanua

Off Manua

Upolu

to Tahaa. It is something like the way we did in Honolulu
—sailed right by to Pearl Harbor, and stayed there a month
before going into the city.

Mrs. Vonnegut is a jolly soul, Tahitian-born but of English parentage. Upon our arrival at the store she promptly
sent for the surrey, and, drawn by a sorrowful but willing
roadster of Liliputian breed, we saw some of the country.
The little bays, with their thatched huts, and the mountains
behind reflected in the water, made entrancing pictures; and
other views with Tahaa and Bora-Bora in the background,
were equally lovely. In many places in the marsh through
which the road runs, grows a beautiful sort of lily. It resembles a hyacinth in form—many blossoms around one stem
—but is larger, and the overlapping petals have eyes like
peacock feathers, with the difference that the eyes in these
flowers are canary yellow, set in blue that shades through
mauve to a lavender which deepens toward the outer edges.
The leaf is almost round, ending in a slight point, and looking like a leaf painted with one masterly stroke of a broad
brush dipped in dark green pigment. Jack picked me one
of the flowered stalks, but it soon withered and discoloured.

We called upon the French Resident, M. Belonne, and his
pretty bride, and drank tea with them on their tree-sheltered
bit of beach.

Returning to Uturoa from our northwest drive, we passed
through the village south, on the way buying a basketful of
live shrimps from a woman who waded in from the near reef
at Mrs. Vonnegut's call. These were for bait, as Jack
planned to fish off the yacht after dark, asking the Vonneguts
to join us.—And while we were fishing, Martin played the
searchlight on the shore for the amusement of the natives,
whom we could hear shouting with delight.

Martin, who travelled southward some miles on Raiatea,
says the country is superb, and that the natives live very
primitively and picturesquely; but Uturoa is not pretty.
The example of the misguided missionaries evidently persisted here, for most of the houses are European, and not

attractive European; while the large white, staring, uncompromising warehouses of the trading companies are an exasperating blight. When Mr. Ellis, nearly a century ago, was carried out of the water, canoe and all, by the welcoming natives, upon his second visit, he found an "improvement" since his first coming that made his soul rejoice: "We called upon the king," he writes, "whom we were delighted to find living in a neat plastered house." Isn't that lovely?—And if said king did not contract consumption or asthma or phthisis, through the unaccustomed restriction of air, it was because he had a stronger constitution than most of his kin and kind.

Raiatea is said to possess some interesting relics of antiquity. One of these is the ruin of an old temple of human sacrifice which was once enclosed by a wall built entirely of human skulls—mainly those of warriors slain in battle. But with Bora-Bora only a dozen miles away, famed for its merry people and pristine life, we did not linger. At one o'clock this day upon which I am writing, April 9, Martin started off the engine and we set over toward Tahaa to take on Mr. and Mrs. Tehei, making our way cautiously in the deeper channels among the coral. It was the brightest of mornings, everything sparkling, a gentle breeze cooling through the warm sunshine, breakers curling white on the barrier reef and the lagoon painted in more hues of green and blue than man can name, "nor woman neither," I found—blues so live and intense that the eye was caught and held as by a very spell of colour; greens brilliant as emerald shot with sunlight, or soft and restful as purest jade. In this riot of silken colour, broad irregular splashes of elusive plum-tints marked where coral rose near the surface. Midway between the two mountainous islands, we all agreed upon Tahaa being more beautiful than Raiatea; and during the day, travelling mile after mile along the dreaming shores of the smaller island, we have strengthened our belief. It is an enchanting panorama of rambling hills and bays and islets, with high Ohiri lending a strong and rugged character to the otherwise verdant round outlines of the land.

Tehei hailed from the cocoa-plumed point agreed upon, and indicated that we were to go back to the village. Which we did, first taking him aboard. Out from the village paddled three large canoes so laden with food and floral offerings that Captain Warren raised his hands in helpless dismay: "My goodness gracious! Where are we going to put it all!" The decks were littered with bunches of prime bananas, both green and ripe; cocoanuts of all edible ages; papaias, green and golden; endless baskets of the homely but heavenly yam; a few oranges; taro; pumpkins; bound and protesting chickens, and a vociferous and reluctant piglet; and lastly, a diminutive papaia tree, cut down in all its promise, set in a kerosene can, and decorated with the rarest flowers of the island, twined around the fruit at the top, and stuck into the pretty leaves. When we were under way, Tehei and his wife formally presented Jack and me with the sucking pig, the chickens, and the gay papaia tree, along with other and not so elaborate bouquets. The fruit and vegetables went without saying; they are automatic hereabout.

Some of the relatives of our passengers wanted to go along too—one, a pretty young wife, her ears decked with large real pearls, entreating Jack with tears in her eyes and arguments that must have been most eloquent if misplaced, judging by Bihaura's disgusted expression at this, to her, breach of breeding. She looked somewhat as she did at her own house when a vahine dropped familiarly in at dinner-time, and tried to sell us chickens!

Tehei appropriated the wheel and piloted out of the harbour, a school of small fishes having great sport in the froth kicked up by the propeller. Bihaura, seating herself upon the deck on a small straw mat that always accompanies her travels, gazed around complacently upon this big "bateau" with its "mash-een," and pronounced it all "maitai," and again "maitai."

. . . And now, I have been writing pretty steadily since

we left Tahaa, and am going to rest and look, until we drop anchor under the green battlements of Bora-Bora.

Lat. 16° 32′ South,
Nearly 152° West Lon.
Aboard the *Snark*,
Teavanui Harbor, Bora-Bora, Society Islands,
Friday, April 10, 1908.

In the sheltered cockpit, writing, I am surrounded, outside the rail, by inquisitive but unobtrusive natives of varying ages. They have been paddling quietly out all forenoon from Vaitapé village (called Beulah by the missionaries), lying yonder in the morning shadow of Pahia, which rises almost straight up 2100 feet close behind. One might suppose that the mountain would cut off from Vaitapé the prevailing wind; but the trades contrive somehow to reach around both sides of the peak, and the climate couldn't be more delightful.

Bora-Bora lies only about twelve miles northwest of Tahaa; but it was after moonrise last night when Martin shut down the engine and the anchor rumbled out, for the harbour is to the west and we had to travel nearly around the island, outside an endless ring of reef breakers to the entrance, a fifth of a mile wide. After the sun went down, Tehei stood in the bow with the captain, Jack at the wheel, and I camped amidships to pass orders above the noise of the engine. We were not sorry we had to go so far around, as we saw more of this matchless isle. We realised in glorious actuality an old engraving of Consul Dreher's; only, the real Bora-Bora is far lovelier than the picture, and infinitely more majestic. Wonderful, wonderful, and again wonderful, I kept repeating—line and colour changing with each new facet of this island jewel. During sunset the land was all rose and opal, turning to cool restful green. The islets on the garlanding reef stood like emeralds against a green lagoon; green hills grew up out of the verdant shore, and behind, the green, green mountain pierced clouds that reflected the universal green. Pahia is the piéce de resistance in all views of Bora-Bora, rising sheer and double-peaked and palisaded, hills leaning against it, and little islands flanking round about. The Nuuanu Pali in Hawaii has been widely painted and photographed, and it is not a whit more worthy than Pahia of Bora-Bora with the perfect composition of its surroundings. It is like a planet, petrified with its ring of satellites.

After Tehei and Bihaura had been set ashore at their request, Jack said to me: "What do you say we go over for half an hour or so?" Ernest took us to the long jetty, and we wandered in the soft cool air, attracted by music, which was accompanied by a concerted, regular *chug* as of some dull and toneless instrument. The grass grew to the water's edge, and on this village green, by the forgotten graves of the decaying Mission church, we beheld an idyllic pastorale of youths and maidens dancing under a spreading *flamboyante* to the strange rhythmic chant. The maids were all in white, garlanded with sumptuous perfumed wreaths of allemanda and blumeria and tiare, mixed with drooping grass-fringes, the men likewise garlanded, and girdled in white and scarlet paréus. They moved in twos and threes, arm in arm, closely around the mouth-organ musicians in the centre, like bees in a swarm. The curious chug-chug was made by a measured grunt-grunt! grunt-grunt! of the dancers. There was witchery in it all—the wheel of graceful revolving forms, twining brown arms, bright eyes and white teeth glistening in a soft and scented gloom that the moon had not yet touched; and the last least veil of enchantment was added by flitting soft-glowing lights amongst the dancers' heads. These spots of soft radiance were curly fragments of phosphorescent fungus, culled from dead and dying cocoanut trees, and set in red and silken hibiscus blossoms, worn over the ears of these flower-like women—curled flowers of captured moonshine, sometimes tender, luminous blue, sometimes evasive green, and again mere phosphorescent white.

One of the girls, encouraged by our Japanese boys who

were gaily mixing with the company, bashfully gave me her moon-blossom from its place over her ear, and it was such an exquisite unearthly thing that I wished I might keep it forever.

A half-caste merchant, Mr. Buchin, who runs a sort of hotel, came over to us and passed the time o' night, graciously placing his services at our disposal.

After clapping a few more dances of the dusky sprites, we walked south along the beach road, like a pair of children in dreamland, peeping into open lighted doorways of habitations too frail to be the abodes of human beings; looking straight up through feathery palm-tops at the moon peering over the mysterious shadowy mountain; and presently we were arrested by music of another sort than that under the *flamboyante* tree. "Himine!" Jack whispered, holding my arm tighter and hastening his steps; and together we tiptoed to a large oval structure—just an immense thatched -roof with walls of low picket. Inside, a lantern and kerosene lamp disclosed by their flicker a group of women and men sitting on a large mat on an earth floor first. spread with dry grass. They were singing himines such as cosmopolitan Tahiti forgot long ago. Vahines composed the front ranks, and from the rear came the remarkable tones of the "kanaka organ," heavy ringing voices booming like strings of 'cello and bass viol picked resonantly by giant thumbs. Three young men, leaf-crowned like wild things of the forest, with a frolicsome-eyed Mowgli at their head, swayed from the hips, their foreheads clear to the floor as they trumpeted, in a sort of sitting dance—like that of the Samoan *fita-fitas* on the *Annapolis* in Papeete harbour.

Singing mothers held children in their laps, and one girl, a perfect type of the heavy-featured, dreamy-eyed Polynesian, looked wistfully through the green grass fringe of her hei, toward where she knew her young companions were dancing free. But she held her important own in the himine, being principal high voice. I do not say soprano, for there are no natural sopranos in savagedom. So, in order to emulate the high tones as heard among the missionaries in their hymn-singing, the native woman forces her chest tones up into the head, producing a true note, to be sure, but a harsh and strained one. I have yet to see a vahine who can take a high tone without wrinkling and distorting her face, and sometimes she even reaches up and holds one side of her face as she climbs the register.

Jack's theory of this difficulty is something as follows: That the lower the race, the less differentiated are the sexes; the women are stronger in proportion to the men than are the women of higher civilisation, and so on down the line of sex characters, even the voices of both sexes resembling.

We were assigned to a bench by a grey-haired elder, and sat there half an hour lost in pure enjoyment of the remarkable harmonies. One himine especially we called for again and again. It was like the triumphant shouting song-cries of successful hunters returning from the forest; or like the victorious pæan of warriors bearing home slain enemies from the mountain.

We trod the charmed path back to our boat rocking in the silver flood, and went to sleep in our little floating home, in our ears the organ tones of Mowgli and his wood-mates, and the wild call of hunters and warriors from forest and mountain.

Bora-Bora, Saturday, April 11, 1908.

Hands full of gifts, we returned this morning to the yacht after early coffee and hot-cakes with our devoted Tehei and Bihaura in their imposing residence, a two-story, four-roomed house. Yesterday the gendarme in authority on Bora-Bora, M. Laborde, not waiting for us to look him up, came aboard resplendent in white helmet and ducks and military medal for "Service et l'honneur," and welcomed us in the friendliest way, inviting us to his house, granting unasked hunting privileges, and offering us "plentee cheval." Whereupon we ordered our saddle case out of the forepeak. Everybody is the same—it is smiles and Ia ora nas, abundantly backed with practical benefits. Never can we balance the score—only can we be thankful for our lucky hap.

So ashore we went in the afternoon, returned M. Laborde's call, and met Madame, a stately French woman (probably the only white one on the island), with a royal braid of brown hair hanging nearly to the floor. Her husband obligingly conducted us to the house of the old chief of Bora-Bora, Tavana Tuhaa, to whom we had a letter of introduction from his cousin, Terii Marama—Susan Bambridge. The gendarme humorously explained that he himself was the French chief, and Tavana was kanaka chief—with a Frenchy little shrug at the obvious lack of Tavana's power. But then, M. Laborde is directly under the Resident at Raiatea, who is directly under—but no more.

At a dilapidated European house we were greeted by a very queen of kanakas, a splendid big woman—the physical aristocracy again. But she was clad in tatters that ill concealed her hideously advanced elephantiasis. She went to fetch her husband, and the two wrecked bodies came together up the neglected garden walk. He is part white, a small, slight man, pitifully disfigured with elephantiasis. They were very quiet, courteous, and unembarrassed by their sickness. We soon left, for there seemed little ground upon which to meet. After this we dropped in to see Mr. Buchin. As we were due at Tehei's for dinner at five, we sauntered early in their direction, passing on our way the big himine house. Bless us, if they weren't singing yet!— or had they rested off in the night?—the same three wood-boys, the girl we call The Type, and the rest. The elder hailed us in, hospitably enough, but with tone and gesture of one accustomed to authority.

Seeing a number of large rough tables piled around, and a great mound of fruit, vegetables, and fowls, we concluded that preparations for a feast were under way. Never did we hazard more widely. After listening to a number of "selections," and to a repetition of our especial favourite, the fiery ferine chorus, the astounding thing happened.

A fine looking man arose from the grass, waved his hand toward the heap of edibles with a graceful flourish, and began to speak. As he proceeded, we at length caught the unbelievable drift of his discourse. He was presenting us with this bounty. But why? We made deprecatory and declining signs, and the orator disappointedly subsided. We were very uncomfortable—we could not accept so great a gift. Why should we? How could we? We could make no fitting return, and we have heard of an unwritten law, that a gift in this part of the world means a gift in exchange for a gift. Also, the yacht would not be able to accommodate such abundance of kai-kai in addition to the quantity already taken aboard at Tahaa.

So we sat and uneasily listened to another himine from men and women with baffled, reproachful eyes, while the grey elder fidgeted with a hurt and displeased air.

The song finished, he arose stiffly and, advancing toward the mooted offering, himself presented it to us in an address with many flourishes. Still we hesitated. We simply did not know how to act. And suppose we had possibly made a mistake in our interpretation of their meaning, and committed an awful breach of etiquette? Judging by the frustrated elder's face, when we again declined the unprecedented munificence, we were already guilty. We felt very foolish; but we lacked information, and were anxious to get hold of some one who could set us straight. To ease the strain, we asked for another himine, after which we retreated as well as we could, hopeful of finding some way to come to a rational understanding over such an irrational situation.

When we reached Tehei's house, he explained, with the help of Nakata, who had been washing and ironing there, that kai-kai was not ready, and that we were to take a walk with Bihaura. Captain Warren and Martin had also been invited, and we five struck south and caught a view of the next bay before sunset.

We passed a "lumber-yard," or so Martin named it, where, upon racks under long sheds, were laid for sale supplies of thatch: Long dry leaves of pandanus are strung on to five-foot lengths of reed, made fast to the reed by overlapping one end of the leaf and pinning it with the midrib of the cocoanut frond run through from leaf to leaf horizontally, until the rafters are covered. Sometimes it takes three thousand or more of these fringed reeds to roof a fair-sized house. The thatching will last about seven years, and no roofing equals it for coolness—or for centipedes.

We noticed before some of the houses canoe-shaped wooden trenches several feet long, full of sago in the making. Farther on we flushed a number of blue heron, as well as snipe, and a few ducks, and promptly recollected Laborde's permission to shoot. Captain Warren took a gun out this morning and we had fried snipe and wild duck for luncheon.

Jack and I had made it up together, on account of mosquitoes, that we would somehow get around the wishes of Tehei and his wife for us to spend the night ashore; but we changed our minds once we were inside our room, not because we feared the mosquitoes less but that we feared hurting our friends more.

Our room was large and many-windowed, and had two wide beds dressed in perfect triumphs of scarlet patterned quilts and snowy belaced pillows. "She noticed we had separate bunks on the boat," Jack whispered. The floor was thick with beautiful plaited mats, Bihaura's weaving; and there was provision in the corner for washing. On the floor between the beds was that red and white basket I had admired on the passage, and which was now mine. Beside it lay some pretty seashells.

They had not wanted us to come to their house until it was quite prepared, this lady and gentleman of Polynesia; and when we went from our bedchamber into the next room where the dinner table creaked with its weight, we knew by these signs and by their tired and anxious faces that they had worked themselves nearly sick. But they were so blissfully, affectionately happy over our appreciation, that their eyes and lips broke into loving smiles whenever we looked at them.

On a small side table stood two newly plaited green baskets full of all kinds of flowers, and beside them a more enduring present. This was a miniature double-canoe carved by Tehei, and rigged with the native tackle for hooking large fish—a long bamboo pole amidships between the two boats. When a fish is caught, the pole is jerked high in air, the line flies backward and the fish is brought to hand. This toy is a perfect representation, even to the shell fish-hook. And to cap it all, a gigantic wooden fish depended from the pole—this last Bihaura's work, carving, pink and blue colouring and all.

Next we were crowned with white tiare and led to the board. The Horn of Plenty had been spilled upon it! There was roast sucking-pig, done to a nicety; and fowl, dressed with delicious gravy and browned onions; breadfruit and the usual native vegetables; raw fish in our pet dressing; fresh-water shrimps; baked fish; banana poi, cocoanut milk —and I cannot remember any more, except the good coffee and French bread, and many kinds of fruit.

The centrepiece was a bouquet of strange flowers resembling ears of wheat, anywhere from one to two feet long. At the end of each was attached a blossom of some other kind, even to white jasmine.

A step forward in intimacy was made, Bihaura taking her place beside me. Tehei declined all urging, pretending that he was needed to look after the cookshed. But he was absent very little. The two were evidently agreed on this arrangement, so we let them have it their own way. Bihaura was so tired she could hardly eat; also, she was in a flutter lest she do something wrong. She watched our every mouthful and the manner of the taking—which fork, or spoon, or dish. But after a while she became more at ease, and later was drinking our health in flagons of cocoanut, and jumping up and down in her seat at our suggestion of bringing the Victor ashore and giving a concert. You see, we are cudgeling our brains for ways to offset the favours we are continually receiving. Tehei never comes near us empty-handed. Martin, noticing that the Seth Thomas clock on the wall, an "octagon-drop," was not working, offered to repair it, and the gratitude of the owners knew no bounds.

We had to be careful what we admired. I remarked an elaborate straw hat tastefully trimmed with a blue feather, and asked Bihaura if she made it. She nodded and said something to her husband, and he took up the hat and presented it to me. Of course I refused to accept it; and so sensitive are they, that they instantly divined the situation, and acknowledged the refusal in good part. But Bihaura went into the other room, and returned with a thirty-foot length of hat braid, plaited of straw so fine that the entire roll hardly covers my hand. This I could take—but not her best *chapeau*. It was a relief that they did not pick up the mats from the floor and give them to us.

After dinner we all sat on the porch, with fairy fungus lanterns over our left ears. Tehei was so weary that he slipped off to the end of the porch and lay down. From somewhere came to me the memory of an old sweet custom in the Marquesas, of friends exchanging names, thereby inaugurating a relationship. So, tapping Bihaura on the breast I said, distinctly, "Charmian," and, tapping myself, "Bihaura." It was an inspiration. She understood, and repeated the formula gravely and reverently, whereupon we kissed as sisters. Jack so approved that he tried it with Tehei. And now we often call him "Brown Brother." This is the favour they love. The worst of it is, that they now try to get even with us for this greatest of all honour we have bestowed!

We suggested himine, hoping that Tehei, on the spot, might unravel the mystery at the singing house. The singing was in full blast when we arrived and we could see aggrievement still on the face of the elder, although he was punctiliously polite. The pyramid of fruit and gasping

chickens was untouched. It was not long before Tehei
brought order out of the chaos of misapprehension. It
proved true that we were expected to accept this friendly
largess; but Tehei, quickly catching the drift of our protest
against the magnitude of it, explained that we should be glad
to have say two of each kind of article. Amity was restored,
and Jack laid aside two hens, two bunches of taro, two clus-
ters of bananas, and so on.

Then we all sat down happily to the music. The captain
and Martin, classically wreathed, lounged on a curving
bench—an Alma Tadema strayed into the barbaric picture.
There were more singers and more sitting dancers. One rose
in the flickering light and performed the most beautiful
dance of welcome, bending his lithe body back, with extended
arms; pressing his hand to his brown breast as he swayed
forward; in every pose expressing that all Bora-Bora
was ours. And through it he sang, with a voice like a bell,
so ringing, so smooth, so rich in tone and expression, that
it stays in my ears like a song heard overnight in a dream.
He was the most captivating boy—captivating and uncap-
turable, in his half-wild spirit. If we had reached out to
grasp the welcoming hands of his dance, I am sure he would
have vanished furtively into the woods, with his sinewy
young body, his red mouth curling back over flashing teeth,
his bird-like eyes, his light, small feet with the toes spread
like a bird's. Sometimes he leaned forward, looking closely
into our eyes in the uncertain light, like some questioning
forest animal or sprite.

I do not believe the grey elder will ever quite forgive the
unintentional slight we put upon him and his followers.
Although he failed in no detail of courtesy, it was but a limp
hand we wrung upon parting. If he could only understand,
as Tehei understands.

. . . The many windows in our bedroom were a delusion,
all but one which had a couple of panes out. And upon bidding us good night, Tehei and his vahine were at great
trouble to shut both doors tightly. When a savage, accus-

tomed to the air of all outdoors, comes to live in a house with windows, he seems to think they are made to nail up— else why should they be furnished with glass?

We got the doors open, meanwhile more than vaguely aware that we were inoffensively spied upon by inquisitive neighbours; but the windows were tighter than the storm-windows in a Maine winter. We had not noticed a mosquito during the evening, so turned into our fluffy beds trustingly. —They didn't sing, they didn't even bite; they just threatened, they alighted, they pestered; and there was no way for the breeze to get into the sealed apartment and blow the wretched things about.

. . . There is no getting around the fact that our host and hostess are suddenly become of high importance among their neighbours. Did they not arrive as guests on the "masheen bateau," and were they not taking first place in entertaining the white visitors? But do not think for an instant that this figures in their kindness to us. One look into their faces precludes such possibility. The little woman sat beside me at the himine, and if I leaned toward her in the least, she would nestle closer, and clasp my hand—bridging with sheer lovingness and trust all time and difference of race. Returning up the moonlit road that night, Bihaura and I with arms around each other, Tehei stalking with exalted awkwardness arm in arm with Jack, with a hundred following us, we were so full that, once alone in our room we could only look at each other with moist eyes. Finally Jack, wandering around with a hopeless look, arms hanging, said in a discouraged voice: "I can't understand it. It's overwhelming. I simply don't know what to say." A minute afterward he added: "Wouldn't it be an *awful* thing stupidly to hurt them in any way?"

It gives new lights upon cannibalism as practised on white sea captains who requited love and courtesy like this with deception and abuses worse than death.

.Sunday, April 12, 1908.

Aside from an early walk with our guns, this has been a restfully uneventful day, if there is anything uneventful about lying at anchor off a South Sea island as extraordinary as Bora-Bora. In the evening we were due to join Tehei and Bihaura, to go to the phonograph concert. Tehei's resuscitated Seth Thomas was pointing to ten minutes before seven as we entered. It had struck me that I should do my brown sister the courtesy of at least one appearance in strictly conventional attire; so I had brought a rose-flowered ahu. I knew Bihaura was pleased, although never by look or word has her perfect ladyhood betrayed sign that there was anything out of the way about my clothes—whether bathing-suit, pajamas, or bloomers.

The machine-made concert in the himine house was such a success that we knew we had hit upon the one thing to square favours. What mattered it that the machine had less springs than usual, warning us, by sundry whirs and clicks and obstinate halts of the crank, that it would throw up the job if we did not look sharp? The man behind, one newly baptised Tehei London, had a warm and perspiring time of it.

. . . The comfort and sense of home Jack and I now feel aboard the *Snark* is inexpressible. My little white cubby is a place of refuge and privacy, clean and convenient. The deck is immaculate with lime-juice, and clear of boats—a roomy, breezy place for work or play or sleep. Think of scrubbing decks with the juice of limes! Why, I help squeeze them in the tub for this purpose, submerging my arms to the elbows in the bleaching, softening fluid. I also tried trampling out the juice with my bare feet, to Jack's great amusement.

There is only one drawback to life aboard—the swarm of cockroaches, large, medium, and small. We have joined the fleet of ''cockroach schooners,'' the attractive name by which Society Island trading vessels are known. We are fighting the bugs, hand, foot, nail, and—I had almost said tooth.

Anyway, I can bring my fist down on a cockroach with the best, provided it isn't one of the largest. My qualms are still insistent that I shall not squash a shell-backed monstrosity full of blood that is white!

Aboard the Snark, at sea,
Society Islands to Samoa,
Wednesday, April 15, 1908.

There goes the graceful white cutter headed back for Tahaa under a cloud of canvas, while the *Snark* surges westward. From the stern of the cutter a white-robed woman waves her handkerchief, and upon the stern rail of the *Snark* Tehei is bowed in prayer and tears—*riomata*, tears and sorrow. He did not know how hard it was going to be, the big brown child-man, this parting from his little brown woman. He wanted to go, and she was willing; but the pain of parting, beginning yesterday, when Jack and I made up our minds to take him, was worse than they had bargained for. She was brave; but to-day, coming to eat the last meal with him, she sat in my room, bent over with grief, while I frantically pawed my belongings to find gifts for her, beginning with a fine hanky to wipe away her tears. Tehei went about with salt trickles running down his cheeks, reiterating "Maitai, maitai ariana," with rebellious courage, when we laid a sympathising hand on his shoulder.

He joined us this morning with his scant luggage, also bringing for me one of Bihaura's enormous tree-cotton pillows wrapped in a many-times-folded mat some seven feet square, and a smaller mat, exquisitely fine. In addition, Tehei brought more vegetables and fruit, and Mr. Buchin rowed out with some South Sea cotton—not the tree-cotton, —a basket of ripe pomegranates, and a parcel of vanilla-beans. Then arrived thirteen chickens we had bought on a wonderful horseback ride around the island—accompanied by presents of fruit until the yacht was fairly wreathed with bananas, pineapples, baskets of oranges and limes, and her decks choked with yams, taro, pumpkins, cucumbers, and a dozen other comestibles. Bihaura's final offering was a sucking-pig—such a homesick, disgusted, obstinate *puaa* never came aboard a ship. It persistently pulls its foreleg out of tether and essays perilous journeys to the rail. Tehei himself cannot make that wee porker fast.

"They have placed us on the High Seat of Abundance," Jack mused, his eyes very blue with feeling.

And now we are really westing toward Samoa, about 1200 miles from Tahiti. We have fair wind and sea, and are glad to be sailing. I am looking forward to a few uninterrupted days for work, and might as well begin right away and tell about yesterday's stone-fishing:

I had forgotten all about the conches that were to rouse the inhabitants in the morning. When the heavy resonant tones broke the stillness, I sleepily wondered if a tramp steamer had strayed in, or perhaps a cruiser; then turned over and slept again. It was just as well. Although the starting-time had been seven, and Jack had given up work, we did not get away until ten.

"Here they come!" Martin shouted, and there they certainly came! It was a gorgeous spectacle. Imagine the deep-blue lagoon, encircled with green islands of all sizes and forms, and, coming toward you a barge that rivalled Cleopatra's—a gigantic double-canoe, "manned" by a round dozen splendid brown girls, all in white with red scarves knotted about the hips, garlanded and crowned like tropical May Queens. In the stern of each of the joined canoes sat a huge muscular savage, likewise crowned, naked to the waist, both smiling under the hot sun like the happiest creatures ever created. On a platform across the bows Bihaura and Tehei, decked in scarlet and crowned with orange-coloured cosmos, swayed and bent, bowed and gestured in the graceful abandon of their native dancing. We could hardly recognise the prim and housewifely Bihaura in this radiant undulating woman; nor had we realised how handsome our swart brother could be. Sometimes they leaned forward from the prow, for all the world like Polynesian Wingèd Victories challenging wind and sea with defiant, irresistible figures of bronze. And all the time they sang, and the girls sang in chorus, knocking rhythmic paddles against the canoes in unison, between dips.

Three times around the yacht they swept, then ranged alongside—a careful undertaking, for a long bamboo fishing-rod was thrust forward from the bows, decked with festoons of flowers. We welcomed the beauties aboard, and after some formal speechifying by Tehei and the boatmen, we all embarked in that gay "bateau." As soon as we were settled on the tiny platform, the fair paddlers got under way, and resumed their singing, while our brown relatives took up their performance where they left off. In the midst of the musical clamour a languid-eyed houri rose, climbed up to us, and, dancing the most alluring hula before me, bent in her dancing and embraced me, the while dabbing my face with fluttery kisses from lips cool and soft as blumeria blossoms. She repeated this fond greeting to Jack, and danced back to her paddle.

Looking down the double row of dusky girls, performing so easily the arduous work of propelling such great loaded canoes, we were almost startled by the seeming varied root-types among them. Yet they were probably pure Bora-Boran from time out of mind. There we saw a face that would have done honour to a North American wigwam; two moon-faced sisters with languishing, sleepy eyes, were strikingly Chinese; while one maiden would easily have passed for a Persian. Another was elusively Japanesque; and a slender paddler on the right was a good American type. And so on down the line: some were intellectual in feature and expression and shape of forehead; some innocent-faced, some sophisticated; some wise, some frivolous; and each one a beauty, with strong, brown body and limbs, inexhaustible spirits, and the desire of fun in her brown eyes.

It was a pull of several miles to the shallow point where the manœuvring was to be, and our garlanded crew sang all the way, with untired lungs, occasionally breaking out

in some old wild cry that had to do with the custom of stone-
fishing. Once in a while a little squall would rush down the
mountain and give them all the work they could handle,
while Bihaura shouted, "Hoé Hoé" (Paddle! Paddle!)—the
word we learned in the surf canoes at Waikiki.

To help along the cheer, I essayed a little hula dance of
my own, for was I not one of them this day, and did I not
wear a white waist and a red paréu and a yellow hei, with
the best! Oh, they were vociferous in their applause and
their cries of "Maitai! Maitai! Maitai nui!" It completely won them, that little tripping of mine off the beaten
track.

When we were hauled up on the white shallows, I was
borne ashore high and dry, pick-a-back, by a laughing vahine,
while one of the jolly steersmen did Jack a like service. The
palmy point was dotted with the tribe, and we were led to
a thatch on the sand, under which we reclined in the midst
of our crew, who took up their himines again, sitting in a
circle. One of the steersmen was an actor and *improvisateur*, delivering himself of the most touching tones of appreciation of our joy-giving presence. Outside gathered the
clans, and on the beach a crowd surrounded the captain and
Martin in the launch.

There seemed to be some delay, some hitch in the proceedings. Things did not appear to be going forward, and we
learned that there had been disagreement among the factions
—one faction would not fish with another, and so forth.
Now, the grand feature of stone-fishing is the number of
canoes—a hundred should be in. the crescent that spreads
out upon the reef and narrows and draws in to where the
women, standing in the water at the beach, holding a net of
cocoa leaves, close the crescent into a circle, and thus capture the driven fish. Only about twenty canoes had answered the blasts of the conches, and here we were, likely to
be robbed of our stone-fishing. At last, through the inter-
vention of M. Laborde and Tehei, it was arranged that the
twenty canoes would see what they could do. We embarked

in the launch, with Captain Warren at the engine, Martin remaining ashore to take pictures.

When the twenty canoes had spread in a wide crescent on the shell-green water, with the breaking wall of thunderous breakers at reef-edge, we could realise the disadvantage of there being so few, and tried to imagine how a hundred would look. There was a flag-canoe, and, when all were in position, a man dropped the flag—a red and white paréu on a stick—from side to side. At every drop, a kanaka at the bow of each canoe beat the water with a stone on a string. It was a remarkable scene of action. Running our eyes along the crescent, we saw the white spray-smoke of the stone-thresh on the water, then the brown forms lifting and swinging the stone again. Tehei, in our bow, swung with the best, and when he lost the stone from its string, instantly followed it overside, promptly rising with it in his hand. I picked up his floating orange wreath and put it dripping on his black head as he emerged.

The line of canoes drew in and in, beating and beating, and we saw the vahines forming their barrier of legs and cocoa leaves. Our launch behaved beautifully until almost the end, when the canoes had constricted into a tight circle and the vahines passed the great string or screen of leaves inside the canoe-circle. Then the engine gasped and died, the rudder at the same time coming down with a crunch on a huge hummock of brown coral. Jack pick-a-backed me ashore, and we approached a dismayed and disgruntled gathering on the beach. There was not a fish in the enclosure —not one! Where were the boiling myriads of fish, big and little, that fought and jumped and struck and bit at the wall of legs—the fish that in desperation dashed themselves up on dry land!

We made a cheerful, if sympathetic, face about it all, especially as we could see that Tehei and his wife felt keenly the failure to show what the stone-fishers could do. It seems that the people here never can judge when a good catch will be made, even when the canoes turn out in force. And the bad luck happened on this day of all days.

Bihaura had by now learned that her mate was going to sea with us, and although she continued to keep the pot of fun boiling, on the paddle home to the yacht she broke down and sobbed with her head on her knees. Mr. Alacot, a genial half-caste merchant who had been in the party, interpreted to us that she was also sorrowing because Jack and I were leaving, and that we had been "so good to her." We asked him to tell her that no one in the world had ever been so good to us as she and Tehei, and that if the yacht were only larger we should take her also. Once back on the *Snark*, with the girls sitting around the after skylight singing choruses for the *improvisateur*, she became more like her usual controlled self. But she clung close to Jack and me, and watched her husband as he danced and sang and tried to interpret to us the impromptu songs and speeches. Nevertheless, we caught him wiping his eyes now and again.

Long ago in Polynesia there was an organisation called the Aeroi Society, that lived by its talents for entertaining; a sort of peripatetic Bohemian Club, going about from district to district visiting the chiefs, with whom presents were exchanged. The chiefs in turn descended upon the common people and farmers, robbing them of their produce in order to feed genius. Besides artistic ability of one kind or another, one of the qualifications for membership in this profligate association was the solemn promise of a man to kill his offspring at birth. One of our steersmen, a well built, slender fellow, handsome of face and winning of manner, certainly was the result of a slip-up in this cheerful custom by some talented member of the ancient fraternity, for the scene aboard the *Snark* was much as the chronicles describe the milder phases of the Aeroi orgies.

Any one who wants to fit himself for unembarrassed public appearance, should come to Bora-Bora and sit under one of these *improvisateurs*. An you can take what he gives you without feeling silly and looking worse, your reputation will be made. I could not. The graceful creature (by the way, he had fée-fée!) would approach, making up the most poetic sounding runes and things with endless and varied repetitions of my adoptive name, ''Bihaura Vahine,'' the chorus meantime shouting enthusiastic responses, my brown sister bowing grave acquiescence to the honour paid me through her, and Tehei assuring me by expressive maitais aside that this man was a prince of poets—''Fine! Fine!'' Oh, the genuflections, the spreading of arms, the waving of shapely hands, the sparkling eyes! And all the while, little individual hulas were palpitating around the ring of sitting singers. These love-dancing people do not have to stand on their feet to dance.

Wada, instead of worrying about so many to feed, thought it all very jolly and funny, and bustled about in his light-footed neat way, hoisting ship's biscuit on deck, opening coveted tins of salmon for the eager inrush, and boiling huge pots of rice.

After a while, Jack and I withdrew forward, the better to orient ourselves and observe this strange act in the *Snark's* drama, performed under a swinging ship's lantern while the boat rocked at anchor in the light of the moon. Even now, so soon afterward, it seems far away and unreal, and wholly sweet and wonderful and unspoiled.

Bora-Bora to Samoa,
Thursday, April 23, 1908.

One year ago to-day we beat our way out through the swirls of the Golden Gate. One minute it seems a very short year, when one thinks of the rush of events; and the next minute, pausing on some of these events the twelve months lengthen into years crammed with novel experience. I know more about geography than I did a year ago, to say nothing of human nature.

And we're getting on, we're getting on, even if slowly.

We could not keep up the six-mile gait struck the first and second days out from Bora-Bora, and since then have been lucky when we could exceed forty miles a day. Winds are light and variable, with a criss-cross sea that makes an all-night sleep a pleasant memory only. We expected to sight Manua by the ninth day, which will be to-morrow; but it now looks like a twelve-days' run from Bora-Bora.

Jack and I were both fairly seasick for a couple of days, then buckled down to work. We feel very luxurious with our unwonted deck room—the boats are on davits now—and a good-sized awning amidships. One of our cots is left on deck in the morning, and we work and read, play cards and nap, as comfortably as if we were in a house. The men follow the sun around with a flap of canvas, and we are in cool shadow all day. Squalls of rain curtain the horizon, but none comes nigh us. All three meals are served on deck on the 'midship skylight, and I do not even trouble to sit up, preferring to rest against big blue denim cushions filled with silk-cotton from Bihaura's enormous pillow. Tehei is quite satisfied with this disposition of his wife's gift. He is beginning to cheer up, although when Martin developed the pictures of the double-canoe, showing Tehei and Bihaura dancing, he leaned against the companionway and wept like a good fellow. Every night at sunset, he kneels reverently at the stern rail and prays toward the East. He is a good sailor—keen, willing, with sharp eye for disorder, and a good hand at the wheel. Little experience as he has known in white men's boats, he is a far better sailor than poor Ernest, whose three years before the mast have left him innocent of efficient seamanship. Along with his uselessness, he has a decided penchant for "bossing" everything and everybody whom he imagines under him—Wada and Nakata for instance. And, last and worst, he has an unpleasant and dangerous disease, which Jack is doctoring and which, on so small a boat, is very undesirable for all of us. We look forward to dropping him at the first available port.

Our supply of fresh food is dwindling to the noble

yam. I enjoy it three times a day, in the variant forms that suggest themselves to Wada's fantastic Japanese brain. Why, to-day we thought we had French-fried potatoes— and behold the hearty yam, done to a nicety in olive oil. Big ships whitewash their yams, which keep for months this way. We have not been able to dispose of all the bananas, and they are dropping overboard with reckless wastage. The hens have delivered only two eggs altogether, so chicken stew and fricassee are frequent.

Never did the *Snark* look so well, nor promise to look better. The men are working hard, painting and cleaning and polishing. Jack has them knock off at 4:30, and the watches are easy in this uneventful weather. In fact, Martin, taking the wheel from eight to ten, has all night in. The engine room is unbelievably clean, and the engine is painted dark green and light brown, with shining brass to top off.

Wada's department has spread to quite a farmyard, although the feathered stock is diminishing by two a day. Two fine young roosters committed suicide by flying overboard, but the rest contented themselves with merely trying out their wings and returning to the rail. The land-lubber crowings at daylight are very confusing to the dream-dull mind. One's opening eye expects to see the "glimmering square" of a house-window. And the pig, the little, little *puaa*. He slipped his moorings under cover of darkness, and we have since speculated as to whether he met his untimely end at the business end of a shark, or cut his own throat with his cloven hoofs.

Jack and I have been boxing daily, as of old, and now, with our enlarged deck space, Martin has taken it up with Jack, who gets more exercise than when he "fights" solely with me. The boxing amuses Tehei inordinately.

Outside of the dawns and sunsets, and Jack's indignation over my impertinent suggestion from below that my ventilator was not a deck ash-tray, the only other special incident I can think of is the bleaching, or attempt at bleaching Nakata's hair. I brought a generous bottle of peroxide from

Papa Williams

Village Beau, Samoa

San Francisco, at his request; but Nakata's enthusiasm to become a blond had not augmented during our absence. However, when we now explained that the black would grow out again soon, he fell into the plan with zest. He was only afraid he would meet Japanese in port somewhere who might laugh at him. But the bleaching of his wiry, purple-inky poll is not easy. We have used nearly all the bottle, the captain and I, and can only detect a dull auburn tone when Nakata stands between us and the sun. In passing, I must mention that we have discovered that Nakata's first name, Yoshimatsu, means "always happy," and Wada's, Tsunekichi, "always good."

Jack spotted a bonita to-day, but failed to supply Wada with fresh fish. Even Tehei's beautiful feather-lure, plucked from the dejected tail of a doomed rooster, did not look good to the bonita.

Two new articles have kept Jack occupied, one called "The High Seat of Abundance," relating our experiences with Tehei and Bihaura, and the other "The Stone-Fishing of Bora-Bora." In *Polynesian Researches,* he had found the following:

"On the arrival of strangers, every man endeavoured to obtain one as a friend and carry him off to his own habitation, where he is treated with the greatest kindness by the inhabitants of the district; they place him on a high seat and feed him with abundance of the finest food."

> Aboard the *Snark,* at anchor off Tau,
> Manua Group, American Samoa,
> May 28, 1908.

I am sitting on a little camp-stool that sways threateningly at each offshore heave of the sea. Around me is a gathering of Samoan gentlemen whose frank admiration of a woman who does not have to bleach her hair to make it brown, is quite overwhelming. You see, these Samoan dandies and their *fafinas* (which is the *vahine* of it here) do have to bleach theirs, and to that end use lime made from coral.

Why, when the big whaleboat came out to us just now, rowed by these splendid kanakas, we were all agog over a magnificent savage in the bow, a man of herculean size, apparently white-headed. He was a veritable South Sea Colonies George Washington. But it was only lime, white, thick, plastered lime made from coral, although his truly grand lines and bulk and crawling muscles were no illusion. Those who have taken off this rigorous bleach are left with hair of various auburn hues that make Nakata's dull flush green by comparison. The reddish hair lends a red-brown to their great black eyes, and a warm tawny tone to their faces. The splendid bodies are clad only in loin cloths, which partly conceal a fine tattooing that covers their glossy skins like tight knee breeches. The upper back part represents a canoe, the two ends reaching in points half around the waist. A Samoan is not a grown man until he is thus decorated. He indubitably must be a man then, by right of pain, if nothing else.

Another reason for admiration in the regard of the circle is my facility with this fountain pen, for I do not waste much time getting over the paper when I am trying to record happenings on the spot. When they first swarmed aboard from the whaleboat, all shook hands and said "Talofa," (reminiscent of the Hawaiian *Aloha*), we replying in kind; and then I made for parts below and fished up Turner's *Samoa*, in the back of which is a vocabulary of native words. I wanted to find out a few things from these new Americans, and began pointing at the words I needed. They were able to read the words, and pronounced them for me, one after another immediately translating into English—as, "*Uru*—English, breadfruit." The rogues—they all spoke considerable English, and had not let on!

Tau Island was sighted this morning, but with light wind it was well into afternoon before we sailed under the lee of the high land. The wind failing, Martin started the engine, which behaved well until we were close to our precarious anchorage outside the tremendous breakers; then, just as we

most needed power, something went wrong. Two boatloads
of natives came out, and towed us with a will to the place
they said was the best holding ground. This is a volcanic
island, rolling up from the shore twenty-five hundred feet,
densely wooded from water's edge to clouds. It is quite
different from any of the islands so far. There is no barrier reef, only the rock reef close in, and no safe anchorage,
in a blow, anywhere on the fourteen miles of coast. We are
in the best, but fearsomely near is the racing surf, a veritable
Grand Prix of Neptune's finest horses. Our Carmel never
flaunted more brilliant turquoise and emerald than do the
glorious speeding breakers of Tau. We are so close that
we fall into the hollows they leave behind as they pile up
ceaselessly on the smoking reef. Catch us risking *our* boats
in any of their indiscernible "boat-passages." Not we.
When we go ashore to yon palm-smothered village, it will be
in a big whale-boat manned by amphibious Samoans. One
of them just now posted me upon local etiquette in the matter of compensation for services such as have been
rendered us: "A little sea-biscuit for the boys? They pull
boat hard. *Ai?*" So Wada is handing up a tin box of pilot
bread from the forepeak, while the square white teeth of the
expectant, smiling natives encircle us. "Some whiskey,
please?" Oh, that is different. Whiskey is taboo. They
know, and so do we. That is one point of perfect understanding.

Wednesday, April 29, 1908.

We did not go ashore, as it was nearly supper time when
we came to anchor. For convenience in running back and
forth, we should like an airship. Our visitors departed well
satisfied with their entertainment, and pulled away singing.
After dark several boatloads came out through the surf, and
passed by in the starlight, singing, always singing; and in the
night we awoke and heard them in the distance, fishing by
torchlight under the Southern Cross, while on the beach
fires burned redly.

The *Snark* rolled heavily all night in the ground swell, and we were driven below by a stiff squall; so there was scant repose. This morning Mr. Morrison, an American in charge of the one store, came out in company with a two-hundred-and-sixty-pound "high man" of the village, who teaches English in the school. His name is Viega, pronounced something like Vee-ahng-ah—this melodious *ahng* sound always preceding the *g* in Samoan. The two invited us ashore, so we swallowed our coffee and toast and made ready. It was very exciting going through the surf, and I found myself studying ways and means of winning ashore over the reef, should we upset. Many boats are broken up, even in the hands of the skilful surfmen. We were reminded of surf-riding in Hawaii, when at length a straight-going friendly roller sent us shooting in.

Borne on the mighty shoulders of the tattooed, red-headed Samoans, we were set high and dry on the broadest, palm-dotted beach we have seen. Viega led us to the house of Tuimanua, the King, who, greatly to our disappointment, for we had heard much of him, was absent super-intending the copra-making on Olosenga, the westernmost of the Manuan group. Later in the day a flashy-looking habitué of the royal neighbourhood, elegantly tattooed and be-limed, broached the suggestion that he send a boat to Olosenga with news of our arrival. We were glad of this, for this pseudo-monarch is the last and most illustrious of the kings of Old Samoa, and we should regret missing him.

As soon as we were in the house, the high men began to drop in, and we sat in a circle and had translated to us by the gentle-voiced and courteous Viega the speeches of welcome made by the chief orator of the village—the Talking Man. Not one of the speakers would have risked his eloquence to his own scant English. Viega, the teacher, was able to do their high-flown language into very good English, with admirable grace and dignity. The Samoans are cere-monious above all the Islanders. Viega's effect is quite overpowering, and I find it necessary to recall my stare occasionally when I am lost wondering how he carries his massive bulk so well. And he is athletic—looks fat, but can easily touch the floor with his knuckles without bending at the knees. It turns out that he practises this and other exercises daily—proving that he has brain as well as brawn. In feature he somewhat resembles Prince Cupid of Hawaii. The profile is good, mouth well shaped over even teeth, and wonderfully sweet when smiling; the forehead is low but broad, and the eyes, very large, are dusky black, with insolently level, heavy lids—the insolence being solely in the lines, for the gaze is kind and gracious. His eyelashes are half an inch long at least. It is the physical aristocracy again, the splendid result of generations of ample nourishment and care and selection. Viega wears a white *lava-lava* (all the same paréu, I can hear Wada comment), a shirt and a white coat.

A room was made ready for us *papalangi* (white folk) in this European and breezy stone house, and oh, yes—I must not forget the 'ava. *Kava,* the Americans say at home, but 'ava is the correct native usage, while the real botanical inwardness is *macropiper methysticum.* There was no postponement in our liking for it, and there is now a note filed away to remind us to send for "pepper-bush" when we are home once more. They made it in a large fourteen-legged calabash called *tanoa,* wrought from one piece of hard wood. The knobby yellowish root is coarsely grated, placed in the bowl, and water added. The mess is squeezed by pretty maidens whose hands are first punctiliously washed—at least, that is what happened while we were looking on. As the yellow root begins to tinge the water, the grosser gratings are strained in a bunch of cocoanut fibre. When the water retains the proper amount of the flavour and colour of the root, the 'ava makers all stand and clap their hands. This signifies to the household that the flowing bowl is prepared, and is also a signal that the house is taboo to intrusion until the drinking is accomplished. Originally the meaning of this clapping included the warning against evil spirits.

A cocoanut calabash is now dipped into the bowl and brought by one of the pretty maidens to the guest of honour. On this occasion it was passed first to me, and then refilled for Jack; Mr. Morrison came next, and was followed by Viega, and thence on around the ring of "nobles," undoubtedly in the precedence of their rank. The same drinking-calabash is used by all, going back to be replenished after each drinker, even if he has but touched his lips to it. But the best observance is to drain it. The person presenting the cup raises it high, then sweeps low, finally bringing it to the level of the drinker's hand. It is a beautiful and stately ceremonial.

'Ava drinking is said to have been the most strict and ceremonious function of Samoa 'Umi in the past, and the pages of her history are redly punctuated with squabbles, feuds, and wars, that arose over the question of precedence in drinking. There is no doubt in our minds as to who will first press lip to cup when Mr. Tuimanua comes to town.

Originally, the 'ava was fermented, but the people were not given to drinking to excess, only taking a draught before meals, like a cocktail; and old men drank it in the morning, believing that it prolonged life. 'Ava is taboo in Hawaii now, on account of the intoxication it produced among the natives. But this 'ava in Manua is newly made for each quaffing, and is the freshest, most mouth-cleansing of drinks, leaving an effect on the tongue like a gargle of listerine—a "delectable toothwash that cleanses all the way down," according to Jack. When my cupful started down, I thought I should not care much for 'ava; but before the cocoanut-shell was emptied, I changed my mind. One cannot name the flavour—that is as difficult as describing the taste of bread-fruit; it is just *rooty*, and somebody said it reminded him of hops. Perhaps it might be likened to a sublimated, unfermented, celestial beer. One writer has said that 'ava tasted like soapy dishwater as much as anything else; but we failed to notice the similarity—perhaps we don't know the taste of dishwater.

Mr. Morrison tells us that 'ava is mildly stimulating, and that some persons find their knees wabbly after drinking a quantity. But Jack and I have noted no effect whatever, except that of refreshment. We are just as well satisfied, too, that our 'ava is not made as of old, when the root was chewed by the Samoan girls. No matter how charming they be, one cannot help preferring to do his own chewing, and, anyway, microbes are microbes.—Oh, surely, we'd have had a try at it, just the same. We could not have let our beloved Robert Louis go us better on a little thing like that.

Although one consequence of 'ava drinking is to check the appetite for food, it is customary to offer food with the drink; but the ceremonial does not impose acceptance of the taro, or breadfruit, or whatever happens to be set forth.

The household of the King is unique. Here, besides Tui-manua and his wife, live Mr. Morrison, and a sister of the King, whose name, Lepepa, means Good Tidings, such as announcements of marriages or betrothals. She certainly looks all of it, and more, for topping her spare presence is a head of short black hair, red-ended, standing out frizzily in all directions like a Fijian's, giving her a look of pained surprise which is irresistibly funny. Lepepa's main occupation, besides being good to us, is keeping this aureole in order, which she does by rolling it up tight in a point on top of her head, pinning it with two or three insufficient wire hairpins. I spared her one of my large bone ones, and she promptly came with a beautiful tapa (*siapo*, here) of her own manufacture. It is done in dark brown designs on dull white, and decorated with big bars and disks painted with a varnish-like vegetable juice. This square siapo is for wearing apparel, held in place by a broad white siapo girdle, picked out in brown leaf-forms.

There are several young girls, related to the royal family, who sleep elsewhere but spend the day in the "palace," ostensibly helping around. Two beauties stood fanning us at table to-day. One, vouched for as full-blooded Manuan, is a variation in her race. Her hair is brown, half its length burned by the sun to a splendid lustreless gold. Her skin is tawny, and her black eyes, long and level, heavy-lidded and indolent, borrow a tawny tone from hair and skin. She has a square-cut neck on her short tunic of bright blue-flowered stuff, and her neck and shoulders and back are matchless in line and texture. Indeed, she is so lovely a thing that she seems fairly to breathe out beauty. Only thirteen she is, with an exquisite budding body; and she lays her dull gold hair on the nape of her neck, dressing it over the ears with crimson blossoms of hibiscus, and looks upon us with a calm sphinx-like gaze that tells nothing except that she is unconsciously a perfect thing fashioned from the dreams and colours that pictures are made of. I wonder if Cleopatra looked so, when she was thirteen. This beauty's name is Liuga, with the tender *n* before the soft *g*. And Liuga means The End, The Aim. Isn't that beautiful?—What does she here in unappreciative Samoa-land, where her fairness is but subject for mirth among her kind? She would be The End, The Aim, of many a white heart if she went to a white man's country, and possessed the mind to inform her loveliness.

There is a fashion magazine in Tau. I saw it lying on the Queen's sewing machine. And if I had not seen it, I should have known it was in the village. The strange garments that have been evolved would make a book in themselves. There is great preference for semi-décolleté and berthas; and as this pinafore sort of apparel seldom goes as far as the knees, a lava-lava of some unrelated material covers from the hips down. Liuga finished off the square neck of her blue-flowered upper garment with wide purple lace laid flat, while her lava-lava is brilliant rose-colour. She is like an Egyptian scarf, a rainbow. There—I am back to her again, when I want to tell about Viega's wife, Sialafua, which means The Road, The Way. She helped in the hospitality this afternoon; a magnificent woman, well up to her husband's weight. I should like to see her in a box at the opera, in full panoply of silk and jewels and bare shoulders. She would create a sensation, would Viega's wife. As it is, she makes a marked impression in a lavender and white *ofu* (Samoan for holoku, ahu, etc.), her black hair done high, and plump taper hands folded in a lap that "ample" doesn't express. She is the daughter of an old chief of Upolu, and looks born to the purple.

When Mr. Morrison had enticed Jack out to the store, the women and girls lost no time surrounding me, and asking, in unmistakable and highly ludicrous ways, if I had any "pickaninnies," which familiar word they have adopted. When I made it clear that I was so unfortunate as to have no family, the good souls left me in no doubt as to their pity for my childlessness. But after some one pantomimed the size of the *Snark*, and the perils that would beset pickaninnies on that overcrowded *vaa* (boat), they sagely nodded that it was best so, and wished me well for the time when my little ship should come home.

Thursday, April 30, 1908.

At last we have seen tapa-cloth in the making. I had begun to look upon it as a lost art, until Jack and I, taking a walk, stumbled upon a *falè* (house) where a pretty woman sat cross-legged before a tilted board, pounding and scraping the wet lengths of stripped white *tutuga* bark—a kind of mulberry—*Bronssonetia sapyrifera*, if you really want to know. After the pulpy substance thus made is pounded into "cloth," it is laid over a board carved in one of the patterns peculiar to siapos. A piece of rag is then dipped into native dye made from tree-bark, and well rubbed over the cloth. The colour remains on the high places pressed up by the carving, and the thing is done. The woman discoursed volubly to us about the process, and we, nothing daunted, replied at length in our own, to her, unintelligible jargon.

The village strays picturesquely along the beach, each falè set up wherever its owner chooses, and his shell-garnished canoe drawn up not far off. There are two roads in Tau running parallel until they converge at the ends of the village. Trees and flowers crowd to the edges, and we saw passing through the air from bough to bough several of those strange furry paradoxes, flying foxes. The houses are beautiful—far superior to those of Tahiti and Tahaa, especially inside. The roofs are domed much higher, and are more often round than oblong, while the workmanship in beams and thatch and sennit is exquisite. Samoan thatch is almost always made from sugar cane, and the eaves of the steep roofs clipped short. The floors are the ground, raised several inches by layers of pounded white coral, with stones set around the edge to keep the coral in place. One stoops low to enter, passing in between the upright pillars. The interiors are lofty and roomy and cool, with a restful gloom; and when rain or draft is to be shut out, mats rolled up under the eaves are let down, a section at a time, or all around, as the need may be. The only furnishings are handsome calabashes lacquered bluish white by the 'ava, rolls of sleeping mats, and short bamboos raised a few inches, which are used as pillows, Japanese fashion.

Upon going into a house, with "Talofa" all round, mats are instantly unrolled, upon which one is invited to sit—cross-legged of course. And the most approved posture, especially when in presence of royalty, is with the right foot resting upon the left leg, well above the knee. Try it. Jack says he cannot succeed because of his stiff knees—stiff from many accidents; so I am doing it for the family, although I must admit it is a strain.

These Manuans are universally good-looking, except for the prevalent disfiguring blindness. No one seems to be sure of the cause. But judging by the myriads of small, clinging, sticky flies that infest the faces of the children, one cannot help wondering if they haven't something to do with it. Some of the prettiest faces are grievously marred by an eye gone white or whitish blue. Hunchbacks of both sexes are a common sight, but they are as jolly as the rest. We noticed a number of men without hands—dynamiting fish being responsible. There is *fée-fée*, but no leprosy. It is a pity there is not more fresh water in Manua. Rainwater is the source of supply, and the natives have no chance to bathe in rivers as all the islanders love to do; and there can be little sea-bathing, on account of sharks. They are not voluntarily uncleanly; they do the best they can, but lack the fresh and shining appearance of people who may revel in abundance of water.

We cannot stir out of the house but a large following of all ages and conditions attaches to our rear. To-day one lusty young fellow took it upon himself to be guide. He speaks English, and says he was once a marine on the *Adams*. He led us into various houses, where we bought siapos and fans, shells and baskets. When some avaricious fafiné wanted a price that our guide considered exorbitant, he assumed a lofty, detached expression and remarked: "Let uss go." And go we would, on to another falé where perhaps a couple of voluptuous damsels volunteered to siva-siva, first placing a dish before us, into which Jack was expected to drop small change. These Manuans, despite the fact that this is not a steamer port, are not so primitive by far as our adorable Bora-Borans.

The children have learned that certain purplish-red cat-eyes, although common as pebbles here, are for some reason esteemed by me; and they come in droves, hands full. Jack pays them a cent for ten desirable specimens, and they scuttle for the store to spend their gains in "lollies." When we reject bad stones that they try to foist upon us, there is a great uproar of laughter, in which the detected one joins with good will. I am minded to plan a girdle out of the cat-eyes. One green one has come to light, but such are rare.

We were gone possibly an hour and a half on our quest through the village, and when we returned, ten of our coppers had already found their way back to the store, where Mr. Morrison was dispensing lollies at eight for a cent. It seems good to be handling American coinage. It provokes the old query: "Do you know where you are?" Frankly, half the time I do not. Down on the broad glistening beach I sit with chin on knees and watch the bit *Snark* tossing just beyond the tremendous barrier of surf, and feel very much lost indeed.

The King's front veranda was the scene of quite an extensive bazaar to-day, when the natives, rounded up by Mr. Morrison at our request, brought siapos and fans and mats for us to buy. All were good natured—congratulating one another when a sale was made, and gaily jeering when an article was not up to the mark. Mr. Morrison, who is the butt of much friendly abuse because he will not take a wife from among them, engineered proceedings, and kept prices down to normal; and we became the possessors of enough mats, fine and coarse, to furnish our floors in summer at home, and to sleep on for aye if we choose. A large mat of fine, soft weave can be bought for $2.00 to the entire content of the seller. Lovely sleeping-mats, child-length, come two for a quarter, while an ordinary-sized siapo that would take three women a week to make, brings half a dollar or less. 'Ava bowls are held very high, because few are made in this day.

When I lay down to rest after dinner, in to me came Soa, one-time *taupou,* or Maid of the Village, now a sober young matron of a few months. She sat beside me on the bed and began to massage—*lomi-lomi,* the same as in Hawaii. Then Lepepa dropped in, with half her unruly hair sticking straight out on one side, and added her kneading. After a time another girl strayed along and joined, while outside on the porch Liuga, head nodding with red flowers, looked through the window and wound up a musical clock for our amusement.

I must tell about the Maids of the Villages. I do not know who is *taupou* of this one, now Soa is wedded; but it is the custom for the chief of a village to appoint a child to the high office, which child is brought up carefully with this goal in view. She must be a virgin of high degree, and she is the standard, the representative, the paragon, of all pure excellence in the community. If she fail in virtue, the chief who appointed her must indeed be powerful to save her from punishment if he would. Her function it is to entertain high guests—to make the 'ava, to be gracious, and to look all her loveliness, dressed for the part.

Now, also in each village is the *manaia*, the beau, the flash-man in whom is embodied all the foppery and manly style of his people. Part of the business of this masculine butterfly is the conquest of taupous of other villages than his own—his guerdon being the number of maids he may win. Courting-parties besiege each village in this game of hearts, and each group must look to it that its taupou be shielded from the charms of the intruder. Her end is to marry a chief who will be chosen for her, and there must be no tripping aside. There are all sorts of intricate ins and outs in the taupou system, and one would have to reside in Samoa a long time to unravel the inwardness of the charming custom.

After supper, still tired, I stretched out on a mat on the veranda, where young girls gathered around, who, I have no doubt, commented upon the cut of my *ofu*. I said "Lomi lomi," and was promptly surrounded, three on a side, twelve small hands hunting out the tired places in my nerves. Even the indolent Liuga took a hand, two hands, as well as the other belle who fans us at table.

Boys from Viega's school drifted over to sing for us, and sat in a row on the grass under a big *fau* tree. Their himines are less varied in harmony than those of Bora-Bora, but very musical nevertheless.

Friday, May 1, 1908.

He came, Tuimanua, in a pouring rain. Early in the morning the word was passed along that he had landed; but

it was some little time before we saw him, for he beached at
a distance in order to dress suitably. When he finally appeared, he walked under an umbrella, barefoot in the rain,
clad in neat brass-buttoned khaki coat, over a white lava-
lava. His wife followed, with Sialafua, and we were introduced by Viega. Then ensued a ceremonial period, during which we sat around in the main hall and exchanged
compliments and courtesies. As for Tuimanua's Queen,
Vaitupu, she is just the dearest of solid, lovable, wholesome
women, with dignity and fine manners. So has her husband dignity and grace, but something more. We had been
with him but a few minutes when we said to each other:
"He is every inch the part." He is tall, well shaped, with
sharp and restless black eyes, fairly light skin, noble profile
and head, firm mouth, slender sensitive hands, and the first
fine feet we have seen in Polynesia—long, slim, classic, even
to the long second toe. His carriage is kingly, aloof, lonely.

We had understood at Tahiti that Tuimanua spoke a little
English; but no word did he utter to us except in Samoan,
which Viega interpreted. Once or thrice, a quick lift of
the Tui's eyebrows or a flash of his keen eyes, made me
wonder how much he really did understand.

Jack and I were getting quite at home in our surroundings,
when Tuimanua made some request of Viega. That engaging creature rose to do his bidding, but passed out of the
room backward and bent double—and he a kinsman, a nephew
of the august Tui. We kept our eyes alert, and when
clapping announced the 'ava, we saw Liuga approach deeply
bent. I do not think the fair maiden likes genuflecting, or
else she has been growing careless in the absence of her
sovereign, for later in the day she failed somewhere and
earned a reprimand from him that sent her backing out of
the room as fast as she could progress in that fashion.

We had been curious as to how this round of 'ava would
be served. Tuimanua indicated Jack to the hesitating cup
bearer, and Jack was obliged to drink first, although he tried
to offer the calabash to the Queen. But Tuimanua's imperi-

ous drawing together of his black brows suggested that the best way was to comply with his wish. I came next to the head of my family, then Mr. Morrison, the King, his wife, and so on.

The formal audience shortly broke up, and Mr. Morrison took us to see Mr. Young and his daughter, who had just arrived in their schooner from Tutuila. The girl we found very sweet and modest, and her father exceedingly interesting, full of travel and experience. By marriage he is connected with the Manuan chief blood, and a few years ago during some lull in succession of rulers on Tau, he set his elder daughter on the high seat. She subsequently died, and her tomb, a modern one, is just outside the house. Tuimanua was next on the throne, and there is no love lost between him and the Youngs. However, neither mentioned the other to us; and when, upon our return to dinner, Mr. Morrison casually mentioned that he had taken us to call upon Rosa Young and her father, the intelligence was received by a well-bred inclination of the royal heads.

There is a vast difference in the way things are conducted since the Tui and Vaitupu returned. Law and order prevail in right regal fashion, and the women stand around promptly. Tuimanua's quick, roving eye detects the slightest remissness in table service—which he has learned in the navy circle at Tutuila—and he makes his corrections with a quiet unobtrusiveness that would bear emulation in many a paler menage.

After the noon meal, Vaitupu took us by the hands and led us into her and her husband's room, where we found a transformation had been wrought. The dismantled black and gilt four-poster was made up snowily, fresh mats laid on the floor, a reading-stand ready by the bed, bearing a good lamp, and upon the floor a heap of Samoan treasures, all for us—siapos, mats and fans; while from her own finger the Queen took three turtle-shell rings, inlaid with silver, and placed them on my fingers. Around my neck she hung a long thick necklace of beautiful diminutive land-shells. But the cream of the pile at our feet was a loose low-necked shirt, made for the use of the taupou on state occasions, plaited of sennit so fine that the woof is like soft cloth, or doeskin. This is a valuable souvenir, being an old specimen, finer than any of the work done in this day. It is trimmed about the neck with a sort of fringe of white bark-fibre, fine and smooth as silk ribbon, and interspersed with small fluffy red feathers of a rare bird. I could not express my delight, and Jack looked positively bashful. It really is embarrassing to have heaped upon one such redundant piles of presents. Perhaps we shall get used to the marvel of Samoan commonplace—although customs may be different beyond Samoa, and the novelty remain untarnished after all.

An elaborate siva-siva, combined singing and sitting-dancing, was rendered outside after supper, and later, as we sat fanning in the twilight, Jack and Mr. Morrison swapping yarns, and Vaitupu caressing my hands in her large, affectionate way, Tuimanua arose and went in. In a few moments a girl came with a message to Mr. Morrison, which was translated as a request that we step inside for evening devotions. We found the King seated at the large table, his head on his hand. There was something pathetic about him, for Tuimanua has a bad illness of the stomach, for which he has been to the hospital at Tutuila. We are told that he thinks he has an *aitu* pursuing him—a malign spirit bent upon his undoing; and from the way he looks about him at times, it is probable that the devil will get him, if fear will kill. This evil presence, like the *kahuna* of old Hawaii, is a dogger of men's footsteps in Samoa, and even Tuimanua, who is more intelligent and enlightened than any of the remaining chiefs, does not escape the stunting, damning superstition, despite his strict devotion to the Christian faith. It is even said he hesitated a year or two before he would accept the chiefdom of Manua, waiting for the people to give up certain barbarous customs. But it is no use. His *aitu* is stronger than his faith.

Viega offered up a long prayer in his musical voice and

language, at the end of which all joined in repeating the Lord's Prayer in the native tongue. It was a picture to remember—the stricken quasi king bowed upon his hands, the nephew of mighty sinew praying like a trusting child, the sumptuous women filling their inadequate chairs in overflowing lines of ease, and, off in a corner, sitting on our now new 'ava calabashes, a cluster of young beauties, gorgeous in colours of cloth and flowers—and a bit inclined to giggle and whisper.

A hymn ensued, and then the Tui indicated to Mr. Morrison that he would be pleased if Jack would tell him the latest news from America—say concerning the elections, and any other matters to do with the Government. In speaking, the King addresses the person to whom he wishes his speech interpreted, quite as naturally as if he expected to be understood. Jack glanced up at a portrait of Teddy Roosevelt adorning the key-beam of an arch, and racked his brain for items to interest the royal interlocutor. When he had finished, Tuimanua went on to state some of his pet plans for Manua, one hope being that the Government might some day send a man to the school who would know *law,* so that the youth of Samoa would be able to learn the newly imposed American laws, and clearly explain those laws to their elders.

And so ended our second May Day since the voyage of the *Snark* began.

Aboard the *Snark,*
Manua to Tutuila,
Saturday, May 2, 1908.

There they go, the grave King, the motherly Queen, Viega and his gorgeous wife, all singing, they and the brown oarsmen:

"I nev-ver will for-ge-ett you!"

—the "Farewell to Admiral Kimberly" that has become farewell to every one in Samoa. Three times they have circled us in the long whaleboat, singing and waving, and now they grow smaller and dimmer as the boat surges with sweeping strokes toward the familiar beach. A few little out-rigger canoes, shell-decorated, float idly about, and Young's schooner dips her flag as we get under way and pass slowly in the light air toward a fair breeze that we see wrinkling the ocean out from under the land.

We did not want to go so soon, but time and the season are pressing. The only reason for pressure of time is that there are hurricane seasons farther on which cautious Jack wishes to avoid. You see, the voyage of the *Snark* is not so foolhardy as it might look. So it's anchor up and away, our light barque freighted with bales of curious merchandise. Which pleasant burthen goes free into the United States, from our own harbour in Tutuila.

Such a busy morning! There was nothing on the yacht fitting for gifts to those who had served us so sweetly; but the store came in handy, and Mr. Morrison, knowing the tastes of every woman in the place, helped us select. The younger maids were gladdened by wool and silk shawls of dainty shades; Lepepa had a new ofu of a coveted print, and some excellent German umbrellas came to light that were just what Vaitupu and Sialafua wanted. Soa had a present too; and I was obliged to send a special messenger for Liuga, who was still under the ban of Tuimanua's displeasure.

. . . And then it was "Tofa—tofa soi fua!" all round— words that bear all the lovable significance of the Hawaiian "Aloha nui!"—with handclasps and cheek-pressures. Tuimanua and Vaitupu, with Viega and his wife and Mr. Morrison, accompanied us out to the yacht, where the two ladies promptly fell sea-sick while inspecting my tiny quarters. Only one at a time could squeeze in, for my cabin door was blocked by the aforesaid bales of merchandise, and our guests had to compress themselves to the dimensions of the narrow mirrored door between Jack's room and mine. I did not think Sialafua could do it; but she did, although piecemeal— literally lifting herself through in sections, the while shaking

with mirth. It was Viega who failed. His mighty chest
stuck fast midway, and he surveyed my inadequate dormitory
from that breathless vantage.

. . . Tau village is now all a blur of palms brushing the
feet of the massive mountains cowled in cloud, and Olosenga
looms near, little-big Olosenga that lifts its minarets 1500
feet from but a mile-long base washed with a spouting on-
slaught of breakers. Beyond is Ofu Island (Petticoat
Island?), misty-green with distance, and trembling in the
westering sunlight. There is nothing like it in all the world
—the ever fresh delight of flushing green isles in the deep
sea.

We have caught fair wind, and the *Snark* is sailing
well. To-morrow will see her resting in another strange
port. It is bewildering, this flitting from place to place. I
am already confusing the memories of Raiatea and Tahaa,
Moorea and Bora-Bora and Manua; and if that be true, what
will it be like when Tutuila, Upolu, Savaii, and the Fijis are
left behind? But it is a joyous jumble of sensations, and
already we are thinking still farther overseas, glimpsing
fearsome night-sailings past the shores of the head-hunting
Solomons; perilous navigating in the reef-netted currents of
Torres Straits, visiting Thursday Island by the way to see
the pearling, and, who knows? to fulfil Jack's promise of a
lapful! And there are Summatra's pearls also; to say nothing of her tigers and tapirs, crocodiles, and great elephants,
with vegetation in proportion, flowers of three-foot diameter,
and leaves to match. And oh, Java—Java with its unim-
agined lures—its peacocks and flying foxes, five-foot bats;
and terrible tigers, black tigers from out of nightmare forests of indestructible teak. And who whispered dragons—
real dragons—or are they only flying lizards? Java has
her flora, too, blossoms weighing eighteen pounds, they
say; and bazaars—think of the India stuffs, and silks, and
goldsmiths who will make curious settings for one's pearls
and cat-eyes and opals caught along the way!

. . . I can see there is to be no sleep on deck to-night in

this big swell, with threatening showers, so I am going below and turn in under the friendly funnel of my ventilator.

Pago Pago Harbor, Tutuila, American Samoa,
Sunday, May 3, 1908.

We are not quite so happy this morning as we should be
in so lovely a haven. Jack sits on a campstool over against
the side of the teak companionway, with a shadowed countenance, and he is not even reading—which phenomenon indicates that he is much preoccupied. Captain Warren, with
all hands and the cook, is sweating exhaustedly for'ard, taking in anchor chain for the third time within two hours.
And it was all unnecessary. We are a grinning spectacle
to the nautical shore, from the Governor in his high mansion
down to the least bluejacket on the beach; and it had to
happen in our own naval station, of all places.

. . . After keeping off until daylight, we entered Pago
Pago Harbor under sail, right in the middle of the channel,
and around the bend of the splendid landlocked port. Indeed, so safe and sheltered is it that we needs must round
the bend before ever we could see the tall masts of the
familiar *Annapolis*, lying at the wharf. We were surely a
fair vision, sweeping in with all sail set, and were abreast of
the gunboat, when we heard her boatswain's whistle and the
order given to "lower the whaleboat." On the instant, Captain Warren let go anchor. He seemed to lose his vain head
over the fact that some one was coming out to us from a
cruiser. Jack had already suggested where he thought we
ought to lie, close in to a buoy, astern of the big ship; but
Captain Warren, as I say, lost his head. It did not improve
his temper when the port doctor came alongside, instead of
the elegant uniformed officers whom he had met in Papeete;
and so crusty was he, that the Doctor grew excusably cool
to the *Snark* crowd generally, and remarked drily as he re-
entered his boat, that we could not have selected a worse
anchorage. A few minutes later, Jack noticed that we were
dragging rapidly down upon an old hulk of a schooner

anchored in the middle of the bay, and Martin was ordered to the engine, while the rest of the men laboriously hauled up our skating anchor. When the hook was out, we moved over toward the buoy Jack had indicated, and which, by the way, the Doctor had volunteered was the best place for us. On the way, the anchor chain, carelessly left with a single turn on the bitts, got away and we were fast again. The boys went at it once more, straining and panting in the heat, for it is arduous work to haul in fathom upon fathom of heavy chain-cable twice in an hour. And all the time the Sabbath-lazy bluejackets lounged ashore listening to a big phonograph and amusedly watching the elephantine manœuvres of a small mismanaged American yacht trying to pick up her moorings.

At last, with great expenditure of gasoline, the captain decided he was where he wanted to be (although Jack warned him we were too close to a coral-rock jetty that ran out from the reef), and down went the anchor. Shortly after, two officers walked out on a wooden pier near by and called to us that the Governor had sent word that we were too close in for safety, and we might carry a line to the Government buoy. So the weary crew set to again at pulling up the chain, and before we had gained the desired position, the anchor got away from them again. And here we are, disgusted, and keenly disappointed with our messy arrival in Pago Pago, after our bright beginnings. Jack said gloomily: "I really think, when all's said and done, I've got more sailor-pride than all the rest of them put together—even if I don't talk about it; and just look at the spectacle we've made of ourselves this morning!" I feel so sorry for him; he spares nothing in order to have things as they should be, and seldom gets what he pays for. And the one and only thing in the world in which he fights for style, is his boat.

. . . These young Tutuilans are a nuisance. They are clambering up our sides in swarms, and we have to order them off for we haven't room to turn around; and they are too sophisticated to be especially interesting. They are perky and impudent—but when Jack pretended that he was going to throw one small urchin overboard, the boy began to blubber. I was much amused a few moments ago when a canoe paddled out, and a pair of exceedingly pretty half-caste girls climbed over the stern rail. When they saw a white woman aboard, their coquettish quest was abandoned with comical alacrity, and they faded away over the stern, returning my smile and wave rather dubiously. A big Samoan came off to us and asked for laundry, presenting a letter from some American officer recommending him to the effect that he had done several washings for him, and that he probably did them as well as any other laundryman. We managed to keep our faces straight, appeared duly impressed, and referred him to the crew.

This harbour is a prize for the American Navy, quite hurricane proof—shut in as it is by mountains. The highest, Matafaa, rises 2357 feet. On the starboard side, entering, a mighty bluff called Tower Rock juts up into the sky. It bears the picturesque local name of The Rainmaker, for whenever clouds are seen about its summit, rain is sure to be brewing. To all appearances we are in a mountain-girt lake.

The red-roofed dwellings of the officers are very pretty, and the Governor's House, set high on a little ridge that projects into the bay, carries out the same colour scheme.

The *Annapolis*, we learn, is leaving on Tuesday for Fiji, to bring back Governor Parker, to replace Governor Moore who is bound home.

Monday, May 4, 1908.

My! but it is good to be in a white-man's house again—to have two big breezy rooms, bathe in a real bathroom in hot running water and cold shower, and to sleep in a bed the rolling and pitching of which exists only in the mind. Even my typewriter sits tight, showing no inclination to fall into my lap nor tilt backward; nor does it exchange capitals for lower case in the mad style it affects at sea.

We climbed the breathless hillock yesterday to call on
Governor Moore, and that gentleman repeated his invitation given in Papeete, to make ourselves at home in the house
as long as we please, whether he is here or not. We at once
moved into the delightful suite allotted, Nakata playing valet
with marked success. The young officers and their wives
dropped in during the evening, and we renewed our Papeete
acquaintance; while the Governor regaled us with witty
stories. His most interesting anecdotes, to us, are those connected with his administration in Tutuila, where he has made
himself respected and admired as well as loved by the people
of our corner of Samoa, barring a few rebellious souls. The
latter seem to be of the sort that kicks against the pricks of
government, and they are not to be found among the pure
native element. One man with whom there has been serious
disagreement, is, as the Governor puts it, "So crooked he
can't hide behind a corkscrew"—which must be pretty
crooked.

In general the inhabitants of American Samoa are fairly
content. As in the case of Tuimanua, who is practically
Governor of Manus 'Uma, or "All Manua," other chiefs
have been made governors of the various districts on Tutuila.
Thus, a chief named Mauga is governor of the Eastern District, and the Governor of the Western District is a half-
white, Fauvae—both, of course, answerable to Governor
Moore. Even Tuimanua has a little colony of Manuans over
across the bay. The *fita-fita*, or policemen, are all native,
usually of high rank, and appointed by the chiefs. They
must be big and physically fit in every way. Governor
Moore's stunning steam-launch crew that we saw in Tahiti,
is a good sample of the fita-fitas we see here.

. . . This forenoon I accounted for some of my lost hours
by bringing Jack's typing up to date, namely a new Klon-
dike story, just finished—"Lost Face." Then came an invitation from Mr. Groves, a socialist who came aboard the
Snark yesterday, to attend a birthday feast across the water.
We accepted, and went aboard the yacht at four, to see about

packing our Manuan curios for shipment. Mr. Groves sent a Samoan to the *Snark*, who rowed us in a chubby little bobbed-off boat across the sunset flood and over the reef that hugs the shore. On landing we were met by Mr. Groves' pretty half-caste wife and a little son who looked as if he had stepped right out of a Sir Joshua Reynolds canvas.

We ascended a short rocky trail to a cottage perched on the hillside, and found great preparation going on for the feast, even Mrs. Groves' ancient sire taking part with zest. Mrs. Groves' attitude concerning him in relation to us was beautifully tactful. There was no embarrassment in her regard of the withered old savage, tattooed and naked but for a scant cloth; but she was half-apologetic for his appearance, with the explanatory but prideful manner in which she might have accounted for some custom of her country strange to us. I must say few of us can lay claim to a finer looking parent than hers; and the daughter has the same clear-cut features.

A bright-faced girl came out on the little porch and made 'ava in a fascinating fourteen-legged bowl, and it was the best we have tasted—a trifle stronger than the Manuan brew. By this time, Dr. Rossiter (in a much more genial mood than the official one in which he boarded the disgraceful *Snark* yesterday), arrived with his wife, and we were all bedecked with wreaths of flowers and vines before climbing farther up the steep to the feast. It was spread on a terraced level strip of hill, and some fifty guests squatted around. I was called upon to cut the birthday cake, a towering achievement of white frosting and pink decorations that taxed my imagination and skill to the uttermost; but I did manage to separate it into over fifty pieces, much to the delight of hostess and feasters. Mrs. Rossiter was appointed to struggle with a cake into which were baked numberless American nickels, while the rest of us offered suggestions and criticisms and generally superintended her.

Aside from the cakes and ice-cream, it was the usual native spread, with fish baked in *ti* leaves, as in Hawaii. The cocoanuts here are nearly as fine as the Marquesan.

The board was deserted early by most of the guests, who were anxious to avail themselves of the privilege of carrying home what they could not eat. Even the native houseboys of the Americans were smuggling away the lion's share of their portions.

Hanging on the almost perpendicular mountainside, a green precipice frowning above us, we had a wondrous view of the twilight lake below—for lake it looked to be, the opposite shore glowing softly with home-lights, and a bugle from the *Annapolis* floating liquidly on the purple air. After the feast we were entertained with a siva-siva in a large native house, where three young maidens, girdled in skirts of leaves and feathers and tapa strips, gave pantomimic dances, somewhat on the principle of the Geisha. Children joined in, moving their little feet and hands in dainty and graceful rhythm. No civilised dancing of small folk is so unaffectedly simple and beautiful as the siva-siva of Samoa. These babes imbibe grace with their mothers' milk, and are practically untaught, strictly speaking. They learn dancing along with walking and talking.

It was "Tofa sui fua" at an early hour, and we rowed back across the ripples of the bay to the eternal singing of the boatmen. I believe these dark boys cannot row without singing. It is said that the canoe-songs of the Samoans are old as the race, but while some of the quaint chants survive, most of these we hear are of modern conception, tinged with the hymn element. The "Farewell to Admiral Kimberly" cropped up again this evening as a matter of course, albeit the occasion was not one of parting. There seems less attempt at part-singing than with the Society Islanders. The Samoans mostly sing in unison, only occasionally dropping into harmonious intervals.

All about us rose the straight black walls of the mountains, as we skimmed over the water, and overhead a tinsel moon and electric stars wheeled among dense pillowy white clouds. It was as spectacular as the doldrum skies, which transcend all rational, sober naturalness.

Upon landing, we went in for a few minutes to see the tiny quarters of the Rossiters, and learned anew what an American girl can do with some yards of flowered chintz and muslin, a few cushions, a picture or so, scraps of cardboard and coloured paper in the matter of lampshades, and an oil stove and chafing dish. The Rossiters arrived in Pago Pago after all the quarters had been assigned, but it did not take the bright "Yankee" girl long to create out of nothing a small and select paradise for two.

Tuesday, May 5, 1908.

Governor Moore bade us good-bye this morning, on his way to Fiji to meet his successor, leaving us in the care of Paymaster Hilton and Pay Clerk Shute. The latter comes from Searsport, and knows my people. It does seem to me that persons from Maine, or connected with Maine, can find more things to talk about than those from any other State in the Union. This is likely to be widely contradicted, I know!

The Rainmaker was busy all morning, and this high house shook with broadsides of wind. So loudly did rain and wind vociferate that we, at work, listening for the whistle of the departing *Annapolis*, heard nothing of it, and she passed out of ken before we knew.

Mrs. Frazier, the Navy Chaplain's wife, sent word for us to go around the bay with her in the afternoon, Jack on horseback, and I in the donkey cart with her. It seemed odd to be talking over a telephone in such surroundings meanwhile looking out over the beautiful green-bound bay. Why, last night, playing Seeling's *Lorelei* for Governor Moore (his wife had written him to ask for it when we should come to Tutuila), I saw through the window the rippling Rhine, while a jutting promontory personified the German Lorelei to a nicety. Such pictures may a casement frame!

But to come down to earth—I had a virulent attack of prickly heat to-day, and in desperation tried the first thing

Lava-choked Graves

Lava Pouring into the Sea, Savaii

that came into my head, which happened to be a thorough lathering of Castile soap, allowed to remain on half an hour. Then a brisk cold shower, and the cure was complete.

Mrs. Frazier drove through the naval settlement and beyond along a road so narrow that only this one vehicle, made to order for the purpose, can travel at all. One other person in Pago Pago has a cart, but forgot to measure the highway before sending for it. It languishes unused in a shed of sugar-cane thatch.

The shore and the feet of the steep hills are dotted with little hamlets of Samoan falés. They are not quite so fine as the Manua houses, but then, Manua was not so long ago the centre of Samoa 'Uma, whence issued the governmental edicts for the entire group. As we jogged through the quiet little villages, resting so peacefully under Uncle Sam's jurisdiction, I recalled something I had read about alert and bloody years when the Fijians came over and conquered the Samoans, driving them from their sea coast homes back into the rugged interior, where they perforce became mountaineers. To this day can be seen the remains of great roads that the transplanted beach-lovers constructed in the troublous past.

In Mauga's village his wife, Faapia, stepped out of her well ordered falé and was introduced to me—a pretty woman, fair for her race, although of pure breed. The aristocracy once more. On our return in the dusk, she spied us and came out again, hands full of tasteful nosegays, which she pinned on our bosoms and set over our left ears, and in our hair.

I saw the handsomest islander—I might almost say the handsomest man I have ever seen. The graceful Adonis of Hooumi pales before this Apollo of Polynesia. Covered only with a red loin cloth, he paced majestically along, as if happy in princely superiority of manhood, his severe straight-featured countenance breaking into the most genial of smiles in eyes and mouth when he answered Mrs. Frazier's pleasant "Talofa." His hair, in sharp-cut contours, was plastered white, and he walked head and shoulders above his fellows.

Mrs. Frazier is very popular along the waterside, and I am sure we said "Talofa—tofa, soi fua," a million times more or less, and heard the words as many times again. We talked of Tuimanua, whom Mrs. Frazier has entertained in her home many an afternoon. And she says he comprehends English very well, although he refuses to speak it. Evidently we did not irk His Majesty, for he sent a letter by us to the Governor in which he said we had been "Very good" and that he had been pleased with us. We are indeed pleased, for we lack words to describe our admiration for so great a man among his kind. Our hope is that the kingly Manuan may die before he ever fully realises how little of a sovereign he is in actuality. It is no pleasure to break a heart and spirit like his—which is a wholly gratuitous and ridiculous observation, because spirits like Tuimanua's cannot be broken.

Aboard the Snark,
At sea, Tutuila to Upolu,
Wednesday, May 6, 1908.

Sit with me here and run your glance along the "iron-bound" leagues of Tutuila's coast, where snow-white surf breaks against the inky lava of forgotten volcanoes, or forces under and out through the crevices of spouting columns. Then follow up along the twilit foothills to where the sinking sun pours streams of gold down guttered mountains, and the clouds and mists of evening swirl and stir the colours into a riot of brilliant green and gold. Then gaze close into the jewelled waves that break and foam against our white boat, and say if it is not a beautiful, beautiful world of shimmering land and flowing water and lambent air. . . .

. . . They watched us out of sight, the wholesome, clean, hearty young pairs of the Navy, first coming aboard to wish godspeed and to inspect the wonderful small boat that had borne us so far. They brought us presents, too—Samoan baskets, and precious eggs; while on the wharf stood our Manuan burdens, boxed and labelled for California.

We took away a new sailor, one Henry, a Rapa Islander (Society Group) who came aboard the first day in Tutuila and helped Tehei manfully, having him ashore in the evening and making that homesick Brown Brother much happier. Henry seems to be an able man, and when he applied for a berth, Jack decided to accept him, for we must rid ourselves of poor Ernest, whose uselessness, and penchant for ordering others around, together with his unfortunate malady, make him most undesirable. We could not lose him at Pago Pago, for he could not pass the Port Doctor. And as there was no vessel there upon which he might have shipped, we can only hope for better luck at Apia. Captain Warren, knowing that we do not want to keep the boy, sharpens his wits on the poor fellow to the tune of a sort of sarcasm that completely robs Ernest of any little sense he has.

Henry speaks half a dozen languages, and is a quick, smart man, about thirty, partially bald, with a wry smile belied by the good natured expression of a pair of sharp eyes that seem to miss nothing. He has been around the world several times, owns to a slight streak of French blood, and was fourteen years at school in Paris.

I do not know what ails Captain Warren, he has grown so careless. We had hardly cleared the passage this afternoon, going out, when zip! went the anchor chain again, and we were bucking against the sea, weighted with the heavy hook. Many things that should have been done in port have been left undone, and we are none too happy over the way things are going. It is a terrible thing to see a man in his position, with the chance of his life to make good, letting the chance slip.

. . . Robert Louis Stevenson's words often come to me when I consider the superfluity of men on this small boat:

"The world is too much with me." There are nine of us, and that is all of two too many in a space 56 feet long, by 15 feet at the widest.

. . . The 'longshore lights are blossoming, one by one, and a young moon is rising in the east. I hear the inviting whir of an electric fan below, and am going to climb into my dainty, clean, comfy bunk and read.

"Goo' ni'!" purrs Tehei from the wheel, and Good Night it is, with Good Morning to come, in sight of Upolu and the smoke of Savaii's unresting volcano.

International Hotel,
Apia, Upolu, German Samoa,
Friday, May 8, 1908.

Such a sleep, and such a rejuvenated sailorwoman this morning! We have just come back to our rooms in the hotel, after calling upon Mr. H. J. Moors in his home over one of his many stores on the island. We wasted no time getting on the subject of Stevenson, and so absorbing was it to hear of that beloved man from the lips of one who knew him intimately, that Jack came near forfeiting his day's work.

. . . At seven yesterday morning we were twenty-five miles off Upolu, but the wind dropped and we did not come to anchor in Apia Harbor until sunset. In the late afternoon, sailing for miles along the barrier reef that frills a green lagoon surrounding the land like a moat, we found the island very lovely—reminding us of Raiatea in its general aspect. There must have been heavy rains, for we saw numerous high waterfalls leaping sheer green walls on the mountainsides.

As the *Snark* slid along, we began to exclaim at the magnificent condition of this German province—the leagues of copra plantation, extending from the shore up into the mountainous hinterland, thousands of close-crowded acres of heavy green palms. There was an orderly prosperity about the country that spoke well for German management. The sunset was a vast miracle of gorgeous suffusing colour, softened by drifting smoke from the volcano on Savaii. We had been watching all afternoon the white slanting column of steam from lava running hot into the sea. Back of Apia, upon a green ridge of Vééa Mountain, the German pilot told us lay Stevenson's tomb.

Under the jolly pilot's direction, Captain Warren's unaccountable resentment of which he did not try to conceal, we made anchorage without aid from the engine. Immediately we were beset by native wash-men, bringing their soiled letters of recommendation. The pilot had but just left, and Jack and I had got into our shoregoing ducks, when a newspaperman came aboard for an interview. He looked upon Jack with adoring eyes from the moment they came together, and has made good this love-at-first-sight by offering us the use of his two race horses—his idols, The Fop and Emélé. He did not urge them upon us when we asked if we could get good horses ashore; but when he found we cared enough for horses to lug our own saddles over the world and back, The Fop and Emélé were ours—only, he suggested that Jack would better ride Emélé. His name is Charles Roberts, an Englishman, who, with his wife, keeps a small inn. He said his house would not be comfortable for us, or he would insist upon our staying there. We packed a grip and went ashore with him, where we inspected his saddles and bridles, hanging at one end of the dim bar-room, and met "The Missis." Every matron here is "the Missis," and I have become "the Missis" also. But then, Nakata has always called me "Missis," probably so coached by Wada.

We put up at the highly recommended International, where we can see the *Snark's* saucy flag in the distance—through the ribbed wreck of the old *Adler,* lying where she went ashore in 1889's hurricane. Meals are served in an open second-story at the back of the house, whence we can look out across the reef to the sea. Mr. Easthope, sitting at one end of his long table, resembles no one so much as the merry Falstaff—a handsome, florid soul with smart white moustaches and imperial, who loses and finds his h's in true

Cheapside fashion. It is whispered that of old he was a pirate and a blackbirder. If this be true, all I can say is that he must have done his deeds with picturesque dash and style, and that he has reformed most gracefully, for never did mine host look or act better the part, with his true wife at his elbow, and his beautiful half-caste daughter never far off. When guests order drinks, his invariable "Whisky for mine," never comes amiss. One can easily understand, after a look at his jovial countenance, how men must be willing to pay for unnumbered drinks for him, just for the privilege of hearing him order them.

. . . It was four o'clock when Mr. Roberts, in his light breeks and topboots, the picture of an English jockey, brought the horses. We were ready, and I was writing, when there came the clatter of hoofbeats in the yard. They sounded so ringing and cheery, those small iron feet of flight, that I cried out in delight and ran to our balcony to look down upon the saddled backs of two of the prettiest golden sorrels I ever want to see. I fell over several things when I flew back to Jack, who waited laughing and commented: "The kid!"

In a few minutes we were mounting, I on The Fop, whose knowing eye and staid ten years belied certain frolicsome traits I was to learn. Jack bestrode Emélé, in whose flaring nostril and white-cornered eye one may read who runs (if he can run fast enough) disaster for him who sits not close and well. Of course both beasts wanted to race, and we had our hands full.

Out of town, we cantered along ferny byways edged with sensitive plant that shrank away from our hoofs, its slanting shudder communicated throughout the green mantle like a nervous chill. The copra plantations looked in thriving condition, the palms, young and old, set in regular rows, acre upon acre, with sleek red and white cattle transmuting ferns and lush grasses into butter-fat. We worked around through a pale-pillared forest of palms and found ourselves on fine hard beach, where Apia's racing meets are held. The ride home was along the beach, when we didn't leave it to cut across arms of lagoons, our animals lifting their feet like kittens above the water. It was a delectable ride, and all-too-short. But the horses, for all their early friskiness, had had enough for one afternoon in such humid climate. They are the only horses we have seen that are clean of sores. If horses are not groomed carefully here, they contract a disease that eats their hides in spreading sores, which also attack the face, sometimes entirely destroying the eyes.

. . . After dinner, we went over and talked Stevenson again with Mr. Moors, and borrowed from his library, which is largely stocked with books brought from Mrs. Stevenson after her husband's death. Then his daughter, Rosa, and I discussed fans and mats and hats, and she filled my arms with a variety of Samoan fans when we departed, while Jack carried away the gift of a Talking Man's fly-brush made of white horsehair on a handle of ironwood. We were much interested in two chair-rugs they had, made from shredded bark and resembling long white goat-hair. The wrong side is merely a fine woven mat. The natives no longer make these rugs, but Mr. Moors thinks he may locate one that we can buy.

Apia, Upolu, Samoa,
Saturday, May 9, 1908.

Stevenson's Vailima, literally "Waters Five," named from the streams that once met on the place, lies about three miles of steady slope from Apia. We started in the early afternoon—although it seems "always afternoon" in this sunny land—Jack with Rosa Moors in a high black jaunting cart drawn by a stout black roadster, native groom behind with a parasol over their heads. I rode a brown mare that Rosa brought, as I am looking for all the exercise possible.

We fared happily along the lovely climbing road, shaded by tropic trees, bamboo, palm, fau, hibiscus, and a dozen more, with little to remind us of our tender quest until we turned into The Road of Loving Hearts, the Ala Loto Alofa of the Samoans, that leads from the main highway to the gates of Vailima. This road was made by the hands of natives of lofty caste, led and helped by the six liberated chiefs of Mataafa's following, who had been befriended by Stevenson during political difficulties with the foreign Powers that ended in the imprisonment of these chiefs. Stevenson's own words will best make clear the value of this gift of labour, and also give a glimpse of his sane sympathy with the Samoan nature:

"Now whether or not this impulse will last them through the road does not matter to me one hair. It is the fact that they have attempted it, that they have volunteered, and are now trying to execute, a thing that was never before heard of in Samoa. Think of it! It is road-making, the most fruitful cause, after taxes, of all rebellion in Samoa, a thing to which they could not be wiled with money, nor driven by punishment. It does give me a sense of having done something in Samoa after all."

This astounding memorial to the Man who Understood, should be marked by some abiding symbol, and England should look to it. For this Road of Loving Hearts, first called by its builders The Road of Gratitude, is a monument far more significant than any tomb of massive proportions. Now, even the board, made and lettered by the chiefs, that once pointed the way to Vailima, is gone. Stevenson—their Story Teller, their *Tusitala*, touched by the tribute, had already prepared a graving to immortalise his appreciation of what his brown brothers had done; but the brown brothers had other plans, and he was obliged to let them inscribe the sign-post with their own words, which, translated, read:

"Remembering the great kindness of His Highness Tusitala, and his loving care when we were imprisoned in sore distress, we have made for him an enduring gift, this road which we have dug to last forever. It shall never be muddy, it shall endure, this road that we have dug."

We are not the first world-wanderers in a small boat who have made the pilgrimage to Vailima. Our friend Captain Slocum touched at Apia in the *Spray,* during the residence of the widow, who presented the plucky old mariner with a handsome set of Sailing Directions of the Mediterranean from her husband's library. Alas, there are now no books nor other personal possessions of the author's left in the great house, which has been added to in order to meet the needs of the German Governor who owns it.

The caretaker was away, and we could not even go into the building, but Rosa took us where we could peep into the great hall. Stevenson had a terrible time planning that house. He would bring his projected sketches and elevations to Mr. Moors for certain disapproval, and that critic regularly convinced his friend that the schemes were unpractical and unsuited to the tropics and his needs. Finally, the homeless Scotsman returned from a voyage to Sydney, enthusiastic over the perfected drawings of an Australian architect who had caught the fine sense of his client's manorial dream. Mr. Moors gasped when the sheets were spread out before him. The dimensions were for a castle, or a great mansion at the least. Poor Robert Louis wilted under the gentle sarcasm of Moors, and came down tremendously on all the measurements except those of the main hall, which he would reduce but little. It was his pet hobby, that hall, and provided with a vast fireplace, to feed a proportionately vast chimney. "What on earth do you want that for?" demanded Moors. "You'll never be able to use it in this climate, and it will cost you a fortune to haul the bricks and stones and mortar up that hill, and to build it after you get them there."

Stevenson was crestfallen but obstinate. He could see the practical absurdity of the fireplace, but what was a living-hall without a fireplace? Besides, that was the way they did it in Scotland, and it made the room look like home. No one could argue against this, so the fireplace went in, and one cannot but be glad he realised his dear desire. He paid for it, and it was one of the few desires he did realise, for all his arduous pursuit of happiness. That Heart of Gold must have been heavy in his bosom, for he once wrote what is a sad admission for his lovers to read—"I was only happy once . . . it came to an end from a variety of reasons, decline of health, change of place, increase of money, age with his stealing steps; since then, as before then, I know not what it means. But I know pleasure still, pleasure with a thousand faces and none perfect, a thousand tongues all broken, a thousand hands and all of them with scratching nails. High among these I place this delight of weeding out here, alone by the garrulous water, under the silence of the high wood, broken by incongruous sounds of birds."

From the upper front veranda we pressed our faces against the window panes of Tusitala's bedroom, over the inner door of which jarred the portrait of the Kaiser. Then we gazed through the glass into the "Temple of Peace," the inner sanctuary where the master wove his spells. How will our own shelves of him look to us when we see them again! Straightway into the back of our eyes will come the vision of a small dismantled room overlooking the slope of Vééa Mountain and the shining sea sparkling through his garden trees.

As we looked around over the present formal garden with its disk of lawn bordered in brilliant box, and its gay-foliaged crotons and dracenas, there came to us the breath of the perfumed things of the land, papaia, frangipani, waxen gardenia, and even the scent of orange blossom. And we thought of how the place must have appeared to its old owner when he began to grapple with the wild for a space that would not choke his dwelling. But he enjoyed his combat with the growing earth. He was "aye a magerful man," was Stevenson, fighting for health in life, since he must live, striving to enjoy that life while it was imposed upon him, gaining upon his work against bitterest odds. His strife with nature was unique—he realised this when he said, in connection with his eternal weeding and other garden work:

"I wonder if any one ever had the same attitude to nature as I hold. This business fascinates me like a tune or a passion, yet all the while I thrill with a strong distaste . . . a superstitious horror of the void and the powers about me, the horror of my own devastation and continual murders. The life of the plants comes through my finger-tips, their struggles go to my heart like supplications, I feel myself blood boltered—then I look back on my cleared grass, and count myself an ally in a fair quarrel, and make stout my heart.''

One child of nature there was, however, that elicited from him no qualms of sympathy. This was the Sensitive Plant, whose pretty acacia-like foliage and lilac-pink pompons are nearly as great a pest in Samoa as is the lantana in Hawaii. It overspreads rock and roadside, height and hollow, and one can appreciate how Stevenson regarded his continuous encounter with the insidious creeper: ''A fool brought it to this island in a pot, and used to lecture and sentimentalize over the tender thing. The tender thing has now taken charge of this island, and men fight it, with torn hands, for bread and life.''

Almost one expects to see his half sad, half whimsical face at an upper window, or his slender back bent over the weeding of the grass. Then the utter silence of all things calls one to reality with a pain at the heart—''Alas! for Tusitala he sleeps in the forest.''

We took no guide farther than the beginning of the trail that rises on the other side of one of the Five Rivers. Rosa Moors wanted to send her native groom with us, as she did not care to make the climb; but we preferred to go alone.

Through the dense bush and forest of the mountain a broad swath has been cut straight up the uncompromising steep, the clearing laced back and forth with a tiny pathway, water-eroded, beset by rock and root and clinging creeper. We set our faces to the hidden goal and plunged up through the cool still gloom, treading blossoming things that resembled violet plants bearing snowdrops, and now and then stepping into a drift of pink petals blown from trees. As we clawed into the stiff ascent we began to be gently depressed with the spirit of the place. At intervals a dove mourned in the woods, and our thoughts turned to the stories we had heard of Tusitala's death—how he was stricken suddenly the very day he had been talking of death and of his desire to be buried on the mount, in the spot where the frail frame of him now lies. ''Why, the man died of too much health,'' Mr. Moors had declared; ''he hadn't been better for years, but his veins could not carry the good blood he had in him. Something went wrong, and a blood vessel burst in his brain.'' And when the natives heard what had happened, and it was verified to them, waiting without, that Tusitala, their Story Teller, indeed lay low in death, they set up a universal wailing that must sorely have tried the endurance of the mourners within.

''How did they do it?'' I panted as we struggled upward —''How did they ever carry him up this place? And what way was there to go—this swath has been cut since?''

Oh, the bereaved Samoans saw to it all, Jack told me—five hundred of them attacked the woods by night, when they heard the wish of their Beloved to be laid upon Vééa, and in the morning the path was ready and the pitiful spot cleared. And they bore Tusitala on their own chieftain shoulders, with lines carried up the mountain as well to help. One white man came into it all, too. It was found after the funeral that the place of burial was outside the confines of Vailima; whereupon the owner, Mr. Trude, promptly made over the piece of property as a gift to the family.

If ever you go to Stevenson's tomb, do not believe the soft-eyed native who tells you that two young palms mark the half of the climb. It seemed ages before we reached those trees, and we breathed ourselves for a fresh start on a tug as long as that we had already come. But it was not half of the half, and all at once, at a sharp turn around a large boulder, I was suddenly confronted with the grey gabled sarcophagus resting upon its broader foundation, and cried, startled, ''Oh, Mate—Mate!'' Then we went forward hand in hand, and tears were in our eyes to think of that little great man lying under the weight of woful stone. A fresh double scarlet hibiscus was upon the foundation slab, where it must lately have been laid by some furtive living mourner, after all the long years. The querulous pipe of a mellow-throated bird came from the thicket close by, as if resenting our disturbing the sacred solitude, and the rays of the low sun slanted through the rustling fau trees and across the grey tomb. On the western face of the gabled concrete are cast in Samoan the words of Ruth to Naomi, with a Scotch thistle and a hibiscus to right and left:

"Whither thou goest I will go, and where thou lodgest I will lodge; thy people shall be my people and thy God my God; where thou diest I will die, and there will I be buried."

On the opposite side we read the verse, with its great simplicity, that Stevenson wrote for his own grave:

"Under the wide and starry sky
Dig the grave and let me lie
Glad did I live and gladly die
And I lay me down with a will
This be the verse you grave for me
Here he lies where he longed to be
Home is the sailor home from the sea
And the hunter home from the hill."

We turned on the brink of the descent for a last look at the quiet stone drifted over by withered leaves, and then dropped to the trail, full of a peaceful melancholy. "Here he lies where all must come, after days grown wearisome," came to my lips; and Jack said in a subdued voice: "I wouldn't have gone out of my way to visit the grave of any other man in the world." It is not going out of one's way in Paris to see Napoleon's tomb, nor to find oneself leaning against Wellington's in St. Paul's. "But this, but this was you," Tusitala.

"Glad did I live and gladly die," wove into our spirits as we let ourselves down the trail, and when we crossed the river again on its narrow broad, we were glad enough over our own aliveness to yearn toward a deep pool under a spreading bamboo tree. But Rosa was calling from the sunset garden, and we hastened to where, on the green wheel of lawn, she sat amidst baskets of peeled oranges, mangoes, and loving-cups of cocoanut ready opened.

It is all over. We have seen Vailima's many porches where our Robert Louis broke breadfruit with his loved brown brothers in days gone by, oh, such a little while in our thought. One thinks of Vailima as with his living presence directing the life there; or, when he must rest, sleeping as he wished to sleep, with patient folded hands, upon the twilight mountain.

A few days before his passing, the Story Teller received this poem from Edmund Gosse:

> "Now the skies are pure above you, Tusitala,
> Feathered trees bow down before you,
> Perfumed winds from shining water
> Stir the sanguine-leaved hibiscus,
> That your kingdom's dusk-eyed daughters
> Weave about their shining tresses.
> Dew-fed guavas drop their viscous
> Honey at the sun's caresses,
> Where eternal summer blesses
> Your ethereal musky highlands.
>
> "You are circled, as by magic,
> In a surfy palm-built bubble, Tusitala.
> Fate hath chosen, but the choice is
> Half delectable, half tragic,
> For we hear you speak like Moses
> And we greet you back enchanted,
> But reply's no sooner granted
> Than the rifted cloud-land closes."

It would seem that all the gifts of circumstance surrounding his death were as poetic as he tried to make his life.

"Glad did I live"—"I have lived, and loved, and closed the door."

Sunday, May 10, 1908.

We have been picking up something of the history of our Tehei. A young woman we have met saw him in town, and they recognised each other, for it seems he was cook on the *Eimeo,* a schooner belonging to her cousin, Mr. Dexter, when that vessel was wrecked, *literally blown to pieces*, in the Paumotus during the 1906 hurricane that swept the Dangerous Archipelago and Tahiti. Tehei and another Tahitian were the sole survivors of the *Eimeo*. They managed to catch hold of a hatch-cover that had been torn loose by the wind, and for three days the two were in the water under the tropic sun, one in and one out alternately, for there was only room on the hatch for a single person to rest high and dry. In the end they sighted the low island of Tahanea, and by waving the rag of a shirt that was left between them, the attention of the natives was attracted, and they sent out a boat. And Tehei never has breathed a word about the adventure, not even to Henry, who could have translated.

Jack rose early this morning and had his work done before breakfast, for at nine Mr. Roberts and Dr. Davis, the dentist, were to come to take us on a ride through the cacao plantations. And lo! Mr. Roberts said Emélé was a little light for Jack's weight, and would I mind riding her? Would I!

We forded a river and struck into the hills where we rode through beautiful plantations, where pretty cacao trees grow amidst springing young papaias that flourish like weeds in Upolu, fruiting in such rank abundance that they are rated as food only for pigs and cattle. No self-respecting hotel keeper would dare place papaias—or pawpaws, or mummy-apples, as they are variously called—on his table. Pig-food indeed! Why, the lack of it and our fondness for it, gave us a distinct and somewhat discomfiting desire to be pigs.—Which we became, to the extent of begging pridelessly for papaia three times a day.

We passed small piled heaps of the cocoa in its crimson-pink shell, and it tastes not badly, even in its crude state. Five kinds of rubber trees are planted here, also. And oh! the woods of Upolu! They are so strange, so unreal, with the tortured trunks of the Malili trees that spread out toward the ground in board-like upright slabs all around, and the native banyans that grow very high before they reach out feelers toward earth. Umbrageous forest it is, on the one hand, so entirely overspread with leafy creepers that one can but think of painted stage scenery; and on the other hand, there are woods gladsome with hibiscus and papaia, fau and climbing palm and fern—until you are breathless at the contrast of grotesque Doréan glooms so near by.

Messrs. Harman and Radford entertained us for lunch on the Upola Company's Plantation, of which they are managers. They impressed us as weirdly unhealthy and spiritless, until we came to learn that only the week previous both had been beset, on different parts of the plantation, by vicious Chinese coolies who beat and jumped upon them, Mr. Radford having several ribs broken. "Gaw' f'damee," blustered Roberts, flicking a topboot violently with his crop to hide his emotions at sight of his battered friend. And Radford smiled as little wearily as possible in appreciation of the other's feeling, for it hurt him even to smile. Such a sad-faced man; and aside from his present condition, I knew he was homesick. "Just to walk along Piccadilly again," he sighed, half-smiling at his triteness, his well-bred thin face turned wistfully toward the open window; and once, when the rest were out inspecting the cocoa-dryer, we fell to quoting Kipling, and he became another man, and they found him laughing and talking volubly on their return. England's men—where does one not meet them! Here a younger son; there a cockney; now a "gentleman adventurer," and then a "gentleman ranker." But oh! the "Broken Men"—they are the saddest. However, not one of the men we met to-day would answer to any of these. Radford is an English gentleman, if ever there was one, and his house-mate, as gentle, is from Australia.

I found it very interesting, sitting with all these men at the lunch table set on a second-story porch and served by a Chinese boy, listening to their stories, which were largely about horses—while our own horses rolled and fed on the grass below. The ride back to Apia was by another way, lying through more wonderful woods high-trailing their mantles of creepers, and underfoot grassy, fern-brushed paths. We ended with a good gallop into town, more than ever grateful for the boon of fine horses to ride.

Monday, May 11, 1908.

There are some odd types here in the hotel, from good Mr. Falstaff down to the funny slim Chinaman, Ah Chong, who slants around the room in stiff little bumps when any one asks, ''Dance, Ah Chong, dance for me.'' There's an ex-sea-captain from New England, who is teased a great deal. He is only eighty-five or so, and has a new wife and a two-months girl baby. The old man was at about the end of his patience with badgering one day at dinner, when I asked him, in a most respectful tone, particularly why he lived in Samoa. ''To raise children,'' he growled back; and I subsided, well informed. But he is proud to talk about his fine, modern home and his family. ''My children speak four or five languages, when they get ready; but they don't always get ready,'' he boasted with inflated chest; ''—though I don't know as it's anybody's business,'' he finished lamely, with a malevolent glare from under his beetling eyebrows, remembering that he was still put out over the badgering, and also that a New Englander just must be contrary. But he is a most kindly soul, beneath the husky shell of him.

Then there is the stony-eyed, pink-skinned, brassy young Colonial whose papa is a wealthy canner in New Zealand, everybody knows, because the son has said so. He walked up to Jack the first time he saw him, asked rudely whence he came and whither bound, from what ship he had come ashore. And, learning at the table that Jack was off the *Snark,* he has since spent his leisure moments gazing fixedly over a cuff-high collar, plainly wondering how that soft-shirted, curly-headed boy came into possession of a name and a yacht anyway. He means well—every one means well; but birth and nature are terribly against letting it show.

Mr. and Mrs. Chappere, from Auckland, are delightful,
and I follow the making of their accent with my eyes and
unconsciously moving lips. Of course, I am quite aware
that they probably regard my Americanese as just as remarkable. Last night, after dinner at the Roberts', we
came home and went swimming with the Chapperes off a
little boat-pier at the hotel. He is travelling for a biscuit
company and knows something about other commodities than
crackers—jewels for instance. We began discussing Australian opals, and he brought out a little hemisphere of fire
and dew that made us catch our breaths at the living colour.
Jack was so interested in the opal that Mr. Chappere presented me with it. I thought I saw his wife check a falling face; so I produced my little handful of bright Paumotan pearls (added to in Tahiti), easily discovered, without
asking, which they both liked best, and so managed to even
the obligation. Every little while I take out my box in
which the drop of blue and rose flame trembles in the moonlight of the pearls.

Jack has picked up some green cat-eyes, and some grey
ones, and I am looking forward to combining them in bizarre
settings when we reach Batavia and the goldsmiths. Compare this adventuresome collecting of trinkets with buying
in the conventional fashion!

Curios are high in Apia, naturally, it being on the "tourist route," the basket and tapa and mat makers catering
to the steamer trade. The Samoan fans are very good, much
heavier, firmer and more useful than the flimsy Tahitian
bamboo ones. There is a great variety, and we are told that
we shall do well on Savaii, where the natives are practically
unspoiled by visitors.

Tuesday, May 12, 1908.

Yesterday we took the ocean drive that leads past the memorial monuments of the heroes of 1899; and we also came
upon the remains of the last of old Samoan war canoes, protected under a long shed. It is a double-canoe, the boats of

slightly different size and build, and must have been an imposing sight in action in the days when it was decorated and manned. Now it is too far gone to allow of launching even for exhibition.

The American Vice Consul, Mr. Parkhouse, had invited us to dine at the Roberts Hotel, to meet the Acting Governor, Dr. Erich Schultz. We also found Mr. Moors there when we arrived, and several others, among them Mr. Miller, editor of the Apia paper, and Dr. Davis and his beautiful Tongan bride. The main intellectual excitement of the extremely good dinner was the trying to convert Mr. Moors from his unguardedly expressed opinion that Kipling's poetry is "jingle." He soon found what a warm nest he was in. Roberts rushed from the room, cursing volubly, returning breathless and gesticulatory with a volume from which, with tears in his eyes, he declaimed "The Broken Men." "Jingle, is it!" he panted, nervously running over the thumbed pages for "Gentleman Rankers." "Listen to this: 'For things we never mention' "—and he went on, his heart in his voice, fanning the air with his free hand in a professional manner that made us wonder if the stage had claimed him at some period in his varied career. Jack read several of his favourites, and I tried out Mr. Moors with the "L'Envoi" commencing, "There's a whisper down the field." The worthy Moors laughed his unembarrassed and spontaneous laugh, and said with twinkling eyes, "Oh, it's all very well, I know. Tell you the truth, I haven't read much Kipling—and I'm willing to admit that all this isn't jingle. But perhaps I don't care for poetry, for all this stuff you've read doesn't affect me in the least." (Here a snort from Roberts, who was standing before a large print of "The Drums of the Fore and Aft," glowingly reading me the text.)

And then the Kipling discussion languished, and Dr. Schultz, on my right, got the folk interested in questions of Samoa. By ten, much in need of sleep, I slipped out, and was driven back to the hotel in Mr. Parkhouse's trap. It was a brilliant moonlight night, with a soft warm breeze, and I wondered where I was, speeding along this strange water-front with a savage coachman, my little boat-home rocking in the harbour, not far from the romantic old wreck, and, to the west, the intermittent glow from a great volcano painting the moonlight lilac of the sky.

And all this day the flags have been at half-mast, on land and water, for the little daughter of a local photographer, who died last night very suddenly of ptomaine poisoning. Mr. Easthope's daugher is going about with wet eyes, and there were tears in Rosa Moors' voice when she talked to me over the telephone about the trip to Papase'ea this afternoon, saying she must return in time for the funeral. This accident will make us more than ever careful on the *Snark*, and more than ever strict with the galley as to serving any stale food. It was tinned salmon that caused the death of this child.

On The Fop and Emélé we started at eleven, Rosa in her cart carrying lunch, and accompanied by her groom, a native maid, and Miss Caruthers, daughter of Stevenson's old friend. It was beautiful country we clawed through, which finally became so steep that we left the horses and went on foot to the famous Sliding Rock. We had to let ourselves down a long bank to get to it, and at the bottom stood beside a mountain stream, just above us a broad waterfall only a few feet in height, and below us the flowing thirty-foot precipice over which we were invited to launch our precious persons, feet first. I was very brave until my bathing-suit was on and the fateful letting-go moment approached, when I found all kinds of excuses for delays; but after watching the groom and the maid go down, followed by Miss Caruthers, all sitting upright with their hands on the rock beside them, I took my place with the bunch and looked at Jack sliding to his disappearance in the dark deep pool. He swam out laughing and shaking his head, and sat on a warm rock a long time jeering at me to screw my courage.

I promised Rosa I would follow her. She admitted that although she had shot the fall hundreds of times, she always dreaded it. This cheered me up, and I waxed boastful over my own swimming-tank exploits of slides and 22-foot jumps, long dives and backward dives—until Rosa went down, and I was obliged to make good. I took one look at Jack's odd expression, half of incredulous fear that I might fail him, and wiggled to the descent. It was successful, despite a bad sidewise start. The natives were much amused because I put cotton in my nostrils and ears. But I had noticed the backward jerk of Jack's head when he struck the pool, and knew his tubes were stinging from the rush of water; and I have not forgotten the month I once lay on my back, as a result of high jumps with unprotected ears and nostrils. Well, I did it! I did it! And they say there's only one other place in the world where I could do it, and that is on the Malay Peninsula, where we have no expectation of going.

Before leaving the pool we girls washed our hair, rubbing lemons into it, even the rind. The Samoan girls do this for its softening effect and also for the delicate perfume. The hair must be dried as quickly as possible, however, in order that the scent may not be in the least musty. One has to work with speed in the tropics, on account of the deterioration of things. My hair now shakes out an odour like orange blossoms.

Wednesday, May 13, 1908.

Last evening Jack delivered his lecture "Revolution" at the Central Hotel, and it provoked a discussion that lasted until midnight. Trust the German every time for knowing something about what is going on in the world political and social. Jack says it was one of the most stimulating audiences he ever had. And to-day at table, the guests are discussing Socialism and plying Jack with questions. Very dissimilar his experience in Papeete, when he spoke under the surveillance of the chief of the gendarmes, in a native

Folies Bergéres—the property owners, under the compulsion of the local authorities, refusing to rent him a hall.

We are bound for Savaii to-morrow, and this afternoon Jack and I were crossing and recrossing each other's tracks in a brief buying-tour. Unless you speak German, be warned that if ever you go to Upolu and hear "The German Firm," accept the name as a matter of course, lest you be called upon to write or pronounce, *"Haupt-Agentur Deutsche Handels und Plantagen-Gesellschaft, der Südsee-Inseln zu Hamburg."*

I bought some shocking lava-lavas with which to make envious the *Snark's* crew, one in particular, in wavy stripes of all gaudy colours that be, causing Rosa to gasp when I shook it out. After the shopping, we drove around town in the sunset, and I met the lawyer, Mr. Caruthers, who told me many things about Tusitala, and gave me a picture of old "Jack," the horse Tusitala used to ride. It is now in Mr. Caruthers' possession, some thirty years of age, spinning out its latter days in pleasant pastures. Mr. Moors tells us that he sold the horse to Stevenson for fifty dollars. But this was not the first time Moors had sold old Jack. He originally paid fifty dollars, and later on, being offered fifty dollars, and not needing the horse, accepted the price. The chance arose to recover the animal at the same figure, fifty dollars, and it again became Moors' property. But he had got into the habit of selling Jack, and again parted with him to a friend for the consideration of fifty dollars. Not long afterward, the friend, owing him fifty dollars on a bet, Moors accepted the worthy horse in payment. The next and last sale was to Stevenson, for fifty dollars.

We have not seen the famous old high chief of Upolu, Mata'afa; but this afternoon while driving, Rosa pointed across lagoons and low hills to a green blowhole in the side of a wooded mountain, and told me that Mata'afa has a very beautiful native place there, which he greatly loves. But it happens that for some time each visit he has made there from Apia has been followed by sickness; therefore the old autocrat has decided (like Tuimanua) that he has an aitu, and has eschewed all sojourning in his favourite falé. And so they pass, and in a little while all the old representatives of true Samoan nobility will be gone. "Drive away from us sailing-gods, lest they bring disease and death," they used to say; but probably now only the ancient fathers of the tribes remember the proverb. The rest are glad enough to welcome both sailing-gods and steaming-gods, for they mean money in exchange for goods and labour, money with which to replace their beautiful siapos with cheap manufactured stuff, the siapo now being made mostly for sale. "The iron of the machine has eaten into the soul of the artisan," as Austin Lewis says.

The Samoans have been a very superior race, with certain strict ideas of morality. The old taupon system is an example of what they strove for. And they took great care that there should be no intermarrying among close relatives. Also, it does not come within our knowledge that they were ever rapacious cannibals. A morsel of a notoriously cruel enemy was not to be snubbed, but it must be borne in mind that the participation in such fare carried an ethical significance.

They are an altruistic people. In their language there is no equivalent for the word poverty, and the nearest they can come to expressing the idea of *servant,* is "one who runs an errand for another."

The Samoans once flattened the noses of their children by frequent pressures, much as the Hawaiian mother even to-day is continually seen moulding the fingers of her babe into taper form; but it would appear that the Samoans have recovered from the old aversion to the "canoe noses" of the whites, for they are now a well-featured race, according to our biases. Sometimes I weary a little for the sight of a fine nostril in an otherwise clearly chiselled face, but one mustn't be too particular!

They have a fascinatingly intricate and interesting mythology. The very name Sa-Moa, meaning "Sacred to Moa," a heaven-born ancestor, gives a line on their concepts. But I cannot take space for the dead in this essentially living screed, so I wish you would read G. Turner's *Samoa,* a book that goes exhaustively into the lore and which will be found anything but dull, with its striking parallels to the mythology of many a presumably enlightened nation.

It is not all beer- and skittles for the erring ones among these Apians. This morning, at work, a strange clanking arrested us, and from our balcony we saw a procession of convicts dragging their chains down the street. They were marked with black disks on the right shoulder blade and left breast of their grimy shirts. Some were Samoans, some "black boys," the universal name for the imported labour from darker isles, such as the Solomons. I saw one guileless-faced Chinaman, and wondered what he had done. That reminds me of another celestial employed by Falstaff. His name is Jim, and he is small and trim and good looking, with heavy eyebrows drawn into a slight scowl. He is just out after doing eighteen months for pilfering from Falstaff's cash drawer; but the proprietor seems to think there is scant danger of a repetition.

Bougainville, seeing the Samoans so much about in canoes, named the group The Isles of the Navigators; but it seems to be the general judgment that these people are not nearly such good sailors as many another race of the South Seas.

We came away from our last visit to Mr. Moors with arms full of books about the Solomons, New Hebrides, New Guinea, and other countries where we expect to touch. The owner takes chances of losing them all in case we should be wrecked. Whenever I look at these books, I get to dreaming of the real raw edge of earth we are so soon to explore.

One pretty experience we have had in Apia—whenever we go on the street at night, an escort of brown small fry springs up and sees us to our destination. The noiseless forms walk close behind in the dust, sometimes one or two coming abreast. Nothing is said, and when we arrive, all disappear softly. They seem to expect nothing, and display

Samoan Falé

Bush Woman, Tana

Taupous, Samoa

little curiosity. Wouldn't it be sweet to discover that this is some ceremonial of hospitality connected with the stranger in their land! I am reminded of days gone by, in Berkeley, when, walking with my escort on fair nights to and from the college dances, a majestic St. Bernard on many occasions padded softly alongside. If he attended us to the Gymnasium, he failed not to make the round trip. Caresses he received, but returned none. Perhaps his life was too idle, in our summer land, stirring in him old instincts of protection. To whom he belonged I never learned.

At sea, between Upolu and Savaii, Samoa,
Thursday, May 14, 1908.

We have just passed through our worst thunder squall, the most terrifying thunder I ever heard, even on thunderous old Mt. Desert Island. It was overwhelming, the silken-blue suffusion of the lightning, followed by frightful crashing of rended elements. This sort of display is very interesting for a while, especially when one is within several feet of a thousand gallons of inflammable gas-engine fuel, to say nothing of a tank of kerosene and two tanks of lubricating oil, as well as 15,000 rounds of ammunition. But one quickly tires of the fireworks, the uncertainty and the racket, and longs for even a dead calm. We got it—the deadest of dead calms, and the shortest, broken like a flash by a double-squall smiting from opposite directions, like one I have described farther back. Now, as I write, the clouds are lifting and breaking before us, disclosing a nearer view of Savaii—a huge squat shape, warted with volcanoes. And from one living crater, like some ceaseless humour flows a stream of red lava, the venous blood of the squat and knobby shape. Already we can see very distinctly the wind-slanted columns of steam rising from where the hot lava meets the sea. Henry is much excited, for the last time he visited Savaii there was but one column.

We left Apia yesterday under power, since the wind, which

has been very capricious the past few days, had played out altogether. We dipped our flag to Mr. Young, who was coming in from Manua, but he was too busy keeping his schooner off the reef to bother about flags, and waved an arm instead. Our engine purred away until we had cleared the long point, Falooloo; then we let the *Snark* roll in a silvery calm, with just enough air to keep on the course. The silver moon rose astern from the silvery sea, half-enveloped in frosted-silver clouds, and from time to time heat lightning flushed the low clouds on the horizon. We slept on deck, our lighthouse a volcano; and frequently Jack and I raised our heads to look at the pillar of flame rising to the brooding clouds and illuminating their under sides in long wastes of fiery light. To-day it is a pillar of smoke that shows us the way. It is so wonderful, so unbelievable—sailing in a white-speck boat in the tropic sea, steering by a volcano.

Our decks are well stocked with native kai-kai, much of it brought by the friends who came aboard to see us off; and a brown and yellow turtle that must weigh over a hundred pounds, lies heavily and sadly in the lee scuppers. If we speak to him, he droops his eyelids and withdraws his head, but displays no tendency to snap. This is the second edible turtle our boys caught in Apia; and so unusual and valuable is such a prize, that the turtles had to be watched nights to keep natives from marauding them where they lay in the water alongside at ropes' ends.

Mr. Easthope's daughter brought a beautiful siapo and handsome fans. Rosa Moors came over the side with basketfuls of oranges and lemons and other good things, arranged as only she, artist that she is, can arrange everything. Charley Roberts, bursting with ill-concealed grief over parting from Jack, smuggled into our staterooms some fascinating long-necked bottles of liquid sunshine from France ("Mere trash, my dear fellow, mere trash!"), while his "Missis" remembered that she had left five dozen eggs in the launch. And there were "roses, roses, riotously," and good wishes by the bale, and farewells between people who may never meet again, but who are glad of having met that once. For the *Snark* is a ship that passes, and passes, and keeps on passing, the round world around, never to return. Why, the gleeful winged thing doesn't even have to return to ports of entry to clear, what of her yacht license, which, by international courtesy, entitles her to come and go as she pleases, like a man-o'-war, unbound by papers of any kind save her Bill of Health.

This morning, looking back with the glasses, we could faintly make out Young's schooner at anchor, still outside the reef. That is where we would have been but for our engine. All our heartbreaking difficulties with the engines fade before our present joy in them—propulsion, interior lighting, and searchlight.

This whole day I have done nothing more practically profitable than take a bath in the violent warm rain that fell with the squalls; and the profitableness of this act is, I believe, a question of climate and open to individual dispute. In general the sea has been too rough to allow of comfort in any occupation. Hunting for braces to offset the rolls is about all one can do. There is one gratifying circumstance aboard—Ernest is missing—gone to Australia on a steamer. Captain Warren ought to be happy, with his detested Frenchman removed; but I can almost believe he misses the luxury of some one on whom to vent his brilliant sarcasms. Henry does not look as if it would be healthful for any one to use him as a butt, Tehei is our brother, and the captain has an inkling that we do not care to lose our Japanese boys. Poor Captain Warren—he would seem to have forgotten how ardently, in Tahiti, he wanted to rehabilitate his reputation, and how much Jack overlooked of his misconduct. And nowadays, he is more or less of a blight upon the gaiety of our adventure.

But we cannot be shadowed very much, in so vivid a life. Think of sleeping under the biggest moon ever seen, with a great sighing leviathan of a turtle at the head of your cot, and an active volcano for guide-post. Then to wake in the morning to a sunrise like the gates of Paradise, with a flight of golden angels in between. . .

The water is flecked with ashes, and as the day draws to a close we can see the fearsome glare of molten lava that plunges over the rim of iron-bound coast. The colour is lambent rose of opal; each moment the wonder grows. After a wintry-grey sunset, followed by coloured hazes of the volcano smoke, we are coming near enough to spy the actual lava-falls as they drop heavy plummets into the sea-wash. Henry's eyes are large with astonishment at the increase of the flow, and he and Tehei exclaim sharply at intervals as some augmented cascade of liquid fire explodes in the breakers, sending up rockets never surpassed by man's ingenuity. We are all exclaiming, for that matter. The volcano is classic to-night, the cone showing clearer, the smoke rising funnel-wise to a great height, now and then blown into fantastic spirals by the high winds. There is something sinister and sullen about the glaring, flaring, unnatural light. The water alongside is 88° Fahrenheit, warmer than the air, which is oppressive with fumes of sulphur. We are now only half a mile from the hell that has so long been loosed upon the ruined land, and are beginning to realise that something dreadful is enacting before us—something exceptional, not yet known in Apia, for we were unwarned of such magnitude of disaster. The wind holds, and we are able to skim along the edge of the tremendous spectacle, each long black land-point divulging greater devastation of liquid fire. Whole plains have been licked up, the red flood forcing under a cooled and blackened crust, and only emerging at the brink where it writhes and twists out of its confines, ever hissing into the sea, like a myriad driven serpents.

To put on paper what I behold is like painting a picture, and I am no artist; but there is fascination in trying to share with the many what so few may see. And now it is grown too dark to write, and I shall give myself up entirely to this terrific experience.

Aboard the *Snark*,
Matautu Bay, Savaii, German Samoa,
Saturday, May 16, 1908.

After we had sailed to a safe distance for lying off and on all night, the calm that had preceded the afternoon thunder squalls returned and left us drifting. I had a good night below, deciding that the universe was altogether too light and bright and diverting for any repose on deck. Daybreak brought lovely new colours, and a transformation of the warty monster Savaii into a colossal milky opal, what of the delicate tints in smoke and mist that obscured its grim ugliness. When the veils lifted, we made use of a light breeze to carry us back near the scene of fireworks, in order to take pictures. The wind gasped out suddenly, Martin tuned up the "masheen," and we steamed as close as we dared to the flowing abomination of lava—the living, moving curse that had come upon the land. Raising our eyes, we saw vast forests standing stark and dead upon the mountainsides, the edge of the blackened coast licked up with red flames from the water's edge, where cascades of slow resistless lava were quenched of their heat. The water in which we sailed was, a venomous yellow-green, while close to the lava it boiled a bright yellow. At an eighth of a mile we tested the flood, and it went up to 90°, 10° warmer than the thick air we breathed, shortly, as if in fear of a pestilence. We were disappointed, upon closer view of the stream of lava that sent up the most conspicuous disturbance of steam and smoke, to find that it did not run over the low cliff, but came out under the surface, an upper crust having already formed. But there was ample opportunity in other places to observe the real red stuff, and red and awful it showed even in the broad sunshine, trickling or dropping into the dancing hot surf that beat loudly against the rocks. This present eruption is overflowing the dead lava of 1905, from the same crater; but three years before, another peak turned loose and destroyed a fine section of the country. An island in the making! And we can see it with our own eyes!

We speculated if the hot water would kill off our barnacles, and whether or not we could stand warmer baths than the sharks, in case we took a swim. Jack climbed into the suspended launch, taking pictures, while we throbbed along the shore, passing the daylit wonders of last night, on and on, every turn divulging new destruction of a land that only yesterday was green with cocoanut and banana, mango and citron. Then we came where we must avoid the reef which protects Matautu Bay from the east, and lost our nearer view of the lava fields. But we could see that the consequences of the present eruption are widespread, and as we approached Matautu, our glasses showed a village smoking by the water's edge under limp and ragged cocoa palms, and Henry cried out in sorrow, for he had been in this village.

Jack did not like the way the yacht was allowed to hug the eastern horn of the reef entrance, but did not interfere. Our good luck was to make through safely, and we found excellent anchorage. This harbour is much exposed at all seasons, but it is only the north and northwest winds one need dread, and between the first of December and last of March, mariners are warned from visiting Matautu.

We bore various letters of introduction to "Dick" Williams, Administrator of Savaii, and had been prepared to find him "a bunch o' good fun," which seemed to be the enthusiastic opinion held by his friends in Apia. It was after three when Jack and I started with Martin for shore, Henry also going along. No boat of any kind had come out to us from Fagamalo village, which was rather surprising. Little did we know the reason that kept every one on land. Henry pointed out Mr. Williams' place, and we picked our way over the shallows of the reef, avoiding the little rips of foam where the water broke on higher coral. The colours were lovely—I can never get over the enchantment of these coral gardens of orange and blue, brown and purple, seen through the pea-green water.

The *Snark* anchored near the middle of the bay, so we had some distance to go, and when we began conning the sandy beach for a place to run in the launch, a picture out of *Pick-wick* came towards us from a pretty concrete house, and motioned where we should land. The launch nosed into soft sand, and we were borne ashore by native policemen, who had donned their helmets and gilt-buttoned khaki coats for the occasion.

We promptly fell in love with the "bunch o' good fun."

"Come on in—the 'ava's just made," he called heartily, preceding us into the pretty house with its arched corridors and doorways. After we had drained our cocoanut beakers, we presented our letters. Mr. Williams tossed them unread on the table, and proceeded to be very hospitable on his own account.

"Now, I'll tell you how I am situated," he began. "Here's this big house, but nobody can sleep in it for the dampness. The concrete was mixed with salt water, and I don't know if it's *ever* going to dry. But come and let me show you where I sleep," leading the way to a long wooden structure near the water. "This is my boat-house, and in this end is my room." We went into a small but light and airy bedchamber partitioned off from the boat, and he continued: "You folks move right in here and be comfortable. —No, that's all right, don't you worry. I can sleep in a native house—they're glad to help me out," he insisted, tugging away at a beautiful native-carved fan of hard wood that defied his efforts to get it off the wall. It came loose finally, and he handed it to me, along with another from the table, and a dainty hair ornament of the same carven wood. Then he commenced planning trips. "Of course you must go to the volcano; and to-morrow morning we'll drive to the next village, back the way you sailed. It's a great sight. The lava has come through and burned most of the houses, and now is taking a new turn that's going to finish it.—In fact, here you've got your launch, and we can run up there by water now, and see the lava at night."

Before we knew it we were in the boat again, Jack steering, Martin running the engine, Henry bulging his eyes over

the rail landward, and Mr. Williams' rotund figure standing
forward to pilot. And mind you—this fatherly soul was
trying to hide from us a deep anxiety for his people, now
being driven out of their homes faster than he can find
shelter for them. Small wonder that no friendly canoes
came out upon our arrival!

It was a new experience to run along in deep water close
to the sand, only once turning out for a shallow spit, and
once again to avoid the delta of a little river. It grew dark
rapidly, and we wondered how we would be able to get back.
Natives kept pace alongshore; and when we approached the
end of the sandy beach, beyond which was the forbidding
coast of fire, brown boys and men splashed into the water
and carried the whole boat ashore with us in it—as they did
the first white men. So many were they, and so curious,
that Mr. Williams thought wiser for Henry and Martin to
stand guard lest they inadvertently do the engine harm.

It was dazing, the nearness and light of the dreadful disturbance; and as we trod the beach pathway, crowded with
sheltering palms, their higher fronds tattered and crisped
by heat and fumes, we could not but shrink from the glare
of the wicked cone that was laving this land. It is making new land—extending the confines of the island, to be
sure; but how many hundreds of years will have to lapse
before palms take root again and green grass clothes the
black nakedness of plain and slope and shore?

Eyes smarting, breath coming painfully, we walked hand
in hand, the three of us, past deserted houses, not yet burned,
and then turned from the beach and made our way through
a marshy place, criss-crossed by fallen palms, to where the
ruin was slowly, implacably advancing. And then I saw,
close at hand, what I have all my life dreamed of beholding
—living, flowing lava from the heart of a volcano, sluggish,
pushing, sticky stuff that forced out through a cooled crust
of clinker, like rose-madder from a tube—such a terrible,
devastating liquid, growing thicker and more darkly red,
more heavily sluggish as we watched, under the cooling of

the air. Lava follows the line of least resistance, of course,
which in this case is the marshy land near the river; and we
could see slow lines of crimson flowing into the water, which
is fast going up in steam—another disaster to the inhabitants. We shielded our faces and tried to get some of the
lava on sticks; but it was too thick by now, and would not
adhere.

The blazing core of the crater is seven miles in a straight
line from Matautu Bay, but the lava, as it runs, covers a
course of twice that distance. Mr. Williams' figures that
by the time it reaches the sea, it is moving about five yards
a minute.

We went back to the path, and continued to where the
main flow had crossed. It was glazed over, and we were
able to step on it with assurance, although it was still very
warm. We picked our way for some distance, in order to
gain better view of a large bight of the sea where red lava
showed in a continuous cascade along the shore.

By this time we were actually shivering in a breeze that
mercifully broke through the suffocating shimmering heat,
and were glad to get back into comparatively pure air. We
passed a large two-story frame house that we had noticed
when sailing by, and Mr. Williams told us it had been locked
up, furnished and provisioned as it was, by the owner, who
was absent.

We re-embarked in the fitful light that filtered through
the jungle. It was tense work, steering in the murk; but
after a little the moon rose behind us, solemnly, slowly,
redly, like a round world of blood wheeling sadly through
the rack and ruin of space. Very quiet we were, overcome
by what we had seen and were seeing, and touched by the
trouble and apprehension of this man who has the care and
keeping of the island in his hand. By now he made no secret of his anxiety—how could he, when he had revealed
the problem he must handle?

No, Apia knew nothing of the seriousness of this immediate eruption, its sudden accession; but the schooner carrying

the news must have passed us in the night, from what Mr. Williams said.

We decided to rejoin the *Snark*, as it was too late to turn Mr. Williams out of his quarters, and we were set against this anyway. It was nearly nine when we climbed aboard, and there was only some tinned corn and boiled taro left from supper, as they had given us up. So I told Wada to make a little fire and scramble eggs with mushrooms, for we were famished. Later, I heard the captain grumble to Martin: "Say—you had a pretty nice supper, didn't you?—Pity I can't get in on some of the good things!"—And he had had the same dish the day before, and always has the same fare we do, as he takes his meals with us.

. . . The men are playing poker in the cockpit, and I have come up for a breath. There are several fish on deck aft, glistening in the now brilliant moonlight. Our delighted kanakas caught them over-stern early in the evening, and pronounced a silver disk-shaped one "maitai kaikai"; but over a large bright-red fish they wagged their dusky heads. In Tahiti it is a poisonous fish, and in Samoa is supposed to be harmless, according to Henry. I told him he would better try it before the rest of us, if he felt so sure it is innocuous in Samoa. Whereupon he showed a smileful of very white teeth and said, "All right—I eat."

This close view of the ruddy volcano is very impressive. It is a lesser peak, in the side of a mountain over 5000 feet high called Pulé, meaning power, master. The crater was about 3000 feet at the first modern eruption three years ago; but Mr. Williams avers it has broken down at least a thousand feet. The overflow does not now come from the lip, but breaks out below—no one knows just where, because most of the issue makes its way under the coating of incinerated earth which so quickly skins over.

Matautu, Savaii, Samoa,
Sunday, May 17, 1908.

Before we had finished breakfast on deck, a boat arrived
with a gift of flowers from the Administrator. They were
ceremoniously presented by one of the khaki-coated fita-
fitas, and were folded loosely into a green plaited cocoanut
frond—creamy blumerias, scarlet double hibiscus, and a
fragrant fluffy mass of tiny blossoms and grasses and ferns.
Now think how sweet a thing for a busy, worried man to
do! I trimmed my big Cook Island hat with hibiscus, before going ashore, and told Mr. Williams that it was a shame
under heaven for some right woman to go lonely for such a
husband. He has the kindest, gentlest ways—and an eye for
a pretty girl, too; but—"Bless me—what would a wife-
woman do here?" he girded. "Women like luxuries, and
society, and diversion—what!—If a woman loved me, she
would be happy here? Yes—well, well; but where is the
woman to love me?" . . . And a little later: "Besides, my
children need me. They're all my children, these men and
women and young folk. They call me Father, and Papa
Williams—yes, they do! And when they are naughty and
are brought before me I stand them up and talk to them till
I bring the tears to their eyes." He chuckled lovably at
some remembrance, and in answer to a question went on:
"How do I punish them? Why, I say, 'Father, do you call
me? Now what kind of children are you to act this way
toward your father who loves you?'—Say, they're like
lambs. They nearly die of shame and contrition. I rule
them by love—I do! I have never struck a man of them
since I've been in this position. But I had occasion to do it
long ago, two or three times only (I've been here twenty-
four years, you know). They have to realise that a man
is strong, if he's going to get any respect out of them.
Yes, I struck them two or three times long ago, and I did
it well. They know I am strong, and they respect me. But
I rule by love—I rule them by love." He was silent for a
minute, and no human being could doubt his next words:

"And they love me, in their way—not very deep, it's not in them; but it's lots of comfort to me. And they know I care for them. I've proved it to them before, in different ways, and I'm proving it now. I want like everything to take a trip with you folks, pilot you around the island— we'd have a great time. But I can't leave, with this sure destruction coming upon their houses. They would lose heart, and get into a panic. It would be quite unexpected by them if I should leave at such a time. I rule them by love. Why, think! there are thirteen thousand people on Savaii, and not one prisoner among them in the lot."

He beamed broadly at thought of this proof of his successful administration. When he passes a humble woman of the common people, he says, "Talofa lava, ta maitai!" which means, "Much love to you, lady." And the "ta maitai," lady, brings the pleasure into her eyes. The village Talking Man lowers his umbrella in respectful courtesy to the Administrator. And the act is without servility.

"I haven't even looked at those letters you brought," he said. "Say—I never read letters of introduction, until folks have left. Letters don't make any difference to me— I don't want them to. I want to treat folks just the same as if they hadn't any recommendation," he twinkled. Then, with one of his irresistible gurgles: "I never had but one unwelcome guest. He made himself unwelcome. Never mind how. But I told him the second day that it would be much better for us to part right then than later. And he took the hint, and went. He's the only one we ever turned away, isn't he, Barts?" This to the tall trader with whom Pa Williams takes his meals. Mr. Barts acquiesced, and both men laughed reminiscently.

Mr. Barts' cottage has several cosy rooms, and he turned over his large bedroom to us, taking a smaller one for himself, so that the older man is not turned out of his boat-house, after all. Every one seems satisfied, and we certainly are. Mr. Barts is an athletic, fine-looking German, with courteous manners, and quiet hospitality. Meals are served outside on the porch, by a Niué Island cook, whom Mr. Barts oversees with a househusbandly eye. Everything comes out of cans—all fresh green stuffs are ruined by sulphur fumes from the volcano, and we are learning new tinned delicacies.

To-day we drove to the deserted village, behind a couple of gasping horses that became so uneasy with the heat and foulness of air that they had to be held when we left the rigs where lava had terminated the road. Retracing our last night's steps, we found that the lava had steadily advanced, burning several native houses. The fine frame one was as yet untouched, but the low wall of lava was almost up to it. Father Williams called to me to keep from under the cocoanuts, which were drooping perilously in the ravaging heat. The relentless molten rock surrounds and eats out their globular bases, and the fair and stately boles fall only to warp and scorch on the unsympathetic new surface of the earth.

It was a fascinating but doleful scene. Looking toward the mountain we saw only the blasted life of the jungle, "the wilderness of birds, the wilderness of God," the Christian natives say—dead, quite dead; and near at hand, in a little stone church, the people prayed for protection from the slow sure fate that was encroaching upon their happy groves and homes, now only a few yards away from the house of praise. Papa Williams looked sadly out of his Irish blue eyes at the pretty church, then at the ugly black bank inching over the green sward, urged from within by red and living force, and remarked dryly:

"I'll bet on the lava."

We stepped warily over the hot and brittle substance that had covered the ground we walked upon the night before, and I was in some trepidation lest my linen petticoats flame up from the fiery blowholes and crevices. We saw nature's cruel manufacture of tree-moulds—such as they show on the slopes of Mauna Kea in Hawaii—the mould left in the earth by the bases of trees burned in the quickly cooling lava. We peered into little hell-holes of vicious white heat that showed the sort of strata over which we were treading. "Step on the smooth, curling, molasses-like stuff," we were advised—the *pahoehoe* lava of Hawaii.

Last, we followed over a black and shining field that stretched seven miles before us—the flow of 1905, much of it now being re-flowed over. Three years ago this August it was seven miles of almost continuous village—grassy houses and nodding palms. This intense jetty blackness is shocking to the senses, used as we have been to the bright slopes of other islands—even in Hawaii, the newer volcanic reaches are brown or dull red. Perhaps the most tragically impressive feature of all was a family graveyard in a patch of green but wilting grass. The mounds are made of coral-lime plaster of pinkish-tan hue, and the lava, by some freak, has piled up many feet on all sides, leaving several of the tombs untouched, while others are pushed against and cracked. We had to descend warm and brittle walls to reach the green oasis of the dead with its wrecked graves. The lime house of the family is not far off—what is left of it; for the lava set fire to the woodwork, and did away with the roof, leaving only the walls, with baffled lava piled up twelve feet all around. In fact, we stood above and looked down into the open interior. The lava had been too sluggish to force into window-spaces or doors. We came to a church that had been burned—a deserted sanctuary in which a native had begun to build his bamboo house, which was scorched but still standing.

Our horses we found breathing hard with nervousness and sulphur, and as we drove home Mr. Williams talked about his life in Savaii and his association with the people.

"Do you see this road?" he said, flicking his whip in the fine coral powder. "It's a fine road anywhere, a bicycle road, and it extended twelve miles, where now is the lava.— But road-building in Samoa has its comical side as well as its serious side. The natives don't see the comical part, and it's my serious duty not to let them see that I think there's anything funny or unusual in their practices. It takes tact

—but tact is merely sympathy, after all, and they know I love them. That's the way I rule them, you see." (Would that all rulers could earn this continuous reflection!) "When I commenced getting the roads in order," he went on, "I would lay my course, as the sailors say, and set the men to work. All at once everything would come to a standstill, and I would be called upon by the workmen, with some friend in tow: 'My father (or my mother, or my mother-in-law, or my first wife's daughter by her fifth husband) is buried where the road is digging. Can you not turn aside?' And bless their souls, I build around the reverend grave. I don't care if the road is as crooked as a cow's horn—we're not going to run a tramway here, and it doesn't hurt any of us to let them have their way."

I recalled some curious things about Samoan burials, although I don't know if any of the old customs still prevail; but there was a time when corpses were embalmed and exposed for months near the mourners' dwellings. Quite the contrary of the Egyptian practice, Samoan embalming was done mainly by women. One particular family of chief-women would be proficient in the art, and do all the embalming for the community—or at least for those of rank. There seems to have been little superstition connected with keeping the dead unburied. It was done more out of respect and affection, to have the deceased near to those dear in life. When a body was eventually buried, however, it was laid in a grave about four feet deep, spread with mats, and provided with a raised bamboo head-rest. Now this was not entirely for the comfort of the departed on his heavenward journey, as is the case with the North American Indian and many another people, but for the very sanitary reason that the living feared contamination from the dead person's belongings, preferring to forego them rather than take risks.

"We'll go in here and have some 'ava," Papa Williams broke in upon my mortuary reverie; and we crossed the lovely river and turned into a group of fine thatched houses still unharmed. We bent low to enter a splendid falé, and mats were pulled down from the polished beams and spread for us on the tinkling white coral floor. The members of the household took their official positions about the interior, for it is a great matter in just what relation to certain central pillars this or that personage disposes him- or herself.

After a smiling and bowing period broken by Father Williams' jokes in the native tongue, and the responsive giggles of the girls, he suggested the 'ava. It was made by two young taupous, she of this village and the other from the newly burned district. The falés of Fagamalo are crowded with refugees, four hundred having poured in since Wednesday. The Administrator has had to provide domiciles for fourteen hundred since August 14, 1905. The people spend most of their time praying and singing in the churches, trying to avert further disaster, and the older folk are wofully cast down over the erasure of old landmarks and traditional spots. The younger ones are more cheerful—they find novelty living in new houses; but there is a shadow of soberness over them, and no dancing is permitted.

Following lunch, we had a peep at the Administrator's 38-foot lifeboat in the shed, and listened to how one time he sailed it back from Apia in six and a half hours—forty-six sea miles. And he told us about the twelve-foot tidal wave of last October that made them all rush out and cut loose their horses when the wall of water was seen coming, which raised a 400-gallon tank full of rainwater three feet onto another platform, without straining a hoop. Savaii would seem to be a stage for Nature's jugglery.

We visited the office in the pretty house of undried walls, and drank 'ava and 'ava, and then 'ava and 'ava again, made by any chance passing maiden called in by Father Williams, a charming chief custom of Samoa. To-day, the girls happened to be from the latest burned village, and they were only too glad of a little diversion. In the serving of the 'ava, a young *beau*, prompted by Mr. Williams, announced each receiver of the cup in turn, and was obeyed by the taupou. " 'The man who has no wife,' he says," chuckled our host, as the calabash was wafted to Mr. Barts. And when Martin's portion was held poised in the girl's brown hand, " 'Boss of the fire,' " interpreted the jolly Irish Administrator of a German province—an allusion to Martin's occupation as engineer. "Frau Lindler is 'The Lady with the Golden Crown,' " Mr. Williams went on, referring to the yellow hair of a newly arrived visitor from Apia.

"How many children have you?" he inquired kindly of a strange female who was peeping in at us out of a shower. "She says she thinks she has two!" he laughed. Then, turning to a perfect beauty who had strayed in, "I never laid eyes on this girl before. She's probably from the last burned village. She can't be a week over fourteen, but she looks all of twenty, doesn't she?"

She certainly did, the ripe and sumptuous tropic creature, sitting quite at ease, calmly regarding the company from under curved lashes that veiled dark eyes made brown by the lights in her sun-tanned curly hair. Over a broad low fore·head, her hair was parted and rolled over the ears, and done in a loose coil at the nape of her round girlish neck. She was the most unsavage savage imaginable, this nut-brown maid of Polynesia who had never been off the island. She would have done credit to any assembly, with her graceful port, splendid pose of head, piquant profile, arch rise of eyebrows, and, above all, the self-contained, unembarrassed manner—a born aristocrat.

"I tell her you say she's the prettiest girl in the world," Mr. Williams informed us, after some remarks to her in Samoan; and then he laughingly added, after listening to something the young lady said to him, "and she says 'Perhaps I am, I don't know.' "—A literal reasoner, she.

Handsome as are many of the Samoan women, to our minds they are not equal to their magnificent men, gods of the seashore who refuse to become slaves. No labour-ships come here—no natural lord of Samoa is going to wear his heart out upon a foreign plantation. Let planters comb the seas elsewhere for "black boys,"—New Guinea, Solomons, New Ireland, New Hebrides. The men of Samoa 'Uma will swing their own mighty shoulders in their own way, upon their own strand, and praise be to them!

Monday, May 18, 1908.

I am filled with unutterable disgust over the sleepless fate that sometimes—although only just sometimes—cuts me off from doing the things I wish to do. Arrangements were made for a horseback trip to the volcano to-day, but I was too tired from a wakeful night to face long hours in the hot sun. Martin was to have been my escort, for Jack has an uncomfortable sore on his foot, which worries us by its unhealable character, especially when we recollect Ernest's disease.

So I sent the Administrator my apologies, and remained in bed most of the day, trying to sleep. Late in the afternoon Jack suggested a stroll, and we visited some of the houses, where we made the owners understand that we wanted siapos. We returned with arms full, and a boy or two beside to carry the overflow. They are the finest and largest siapos we have seen. In one falé we surprised three men building a long canoe, squatted on the mats hospitably laid for us, and enjoyed watching the adroit joiners. The best canoes are not the stiff dugouts, but these ones made in closely-fitted hand-hewn planks, bound and laced together with finest skill with cocoanut fibre. The Samoan is a clever wood-worker, and his "nails" are strong and beautiful sennit of cocoanut, cleverly bound and woven.

Father Williams was called to Safoto, a village west of Fagamalo, to arrange about sending some of the refugees there. But the suggestion was not his. In the morning, boats came here bringing welcome invitation to the homeless. Jack and I saw these boats returning from inspection of the lava—fine long whaleboats propelled by forty oars, their splendid crews, the cream of Polynesia, singing part-songs as they raced one another in deep water along the edge of the sand. These men are almost round-shouldered with powerfully developed muscles. But this muscle-training has come from labour of love, at paddle and oar and fishing, and not from degrading toil done for mere money and at command of a master. And their lives show that their endeavour is for the good of the mass rather than for selfish individual ends.

Waiting on the porch near dinner-time for the return of Father Williams, we watched the men and women passing in their leisurely fashion, and exclaimed over and over at some remarkable type, Hebraic, Oriental, Greek—they were all there—noting again the physical superiority of the males in general over the females. These have not nearly the fine carriage and gait of their mates, and we could look in vain for the queens of the sex one sees at every turn in Hawaii. We kept nodding "Talofa" to the strollers, some of whom would stop at the gate, or come frankly in to shake hands, with renewed assurances of "Talofa lava." Among such neighbourly callers was a trio of half-naked young girls who pursued the not unusual course of talking at length regardless of discrepancy of tongues. After bowing and smiling a while at them, which only increased their flow of words, Jack adopted their method, and in a flatteringly genial tone took up the defensive:

"Yes, yes—I comprehend conclusively the unanswerable mathematical logical significance of your considerate equilateral triangulation; but your deductions are unintelligibly misleading."

The maidens betrayed a hint of puzzlement, but rose to the situation and nodded and smiled—while I died several deaths to hide my laughter.

"Now, on the other hand," Jack went on gravely, "what is your unbiased judgment of the hypothetical transformation of astronomical hypothenuses of nebulosity?"

He paused long enough to control a smile at my interpolation that he resembled Zangwill's "dictionary in distress," then proceeded in an argumentative tone tinged with becoming deference:

"It is no use losing cognisance of the irrefragable pertinacity of the lachrymal pabulum. Nevertheless, I consider that no indulgent incorrigible metaphysical matriculate will negate the anterolateral angelolatry of strategic Zoroastrianism."

It began to dawn upon the polite trio that perhaps they had been making the same mistake as he, and when my wicked man continued—"Do you not realise, that your incomprehension detracts lamentably from the evolving of my trigonometrical prestigitations?" they faded softly and smilingly away, but without loss of dignity, their "tofa soi fua" uttered with perfect poise and calm. What an actor was lost when Jack London decided to write for a living!

Then everybody came for supper, and my tender conscience was soothed by Frau Lindner's assurances that she had been rather glad I did not go to the volcano, as it gave her an excuse to stay behind! Martin and the rest of the party were weary and unsuccessful. They never reached the lip of the crater, for it rained hard on the mountain and there was no use going the rest of the severe climb through volcanic sand, only to miss seeing the inside of the crater on account of cloud and rain.

After dark we visited the lava-flow, and passed scores of natives drifting in the same direction, bulking large and shadowy in the wavering crimson light. Mr. Williams stopped at a house and called out a little maid, taupou of a deserted village. Her name is Ufi, signifying The Yam, and she is sweet and wholesome as a whole garden of tropic edibles, with a flower-patch thrown in. It is fortunate she lives in a country where women are esteemed above food, or she might fare ill at the hands of some epicure of a high chief. Papa Williams had already told us he had the dearest little girl in Savaii to show us. And never saw we a

dearer. She is not more than fourteen, built squarely and
solidly, with healthy hard limbs and firm virgin breasts; and
her neck is like a doll's or a baby's—round and short and
kissable, like her round brown cheeks that flush to blood
pounded by a stout little heart. Taupou of taupous is Ufi,
so lovable and healthy and deliciously, adorably young that
Frau Lindner and I could not keep our eyes from her, nor
our caressing hands. Our cart broke with its load at the
bridge, and we walked on, the little frau and I on either side
of Ufi, stopping to kiss her neck, her apple-cheek, or pat her
wonderful coiffure—the out-ended fluffy hair that measures
at least eighteen inches across. She accepted our adoration
composedly, in turn patting our white arms with tender little moans, saying "Lelei" in a soft, misty voice, and smiling
affectionately at us.

Terrible were the ravages of the eruption. Over yesterday's lava, well into the sea, ran new streams, issuing like
tortured reptiles white with agony, turning to flame-colour,
then rose, and crimson and wine, the blackening coming on
slowly, as air and moisture reduced the moving matter to
dead cinder. The men approached a curling coil of the indescribable impossible fluid, and plunged sticks into it, while
shielding their singeing faces. The boiling-hot lava thus
caught was stuck into the water, and came out black and
steaming, brittle as blown glass. Of course we had to
imbed coins in red-hot fragments which soon became jet
black, ragged-edged curios; and when we could no longer
endure the searing heat, we started back for Fagamalo, making love to Ufi en route. Half way, Mr. Williams led us
into a spacious falé for 'ava. The family were nearly all
asleep behind high partitioning curtains of siapo—an arrangement we had never before seen; but they were only too
willing to entertain their beloved "Father" and his sisters
and brothers, for so it pleased him to introduce us. I lay
down, my head on Ufi's chubby tattooed knee, and when I
murmured lomi-lomi, a bevy of small shapes rose in the
changeful gloom, and I was surrounded by punching, slap-

ping, kneading gnomes, their bright, mischievous eyes all that was distinct of them. Nothing would have suited me better than to stay behind with these soothing comforters in the big grass house.

Tuesday, May 19, 1908.

Fresh from a glorious night's sleep, bright and early this morning I walked through the green village among the grass houses, glancing into the cool shadow of the interiors, where the waking ones raised auburn-bleached heads from bamboo "pillows," and blinked good-naturedly in the red-gold sunrise. Under my arm was a bundle of white muslin—twelve yards of it, bought of Mr. Barts; and I was bound to the falé of Andy Brunt, a half-caste trader, whose native wife had engaged to print my cloth in siapo design of indelible virtue. The handsome fafiné sat on a mat, laid before her the carven mould and sent for her bottles of pigment made from bark of trees. Then she pressed scraps of cloth on the pattern and smeared them with other scraps dipped in the colouring stuff, until I found the tint I wanted. This afternoon the twelve patterned yards came back, and some day I shall startle my household with a gown of tapa that can go to the laundry without risk. The Brunts also had one of the remarkable rugs of "vegetable fur," such as we saw at Mr. Moors', and which he was unable to duplicate for us. The Brunts' one we bought for $20.00— a very reasonable price.

During the day the villagers trooped to our house with bales of siapos, and we held a bazaar surpassing that at Manua. And such goods as we found here in Savaii—siapos of undreamed proportions—a single one would hang the four walls of a room. And there were oblong calabashes wrought from a kind of ironwood, called *ifilélé*. We selected only the best of everything, for we must not hamper our space aboard during our run to Fiji.

At sea, from Savaii, Samoa, to Suva, Fiji,
Wednesday, May 20, 1908.

Things are not improved aboard the *Snark*. And the fact that the sea is angry and that it looks like the beginning of a gale, does not help matters. Jack has now definitely decided to get rid of Captain Warren at Suva, and take over the navigating of the yacht. I am worrying about his weighing himself down with added work and responsibility; but it seems as if his responsibility is growing anyway, captain or no captain. Warren becomes more deliberately worthless every day, and we really do not feel safe with him in charge. Jack waited hours to-day to see if he would not take in the lifeboat, which was getting pounded by the big seas—indeed, she was lifted a foot or so every time the *Snark* heeled down, and the resultant jerk threatened to carry away the davits. A suggestion was ventured by Jack that it might be well to swing the boat in on deck, but the captain resented this, and said very briefly that it was perfectly safe. Poor Jack watched the imminent wrecking of his valuable property for a little longer, and at last said quietly but in a way that brooked no discussion, that the lifeboat would better be brought inboard. It was done; but it took over an hour. Jack wanted to prove how long it would take in case of need, as he mistrusted certain Roscoe-like optimistic assurances that fifteen minutes would do the trick. It was an ungracious obedience accorded, and once, in the midst of the sweating endeavour, in answer to some remark of Jack's that had nothing to do with the work in hand, Warren snapped:

"You told me to get the boat in, and I'm *getting* it in!"

He snarled repeatedly at the boys, all of whom were helping, and when the boat was lashed on deck, we heard the following:

"Where're you going, Wada? Come up out o' that! *Wet*, are you? Well, I guess you're not the only one who's wet. I'm wet as you are . . ." and here followed some expressions of his feelings that I need not repeat. Wada, with recrudescent hate in his eye for which no one could blame him, dragged up the companionway and went forward. He was not needed on deck, he was needed below; yet his master had to exert his own thwarted authority on some one, and Wada having been whipped and cowed once, was the only one he dared vent upon. Emotional maniac—that's what he is. Why, one day in Papeete, he mentioned Wada with tears in his eyes, and his voice broke and trembled as he said: "That Wada is a *man*, sir—he's a man, clean through!"

So poor Wada hung around on deck a few moments, and presently, standing at the companionway he called back to the cockpit in a tense, high voice:

"Can we go down now?"

The captain sprang half over the cockpit rail. His venom went to his head like a strong spirit as he cursed Wada, and then, remembering me he apologised in his oily way: "You can see how it is, Mrs. London—he's getting out of hand."

Oh, yes; I could see how it was—perfectly; and I didn't love J. Langhorne Warren of Virginia the last least little bit. Also, I knew that if he had not controlled himself, if he had got over the cockpit rail, Jack and Martin, backed by the kanakas, would have reached for him before ever he could reach Wada.

But aside from the slack way the *Snark* has been run for months, we have an even sorer grievance, based upon the conduct of our captain ashore. As Wada once put it to Nakata, not knowing he was overheard: "The captain of the *Snark* ought go around like captain of gentleman's yacht —but no, he act like common sailor—everybody laugh and talk about him—natives they laugh." And this is true. He boasts frequently and proudly that he is "Captain of Jack London's yacht, the *Snark*," but he does us no credit. At Fagamalo, he so vilely outraged the hospitality of our hosts and his, in ways that concern the high and strict moral customs of the land, that our indecision as to disposing of him was forced to an issue.

This morning we sailed out in a light breeze about nine o'clock, and cleared the land. Father Williams and Mr. Barts came aboard with us, also Ufi and her taupou mate, who had especially asked. We departed laden with fans and hardwood canes, Solomon Island spears and a debonaire little red god of those same islands, all gifts from the two gentlemen. We intended to sail yesterday; but some one suggested poker, and Jack delayed over night. The men played until midnight, and I slept peacefully in the next room, lulled by the blissful manipulations of two strange sweet damsels, sitting cross-limbed on the mattress on either side of me. When I am rich I am going to have about me relays of Polynesian lomi-lomi experts.

Before we left the house, the Administrator went to the lava flow, and found the church banked high, all inflammable material consumed. So his bet would have been good. The lava is working down toward Fagamalo, and Mr. Barts said he intended to begin packing his goods and belongings as soon as he saw us off. It made us very pensive to imagine this pretty village, in which we had been so at home, gone to the ruin of ashes and lava. "My poor people!" Father Williams mourned, again and again, underlip a-tremble. Hail! Father Williams—you are a joy forever; and long may you administrate Savaii.

Thursday, May 21, 1908.

The sea, which began rising early last evening and necessitated taking in the lifeboat, continued boisterous, with plenty of wind; then we found this morning that the barometer had dropped from 29:95 to 29:85. I am verging on nausea, and Jack has already been head-over-rail. His disagreeable sores are not improving. "For a man to live the way I do," he grumbles, "and to catch things like this—" Whereupon we recall French Ernest, and also look askance at Captain Warren's hands, which are unpleasant with sores that will not heal. That gentleman has hardly spoken all day, which renders meal-time very genial and sociable—also other times. We have dubbed him The Blight. He sits and sits in the cockpit, sometimes steering, more often idle beside a man at the wheel, and glowers, just glowers. What can he be thinking of? There is no discipline aboard, no work cut out for the men. Henry and Tehei sit and sit, doing nothing when they are not steering; no polishing, no scrubbing, no sailorizing. At first they hunted around for work, the willing pair; but few men are going out of their way to do anything for a master who requires nothing of them.

The Apian turtle expired at nightfall. We weren't ready for him to expire, but he fooled us. Martin thinks the lifeboat squeezed him, for about the time the captain was struggling with his temper and the boat, the turtle heaved an unearthly sigh, and to-day seemed very listless, with drooping eyelids.

The barometer rose again this afternoon to 29:95, although the weather looks about the same. We are sailing fast, and the decks are awash amidships, but dry forward as usual. Wada has to keep his decklights screwed tight and has a warm time, although our thermometer is dropping slightly.

In the slate and silver of twilight I was taking a brisk ride on the weather quarter, balancing on the broad teak and brass of the rail, and watching the surging whitecaps— "flocks of Proteus"—when the most extraordinary thing (for the *Snark*) happened. It took out of me all exhilaration in the rushing Trades, the speeding boat, and the bulky seas, when one of the latter, rising straight up alongside, was a little too quick for the *Snark's* sleek avoiding stern, and broke over my head, curling down with surprising weight. It wasn't warm water, either. Of course I was drenched, and the shock and chill made me almost hysterical. But in a few minutes I was dried and clothed in oilskins, and Jack took me forward to the lee shrouds to watch the big waves. The water washed to our knees, clear over the rail, and we climbed higher. I wish I could tell of the glorious tang of life in these moments, when our brave little ship is holding steadily, stubbornly, through thick and thin, and we talk of our plans after Suva. Everything now is "after Suva." Jack looks cheerily at worn and neglected tackle (rings on the forestay dangling loose, lashing on mizzen boom jaws gone entirely, the peevish smouldering eye of the captain taking no care), and says, "When we get to Suva, I'll do so and so." After Suva, the decks over the galley will be washed first in the morning, so Wada will not have to prepare breakfast in that awful heat. Suva is our Mecca, and, after Suva, Paradise.

Except to say that he would like the mainsail taken in that we might have some rest during the night, Jack has not further interfered with his captain's management. But there really is no management.

Although this has not been a red-letter day, and some of our blessings would seem to be in disguise or saving for the future (e'en "after Suva"), we are glad to be riding close to the mysterious ocean in our intimate small vessel, rather than borne aloft in a "modern wedge of steel," a "floating hotel," on which the sea is primarily a medium of convenience for getting somewhere—like the undulating and beautiful earth under a fast automobile. Give us the small but doughty *Snark*, every time!

May 22, 1908.

One hundred and twenty-seven miles in the past twenty-four hours, under jib, staysail and mizzen. The gale has moderated somewhat, but we haven't dared the mainsail as yet. The sun is perceptibly going north, and we notice a slight coolness of wind and water as we sag southwest.

May 23, 1908.

One hundred and fifty miles.

We do not say much about the captain, but tacitly distrust him more and more, the farther we fare toward the mess of reefs we know is before us. We have a canny wariness of reefs by this time.

Henry caught a bonita to-day on one of his own big pearl-shell hooks, and we had it served in various ways—baked, with tomato dressing, and sliced raw, native fashion, with French dressing—better than any raw oysters in Christendom or Heathendom; and chowder for supper.

May 24, 1908.

The *Snark* may shake herself into kindling wood for all the captain cares. To-day the main boom tackle parted, shortly after the mainsail was set, and the big sail jibed over—always a dangerous contingency. Luckily the gale had eased. The poorly-lashed boats move and grate. Decks and tackle are untidy, and as we surge along we can hear the regular scraping rhythm of our large anchor, which is hanging outboard and knocking against the bow. The man must be crazy. He knows the anchor was not stowed on deck when we left Savaii—which has always been done hitherto, as a matter of course—and that it is wearing the planking thin. Surely is he stretching his length of rope that Jack has given him, for he realises there is no more rope. He was heard to-day muttering, "I guess I'll get my walking papers at Suva!" He is incredible. But we do not act as if anything were out of the way. We chat cheerily at table, play cribbage and poker and casino evenings, quite as if he were normal and approved.

. . . Land! Always new, always fresh, this illusion of discovery. Out comes the chart, and the sextant is ready to hand for the first rift in a stubbornly overcast sky.

May 25, 1908.

If we of the *Snark* are out for sensations, we certainly caught up with a few yesterday. The combination could not be surpassed—a small boat entirely lost in a no-

toriously bad tangle of deep-sea reefs, with a skipper who
had not only lost his head completely, but who sat down
with it in his hands, piteously admitted his befuddlement,
and made no effort to brace up.

Now, here is the situation: Nanuku Passage, the ship
channel into this vast archipelago, is roughly sixteen miles
wide, formed on the southeast by the islands Wailangilala,
Naitamba, and Yathata, the northwestern side bounded by
Nanuku Reef and islets, the small island of Ngamia, and a
large island, Taviuni. We were sailing a southwest course,
running before a breaking gale, and keeping a sharp lookout for the entrance islets. Captain Warren made a six-
teen-mile miss in his calculations, so that in the middle of
the forenoon, yesterday, he picked up the westernmost of the
islets, the Nanuku Islets, whereas he thought them the east-
ernmost, Wailangilala, Naitamba, and Yathata. On this
disastrous basis, he turned and ran to the west of the westernmost, thinking he was entering the Passage, whereas he
was running away from it.

Swinging along fast and free, we were all interest in the
pretty low land dots, covered with trees, when, above the
rush of wind, like the crack of doom came a sudden crash of
breakers and Henry's screech of "Breakers ahead!" They
were so close that only a terrific spurt of intelligent and
concerted energy on the part of every one on board (Jack
waited not on any captain this time) saved us from annihilation. We just, and only just, evaded the creaming ledge,
and doubled back on our tracks, literally very much at sea.

Resuming our southwest course, we barely escaped another bursting ledge of coral, and turned back again. And
every time we resumed our course, we got into trouble. In
the early afternoon, running deeper and deeper into the
labyrinth, no matter which way we steered, Jack, thoroughly alive to the peril, suggested that there was only one
thing to do, as the sun was showing signs of breaking through
the grey sky—to get our certain position by the Sumner
Line. This is a very useful method, as we have proved before,

when you are trying to find your longitude and are unable, on account of an overcast sky at morning and noon, to obtain your latitude. Warren was shaking, and said he was unable to take observations. Jack secured one at three o'clock and another at five, and asked Warren to work them up. He tried, gave over, saying he was too nervous; so Jack turned to and did it himself, finding our position to be a little south of the Ringgold Isles. We had worked through and around the sunken tangle of Nanuku and Nukusemanu Reefs, which enclose a sort of long lagoon full of scattered dangers which we had almost miraculously avoided, considering the lively breeze.

It was well after five when the sights were worked out, and we seemed to be clear for the time being; but after a few miles, we discovered coral underneath us, too close for comfort. This was Budd Reef, about eight miles westward of the central part of the sunken reefs connecting Nanuku and Nukusemanu Reefs. Budd Reef, according to the Sailing Directions, is thirty-three miles in circumference, much of it sunken, enclosing a deep lagoon with several islets in it. We sailed by two or three of these islets, heliotrope-green in the imminent twilight, and Jack saw what he thought a good anchorage. But Captain Warren demurred, and we kept on, the coral visible at all times but a few feet under our keel. The swift twilight overtook us in this position, and it was decided to beat back and forth all night in the lee of these islets, and set our course for Suva in the morning. This was taking chances, but what else could we do? Sympathetically we thought of the old explorers, Tasman, D'Urville, Bligh of the *Bounty,* and of course Captain Cook, who wandered likewise in these forests of coral, and although we had charts, little good had they done early this day, with Warren's erroneous position. Small solace would have been ours, had we been wrecked here, to know we were not the first yacht that had been.

It was a queer evening. Warren refused to dine, and kept at the wheel, tacking back and forth in a fairly moderate sea; the rest of us finished supper, sat on deck a little while, watching the glooming islets, and when Jack and I went below, he unpacked his two old square grips that have been our familiars on many a trip, gave me one for myself, and repacked his with manuscript and notes, and his gold. I was blithely instructed to stow my own valuables in the other grip; and, this done, we kissed good night and retired peacefully to our little bunks. I think we must have been tired, or resigned, or both; for never on the long voyage of the *Snark* have we put in a better eight hours than on this risky night.

The mornings are so wonderful, so various. There never was another in my life at all like this. Coming on deck at five, the trade wind flooded me through and through with unwonted coolness—a coolness without bite, a coolness liquid and suffusing, with no hint of sharpness. The whole universe was heliotrope, a flat tint laid upon the bowl of the sky where a gold sliver of new moon was painted above the two hilly islets showing softly green through their darker heliotrope. Small creaming waves rippled by on long swells that were grey-purple with a flush of red from the shallow coral. It was like some gently-coloured pastel, with the underlying details and colour growing as one gazed.

Captain Warren looked a wreck. He is only a child; but he is not a good child. In spite of his flunk the day before, he now regarded us with a white expectancy of praise for his wan hours of watching. "I never closed an eye all night—I brought you through safe!" he quavered. Sheer luck it was that saved us, not he, for it had been simply hit or miss chance in the dark; and even as he spoke, Henry at the masthead yelled "Breakers!" and we had to hustle mightily to skirt the streak of white water close upon us. (Jack has only now confessed to me that during the sixty days' traverse to the Marquesas, he more than once found Warren asleep at the wheel in the night.)

At six the mainsail was hoisted, and in a fair breeze our

intrepid keel cleared the uncertain lagoon and swept southeast for Somo Somo Strait, on our starboard Vanua Levu,
next largest of all the Fijis, and Taviuni, fourth largest, to
port.

It has been a happy day. Jack has smiled all over, stepped
merrily, and hummed at his writing; and more than once
we have looked at each other and chuckled over the manner
of our retirement last night.

We breakfasted on deck, not wanting to miss anything;
and then I brought my books to the cockpit, to study up a
little on Fiji. I found that there are two hundred and
fifty-five islands and islets of all constructions from low
coral to high volcanic, in an area of 8000 square miles, and,
dull slump from childhood horrific connotations of "Fijian," that the natives are "nominally Christians," reformed
of cannibalism and other sweet practices of less than seventy
years ago, such as the binding of live human bodies to
lengths of banana trees, for boat-rollers to launch great
war canoes—to the music of mortal shrieks accompanied by
crunching bones and tearing flesh. But there were merciful
impulses among the Fijians, as displayed in the following
custom: When parents had lived so long that it was deemed
a kindness to kill them, their devoted children affectionately
bade them farewell with kisses, before wrapping the living
bodies in fine (but not too fine!) mats, burying them alive,
and faithfully treading down the squirming graves. These
lovable deeds were invariably performed when the yam and
taro were in season, so that great feasts might be enjoyed
to celebrate the timely passing of the beloved.

It is small wonder that few persons know the accepted
spelling of Fiji. Here are several that England had to
select from: Beetee; Fegee; Fejee; Fidjee; Fidje; Fid-
schi; Feigee; Vihi; Viji; Viti—and the natives call themselves Kai-Viti. We civilised people are Kai-Papalanhi.

The Fiji Islands grow sandalwood, tobacco, breadfruit,
bananas, and all the rest of the tropical blessings, and in ad-

dition are especially suited to cotton-raising. It is interesting to read that some of their cotton was used in our Civil War.

The more I dip into the South Pacific Ocean Directory, the more I believe that to me it is going to take its place as the most fascinating of all books. Few volumes four inches thick are casually attractive; but once studying this one's pages, in connection with an adventure like ours, nothing can equal it for romance. The personal opinions of the compilers lend a pleasant spice of humour—as, for instance, one writer, after noting that the Taviuni inhabitants were formerly the most cannibalistic of all the Fijians, with practices quite too revolting to mention, tacks on the gratuitous observation: "However, they stand as records degrading to our nature."

Somo Somo Strait is four and a half miles at the narrowest. The big mountainous islands rise four thousand feet, hooded in rolling glories of tropic clouds. Here and there waterfalls drop their white plummets or blow rainbow veils across the green steeps.

Not the least of yesterday's impressions was the absence of life on the islets among which we were lost, and this morning we saw our first Fijians. Well for our peace of mind that we knew them to be friendly, for the bushy-headed, negroid-featured, staring-black-eyed savages were not reassuring on the face of it. A cutter put out from a village on Taviuni, under a cloud of canvas, and as it drew near we could see the white flash of their grins as the men shouted and waved to us. We waved back, and put our best foot forward for a spurt with them, although knowing well that the *Snark's* sail-plan was not for racing with sloop-rigged vessels. As the woolly piratical-looking crew gained on us, Captain Warren ordered Martin to start the engine. This did not strike us as a sporting proposition, and we said so; but Warren coaxed, Jack shrugged, and Martin went below. We could see gesticulations of surprise on the driving

cutter as we gathered speed, which changed to derisive point-
ings and laughter as they finally won by in spite of our
engine, and heard its chug-chug.

Nearing the end of the warm afternoon, our breeze
has dropped to a mild summer fan infinitely restful after
days of buffeting. Jack is reading under the cockpit awning, which is stretched for the first time since Samoa. He
has finished his story "Chun Ah Chun," one of a collection
of Hawaii yarns that he will entitle *The House of Pride*.
I have completed the typing of it and, drawn by his subject,
have put in a couple of hours on the shaping up of my own
book of Hawaii.

Koro Sea, Fiji Archipelago,
May 26, 1908.

In all our "Snarking," to-day occurred our first "gamming"—exchanging calls with another vessel at sea. We
were skating quietly over the Koro Sea, in the heart of this
vast archipelago, the water smooth as a blue jewel, crusted
in rough-cut gems—these the distant summer isles of green
and gold that encircled us. From one of these, Koro, we
made out a speck of a white-sailed boat coming our way.
It proved to be a, cutter much like the one we raced yesterday, but only a single shock-headed native was visible. He
shouted and gesticulated, and a white man stuck his head
up from below, rubbing his eyes sleepily. A yawn paused
midway as he caught sight of us:
"What ship is that?"
"*Snark*, San Francisco!" Captain Warren returned.
The man sprang to the rail and yelled excitedly:
"Not Jack London's yacht!"
Being assured by us, he fell into his small boat, while all
hands were called to take in our spanker and spinnaker—
the latter set for the first time in many a long day. Then
we lumbered ahead creakily under short canvas, and had a
good deep-sea gossip with our Yankee visitor, Frank Whit-

comb, who was so elated over meeting Jack—evidently an idol of his—that he could hardly talk coherently. Every time he started to answer questions about the islands, he would break off with something like:

"Well—Jack London!—I can't believe it!" And again, "To think of my ever seeing Jack London and the *Snark!*" And over and over: "This is the greatest day of my life, I tell you!"

He was enthusiastic over the lines and compactness of the yacht, and kept repeating, "Now this is a proper boat, this is." Or "My! but this is the kind of boat I'd like to have to cruise around here in!"

He paddled back to his sloop, and returned with welcome potatoes, onions, yams, and some taro. Then, after an exchange of addresses and some bottles of our Tahiti wine, and the promise on Jack's part to send him a *Snark* book when it is published, he departed, reiterating to the last that it was the happiest day of his life. . . . We may never meet the good-hearted fellow again; but this brief kindly contact will be unforgettable.

.   .   .   .

Suva, the capital of the Fijis, on Viti Levu, the largest of the group, is a much visited port, so I shall briefly run through our delightful week there, on to the day when our new skipper, one Jack London, took the *Snark* out of Suva Harbor, bound for the difficult New Hebrides, with their cannibals and burning mountains.

We received a most lovely impression of Suva as we throbbed through the reef entrance and crossed the long harbour. The quaint English town rises terrace upon terrace against green hills, the houses smothered in splendid trees. Viti Levu is eighty-five miles long by fifty-seven wide, its beautiful mountains climbing to a height of 4000 feet, capped with the inevitable tropic clouds.

The Harbourmaster, Captain C. Woolley, with open-armed hospitality came out to pilot us to an anchorage. Captain Warren, soiled, unshaven, unbelievably unkempt, insulted him with a cold shoulder and the ungracious suggestion that he guessed he could bring in the ship without any help. I saw Jack flush painfully; but Captain Woolley, recovering from his surprise at such treatment from a yacht-master, smiled a little smile and said:

"I am not going to charge anything for conning the *Snark* in, Captain!" and turned to Jack and me. He piloted us to a very convenient anchorage to the boat wharf, and made arrangements for Jack and me at Mrs. MacDonald's Hotel.

Captain Warren went ashore shortly after our arrival, quite unconcerned over the condition of our pretty bow (the anchor had worn clear through the planking), and of various other inexcusable damages. He did not go near the yacht for two days, accumulated many drinks, and strutted around town like a pouter pigeon, meanwhile bragging that he was captain of the *Snark*. The first time he went aboard, it was to show off his command to a guest—when he was informed by a delighted Wada that his things had been sent ashore to the hotel by Mr. London's order, and that there he was to report. He reported, and I confess I was eavesdropper to the interview that culminated in his dismissal—on the captain's part entirely a whine that Jack was influenced by the fact that he had been in the penitentiary. However, Jack left no honest doubt in his mind that that was the very reason he had been kept on from Papeete —to give him his opportunity. Within a couple of days, Warren had secured a chance to work his passage on the five-masted schooner *Samar*, in port, bound for Australia. He quit us several hundred dollars overdrawn—all of which was part of the "rope" Jack had given him.

As we entered the harbour, the British Cruiser *Cambrian* steamed out, taking the High Commissioner of the South Seas, Sir Everard Im Thurm, on a tour of inspection to the west. Captain Lewes of the *Cambrian*, and his wife, Jack had met in Korea; and now Captain Woolley invited us to join a party the following day in a walk out on the barrier reef at low tide, the party to include Lady Im Thurm and Mrs. Lewes, the latter having stayed in Suva to keep Lady Im Thurm company at the Government Residence. We gladly accepted, and during that novel tramp learned things about reefs that made us more than ever anxious to avoid them in the *Snark*.

We occupied two cosy little English rooms at the hotel, with four-posters and candles, and Mrs. MacDonald made us feel quite at home. She has lived in the Fijis for many years, and distinctly remembers times when the natives were not nearly so "nominally Christian" as now; and many and absorbing were her tales over afternoon tea in her shady green balcony, of the sailing she did with her husband years ago to the various islands.

The steward in the hotel dining-room is a diminutive Solomon Islander, called Johnny, who grew up here. I can see him yet, ludicrously dignified and condescending, forced, from briefness of stature, to look aloft when every instinct of his courteous hauteur calls for a downward glance. He has a funny thin-lipped mouth, big staring black eyes and a button of a snub-nose, his seal-brown countenance shadowed by a tremendous black poll of inky wool sharp-carven as a wooden image. Johnny announces meal-time with a stately solo on a large cowbell. Meal-time! How we did consume the fresh vegetables, and real cream, and cheeses, to say nothing of good red English beef, broiled wild pigeons, and many kinds of fish. At our table sat a kindly old man, Mr. Watson, who has kept a curio shop here for many years. He found me a few fans and things, and clubs for Jack; but he had to make quite a search for them. Fans are especially scarce, as the natives, now they can buy white men's commodities, have almost given over fashioning the old-time articles. The Fijian fans are much heavier and better woven than any I have yet found—compact and firm, with thick short handles. Jack's clubs are exceedingly fine, carved out of rich-coloured hard wood.

At table, Jack had the seat occupied by Madame Melba on her last visit. Suva is a profitable port for artists. Madame Carreño is a great favourite, and I met one of her pupils at the Warden's one day. One of our most vivid memories of the place will always be Blanche Arral, the Belgian concert soprano, and her husband Herold Bassett, who were at another hotel, surrounded by the most entrancing "boxes" labelled "On Tour," a French maid, a skurry of fluffy blue-blooded Skye terriers, and a cluster of blue-eyed Siamese cats presented the diva by the King of Siam. They are a fascinating combination, the Arral-Bassett; and her tropical wardrobe—I spent an entire afternoon of sheer delight in it. Suva was buzzing with enthusiasm over Mme. Arral's voice.

The main street, along the water front, as seen from our balcony, was always alluring with its procession of strange life. The contract labour here is largely Hindoo, and the heavily be-turbaned men and heavily be-silvered women looked very foreign even among the natives. One conspicuous custom of the Hindoos is their public shaving at the shore edge of the street.

The Fijians are very different from our Polynesian friends, sharing, as they do, in the Melanesian strain, which renders them darker of skin and negroid of feature. Our next islanders, the New Hebrideans, are sans Polynesian, and are rated as the lowest of the Melanesians to boot. The Fiji men struck me as far superior to their women. It is said, however, that the chief-women in Fiji, especially among the mountaineers, are strikingly beautiful; but we saw none of them.

And through this driftage of varying blacks and browns up and down the long thoroughfare, the big equipages of

elegant, luxurious Englishwomen clank by, and everywhere
is the military neatness and impressiveness of English atmosphere.

We worked hard in Suva, answering mail, and doing our
regular work as well. One item of news from home was
that *The Pacific Monthly* was to bring out serially Jack's
novel *Success*, which they have decided to entitle *Martin
Eden*. But our work did not prevent us from making some
very pleasant social contacts. We were entertained at the
home of Mr. and Mrs. Griffiths, of the Fiji *Times* (she is
from Texas, and edits this bright sheet, besides bringing up
her seven children), and they also took us on a pigeon-
hunting expedition, where we saw many miles of the rich
tilled and tillable lands of the island. Lady Im Thurm's
and the Warden's and many another card were left at our
hotel, and we met the townsfolk at teas and receptions—one
of them at the Government Residence; and there was one
evening's dancing at the house of Lady Im Thurm's secre-
tary, Mr. Rankin, where we saw a native dance which somewhat resembles the Samoan siva-siva.

It was very cool in Suva, so cool we were threatened with
colds. There is dengue fever here, too, and Jack and I were
of no mind to repeat our Florida sufferings with the same,
which we knew under the name of Boo-Hoo Fever, from its
ability to make one weep at the most trivial things. Earth-
quakes are also among Fiji's attractions, and we had a good
stiff one; but there are no active volcanoes, alas!

Besides the pigeon-shooting trip, our only other exploring
out of Suva was to Rewa Town, a famous native village up
the Rewa River.

We started in the morning on a little river steamer that
made us homesick for the Sacramento, and, as we got under
way, the schooner *Samar* was shaking out her sails for departure. Passing the *Snark*, we waved our hands at Wada,
working on deck, and pointed toward the big schooner's

preparations, for Wada knew Warren was to sail in her. Wada misunderstood our gestures, ran to the flag-halyards, and dipped the flag three times. Jack and I laughed, wondering if Warren thought the salute was for him. Before we entered the river, the *Samar* was under way, every sail drawing, and that was the passing of our third and last captain of the *Snark*.

We were well conducted on this bit of tourist route, by our native guide, a natty youth with the fuzziest of head-dresses, brushed stiffly up and cut in the usual sculptural fashion. He wore a white shirt and a coat of very visible stripe, and carried a cane with a nonchalance that would have been impressive but for bare legs and feet, and his nether garment, which was a white lava-lava.

Our attention was much taken up with the other passengers—bushy-haired natives with leaf-tobacco over their ears, and a little Hindoo huddle of women and their delicate-featured, turbaned men. These little women bore gorgeous ornaments, for thus do they carry their own and their husbands' wealth. Silver is beaten into anklets, armlets, bracelets, earrings, and every other conceivable decoration, and gold coins are immediately appropriated as ornaments.— And thus the Far East toward which we are reaching, lures us on our way.

It is twelve miles by steamer to Rewa Town, and I do not know which of the several mouths of the stream we entered. It was narrow, and edged with rooty mangrove swamps, and our little steamer poked her nose into them more than once and had to back out. The Big Water, as the natives call the main river, is dotted with fairy green islets, exquisitely reflected in the smooth stream, and we passed gay boatloads of natives. The river, now flanked by valuable sugar-cane plantations, rises some forty miles beyond Rewa Town, in the mountains—very dangerous territory for explorers not so long ago.

We landed on a flat bank of rich black earth at the village, and immediately noticed our old Samoan acquaintance, the sensitive plant, which shrank inhospitably from our feet. Ratu Joni E. Malaitini, the Roka, or Chief, of Rewa, took gracious charge of us. He is another specimen of the physical aristocracy—head and shoulders above the common people, and straightens up with a proud "I am!" when asked if he is pure Fijian. We noticed the humble salutations of the women to him as he paced along.

The first point of interest was the English church built by the natives—a beautiful structure with two square towers, like Westminster, and a rounding back, on the lines of Notre Dame. In the vestry we noted big savage war-drums made from logs—now used for the peaceful call to prayer.

Fijian houses are very fine in workmanship, the chief-houses having great beams covered with the finest sennit of cocoanut fibre. Roofs are sharply peaked, or gabled, and of immense height, the ends curving up, Japanese fashion, with black ridgepoles. The thatch is sugar-cane, and the outside walls of the houses are covered with some sort of dry brown leaves. Interiors are very dark, smoky from floor-fires, with but one door and a couple of small deep-set windows. After accustoming our eyes to the acrid gloom, we could see the lofty sennit-beamed ceilings, and judged some of the ridgepoles to be as high as fifty feet. Along the irregular paths among the houses rise occasional carven king posts, some of them thirty feet tall, of splendid hardwood. We longed to send one home as a souvenir.

Into the most imposing of these remarkable buildings we were conducted with great ceremony, and presented, with still more form, to a shrivelled object in the centre of the long floor, disposed upon thick-woven mats. It was the old chief, Ratu Rabici, the most ancient thing I ever saw alive. He was shaking with years and alcohol, being a noted toper; but in spite of his emaciated mummy-face, with its lacklustre eyes, large ears, and a monkey-trick of scratching his protuberant ribs with a skinny claw, he managed to convey to us something of his unmistakable kingliness. I was dying to question what might be his honourable tally of human feasts, but realised that, even were I so rude, I would not get the right answer.

It was good to be out in the blowing sunny air again, among the breadfruit and tree ferns, where we found women making pottery—some of the older ones with a finger or so missing, it being an old custom to cut off a finger in token of mourning for the dead.

In one of the more modern native houses, full of light and sun, reclining on deep-piled mats we partook of one of the best native feasts we had had south of the Equator. And while we ate and drank at our ease on the satin-smooth hand-woven mats, from somewhere came young voices singing Christian hymns. One of them was "Pass me not, O gentle Saviour," and I smiled to think how old Moody and Sankey would have beamed to hear it in this outlandish environment.

.   .   .   .   .   .

Aboard the *Snark*, Fiji to New Hebrides,
Saturday, June 6, 1908.

You might think that *Snark* departures had by this time lost their novelty. Not so. Our departure this morning from Suva had all the snap and go of a new adventure; and rightly so, for it was literally a new adventure. Jack was captain, Henry (who had had desertion in his eye "before Suva") was now mate, and the newest thing aboard was the spirit that sailed with us. It was "After Suva," and Jack was happy. Every one was merry; every one had reason to be. The Blight had been wiped out, and Mr. London was skipper. Tehei for the past week was so happy over the prospect, that, when Jack raised his pay, the dear child-man begged to be allowed to work for nothing; but "Nothing doing!" was Jack's reply. Nakata was all teeth, and went about his work emitting happy little noises. Martin wore a face of extreme contentment; and Wada hummed in his hot little galley.

Anent Jack's taking command, Martin tells the following

ludicrous conversation between himself and the "manageress" of a hotel in Suva, who volunteered that she'd heard in town that the *Snark* was going to sail without Captain Warren. Martin answered that this was true, but that Mr. London was going to be skipper.

"I should think you'd all be scared to death to go without a captain—I would!"

"But Mr. London is going to be captain," Martin repeated.

"My goodness—it doesn't seem right for a little boat like that not to have a captain!" she pursued, with feminine disregard of any one's speech but her own.

"Well, we all think Mr. London is a better captain than any the *Snark* has had yet," Martin warmed up. "He can navigate all around Captain Warren, and—"

"Oh, it doesn't seem to me safe for you fellows to trust yourselves at sea in a boat like that without a captain."

Martin ground his teeth and forthwith discovered he had business down street, leaving the woman to vapour over the dread future of the *Snark*.

Our first memory and our last of Suva Harbor will always be of the unremitting kindness of Captain Woolley. He saw us safely out as he had seen us safely in, and rendered us a thousand other kindnesses.

The northwest trade was blowing a youthful gale, and as our course was southwest, we boomed along before it. In order to make good time, and sail free of the honeycomb of reefs to starboard, Jack set the spinnaker. We rushed along with a corkscrew sort of motion, our copper heel in a churning cream of foam. Pretty work it was, steering through the blowing world of sea, and we were not alone in it, for there were many little white cutters in sight.

. . . It's going to be a rough night, and we shall miss Mrs. MacDonald's fluffy, stationary beds.

June 7, 1908.— 150 miles.

And it was. I fell asleep toward morning, and was dreaming heavily of a free-for-all fight of the *Snark* crew with Captain Warren, when I was shaken awake by Henry's laugh on deck—a musical yet rollicking gurgle of utter content, like an American negro's. And when I came on deck, gentle Tehei was singing a himine at his work. Henry unearthed some hitherto unheard-of (by us) navigation books, and pottered with them at odd moments. The morning faces of all hands brought to our minds that this is the first time we've ever had a true "Snarking" crowd aboard.

Jack slept but three hours, owing to a bad cold as well as the responsibility of the boat, and did not try to write to-day, but busied himself getting hold of everything, and, most important, brushing up on navigation. He gave us all a serious talk about our individual responsibilities, at the wheel, and such matters. Watching him to-day, it puzzles me how he is going to accomplish all he has laid out, in addition to his writing.

Nakata and I figured out additional little conveniences for Jack in his stateroom—a pencil rack here, a book rack there. I took the chronometer time for him when he was making observations. I have a feeling that he has not been altogether satisfied with the way they have worked out.

No land in sight, not even a reef. Wind increased until Jack ordered the spinnaker and headsails in, and in the afternoon we sped under mainsail and spanker.

We are so full of plans. Adventure looms bigger than ever; and why shouldn't it, with our first cannibal islands but a few days away?—and volcanoes. I shall take my volcanoes in quite an easy matter-of-fact way ere long! Captain Cook—of course—discovered Tanna, with its living crater, on August 4, 1774. Read what he wrote about it and wonder if we of the *Snark* are at all bored:

"At daybreak, August 4, we saw a low island (Immer) to the northwestward . . . having passed close to it during the night, and a high one nearly east (Futuna) at the distance of eight or nine leagues. The large island (Tanna), toward which we still directed our course, extended from N.W. to S.E. and consisted of a high range of mountains. Towards the southeastern extremity, at the end of a secondary range of hills, we discovered a volcano, of which we had really seen the fire at night. It was a low hill, much lower than any in the same range, and of a conical shape, with a crater in the middle. Its colour was reddish-brown, consisting of a heap of burnt stones, perfectly barren, but it afforded a very striking sight to our eyes. A column of heavy smoke rose up from time to time, like a great tree, whose crown gradually spread as it ascended. It is the most powerful volcano in the group. The whole island, except the volcano, is well wooded and contains abundance of fine cocoa-palms; its verdure, even at this season, which is the winter of these regions, was very rich and beautiful.''

In 1872, Commander Markham visited the crater, which was found to be about 600 feet in diameter. The officers of H:M.S. *Pearl,* in 1875, found its height to be 980 feet. Mr. F. A. Campbell says: ''This volcano is a splendid lighthouse; there is no mistaking it; the noise of its eruptions is heard distinctly upon Aneityum, fully forty miles away.''

Monday, June 8, 1908.

The coolness of the weather has made us hunt for blankets at night and warm raiment by day. I have caught Jack's cold, a sore throat, and neuralgia in the face.

There was a sharp squall in the afternoon, followed by calm, and the warmth was grateful to us with colds.

The day has ended very joyously for Jack. Without going into technical details—I should promptly be swamped if I did—he has discovered why he was going wrong in working out his sights since we left Fiji. He had forgotten one very important factor: that a degree—sixty miles—is only sixty miles at the Equator; and that the world is smaller and smaller around the farther one is from the Equator. Down here, in 19° South Latitude, he had been figuring sixty miles to a degree. As he says, any one who wants to break all speed records circling the world, has only to sail around in a fast steamer in the latitude of Cape Horn!

Just the same, Jack will not feel entirely satisfied until day after to-morrow, when, according to his calculations, we should see our first high New Hebrides island, Futuna.

Tuesday, June 9, 1908.

A shark! We lured him and caught him with all the customary excitement. He was a five-footer, and no one who ate a steak from him at breakfast had any criticism to make, either of meat or cooking.

Quite calm all forenoon, with low rain-curtains on the eastern horizon. About 3:30 the wind came out of the southwest, and the sea made up. Barometer falling.

We play three-handed Hearts evenings. But Jack and Martin are having everything their own way, while I mourn my bad luck.

Wednesday, June 10, 1908.

We're all a-tiptoe now, to see how right Jack is. Land must be near, for there is a lot of flotsam on the water, and many brown-and-white birds about. The night was rough, as the *Snark* shuddered into the big seas, but all slept well, except Martin, who has caught our cold. Wind lessened toward sunset, and barometer is 30:10—which we find is normal here.

We have been loafing about the cockpit in a burnished gold sunset, talking about our landfall to-morrow. Jack smiled his wise little smile at my jibes, and said:

"That's all right, my dear; but you watch my smoke. I tell you that about six to-morrow morning you'll see the prettiest classic blue cone your heart could desire, rising a couple of thousand feet out of the sea to the southwest."

He altered the course so that the *Snark* should pass Futuna ten miles to the northward, and the last thing he said on going below, was to Wada:

"Wada San, your watch to-morrow morning, you look sharp, you see land on weather bow."

Aboard the *Snark*,
Port Resolution, Tana, New Hebrides,
Thursday, June 11, 1908.

We are so proud of ourselves. Not that we mere mortals have anything to be proud of, except our godlike skipper, one J. L., whose mystical rites and figurings bore out his prophecy and guided our "frail barque" into this turbulent harbour. Turbulent does not refer to the waters of Port Resolution, but to the bottom thereof. Not long ago, inside forty years—large ships could anchor here, and now only vessels of our draft can float free. Each new survey has been put out of line by the upheavals of this restless island. And one is never for a moment unconscious of its instability, what of the intermittent dull rumble of the volcano. The 1901 Sailing Directions are the latest we have; and it would be more interesting than comfortable for us if it were now about time for the bottom of the bay again to heave up and strand us high and dry.

The *Snark* logged a steady six knots all last night, but Jack confesses he slept little. He kept waking and thinking: "Just suppose I am wrong, and run into the damned thing!" He went on deck at three, during Henry's watch. The log recorded forty-two miles. At 5:30 he went up again, and Wada, at the wheel, had seen no land. Jack planted himself on the cockpit rail and gloomily stared southwest. I rose at six, and joined him just an instant after he had spotted the dim but unmistakable high cone. And it was exactly where it ought to be! I could have wept with delight, but remained very still, for Jack was still, too, although pleased clear through, with that little half-bashful smile he wears when he sits under praise. It was a great moment, in its small way, and it is the small things that make great contentment. This was his first unaided landfall, as captain and navigator of his own little ship, with the burden of lives in his care.

We could not go below, but sat and dreamed our dreams in the growing day. The west was all silver and rose, the east steel and lilac, with low clouds scrolled back like Gargantuan rolls of sleeping mats, and to the south Futuna grew like a mirage on a clear horizon, or a Japanese painting on grey silk. The ocean, grey and dull-glossy, and slow like a flow of lava, seemed to show the bulge of the earth between us and the island. The sun rose suddenly, an irregular molten nugget of intolerable brilliance bursting from a low grey cloud lined with gold. The cloud-mats became bales of precious stuffs of undreamed dyes. Then all dazzling hurt of colour and gilt toned into the soothing pearl and blue of broad morning, the sea into a rapture of azure, and we all woke to noisy congratulations over our fair prospect, at a ripping good breakfast of hotcakes and shark-steak.

Jack had said we would pass Futuna at ten miles. At eight o'clock he took its distance by the sextant and found it to be 9.3 miles away. It is a steep truncated cone, 1931 feet high, ten miles around, and not peopled from the New Hebrides, but by some Polynesian canoe-drift.

Henry, aloft, had sighted Tanna at seven o'clock, dead ahead, and during the day our steady six knots brought us into better and better view of the towering smoke of the volcano, Mt. Yasowa. To the south we had Aneiteum, and to the north Aniwa.

As we approached Tanna, Jack bade me take the wheel, sent Henry aloft and Martin below to be ready to throw on the propeller. With his glasses Jack swept the land for miles but could detect no opening in the crashing, unbroken rock coast. He took his compass bearings—one of Futuna, another of Aniwa, laid them off on the chart, and found the

Snark's true course to be straight for this apparent ruin. He had me hold on until we were not more than an eighth of a mile from the thundering surf, much to the concern of Tehei and Henry, who declared there was no entrance. Then I was directed to steer parallel with the coast. They were taut minutes, I'll own—taking orders over that huge oily swell, so near to swift destruction. It was not as if this were a solid and dependable island of staid habits. Our only information about the reef passage was seven years old, and we did not know what had happened since, or when we might grind on disastrous bottom.

But Jack kept on abreast, and presently we recognised certain landmarks described in the Directions—a yellow sandstone bluff and a pyramidal rock; then, just where it ought to be, a narrow opening appeared, but outside of it a line of breakers. Henry and Tehei regarded it with troubled eyes. As we ran on, still abreast, we saw that the line of white water overlapped the line from the other side, and a narrow place showed where the sea was calm. I put down the wheel, Martin threw on the propeller, and to Jack's "Steady!" and hand-movements, I steered in, full of relief, while the boys took in sail. We rounded a little point and saw the mission station, and when Wada, at the lead-line, reported "Two fathoms!" I put the wheel down, Martin shut off the engine, and the anchor-chain grated through the hawse-hole. It was five o'clock. Henry gravely paced a few measures of a hula, Nakata pirouetted and flashed his teeth, and then we were diverted by the things that were putting out to us from all directions.

They looked like an all-star troupe of comedians made up for a minstrel show. All were undersized, except one, a Futuna boy who was tall and large and handsome, with laughing eyes wide-set, and a mouth all smiling Polynesian curves. One Tanese, a spry, slender soul, with near-set black eyes, wore sideburn whiskers combined with a fierce moustache. Another, a holy-mannered, fanatical-eyed elder of the church on the hill, had a fringe of thin black whiskers halo-ing his rotund countenance, the lower part of the fringe growing beneath the chin in a way that made him resemble an American backwoods farmer gone wrong. But he proved a lovable chap. The rest of the men were all individuals of one kind or another of striking personality; most of them spoke English of sorts, and all were connoisseurs of sea-biscuit and tobacco.

And yet, five miles back in the bush, the savages are unreclaimed ancestor-worshippers who eat one another to this day, although Mr. Watt, the missionary, assures us that an European is perfectly safe anywhere on Tanna. It is thirty years since a white man was killed here, and he was shot, and not kai-kai'd. He died in the house where Mr. Watt lives.

From the little station in a bight of the bay, came the Scotch trader, Mr. Wyllie, with gifts of fruit, and we kept him for supper. He is a vast ashen man, with ashen brown eyes very wide apart, ashen hair, mobile ashen mouth and a classic ashen nose. He looks as if the tropics have burned him to this ashen hue.

Mr. Brown, a Christian native, "Joseph Brown, please," elder of the Presbytery, came out with a message from Mr. Watt, that owing to prayers ashore, the supper hour, and the lateness of our arrival, he and his wife had not come out, and hoped we could return with the bearer. Tehei, blissful and self-conscious, ran the launch for us. As we climbed up the perfumed twilight bank, a woman spoke to our guide softly and inquiringly from a gloom of bananas, then fled before, white-robed, laughing and calling back tantalisingly to him in a love-toned voice.

Port Resolution, June 12, 1908.

There's certainly something disjointed about it—so lovely a land, and so low an order of inhabitants. The beautiful harbour, like a pale flawed emerald, reminds us of Taiohae, the painted-scene walls farther removed. Distant classic

Mount Mirren rises opposite the narrow reef entrance, and the verdant flanking hills fold down on either side—a most gratifying composition for a picture. The missionary's dwelling is on Point Resolution, and across the narrow bay boils a hot salt-water geyser, whence Mr. Watt and his family derive their bath water, in barrels per native canoe. This may be the very geyser where vanquished foes once were parboiled and devoured—a different way of preparing "long pig."

And the natives: As I write, near by but not too near (they may be clean but they don't look it), squat a half-dozen of the strangest human beings I ever beheld outside a feeble-minded institution. We had heard they were the lowest of the Melanesians, but they excel all expectations. Bodies are thin and unbeautiful, with bulges in the wrong places; legs show thin and crooked, and their generally evil, low-browed malformed Black-Papuan faces are curiously repulsive. One old fellow, a trifle less unpleasant than the rest, has an expression that is intended to be benevolent, on a nut-wrinkly face with unsecret, sky-turned nostrils, the eyes most remarkable with the vacillating intentness of a monkey, while he endeavours to compose his attention on the typewriter, at which I have been working on deck. He is quite the nearest to a chimpanzee that I've ever seen. The gaze focuses, wavers, comes back, and his lips narrow and widen with an undeveloped attempt at a human smile. The only way to fix an image like this, is to sit right down and write.

Another old baboon is titillating in a hysterical rising-and-falling squat, aft where Jack is showing him a kaleidoscope. Nervous little lean brown arms of others are reaching for the thing, and there are lingering low cries over the changing figures. Jack looks a white giant among them. "And God made them!" he passed across their kinky heads to me just now—vast contrast to the chiselled heads of Fiji and Samoa. Their talk matches their shifting eyes—nervous, crafty little short sounds, and no arresting words.

About twenty different dialects are spoken in the New Hebrides, sometimes several on the same island. As no steamers can enter here (they must lie outside if any one wants to land in a boat), the island is seldom visited. So we and our foreign vessel are a whole vaudeville show to these near-Simians. There is nothing even "nominally Christian" in the appearance of this gathering. New Hebrideans are all looked upon as treacherous, although the Tanese are milder than most. In the history of the islands, when the missionaries treated with the natives, the latter would only go so far as to promise that they would not harm them with their own hands; then they would hire other natives to do the murdering—a grim observance of the letter of the agreement. Natives of the northern islands have been especially ferocious toward intruders, and the list of slaughtered missionaries is a long one. Mr. Watt has quite a congregation in his mission, but a good portion have the Futuna Polynesian strain.

Mr. Watt is a big man of sixty, kindly and obliging, and has already this morning added to last night's offering of pleasant fruits and vegetables. He also offered us the use of his cool dark-room. Mrs. Watt is his second wife—a buxom woman of forty. They have two young children, and all reside in harmony in a comfortable house almost in the shadow of an imposing white monument that marks the green resting-place of the first Mrs. Watt—in the very house garden. The present Mrs. Watt called our attention to it on our stroll. Mr. Watt, from whom we naturally expected to drink endless absorbing reminiscences of early precarious years on Tana, either does not care to talk, or else has no imagination. Perhaps he is like Conrad's good skipper in *Typhoon*, who entered "Dirty Weather" in his log, after passing through the core of a great circular storm.

Later. . . . After another visit at the Watts' to-day, where we were refreshed with rose-apples, sour-sop and sweet-sop, cocoanut water, and saw breadfruit and banyan and banana trees in abundance, we went to the head of the little three-quarter-mile bay in Mr. Wyllie's flat-bottomed skiff and visited him in his store, on a tiny blue reedy lagoon surrounded by dense tropical vegetation. An old paralysed black heathen sat on the beach where we landed, and looked at me and my camera with sullen, unsympathetic gaze—sans fear, sans interest, sans understanding, sans everything. It would seem that the only idea these people ever possessed was to kill. With that ambition quenched by the joint French and Australian colonies, they resolve into mere nonentities. Evidently all their craft went to the one passion; and their general lack of clever house-building or mat-weaving, or ornament-devising, would bear this out. Mr. Watt pointed to a coarse mat on his floor: "I taught a Futuna woman how to make it," he said, "and the Futuna woman was largely Polynesian." Simple, suspicious, blood-mad people they were. Robbed of their natural quarry, they are rapidly decreasing. Mr Frank Stanton, a younger trader with Mr. Wyllie, told us to-day that right before you, in apparently ordinary conversation, they can plot to take your life, using sentiments already agreed upon, about common things. This came out after a little incident that happened at the store. I was imitating cat-calls to mystify the fox terrier, and a small Tanese boy in a group outside elected to think I was making fun of him and his companions. You should have seen the black looks of the murderous mites! Many a white head has been lost for less offence.

. . . The bay is the tender milky green of absinthe with little vagrant flaws of wind ruffling the wavelets with sparkling white. A softly flooding tide rocks my boat of dreams, and the air is full of intangible lights and subtle rainbow tints as sunset begins its painting of land and sea. It is good to be alive, on the highway of the sea, with its crowding waves upon the backs of waves; and it is good to be snugly cradled at anchor inside the silver-rimmed breakers.

Port Resolution, Saturday, June 13, 1908.

Late afternoon, and I am dangling my feet in the water over the side of a skiff, to rest them after the unwonted heating and blistering they have had tramping to the volcano, six miles away.

This morning we were roused early by natives dynamiting fish near by in canoes. Immediately following the blast, men dive overboard and bring up the stunned fish, while others spear the fish from the boat as they float up.

While we were packing lunch for our trek into the "bush," the missionary came out with drinking cocoanuts, lemons, and two wild ducks, which made Jack very desirous for supper time. Mr. Watt was accompanied by two Aniwa housemaids, who wanted to see the *Snark*.

One of our two thin-flanked Tanese guides was a "returned Queenslander"—a native sent back from the plantations when Australia "went white." He could not be convinced that the *Snark* is not recruiting plantation labourers.

Each new wonder island I have thought the last word in beauty; but to-day's impressions eclipsed all others. We plunged into an abrupt wilderness of trees and hanging, creeping, trailing, veiling things so green, so spectacular that I was soon tired of exclaiming, and moved in a trance. There is almost as much child-time romance and glamour to me in a banyan as in a volcano or an atoll. And to-day I tangled in the incredible downward tentacles of innumerable real, true banyans that covered broad spaces of the rich earth. Along the way grew little odourless white violet-things, and a running vine with a violet leaf and red berries, and there was a hardy vine with a morning-glory sort of blossom, pink-purple and white. It lies on the ground, clinging, and wickedly trips a tired foot. Another vine we called a "live wire," for it stings to sudden caution.

We pushed aside giant brakes, and made our way under

Houseboys at Pennduffryn

A Dream of the Southern Seas

the finest tree-ferns we have ever seen, even in Jamaica—
and one heavier and darker green variety here has a tall
trunk spotted leopard-like, the spots being round indenta-
tions at close range, and the fronds look as if stamped from
deep-napped green plush. These are so abundant in places
that, as Jack remarked, "One can't see tree ferns for tree
ferns." There is a fine cane growing here, too, something
like the Marquesan, and it flowers and feathers out like pam-
pas; and one species of palm showed bright and hard in the
soft general green, with big fronds apparently clipped
squarely off short of their legitimate points. Strange para-
sitic, clambering, choking things veiled the forms of the forest, and one of them fairly *furred* the limbs of the large
trees.

The eerie stillness of the jungle was shattered now and
again by explosive grunts of startled pigs, which, although
nominally wild, are the known property of various natives.
In fact, the whole jungle is a wild-pig run, the ground everywhere, under the larger trees, thoroughly snout-ploughed.
Trudging over the black-rooted, bountiful earth, we were
aware of the slow flight of flying-foxes overhead, softly,
heavily flapping their velvet wings. And at irregular intervals would come the growl and rumble and shock of volcanic explosions.

A big father of banyans marked where we should strike
up hill to the right, and shortly we were in an altogether
different environment—volcanic sandy lands of coarse
grass, interspersed with hot steam-geyser sections where we
walked on a crunching crust. Once I broke through to a
boot-top in natural red paint—red-hot, too, it seemed to me
—and simultaneously burst a deafening reverberation from
the crater as if I had pressed a button. I wasted no time
getting that boot off. Coming home, Jack stepped into a
nasty red-paint hole and the steam rushed forth so hot and
strong that my helping hand was scalded. The guide pointed
out a spot where a white man had heart-failure. I couldn't
blame him, if his heart was weak, for I was unable to control

the sting of nervous fright from heart to finger-tips, every time the monster let loose that awful roar.

Off to the side we glimpsed pretty sandy sinks, and little round fairyland valleys where the trees were ferns, and threw lovely lacy shadows. The first views of the volcano, from some trick of atmosphere, were very unreal, and seemed an endless distance away. From the crater rose a milky-opalescent quiver of smoke, swirled by pearly puffs from some special impulse at the depths. There was something uncanny about our progress. We traversed a little plain of iron-coloured sand, wind-rippled, bounded ahead by a rose-bed bank where mocking voices repeated our every word, word for word, but changing the inflections—spiritless, bodiless, the like of which we had never heard before nor shall ever hear again.

I did not know our guide "boy" was plum-coloured, until I got him into surroundings of plummy-brownish old lava. Flesh, scant raiment, and lava-lava, all were plum—even his eyes plum-purple. Once, returning, he went ahead down a narrow gulch defile where all the ferns were dead and red-brown and touched to Etruscan gold by the late sun, and the half-wild creature was likewise gilded.

We did not feel the altitude—it is less than a thousand feet to the top of the crater, which is nearly two miles around by now. Panting up the creaky final steep of coarse sand, to the crusty edge, Jack and I speculated as to just exactly what our judgment would be to do if the earth should suddenly shake and crumble in a real eruption, as it has done before and might do again. Jack said, "I'd grab your hand and hike down the slope as fast as God'd let me!" We had but just gained the ragged summit and made ready to peer into the maw as the smoke should clear, when there was the most infernal crash and burst and shake of ground. Without a thought but escape, we just exactly "grabbed" hands and went down that fearful, reverberating, grinding incline on our flying heels for a dozen leaps or so, until we suddenly realised what a scream our involuntary action was. We halted, looked at each other, and began to laugh. And we laughed and laughed until we cried, and sat down to laugh, and rolled with laughter, and laughed all the way up again. Partially we were comforted by the fact that our two brown companions had fled faster and farther than we, and they have been here countless times. One of them, indeed, refused to come back; but the other, with a long feather in his wind-tossed, scraggly wool, looked no end picturesque on the sharp edge, with the far wall of the crater, smoky-dim, for a background.

This time we were not to be driven away by any pyrotechnics of old Yasowa, and waited hand in hand at the brink for the void of smoke to dissipate. And then, we gazed down unspeakable depths and glimpsed a ragged red ridge losing itself in the lower abyss of fumes and smoke. Doré would have revelled in it. Following around the crisp and crackling edge where the sand fell away from the hard, old lava, we began to realise with grim interest that our foothold was the uncertain roof of the main vent of the volcano, which curved down and back underneath. We could make out two holes, with a saddle-ridge between us and the smaller hole on the opposite side of the crater. Now one would explode, now the other, and rocks would fly up swiftly, growing larger and larger to our vision, then sink apparently slowly, softly, or run down declivities where they had been shot. White smoke and steam would fill the great hot well, and we would sit and wait for it to clear. The only way to describe the sound is to suggest a titanic grumbling, gnashing being trying to free itself from pent chambers of earth; or, less fancifully—cannon of all sizes and sounds, accompanied by musketry; then add to both fancies a violent thunder-storm breaking over the deafening clatter of a busy day in a boiler factory.

Our lunch was eaten sitting with backs to the crater, and we never lost the rhythm of mastication when the dogs let loose in the kennels underground. From here we could see the green world of island stretching out across blue-shadowy valleys to Mirren and the other high peaks. Tana is only seventeen miles long by seven in width, so we gained a comprehensive impression, with the blue-flushed horizon ringing us three quarters around.

I was a footsore sailor as we followed down the mountain behind our savage guide with his triumphant cock-feather atop, and his swinging, slashing bush-knife clearing short cuts through dense growths.

The Watts bade us in for tea; and now I am going to climb aboard and ask my gentle friend Tehei to lomi-lomi these broken ankles; for to-morrow is another tramp, to a native village in the mountains. Jack's feet are tired also; but he is not making so much fuss about it.

Sunday, June 14, 1908.

We are tired again to-night, and Martin also, for we walked and climbed a twelve miles round trip to the bush village. The latter, in addition to scratches, is fuming because the Reverend Watt quietly but firmly declined to lend his dark-room on the Sabbath, because of the deleterious effect it would exercise upon his congregation. Martin, muttering that he never heard of a native who wanted to work on *any* day of the week, no matter what the example, went to developing the day's films in the hot *Snark* bathroom; result, mostly failures. We are all heartbroken, for the pictures we took of the queer hairy human animals in the bush would have been invaluable to us. Martin will never forgive the missionary.

Jack started the day with a hair-cut, Henry at the helm —I mean the scissors. I put tapes around my lame ankles, and laced my walking boots tighter than yesterday. Said boots, a sailor shirt, broad hat, khaki riding breeks, and a 22 automatic rifle for sport, made up my equipment. Martin remarked with a smiling eye that Mrs. London looked "very pantesque this morning." Which rather personal observation may be indulgently allowed, for Martin has ever been the soul of impersonal comradeship and delicacy toward me. Indeed, the tacit taking of me as ''one of the boys'' has been one of the most charming things about the spirit aboard the *Snark*—combined always with the ready hand to help and protect ''the best man aboard,'' as Dutch Herrmann would say. I remember, one time when I was railing to Jack about the way Captain Warren had thrown us down, Jack chided:

''Yes, I know; but don't forget one thing: he was always good to you, not only in his personal treatment, but in turning over to you any loot of any sort—whether it was a mat some one had given him, or a pair of gold-lipped pearl shells, or a pearl.''

. . . We got away at nine, this time in care of Mr. Stanton —a true-blue-eyed, serious mannered, clean young Colonial, the type of earnest, self-respectful Englishman, made of grit—so much so that he can never grow fat. He has suffered terribly from the malignant, devastating malarial fever that all have to reckon with who dally long in Melanesia.

The country traversed yesterday was quite unpeopled so far as we could see. But to-day we passed occasional slovenly grass huts, some of them enclosed in pandanus-plaited fences—the only decent workmanship of any kind that we saw. The women were deadly unfeminine—nearly resembling the men in face and voice, ageless, sexless, dirty; and they and their men displayed an ungracious inhospitality that made us think vividly and lovingly of the Societies and the Samoas. In spite of the scant differentiation between the sexes, these men are notoriously jealous of their females, and special scrutiny of the latter on our part was met by ugly scowls. If any savage smiled, for any reason, it was momentary, monkeyish, and instantly over.

Our way-led to the left this time, and shortly I was forging ahead, for I love to go first along a trail, first in a new vista with a sense of breaking my own trail. I fear there is little of the burden-bearing, heel-obedient squaw in my make-up! We travelled beautiful ferny trails where we had to use both arms to press aside the enormous green fronds. But the woods were not so spectacular as on the volcano side, and many a time Jack and I could nurse a homesick feeling on the familiarity of this scene or that. I even discovered five-finger ferns.

Flying-foxes drifted aloft, and we heard querulous little chatterings among parroquets we never glimpsed in the thick foliage; and there were myriads of wee green canaries flitting and twittering among the lower leaves, and strange small black and white birds with snubby heads.

The chief articles of export of the New Hebrides are copra, small shipments of coffee, bananas, maize, sago, and, in latter days, diminishing quantities of whale oil, sandal-wood, and bêche de mer. Traces of gold, nickel and copper have been found, and Martin spied something that he declared was coal. We saw copra drying on patches of volcanic rocky ground hot in the sun.

When we sat to rest in the shade, Jack and Mr. Stanton talked about wars, in Korea and South Africa, and swapped experiences.

It is like wandering in Eden, to trip along in the wilder parts of this blossoming isle. As we began to ascend mountain fastnesses to the village, I wondered if Jack's and mine were the first boots up the uncanny runway, for Stanton went barefoot, and Martin emulated him. This runway was a matchless approach to a mountain stronghold, for the narrow perpendicular sides were above our heads, and the point where we emerged in a high meadow containing the village, would spell unavoidable death for every single person who should show himself, were the natives hostile. Stanton had assured us of our safety from any tricks, but based the assurance upon the fact that he knew the head man, who was in debt to him for certain favours, and we were expected. Just the same, when we came in sight there was an alert movement ahead, of all the figures on the short fine grass where they lay about, and subdued exclamations from some grimy hovels of grass, mere roofs without walls, off to the right where we caught sight of the disappearing backs of women.

I had never seen animal-hairy humans, and the score or so of naked men that gathered shiftily and uneasily to meet us, were for the most part very fuzzy indeed. It was almost a fine black fur that matted their chests and limbs. They were better formed and fuller-fleshed than the saltwater natives, and their faces showed more diversity and character. It was rather startling to note that some of the faces were painted—strange countenances reminiscent of old civilisations—a notable sprinkling of a Phœnician type; a decided suggestion of the Hindoo; and one bearded old patriarch, despite unspeakable encrustations of filth ("Sty-baked" Martin put it) was a veritable Moses of the old Masters—in miniature, to be sure.

After a protracted pow-wow on Stanton's part with his chief-friend and the council, it was granted that we might photograph the men—but not the women. Any attempt of Jack or Martin to take a snap at them where they crept among the houses to look at us, was met with undisguised scowls and mutterings. I was allowed to approach the low plaited fence, but when I trained my pocket kodak, there was an instant disturbance behind me among the men. So I smiled and nodded submission and kept the lens in the same direction, but turned my own side toward the women, snapping them while I enthusiastically admired the prospect up-mountain.

The women were shyly friendly with me, from over the plaited screen, and did a great deal of giggling. The chances are they had never seen a white woman, as it is very unlikely that they are allowed far from the village, and we are told that no white woman has been in the village before me. The babies were round and dimpled brown cupids, their ear-lobes scooped out and filled with hair-pins, bone rings, safety pins—all sorts of "truck" brought home by the foraging fathers; and strings of shells girdled their pot-bellied little loins. These people are polygamous, and the wives are equally fond of one another's children, even in the same plural household. One old lady, fat and black and fuzzy, was the picture of a southern mammy.

But the gathered clan of obscene, hairy men on the grassy meadow-slope, their only covering a string or a strap, and a wrapping or bandage of astounding phallic advertisement, was a far wilder sight. They were so uneasy, so shifting—lying down, getting up, moving here and there and back again, like a band of monkeys, and never turning their backs to us—a trick of caution that white men would do well to imitate in this corner of the world. We were quite aware that our unwilling hosts were armed, too, with spears and bows and arrows, and they evidenced their consciousness of our rifles by undisguised covetousness of them.

We did not stay long, and I for one breathed easier when we were clear of the descending runway and in the open once more. We lunched under a banyan, took a good rest, practised with our rifles on tiny leaves on top branches of high trees, and reached the traders' store in good time to pick up Mr. Wyllie for supper aboard the yacht.

Aboard the Snark,
Tana to Efaté, New Hebrides,
Monday, June 15, 1908.

At three this afternoon Martin started the engine, I went to the wheel, Henry to his post at masthead, and Jack forward to con. We had intended to put in at Wysissi Bay, a few miles from Port Resolution, but changed our minds after we got outside, and set our course for the port of Vila, on Efaté, or Sandwich Island.

This forenoon Martin, Nakata and our two Polynesians took the volcano trip, all barefoot. Wada did not go, as he has developed a sore on his leg, from a cut he got on the coral—like the ones Jack had. They are known as Fiji sores, and Solomon Island sores, so the doctor in Suva told us.

Some one called them yaws; but Stanton says yaws are a much worse thing. One's skin is thin and tender after a while in the tropics, and the least abrasion, say from scratching a mosquito bite, is apt to become infected, most likely by flies, whereupon trouble begins, and the difficulty of healing is appalling. Jack and I had been so alarmed about his sores that we had privately talked about laying up the *Snark* in Fiji and taking steamer to Australia and the doctors. But Jack is not one to be idle while he waits. He read up in our little medical library aboard, found nothing like his trouble, closed the books, opened the glass doors of the medicine chest, and selected the most violent enemy he could locate with which to fight these malignant and active ulcers. "Corrosive sublimate" sounded more fiery and radical than anything else, and he started dosing the five sores on his instep and ankles (where he had scratched Samoan mosquito bites) with wet dressings of a solution of corrosive sublimate, occasionally alternating with peroxide of hydrogen. Four of the ulcers were entirely well by the time we reached Fiji, and the last is almost closed up—all of them thoroughly healed from the inside out.

There are myriads of flies in Tana, and many of the natives who came aboard had ulcers, so it is probable Wada got his infection by these means. Jack has warned him, and Martin and the others, to use antiseptics on the fresh abrasions they got on the volcano trip, but they do not seem impressed. I am not afraid, for I practically never "catch" anything.

. . . I was up early this morning, in time to see the sun gild the tops of the green, green hills, and light up the heliotrope of the bay. Mt. Yasowa boomed dully, and natives were dynamiting fish. Henry and Tehei went out to get some for our breakfast, and came back grinning from ear to ear, with small mackerel, and a long fish with a red-tipped sword on its nose. A bevy of low-chattering, watchful naked cannibals paddled out aboard, and one of them, who seemed a wag among them, a canny-uncanny wizened ape, insisted that he had seen Jack before, to our gales of glee.

Everybody came to see us off, and brought basketfuls of fruit and vegetables; but so far as the kindly Reverend Watt was concerned, Martin remained unforgiving of his ruined pictures.

We ran the engine for three hours, then set sail; but it soon fell calm, and we are now drifting, with plenty of leeway. We are all very alert, for it is no joke to be wrecked hereabout.

Yasowa flared into the sky as dark came on, and then a big bright moon rose, so we have ample light for our night watches.

Tuesday, June 16, 1908.

At six I was on deck, and our patent log told of thirty-six miles to the good since we stopped the engine yesterday. We lay west of Erromanga, called Martyr Isle, from the many missionaries horribly butchered by the cannibals, and were drifting on a flat, grey sea, with no wind. Behind the long black island, grisly mysterious in the half-light, the fires of the sun were kindling,—lifting, flaring, fading, burning again, then changing into an unendurable splendour of blue and gold, in lateral bands, the massy clouds above shimmering gold and palest green, with palpitating purple shadows. Then followed broad fanrays of intolerable gold. To the southeast, Tana was shrouded in a blue opal mist, throbbing with liquid rainbow colours. The whole universe palpitated in an excess of passionate colour.

A little wind sprang up abaft, and we rippled ahead over a beautiful sea while the world resumed a normal appearance. Jack and I boxed in our bathing suits, treated each other to a salt pailing, feasted on hotcakes and Papeete honey, and put in a good day's work. About four the sea began to make, and we partook of Wada's wild duck and plum-duff dinner on a rolling boat.

At sea, New Hebrides to Solomon Islands,
Friday, June 26, 1908.

This is the day we should have sighted San Christoval Island in the Solomons, but the weather has been so beastly, with such dense cloud and mist where land ought to be, that we have had to be very cautious lest we run into some unseen peril of rock or reef. We have lain off and on all night, and heaved to at daylight to watch for a rift in the tiresome smoky cloud to show us the land. It must be near, for to-day a butterfly tangled in our rigging, and we have seen a number of white land-birds.

Remembering the *Snark's* refusal to heave to on that memorable night out from San Francisco, and in spite of better luck on a later occasion, we were a trifle apprehensive. This morning when I awoke and realised that the men were inducing this manœuvre, I called up to Jack:

"Won't she?"

Came his puzzling response:

"Isn't she?"

I repeated:

"Mate—won't she heave to?"

"*Isn't* she hove to, Mate?" he returned, and I scrambled on deck to find the little old tub safely and successfully hove to in a misty-moisty world of wet, and Jack grinning with achievement.

While all eyes are straining for the four-thousand-foot outlines of San Christoval, for a landmark, the course we want to make is between two small islands near the southwestern end of San Christoval—Santa Catalina and Santa Anna, four miles apart. Jack has decided to run in to Port Mary on Santa Anna, the western of the two, as the old sailing directions state there were a trader and a missionary there. We do not know what may have happened since, but are going to take chances. Nakata is cleaning the "arsenal," just to have it in efficient order. Mate is ill, and I can see he is anxious to prove his navigation correct, for this is not a reassuring place in which to go wrong. He had little rest last night, for thunder squalls were almost incessant, from ten o'clock on. The thunder was sometimes like a steady drumming, or the thrumming of gongs, and the lightning burst the bonds of the dark with brazen contempt for everything human or made by human hands. The forked and streaked thunder-bolts rove high heaven and shot crashing into the sea. Oh—one presses close to the nakedness and smallness of life at such times. Hour after hour the noise and illumination continued, and I caught myself in forbidden self-pity of nerve-weariness and eye-weariness. I had tried the cockpit floor, along with Jack, in our oilskins; then I fled to the dry white privacy of my stateroom, and pitied him wet and sick outside. I tried to sleep, but the lightning had crept inside my head, behind my eyes, into my very soul.

. . . At Vila, I was too occupied trotting about to write, and have been working hard these seven days at sea since leaving Vila. We arrived there on Wednesday, June 17, in a fine rain so dense that Jack made port by judgment rather than sight. It was squally, with a rushing, foaming, following sea. The engine chugged away sturdily, for a change; I steered, and Jack peered ahead for breakers. The mists parted and dispersed only as we slipped into the green land-locked harbour, and we bit into good anchorage in thirteen fathoms, to discover ourselves with plenty of company—nine or ten small vessels, five of them ketches, the others sloops and schooners, scattered the mile and a half breadth of the bay. And, of all things, Jack's friend Captain Lewes and the *Cambrian* had just steamed out.

I noticed that the French Residence and a French schooner flew their flags at half mast, and I pulled ours part-way down. The grewsome result was that the French captain of police, Paul Mattei, put immediately out, expecting to find some one dead aboard! It turned out that the captain of the French schooner had lately died.

Natives flocked aboard, a less scrubby lot than the Tanese,

but not much to boast of.   These Efaté islanders are among
the better sort, possessing a slight strain of Polynesian.   We
traded tobacco sticks and bead necklaces and things for
rather fine-woven basket-bags, and a fluffy dancing skirt of
shredded fibre dyed a plummy wine-colour.

We called upon the Acting English Resident, Mr.
Jacomb, an Oxford man, and upon the French Resident,
Charles Noufflard.   They returned our calls next day, also
Captain Harrowell, English chief of the native constabulary,
and we were entertained by them ashore.   Captain Harrowell seized Jack's hand in both his and cried: "And
this is Jack London!—Why, he's a household word in England!"   We dined with him and Mr. Jacomb, all in faultless
evening dress, with noiseless Chinese servants, and a white
silk punkah waving overhead.

M. Noufflard had us to lunch—all charming apology because he had just arrived and his household was not yet
running smoothly.   However, he had enough of his Parisian
treasures unpacked to set a beautiful table, which was served
by a shy native house-boy trained by Noufflard's predecessor.   At both of these meals ashore we were honoured with
cocoanut-palm salad—made from the very tip-top of the
tree, which loses its life thereby.   "Funeral salad," Martin
cheerily dubs it.

The English cruiser *Prometheus* arrived on the 18th, and
by her courtesy we had her blacksmiths aboard to do some
repairing,—a broken spinnaker boom, and other items.   And
Jack and I went over with our chronometer to rate it.

The British Colonial officials are strict, and our yacht
license availed us nothing; we were obliged to clear, like any
merchant vessel.   We did so, and got away on June 20,
sliding out under full canvas, dipping our flag to the
cruiser, which dipped and cheered in return.

That night there was a red glow in the eastern sky, probably Ambrym volcano.   Next day we could see two beautiful smoking cones rising out of the horizon—the most
wonderful experience.   One was Ambrym, the other Aoba,

or Leper. Island, 4000 feet high. Big Mallicolo, on our port side, tempted us repeatedly to put into its fascinating green baylets; but we were anxious to get ahead to the Solomons, where we might find a doctor.

Jack has gleaned enough from our medical shelf to feel confident in diagnosing his trouble as fistula—caused by he knows not what, unless it be some infinitesimal fishbone. He has a new crop of sores, too—and ample company, for Martin, Wada, and Nakata, who disregarded all advice about corrosive sublimate, are all now nursing bad ulcers—Nakata, especially, has our sympathy, for a large space on his calf, which he inadvertently burned with a hot iron, has become infected. Jack has his sores well in hand; but the others are praying for stronger and stronger cures, even corrosive sublimate being too slow for them. Wada talks in his sleep, and dreams of happy days in Papeete with his native sweetheart.

But Henry and Tehei are gloriously healthy. Tehei has been catching fish—big rainbow-bubbles of bonitas—and his yells of joy as he lands them blobbing on the deck, are a tonic to all on board. Jack says it's worth a hundred dollars to hear Tehei catch a bonita.

We sighted one of the Banks Group on the 23d. They were discovered by Captain Bligh, in an open boat on May 14, 1879, during his remarkable voyage from Tofoa to Timor, after the mutiny of the *Bounty*. They did not dare land and expose themselves to the atrocities of the cannibal natives, preferring the perils of the open boat.

Jack finished an article, which he calls *The Amateur Navigator,* and is now at work on a Hawaiian short story. He is certainly doing all a mortal man could accomplish.

One evening we were playing cards in the cabin, when Jack, who was facing the open door into my room, exclaimed in a tone almost of awe:

"Great God!"

I went cold, and followed his bulging gaze, expecting to see nothing less than half the warm South Sea pouring in.

What I did see was hardly more reassuring—an enormous centipede, fully six inches, making unerringly up the bunk-side for my pillow. Martin nailed it with Jack's big office shears, and was so calm about it that I asked him why. "Oh," he said, "I don't mind them. In Tahiti, the first day I got up, after six weeks in hospital, I sat on one. It didn't hurt much."

Our course from Efaté had been nearly north; but passing between the Banks Group to starboard, and big 5000-foot Espiritu Santo to port, we quit the New Hebrides and set the course northwest for the Solomons. We were content to be well away from Santo, as it is treacherously reefy, and the natives bear an especially unsavoury reputation, being the very aristocracy and autocracy of the New Hebrideans, athletic, strong, cruel, and well supplied with offensive weapons.

Oh, it is a wild part of the world, this—wild peoples, wild weather, and a wild boisterous sea at times. On the 24th we white ones all fell ill with violent headaches, as if we had been poisoned. Not the least of our comforts were Tehei's ministrations with his gentle hands, in hours of lomi-lomi—his *tauromi*. To our repeated mauruuruu's he would nod and bob and smile with the most benevolent manner.

It all wore off next day, but we felt weak and "rocky," according to Martin.

In addition to the myriad other things he is handling, Jack has a navigation class of two, Martin and Henry. I am glad of this, for we would be in parlous pickle if Jack were, say, too ill to navigate. While this is going on, I work with Nakata and Tehei at their English. Nakata is nothing short of brilliant, and has already gone far past Wada in our speech; but Tehei is despairingly an infant, and can hold nothing in his head over night.

Aboard the *Snark*, Port Mary (Upuna),
Island of Santa Anna (Owa Raha),
Sunday, June 28, 1908.

Curious Sabbaths these, at the ends of the earth. A week ago we were in the bush village on Tana, and now, here we are at last in our first port in the Solomon Group, inhabited by the most bloodthirsty and treacherous of any known savages—head-hunters who prowl for prey by night, on land and sea, rarely attacking unless their victims are at their mercy without risk to themselves. And this is going on to-day—indeed, on the next small island to the northwest, Ugi, where we are bound, the trader before the present one was surprised and murdered by a canoe-raid from the big bad island of Malaita—the worst in the world.

We are anchored in eighteen fathoms, with 250 feet of chain. In fact, the good old hook is in a hole in the sandy bottom; and we are about four cable-lengths from the beach village. The bay is on the west side of the little island, which rises 500 feet and is beautifully wooded.

Yesterday we were a tired and yawning lot of *Snarkites*, after another shouting night of thunder. The sky was terrific, brilliant intermittent flashes opening up deep heavens of illuminated cloudlands, followed by fierce hells of lightning-bolts and pitchy dark. We lay off and on again that night of the 26th, and yesterday was calm and lovely as a day in the Doldrums, the ocean like a billowing breadth of woven blue fabric, so fine were the rippling wrinkles, strewn with tiny violet Portuguese men-o'-war. All day we could see San Christoval; but our "tempery" engine saw fit to go on strike, and there was no wind. We worked as usual, and Jack was much gratified to find in his books a diagram of a different application of the Sumner Method, which he had already reasoned out independently for himself the previous day.

At sunset Santa Anna pricked out of the horizon—"Exactly where I wanted it," Jack affirmed. There was nothing to do but heave to again for the night, the isle of our desire melting in copper mist. Over the mainland—San Christoval—there were gigantic piles of smoky cloud, letting forth great bursts of sunset flame—reminding one of mighty sacrificial fires of the gods of the Solomons at cannibal rites. Out of the gorgeous chaos of colour and fire, there upthrust a lofty cloud-pillar like grey marble, that slowly blossomed out two broad wings of gold from its head. Never was anything like it in the kaleidoscope of the sky. And off to the east a false beautiful sunset flaunted fanrays of vivid azure against a background of palest rose-tourmaline that burned to ashy crimson. Higher up grew fairy mountain ranges of pure gold and ruby, with delicate straight cloud-lines drawn across. Tradewind clouds puffed up like pink roses out of the soft purple and rose sea, and to the south a city of dreams glinted on the horizon. Close at hand myriads of fish leaped in the coloured flood, and subsided only when the brilliancy went out of the world. Then San Christoval bulked ominously in its cowl of cloud, and we could not but imagine the benighted bush-heathen in their mountain lairs, killing and eating, hating and loving—with scant love—fattening their little women and children for the feasting. There are some much-hackneyed lines in "Greenland's Icy Mountains" that come unbidden in the face of the facts of life in Melanesia.

When morning broke, this Sunday morning, we found we had drifted slightly but made no headway. It is vast comfort to find our sinned-against *Snark* doing the normally-expected, and not the "inconceivable and monstrous!"

Martin started the propeller at 6:30, and Jack set our course for Santa Anna, or where it should be, for only squalls could be seen in that direction. We "steamed" for seven hours, without a dissent from the engine, at first on a calm sea, and later with a brisk trade wind in addition. "Just see us kite!" Martin panted from out of his diminutive hatch. The sparkling water was littered with flotsam —seaweed, fruit, banyan-leaves, twigs, grasses, cocoanut shells.

We were puzzled by what appeared to be a long yellow shoal ahead, and I confess to a little prickle of nerves when our bow cut into the discoloured water—merely a calm streak yellowed by a peculiar light effect from the sky. Over the long glassy swell of it we fared, flying-fish darting about, every one alert, and Henry and Tehei dropping vowelly exclamations, their eyes sparkling. One or the other was aloft all the time. Jack was tense and keyed-up, and I could see he was suffering physically; but he was living high, just the same, and his eyes were blue and snapping.

As we neared the channel between the two small islands, we noticed lines of black dots on the long low points reaching out from either island. Through the binoculars it was with a real, scary thrill I made sure that the ones on the port bow were moving back and forth restlessly. Soon the glasses showed them to be unmistakable human beings— black, naked, gesticulating, and increasing in numbers. The dots on the Santa Anna point of reef proved to be merely rocks. I can assure you that every man of us—including myself—knew exactly where his gun lay. There is nothing too bad that the books can say about the Solomon Islanders, and from Samoa on, the word of mouth confirmations have been a-plenty, so we were wide-awake and cautious.

No canoes put out, however, and we sailed on, I at the wheel, rounding the reef of Santa Anna and, finally, in a sudden, whipping rain-squall, passing through the narrow entrance. I'll never forget the picture, while I stole glances from the compass by which I was steering my very best, guided by Jack's hand-waved directions and frequent shout, over the noise of the engine: "Steady!" Across the jagged jumble of outer reef along which we slid looking for the passage, with a background of palms and lofty thatched roofs and a wooded hillside, rose stately the most beautiful canoes, more beautiful than Venetian gondolas—elegant of body, with high graceful ends, carved, painted, outlined with white cowrie shells, and manned by woolly-headed, gleaming-bodied, excited blacks. It was all so savagely beautiful, so unreal—so much stage-scenery faultlessly executed and acted. And we were hardly at anchor, directed to our present holding-place by a native who spoke a queer sort of English, than we could see a bevy of similar canoes approaching from Santa Catalina. It would seem that few vessels enter the Archipelago from the eastern end.

The islander who piloted us to our anchorage, gave his name:

"I Peter. I Christian."

But he looks it not. And it turns out that, being the worst of the boiling at Port Mary, and even now awaiting judgment from the Commissioner for threatening the manager of the Company (for whom he gathers copra) with a spear, he was the only one who mentioned his claim to religion, or took the trouble to be decent to us. He does not know why we are here, or who we are—perhaps to watch him, for all he can tell. Very ingratiating he is, very nonchalant and careless, in an elegant sort of way, and, as he is likely to be useful in finding curios for us, we meet him half-way. He has the most remarkable eyes, brilliant, shallow, wicked, with a soulless glitter of utter consciencelessness.

Peter explained, in what is called bêche de mer English, that there was only one white man here, Tom Butler, whose shack we could see ashore, and that Tom Butler was away getting copra on the other side of the island, and would be back to-morrow. But Tom got wind of us and returned today, rowed by two black "boys," in a whaleboat. He is as near a dead man as a live man can be—a ghastly object. He wabbled aboard almost helpless, a dead hand bumping against the gangway ropes—some tropic ailment having robbed it of all sensation and power.

"Lucky it's not your right hand," Jack sympathised.

"But I'm left-handed," Butler quavered with a sickly smile on his bloodless face. He resembles a white-faced, snub-nosed, freckled Irish school-urchin, and his one obsession is his friend the trader at Ugi—"Jack at Ugi." All the sense he seems to have he expends in being kind to us with what is left of his Irish good-heartedness. After one becomes used to his graveyard personality and the wandering bluish gaze that slowly focuses as he gathers his faculties to answer a question, he does not bother one's sympathies much, because what there is of him is perfectly self-satisfied. But conversation boils down to something like this:

"How's copra here?—much of it?"

An eye-focusing pause.

"Oh, plenty; but Jack at Ugi got out a hundred tons last Christmas."

Or:

"So you have no missionaries here any more?"

"No—no—but there's lots of 'em down at Jack's at Ugi."

"Pretty snug little harbour this," Jack remarks.

"Sure—yes—but there's a better one down at Jack's at Ugi."

Christmas is the one event of the year to Butler. He spends it with Jack at Ugi. He looks forward to it, and back upon it. Indeed, he practically never opens his mouth without working in some reference to Jack at Ugi.

We went ashore with Tom Butler in the whaleboat to his shack—a ragged wooden cottage with thatched roof. He was too weak to open his double-padlocked door, so I did it for him, and then poked about the premises seeing what I could see, while Jack, very much under the weather, lolled supine in a rotting canvas chair on the rickety porch. Then there dropped in the queerest bunch of callers I ever had—stark naked women and girls, with close-cropped woolly heads and horrid blackened teeth. The young women had rather pretty figures, except for a peculiar horizontal elongation of their breasts; but any facial beauty they might have is sadly marred by their unlovely cropped heads, which make them resemble microcephalous idiots. One Neapolitan-looking girl from the other side of the island, must have been a sport, or had some Polynesian (she did not look like a half-caste), for she had fine, wavy brown hair several inches long standing out all over her head, softly. The men allow their own hair to attain a sizable fuzz. Did I say the females were stark naked? The maidens usually wear a single strand of twine or cocoanut fibre around the waist, the matrons being distinguished by the addition of a single string dependent in front. Very much overdressed wives attach to their waist-string a grassy fringe fore and aft, about six inches square. I tried to bargain for one of these "dresses," but the woman shot a terrified glance at her man as she vehemently shook her head at me. Tom Butler explained that it would be a mortal offence for her to part with her fringe.

Three slim virgins volunteered a dance, to the music (?) of a jew's-harp at the mouth of one—a slow-stepping hula in which the dancers incline backward from head to knee, the lower-leg and feet angling to keep the curious balance. This performance took place surreptitiously in the cottage, as it seems the males do not approve of strange white men witnessing it.

I have always idolised the human form—filled my house with copies of Greek statuary, collected pictures of nudes, and revelled in the beauty of the cinctured native peoples we have seen on this voyage; but I must confess that there is a startle when one first sees women going about entirely naked. I shall become used to it in no time, I suppose; but the initial impression is a bit of a shock. The men here all wear a loin-cloth, no matter how short it may be of its purpose.

These people are as different as can be from the monkeyish travesties of human beings on Tana. They are well-sized, and well-formed, muscular, graceful. Their shoulders are peculiar, however—massive enough, but lacking the squareness we admire. They round down upon the arms instead of outjutting.

And oh, the ornaments! We have become more or less inured to the lovely practice of civilised women piercing their ears; but here, when you see the lobe-hole stretched

until it accommodates a wooden disk eight inches in circumference, it makes you think.

. . . We have returned to the yacht laden with yams,
cocoanuts and papaias. The bay is beautiful—never did I
see water so brilliantly, luminously turquoise—with a dazzling band of white beach that is not white but cream, not
cream but pink, a rim of sparkling foam at the water's
edge breaking against the ornate canoes hauled up, and
lovely emerald arboreal foliage behind, palms, papaias, hau
trees, and luxuriant thicket, broken here and there by the
sombre, uncanny roofs of the canoe houses where dead
chiefs are hung to dry.

Monday, June 29, 1908.

We had to keep anchor watches all last night, for it was
squally, and the bottom is rather skaty. In case of dragging, we hoped the anchor would hold against the sides of
that hole it is in.

Also, it is well to keep watches here on general principle.
While the natives of this outlying island are fairly well
disposed, Tom Butler says that raids from Malaita are always imminent, under cover of darkness and squalls, and
nothing is more to the taste of the Malaitan head-hunters
than to "cut out" a schooner laden with tobacco and other
loot.

It has been drizzling stickily all day, and we have stayed
aboard rocking gently to our long cable. But don't think
that we have been idle. The word went forth that we would
trade stick-tobacco for curios; and in no time it was easy
to forecast that the oldest treasures of the village would
soon go up in tobacco smoke, for although no women came
out, their choicest ornaments did—evidently seized upon
by the men-folk and brought for barter.

They wanted beads as well as tobacco; and in short order
we learned that the changing styles in adornment, of which
we had been told, is no myth. Just now the fashion calls

for a medium-sized bead—a small-pea size, and the people have evinced a most unaccountable—to us—aversion to certain handsome necklaces of graduated turquoise-blue beads. They will accept them as a gift—they'll accept anything that way; but if we indicate an exchange, they shrug and grin half-insolently.

All day they have clambered over the side, eager, avaricious, bringing treasure undreamed in carved nose-rings of thick turtle-shell; baskets ("bastiks"); shell-like flowers; garters of small white cowries on bands of finest cocoanut-sennit; elongated black cannibal calabashes showing more than the beginnings of art—indeed, the scrolls and figures on the ends are almost classic; beautiful giant "clam" shells with fluted lips, the insides like purest white marble polished to satin gloss—full of delicious meat, raw or cooked; and two actual clam-pearls—one large and round, one acorn-shaped, the surfaces like porcelain; bracelets from the island of Rubiana, of delicate-tinted, hand-wrought shell, finely etched in patterns—each bracelet must have taken months to make with stone tools; armlets worked out of the big white clam shells, that Tom Butler avers it takes a black a year to do; and one native, an athletic young hunter, brought bush-pigeons, trading them for a delicate flowered silkaline kerchief, which he now wears dangling from a greasy belt, against a dingy and very dirty lava-lava.

Jack took a fancy to buy back their beads of other days and modes, and we have a heap of rococo things such as armlets and broad girdles—the large beads wrought into fine plaited sennit. One is all green beads, another bright blue, another red and black—things beautiful enough to scheme a gown on.

Many a curio we bought right off its wearer, this lending an added value in our eyes. I can see some early antisepticising of the articles—such as one irresistible bead garter that was untied from a sore leg! Tehei is even now washing our dozens of Rubiana bracelets and the turtle shell nose-rings.

These people are "Black Papuan," but not as black as the New Guinea Papuan, so say the books. And in their dark-skinned visages one sees as it were all the features and combinations of all the varied white races of Europe, as well as the Orient. A fattish old soul, contemplatively puffing away at a clay pipe, was the perfection of a stolid bleareyed German, but for his colour. Another, for all the world a comical little Irishman, tried to palm off a very rotten calabash, and joined in the insane, brief cackle of merriment that went up from his fellows when we threw it aside. Still another was a typical Mexican—all he needed was a sombrero. One boy was the image of any city rowdy, on whom we kept a wary eye; but the more we saw of him the better we liked him; he was merely a good "mixer."

There was a pretty, impudent American-faced chap, of the weak and conceited sort that can get very nasty on occasion; and there was every sort of Jew on earth. One Moorish old chief, too dignified to barter directly, went home and sent his ornaments by some one else. We even found strong resemblances to numbers of our American friends! A thin, yellow-brown variation, with a few grey bristles on his lip, was the vegetable Chinaman of my childhood.

Peter was much in evidence, excessively dandified, and on easy terms with us. We found another Tomi than Taiohae Tomi—a good-looking, intelligent fellow, high with the chief, to whom we made presents, and who is also, with Peter, drumming up curios for us. Our private opinion is that they are a proper pair of villains, although too wise to get into any trouble with so well-armed and mysterious a craft as ours.

And then there's the Devil. His diabolical face and body seem at variance with an unusually mild and harmless disposition. Martin was just pouring an avalanche of stick-tobacco alongside Jack sitting on the deck-cot, when the Devil, in a canoe, squinted his basilisk eyes over the teak rail. "My God!" said Martin, and froze to the vision.

Jack looked at the thing and said: "I wouldn't call him that, Martin!"

It came over the rail, and sat down upon it. It wore a soft, old felt hat, that drooped limply around the face. The eyes are what I call half-moon eyes—the iris high on the ball, and partly covered by the upper lid. The thing is horribly near-sighted and squints its face into the most infernal expressions. On the top of the end of its nose is a tiny carved sliver of bone, set in a hole long-healed for the purpose, the sliver curving up like a diminutive rhinoceros horn, the sight of which makes one wrinkle one's own nose with involuntary and misplaced sympathy. Jack handed the Devil a small iron puzzle, and he snatched it with hooked fingers. I looked for a barbed tail, but found it not; and the feet were just as spraddly and hand-like as those of the rest of the spawn. He sat for hours over that puzzle, squinting ferociously. I was obsessed to decorate the creature, and hung about its neck the most delicate opalescent and blue beads. I took a picture of it, too, and then got it to remove its funny schoolboy hat. Lo! its hair was a yellow-bleached fuzz all over the crankiest conical head ever born.

Peter wears the nose-spike, too, and also one of the popular nose-rings that hang over the mouth and is of considerable irk when eating.

In addition to the disks of wood or clam-shell in their strained ear-lobes, the men have found other rich possibilities of disfigurement. They pierce holes along the edges of the ear, and in the topmost hole thrust a stick of polished white wood the size and length of a pencil or a sturdy section of macaroni. From the other perforations in the tormented gristle depend little bunches of small beads and porpoise-teeth, dangling coquettishly and ticklingly into the hollows of the organ of hearing. This dainty custom obtains with both sexes. They scorn not the tin keys that come with canned goods, nor the wire handles of tin pails, nor yet large rusty nails. The weighted lobes frequently hang nearly to the shoulder, and some are torn clear through, hanging in two shreds. One haughty councillor of the chief struts unapproachably with a white door-knob bumping on his grimy chest. Another, high in diplomatic circles, has a really handsome thing on his breast—a round flat disk four inches in diameter, of snowy clam-shell, worked thin by untold labour, and etched deep with symbolic figures. I am simulating a careless and rather contemptuous attitude toward it, a feeble interest, for it is evidently of vast value to the owner. But I think that by weight of tobacco and beads cleverly displayed whenever he is around, the great man may talk business.

They do not know what to make of the cameras, and are in dread that the black cases will go off. Nevertheless they brace up to the ordeal, although with an awful fixity of gaze. The deck, during the trading, was fraught with the most laughable un-misleading stage whispers concerning values of articles. It was very plain, among other things, that I was a great curiosity, and my comradely relations with my husband a source of wondering speculation. I believe they considered it surprising that the wealthy owner of so much tobacco should have but one wife anyway.

And in all this mêlée, trading, sorting, cleansing, and packing away our clutter of curios, we were ever courteous, careful not to antagonise, and we unostentatiously avoided letting our visitors get behind us.

Tuesday, June 30, 1908.

Another squally night, another forenoon of trading under the awnings; and as Jack was feeling much better, we had a jolly time. One filthy native produced a gold sovereign and offered it for tobacco; but that sort of thing is outside our sphere as a pleasure yacht, for we may only exchange commodities, and sell nothing.

Nakata went ashore to do the washing, where we found him in the afternoon, near the trader's cottage, cross-legged before a flat stone, scrubbing away, and opposite him two nude females likewise engaged, and all getting acquainted in bêche de mer English. Wada, hearing of the social perquisites of laundering ashore, firmly but inconspicuously gleaned every washable article on the yacht, and departed for the chaste strand forthright.

Jack, Martin and I wandered along a sylvan pathway under the palms, to the village, and found it quite unlike anything we have yet seen. The straggling oblong houses have very low sides and long-eaved roofs. Doors do not extend to the ground, but are reached across a waist-high, roofed platform resting on logs. There are no windows whatever, and the interiors are dark and smelly. Children squat and squabble on the platforms, while shy women lurk in the shadows behind. Tomi, whose house is rather superior, introduced us to his two wives—the first plural wives I have ever met. They were appropriately gowned for our reception, in single strings of tiniest coloured beads on cotton thread.

We noticed innumerable sores on both men and women—mainly on the legs, which invite more abrasions; and Martin groaned in disgust and sympathy, meanwhile spreading his shin-bandages a little wider, for there are myriads of busy flies. As the men gathered around, we noticed several who were minus a leg or an arm.

"Him fella boy bite 'm fella shark," was the unmistakable explanation. And the rascals deliberately advise us that swimming here is absolutely safe!

We are grappling valiantly with the current speech. This morning, having traded for a basket I particularly liked, Jack addressed the former owner as follows:

"You catch me fella one fella bastik all the same along this fella bastik—savve?"

And "How much you want along this fella or that?" is the beginning of a haggle.

Tom Butler's conversation is largely composed of this jargon. He says "Man pig and woman pig," "Man fowl, woman fowl," and, in describing a short distance, "A long way a little bit."

The women in general are very like the men in manner, after they have quickly conquered their bashfulness. They are beasts of burden, carry loads, and do heavy work, while the men "do the jamboree." And speaking of jamborees, we indicated in lovely bêche de mer that we should appreciate a dance. By now, anxious to please the possessors of so much tobacco, beads and "calico," they were willing to let the women perform for us; so we were led to an open space, where we sat about on the grass (fervently hoping there were no sore-germs in it), and saw a strange weaving circle through the most remarkable and not unbeautiful gyrations. We could only guess at the various significances of it, the stealthy, graceful hunting-step of Peter and Tomi, the monkey-movements of the pot-bellied brown babies, and the delicate sensuous danse au ventre of the girls—all to the quaint humming vibrations of the jew's-harp.

We tendered appropriate presents to the dancers, and then Peter and Tomi stole Jack and Martin, Henry and Tehei (who had followed along), and took them to a couple of the big canoe houses—long gabled roofs supported by carven posts. The sides are low, with equally low front walls, the big end-spaces above wide open.

The nearest view I am supposed to get into these sacred edifices is from the water, for no female foot is permitted, on pain of unnameable punishment, or death, to defile even the ground in front. At the first house I went a little nearer than was prudent, in a vain attempt to filch a peep inside, but murmurs from my following of dark heathen made me turn leisurely away as if I had never thought of such a thing. Jack is teasing me because I am of such an inferior clay and sex that I cannot follow him. He did not see much, however—the carved kingposts with obscene figures atop (there is one twelve feet high at a "four corners" in the village), a handsome canoe or so, and a

A Tambo Canoe House

Mangrove

grisly package suspended from the ridgepole, said to contain evaporated remains of chiefs. Henry still insists: ''I smell something that first place.'' Jack says he only imagined it. But in the second canoe house (I did manage an angle where I could obtain a glimpse), there was ample odour of a fresher sort, for a pig, on its back, was being singed, with a lot of men bending over it in the smoke.

I found more curious relics to-day, among them several black wooden trays, carved into fish shapes. I can picture a planked striped bass on one of them some day, in our Wolf House in the Valley of the Moon. We came upon a comically industrious group of artisans under the beach palms, working feverishly on new imitations of the ancient oval calabashes we like, as well as some small and laughably indecent wooden figures, which were being painted with natural pigments. The workers grinned sheepishly when we caught them manufacturing ''antiques'' with which to beguile our tobacco. Jack contemplated them for a while, then observed:

''They're like the man who was so greedy that when he was wrecked on an uninhabited island, it wasn't ten minutes before he had his hands in the pockets of the naked savages.''

There is no true hospitality nor generosity among these savages. It is an eye for an eye, a tooth for a tooth, quite literally sometimes. One old man, at the dance, asked for tobacco, got it, and later gave me a yellow-and-red fine-plaited armlet. It is the only gift we have received. This man, Butler tells us, is an unprecedented old murderer, a terror in the islands, and has killed more men than he can remember. And he, as well as others of his tribe, continually warn us against Malaita—Mala, they call the island.

I washed my hands very thoroughly after returning to the yacht—not because the hands I had perforce to shake were the hands of murderers and man-eaters, but because they were such unsanitary hands!

The *Snark* is a pretty vision from the beach, riding at

anchor, shining white, scraped and brassy, all trig and trim, with long booms out on either side, and the life-boat and launch moored thereto. No natives are allowed aboard in Jack's absence, but there are always a few small canoes hovering about.

We are reading *A Naturalist Among the Head Hunters*, by G. M. Woodford, and it is like a half fairy tale and half ogre tale. The Solomons, by the way, were so named because their early discoverers believed them to be the source of King Solomon's wealth of gold. Mendaña saw them first, only seventy-five years after Columbus discovered America. Woodford tells of the great beauty and variety of the flora, and the insects interested him vastly. This is not surprising, when one learns that the butterflies were of such proportions that to secure them he had to use a shotgun of some sort. In the 80's he sent home to England many skins of birds new to science—rare pigeons, parrots, and so forth; and lizards and rats several feet long. And as for the people—after years spent among them, he concludes that the longer he lives the more he realises that he possesses only the most superficial knowledge of them and their customs. It is as intricate a puzzle as Lafcadio Hearn encountered with the Japanese.

Wednesday, July 1, 1914.

Jack is so improved that we have been jubilant to-day. There was more trading in the forenoon—Jack has not written, these Port Mary mornings, because of the rich opportunity for curios; and Martin and I labelled the things and sorted them for packing.

Wada reported, concerning his wash-day ashore: "Those girl no like Papeete vahine—no hair on head—no good sing, no good that monkey-talk English."

Henry and Tehei rowed over to join some natives who were dynamiting fish, and brought back a few plump and toothsome mullet; but Henry shook his head portentously, and explained:

"Never I see such t'ing. Dynamite go, fish stun, I grab fish, shark he come quick—like that!—and take fish right out of my hand. No more for me!"

It is true—the harbour sharks, instead of fleeing at the detonation, know it as a dinner-gong and gather to dispute the feast.

Peter and Tomi, our two villainous but obliging colleagues, got up a big dance ashore, and thither we went after dinner, laden with a sack of prizes. It was a very pompous affair, with a bevy of dancers and quite an orchestra of heathenish wooden instruments. The performers started in two long lines from a weather-beaten carved pillar, then moved around the clacking, intoning orchestra in opposite circling rings. The figures were much the same as yesterday's, but more elaborate. The dancers were all gay with cocoanut foliage and flowers, beautifully disposed in girdles, armlets, garters, and wreaths for their heads. The steps are very like those of the Igorrotes. Jack and I reclined and watched and dreamed, laughed at the frolicsome bronze pickaninnies, and were glad we were alive.

After the distribution of presents, we returned along the sylvan palmy path to Tom Butler's, where we paid our farewell call. There is not much left of the old man, but all there is left is all good, and he has been more than kind to us. His last words to us were:

"Now you'll see Jack at Ugi. My word, but he'll give you a good time—plenty of milk—he's got cows, you know, and better bullamacow than yours. Good luck to you—" and he waved his live hand.

"Bullamacow" means beef. It is surmised that when the first bull and cow were brought to the islands, they were introduced as "a bull and a cow."

Ugi, Solomon Islands,
Thursday, June 2, 1908.

This has been one long day of nature-beauty and human interest, with the ever present spice of anticipatory danger

from earth and its inhabitants. We have not apprehended
the latter very much—what most worries is the unreliable-
ness of reef-charting, and uncertainty of nature in the matter of tides and currents. The Solomons stretch northwest
and southeast for nearly a thousand miles, with an area of
15,000 square miles—more than twice the area of Wales.
There are nearly a dozen principal islands, and a lot of
lesser ones. And in this long tangle of islands great and
small, weather conditions and all other conditions are such
that it would seem if a man could sail safely through them,
he could sail anywhere.

Jack was called at 5:30 this morning, and before Martin
had coaxed the engine to work, we were half out of the reef
passage under sail, and, once clear of Port Mary, picked up
a good breeze—which they call the Southeast Monsoon. It
is stimulating to sail before a wind with a name like that.

We breakfasted on pigeon and mullet, while engine and
wind swept us along the green coast of San Christoval.
Ugi, which is the larger of two, called the Isles du Golfe,
lies to the north, about midway of the big island, and we
wanted to make it before dark. Night sailing hereabout is
very undesirable. All of us were unremittingly on lookout
for rocks and shoals and reefs, and we saw them a-plenty.
There was black weather ahead for a while, ugly squalls
with whipped-white seas, and San Christoval was swathed
in dun clouds. As the day cleared, and clouds lifted and
melted away in the sunshine, the island unfolded a kingdom
of hills and mountains, billowing and jutting up from the
water's edge to over 4000 feet, the mist-wreathed valleys
looping garland-wise among climbing green peaks that
"stood up like the thrones of kings." There was a savage
royal beauty about the land, as the clouds tore apart from
the face of it—"Ramparts of slaughter and peril, Blazing,
amazing, aglow."

Henry has learned who it is we quote so often, and this
morning remarked sagely:

"That man Kipling he good—he *know* things."

By noon all was veiled in mist and rain again, which in turn cleared away from the water's edge, lifting, lifting, like a slow curtain, revealing tier upon tier of rounded woodsy hills.

After dinner, Ugi showed up ahead like a little blue velvet hat on the water, its top being flattened; and we made out some dots of islets on the starboard bow—the Three Sisters. We glow with pleasure and reassurance when we can positively identify any landmark.

About the middle of the afternoon we discovered a whale-boat coming from the mainland, and presently welcomed aboard Frederick A. Drew, missionary of the Melanesian Society, Church of England. Whalers once frequented the harbour of Makira on the western side of San Christoval; but now, on all this island, seventy-six miles long by twenty-three at the widest, Frederick Drew and one trader, Larry Keefe, are the only white men. Mr. Drew was a picture standing in the boat as she neared, rowed by three handsome San Christoval mission boys. He is the slight, strong, blond type of wiry young English rover who has grit enough to go anywhere and do anything. He met us with frank blue eyes and friendly smile, and immediately he stepped aboard everybody was laughing in the best of fellowship because he wore the familiar badge of Melanesia—a white rag about the shin. Promptly arose a discussion between him and Martin as to the best cures, Mr. Drew backing Jack on corrosive sublimate, and Martin arguing for blue-stone, probably thinking it more efficacious because of its exceeding painfulness.

Mr. Drew's three black youths are beauties, with soft, shy manners and chastened sweet expressions on pleasant-featured faces. One of them, with a strikingly Egyptian profile, wears a little crucifix "to keep a man from harm." I wonder what the foreign talisman really means to him.

Of course we had them all aboard—the black boys taking turns steering the whaleboat, which we towed. Mr. Drew showed us to the best anchorage off Eté Eté, the native village, and we shall celebrate the Fourth of July with a general try-out of our guns, hoping for a salutary effect upon the Ugi inhabitants, for the other side of the small island is peopled by the Malaitans who have killed many traders at Ugi. The long-ago first labour-trade ship that visited Ugi, the *Colleen Bawn*, disappeared there. In justice to the Ugians, however, the crew got no more than they deserved, for the doings of the slave-traders were not nice and pretty.

"Jack," alas! was not "at Ugi," but Mr. Mansel Hammond, an Australian, is, and a good sort we found him, plucky fellow. We invited him and Mr. Drew for supper, and kept them painting local colour until after dark. "Jack," whose other name is Larkin, has only escaped probable butchery like his predecessors ·"at Ugi," to go away somewhere to die of heart disease, taking his native wife and half-caste child with him. Perhaps Tom Butler may pass quietly away without ever knowing. Half dead as he is, I am thinking the one thing that could hurt him would be to know of misfortune to his Jack at Ugi. On the other hand, so godlike to him is Jack at Ugi, that he might believe no mortal tale concerning him!

Ugi, Fourth of July, 1908.

We haled forth every dispensable bottle, match-box, piece of cardboard, cocoanut shell, and went at a demonstration of marksmanship that ought to make us taboo from any "monkeying" in these parts. Mausers, automatic rifles, Colt pistols, Smith & Wesson revolvers, and Mr. Hammond's Sniders, all proved whether or not they were rusty.

Mr. Hammond keeps us supplied with generous gallons of fresh milk, rich and spicy-flavoured, white-man's vegetables, and papaias and limes. We have him to all meals, and yesterday morning went ashore with him. Eté Eté village is off to the right of the well-kept, white-painted trading station on stilts, with a score of enormous bulls and cows browsing near by in long, lush grasses. We found the native houses similar but superior to those at Port Mary, and the natives generally of a better class. All the "boys" look young, as if they had stopped aging at twenty—until they are very old. It is hard to tell a youth of twenty-one from a man of forty.

The old chief, Ramana, is a character. He told me with cackling glee and horrible grimaces, of the numerous white men he had killed in his day, when "him fella white man gammon along him fella mouth too much." But you cannot get any of them to admit they have "kai-kai'd" human flesh. They know our abhorrence of this practice, and look sheepish and silly when questioned directly. My introduction to old Ramana was unexpected and rather startling. I approached the little canoe which he was hauling out on the beach, and took hold of the curved prow to examine its carving. The slender curve broke off in my hands, and I jumped at the grunt the old man let out. But he laughed at me—women are foolish cattle anyhow, he thinks. I must not shake his sacred hand (goodness knows I am not anxious!), for he is taboo to the touch of the lesser animals.

We visited the old rascal in his house, almost as big and imposing as a Port Mary canoe house, and upheld by similarly wrought hardwood posts. Jack bargained with him through Mr. Hammond for eight of these pillars, for they are magnificent curios—the figures Egyptian in effect, the carving wonderfully good. One represents a man sitting on the tips of a shark's open jaws, the square, well-carved hands resting on his knees. One old god laughably resembles our Dante-esque poet friend, George Sterling.

Ramana wanted spot cash silver shillings for his goods, and his hoarse whispers aside to the trader, to put up prices and protect him, were very human indeed. He was well pleased with seven shillings for five of the posts, and I forget what we paid for the other three, one of which Martin spoke for. There were several less ornate poles in the building, with capitals half-Gothic and some nearly Doric. But we had to consider our already cluttered space aboard, and reluctantly turned to smaller curiosities such as calabashes, nose-rings, bracelets, and kai-kai spoons that looked like beautiful shoe-horns of turtle shell, nautilus, and mother-of-pearl.

Ramana led us through quite a maze of little streets into a mysterious, dusky, musty old ruin, and, when we grew used to the unwindowed gloom, we made out, high on a shelf, an enormous black calabash with scrolled ends. They lifted it down, in a rain of dust and crawly things, and it was big enough to hold a whole roast man—and probably had done so on more than one grisly occasion. But it was so very ancient that it fell into pieces when we turned it about. I was very loath to give it up; but Jack convinced me of the futility of getting it home in any kind of shape. I was comforted presently when Ramana found another half as big and in good preservation.

At every cross street in Eté Eté stands a tall kingpost, brown and weather-beaten, with an image on it. One of these has a face composed entirely of scrolls—like an English judge with his wig over his face.

In some houses, it was explained to us, each supporting post is owned by a different "boy." I shall always be wondering how long it will take for old Ramana's depleted palace to collapse.

Plaited grass bracelets decorated the eaves of one dilapidated roof. Everything is falling into decay and disuse, and many of the places are empty, for the people are dying off slowly but steadily. There are few children born, and most of these have dreadful perforating sores. We saw one pretty baby sitting, actually sitting on buttocks that were nearly corroded off with running corruption. It turned whimpering from us on the high platform under the eaves and crawled away; and, as like as not, a healthy native was soon sitting in the filthy, infectious spot.

A scant few of the natives have soft brown hair, like the girl on Santa Anna. The women here at Ugi wear a long chemise-like garment, but are otherwise much the same in type as the Port Mary ones.

The village must have been very beautiful in its heyday, with its king-posted corners and handsome thatched houses. And there is a thatched fence enclosing the village, over which one goes on stiles made of logs. Men have their dogs here, too, a sneaking breed resembling the "dingo" of Australia, and looking to *us* like our California coyote.

We dipped a little way into the woods, which were very lovely, all lighted up with red and yellow flowered trees, and warm like a conservatory, with little lizards rustling the stillness as they darted across the paths and up the viny tree trunks.

In the afternoon of yesterday, Mr. Hammond took us fish-dynamiting around a point of the island. We rowed in a painted world of water and sky, the emerald and sapphire deeps so clear we could see the shadowy white sand below, and uprising from it entrancing coral gardens—great hummocks of flowered colour, brown with blue tips, red and yellow. Certain of the bunches spread as high as forty feet from the bottom. Sometimes the forms branched, and sometimes grew in mushroom shapes. In the lovely opal spaces between and underneath, all sorts of brilliant coloured fish hung, or darted about as we stirred the surface. One expected golden-haired mermaids to swim out in the tinted underglooms of the coral.

To-day, after our noisy forenoon, we have traded peacefully on deck, the natives bringing out things they learned yesterday would tempt us. We have more of the Rubiana bracelets, and a couple of exquisitely fine basket-bags from the Santa Cruz Islands. Jack is happy over scores of beautifully wrought pearl-shell fish-hooks, great and small, and we have packed them into carved boxes of wood and etched bamboo, with sliding tops. These boxes are used for lime, which the natives carry and eat frequently. We saw one or two doing this at Port Mary.

Jack has traded my much-jeered-at Apian lava-lava, the snaky horror of undulating coloured lines, to a tall fellow who went over-rail into his canoe and put it on in place of the dingy small-cloth, hung back and front, in which he came aboard. He holds the new lava-lava in place by a broad thin hip-band of shiny bark that makes him look like a bronze figure with a metal girdle close welded.

Some of the men are pot-bellied and unlovely of line, and some are degenerate of feature, with small heads, and receding chins with hollows underneath. But these are off-set by many fine specimens. One of them stood at the bow of a whaleboat, tall, lustreless black, supple, poised with a stick of dynamite in his hand, and we pleasured in the grace and precision of him in the throwing, and the perfectness of his dive after the gleaming white-and-silver fish that popped to the surface after the detonation.

When our guests were gone this evening, and the crew were breathing deep in slumber on the deck amidship, Jack and I stole aft and sat on the rail in the starred darkness of sky and water—just sat and talked low of the romance of the adventure of "Man, the most unseaworthy of all the earth brood," and we joyed quietly in our fortune that we care for "the old trail, the out trail, our own trail," that calls us over the world.

Indispensable Straits,
Sunday, July 5, 1908.

We put merrily to sea again this morning, carrying five nationalities—for Mr. Drew and his black boys accompanied us, and all took part in the working of the ship. The engine started off well, but exasperatingly quit shortly afterward. "Adrift in the cannibal isles," Martin popped up from his tiny hatch, getting a breath of relief from the conglomeration of gases below.

There is an ill-concealed, amused interest being manifested toward me. An Ugi mosquito bite has refused to heal, and although I am obediently saturating it with corrosive sublimate, I do not believe it is a "Solomon Island sore.'' But Jack and the chortling, doctoring crew hold other views.

. . . In a wonderful sunset of all the blatant colours of the East, Mr. Drew held High Church service, his black disciples taking part, with our Tahitians reverently kneeling by. Japan hovered on the edges, respectfully curious. The Egyptian scarfs in the sky faded to changeable silken veils, and we slipped along in a world of trembling azure isles, while the moon blossomed large and golden in the east. And then, in the midst of savagedom, there floated up from the phonograph in the cabin, ''Guide me, O Thou Great Jehovah!''

July 6, 1908.

Jack kept the deck all night, for we had the slightest of breezes, and treacherous currents almost carried us on Mura, an eighty-foot-high islet with a nasty reef. How we did strain our eyes on the dim dun shape, and strain our ears to the swish of the light breakers, and pore over the unreliable chart on the cabin table! Morning found us about parallel with the northeast end of San Christoval and the southwest point of Malaita, which stretches over a hundred miles to the northeast.

Looking over Captain Warren's log, I find that he never kept it after April 19, at Pago Pago, Tutuila—and then only put down the date, without note or comment.

If we should be wrecked now, what a floating museum would be all about, for we are laden with spoils, even to the life-boat on deck, which carries the precious old calabashes.

A mild breeze came up in the afternoon and we set the spinnaker. Shortly after, Mr. Drew's whaleboat line parted, and every one jumped to Jack's orders to take in spinnaker and work back for the boat with its apprehensive black steersman. It was surprising to find how scared he was; but Mr. Drew says these people get into a ''blue funk'' very easily, and are not to be depended upon in time of danger.

Pennduffryn Plantation,
Island of Guadalcanal,
Solomon Islands,
Thursday, July 9, 1908.

Here I find myself, in the queerest situation, in a big house with a retinue of servants culled from cannibal tribes, on a copra plantation in the heart of the Terrible Solomons. I am guest of the English owner and his Australian-French manager, and my own man is gone across the water properly to enter the *Snark* at the port of call, Gubutu, on Florida Island (Ngéla). Incidentally, this will be the third night Jack was ever away from me. As the *Snark* is to be left at Gubutu to be scraped by native divers, Jack must return in the whaleboat; so both he and our host, Mr. Harding, convinced me to stay comfortably ashore and rest up, as the return trip in the open boat means two or three hours at best in blistering sun and glare. Such a life it is! We found night before last that we could not make Gubutu before dark, so dropped anchor in eight fathoms near this plantation house, which Mr. Drew knew.

Mr. Bernays, the manager, came out, and was mightily pleased to find we were the *Snark*, although he laughingly assured us he would be fined by the Government for coming aboard a vessel that had not entered at the port of call. While we were talking with him, the plantation cutter *Scorpion* rippled softly alongside, just in from some other island, and Tom Harding called across. Bernays explained us, and Harding, meanwhile voicing orders to his crew of black boys, invited us ashore for the night. A most picturesque figure is this handsome Englishman, of medium height and weight, with blue eyes and black lashes and hair, a cupid-bow mouth with even teeth and a small moustache. He is clad in white "singlet" and white lava-lava with coloured border, and barefoot. On his head is an enormous Baden-Powell, and in his ears are gold rings which lend a Neapolitan touch, while from his neck depends a gold chain with a locket in which he carries a miniature of his wife, the Baroness Eugénie, a Castilian. The lady is now in Sydney, and her husband has given me her rooms and her particular servant, a bushy-haired brown Malaita youth of fifteen, in singlet and lava-lava, a white shell armlet, and a string of blue beads around his neck. His name is Vaia-Buri, and he has a partly concealed superciliousness in his port that makes one speculate on what he might do if he weren't afraid to do it. Nakata, whom Jack left with me, is vastly interesting to the blacks.

Mr. Harding's partner, George Darbishire, is also absent. Their business is trading and copra, and there are some five hundred acres under cultivation. They have three vessels— the cutter *Scorpion,* a ketch called *Hekla,* and the schooner *Eugénie*—pride of Harding's heart, built on his idea of American lines.

The house is composed of four houses, two very large, and one small one off Mrs. Harding's quarters, used as bathroom and dressing room. The cook house makes the fourth. The buildings are enclosed in a long "compound," and no strange "boy" is permitted therein. Also, no native boy except a house-boy is ever even allowed on the porches. "Can you trust your men on the *Snark?*" was one of Harding's first questions to Jack.

As a precaution against escapes from the plantation, or worse, our whaleboat had to be sent back to the yacht for the night. They tell us of shocking murders of late, several schooners having been "cut out" and burned, and their masters killed. The latest outrage was early in June, at Marovo Lagoon on the Island of New Georgia to the northwest, where the captain, Oliver Burns, was tomahawked, and his vessel destroyed.

In my charmingly furnished boudoir there is a rack of rifles, always loaded and ready, and I am to keep my revolver with me night and day. There is always danger from an uprising of the plantation boys.

It would look as if we had really arrived. . . .

Day before yesterday's sail was in a fair breeze, along the coast of this magnificent island, Guadalcanal, with dread Malaita looming to starboard, and Ngéla, our destination, dim ahead. About noon we passed a little islet, Nura, which looked to be under cultivation. The water had lost its deep sea tones, and was sparkling grey under the hot sun, and in the late afternoon we saw a sharp demarkation ahead, as startling as that off Santa Anna. This time it was no trick of light, but actual discolouration from river waters. The plantation is bounded to the west by the Balesuna, a shallow tropical stream, and there is a sort of slough to the east, where alligator traps are always set.

As we approached Pennduffryn that night, I hated to take the wheel and ponder the compass, night was so beautiful and there was so much to see. The mountains, away back on the other side of the island, rise to 8000 feet, the nearest peak, Lion's Head, thrusting up superbly into the sky. There was a deafening chorus of crickets from the shore, and I could hear the neigh of a horse. Harding has two slender thoroughbreds, by the way, and a shed outside full of saddles and gear.

These four houses are high up on piling, with an arrangement of iron pans on the piles to keep out ants. Looped lengths of spare anchor chain, painted black, are slung on the floor-beams. Sometimes we can hear the horses fussing around underneath, out of the steaming sun. One lives in a succession of temblors, for every human step rocks the stilted dwellings. From the high verandas that encircle them, one can observe the immediate life of the compound. The three main buildings are in line, first the bathroom, then the house where are my quarters, a large drawing-room, and several other bedrooms, and the last house has the offices and a big men's room, one ell containing the long eating table, and an English billiard table in the main part.

Jack and I slept late this morning in the Spanish lady's pretty room; and when we were ready for breakfast we summoned Vaia-Buri, who served breakfast on the veranda

—fresh soft-boiled eggs, coffee, and "scones"—what we would call soda biscuits, and hard as stones. The Solomon cook has a terrible time with his memory. Never is he known to make anything twice the same, except split-pea soup, and the discouraged planters have it at every meal.

Yesterday we brought all our curios ashore, to be boxed for San Francisco. We also added our phonograph to the three already in the men's room, and Claude Bernays threatens to wear out Caruso's record of the Brindisi Drinking Song.

Although less than four years built, this establishment has an old and settled look. It must be because of the comfortable scale on which it is conducted, and the luxuries of civilisation that crowd the drawing-room. In fact, the fine curios all about strike one as rather foreign! And just about the time you are thinking that, a chorus of blood-curdling shrill yells raises on the beach, and you run to the veranda to see a whaleboat rushing out of the breakers and up to the compound, on the shining shoulders of fifty black boys.

Mr. Harding took me for a walk this afternoon about the plantation, a bewildering network of palmy paths among flourishing young cocoanuts, and little bridges over waterways, for the ground is frequently inundated. The palms are young and squat, but extremely luxuriant. There are acres of Ceylon rubber trees as well. Little white cockatoos flitted among rustling foliage so green it cast a green shadow. One field is given up to vegetables, tomatoes, corn and potatoes. Think of having corn on the cob again, and string beans! I saw the boys at work, and they did not look enthusiastic. I noticed a new kink in decoration—pig-tails, freshly severed, pulled through the holes in ears and noses! They also wore in artificial orifices safety-pins, wire nails, metal hairpins, rusty iron handles of cooking utensils, and some had cheap "trade" penknives clasped on their woolly black locks for safe keeping. On the chest of one sweating labourer I noticed the brass wheel of a clock.

These men work hard and long hours, on a fare of sweet potatoes (*kumara*), nothing but sweet potatoes, boiled. Some of them have to walk half an hour to the midday meal —sweet potatoes. Sometimes they may catch a fish, or come by a few bananas. But sweet potatoes form practically their exclusive diet. Any stealing of cocoanuts is severely punished. It is the "rule of the strong hand," and one can only look and listen. Comment would be silly and futile.

I saw the barracks after working hours, the "Marys," as the women are known here, about the cooking of the dinner of sweet potatoes—which, by the way, are not very sweet, but like a cross with a white potato, and of excellent quality. The men lay around resting, or were squatting in small low houses, some of them playing on plaintive little reed pipes. The Marys are not pretty, and are held in low esteem by their menkind, isolated in disgrace when sick, as things un- clean. A few pot-bellied babies sprawled about. Harding told me of a delegation of boys who came to him one day and demanded that the drinking-tank should be emptied, wasted, because a woman who was not sick had taken water for one who was sick. "One fella Mary, she take watter along one fella Mary she sick too much. No good!" Harding tried to treat the matter lightly, and faced mutiny. So the perfectly good contents of the tank were thrown out and the tank re- plenished with undefiled water.

Besides sores, and bush-poisoning, and a disease called *bukua* (pronounced buck-wah) that makes the skin grey and in a pattern like ringworm, the plantation hands are subject to an acute and terrible dysentery that takes them off fast. I saw the hospital—a long thatched shed furnished solely with an inclined bed of hard board the full length of one wall.

At sunset, before supper, Mr. Harding took me swimming down by the little jetty, where the sea spread white ruffles, frill upon frill, on the creamy-pink sand. We supped in the drawing-room, he and Mr. Bernays and I, all in evening dress. We were served by Vaia-Buri, who is very meek and lowly in the presence of "big fella marster belong white man," and another house-boy yclept Ornféré, a delicate-featured, poet-browed lad. Never did a formal dinner party hear such commands as Harding and Bernays gave the "niggers," as they habitually style the boys. Harding desires a bottle of claret:

"Vaia-Buri, you savvee go catch along him fella bottel belong me fella—quick!"

Or:

"Ornféré, you fella go sing out along Vaia-Buri tell him fella he come along me fella. Savvee?"

Sometimes a few extra "fellas" are peppered upon the commands, as if the speaker were determined at all personal cost to make a complete maniac of the bewildered and scared idiot before him. Harding elucidates at length that it is the height of foolhardiness to be pleasant or appreciative with them; that they regard kindness as fear or cowardice, and are likely to take serious advantage of it; that a Solomon Islander's first thought upon meeting a white man is: "Will he kill me?" And, if his judgment reassures him, his second thought is: "Can I kill him?" They have a passion for head-hunting, and the next thing to a white one is to remove any other kind. If a recruit dies on a plantation, his tribe require a head from the plantation; and it does not matter much whether it is a big fella marster's head or that of some other recruit. They await their chance patiently, and frequently get their head.

The recruits sign on for from one to three years, at £6 a year. But when a man's time is up, he is more than likely to be in debt to the plantation store ("sittore") for tobacco, "calico," knives, and beads, or else to have forfeited his wages in fines for misbehaviour.

Not unnaturally, they are arrant thieves, and appropriate everything they can lay their hands on. The boat-houses are kept locked at night to prevent the men from stealing the boats and running away. Harding told me of a native who died, and whom he buried alongside the boat-house, as the boys would not go near a dead body. Then there was almost a mutiny, the boys vociferating that devils were knocking at their door-posts and that the Marys had run away in fear, and the children were ailing. When they become restless on the plantation, no white fella marster is rash enough to combat their panic or their taboos—*tambos* they say here. Harding had to exhume the corpse unaided, as no boy would touch it, and bury it in another place. Strange to say, the minute he began filling in the shallow grave, several husky blacks jumped in and began to stamp it down.

But the most remarkable thing Harding has told me, is that a little way south of Guadalcanal are two islands, Bellona and Rennel, where the natives, of pure Polynesian blood, are still living in the stone age—a very rare state in this day and year. To the north of the Solomons, also, are two islands, Lua-nua and Tasman, with a nearly pure Polynesian population, but these are in touch with civilisation, as steamers call there. Mr. Harding says that Jack and I will make the mistake of our lives if we do not stay around here a few months, making Pennduffryn our base for cruises that are unmatched by anything left in the world. I am so fascinated by the prospect that I have promised to do something I seldom attempt—coax my husband. Now that Jack is feeling so well on the mend, the only reason we should hurry through the Solomons is to anticipate the bad weather season in Torres Straits, and get on up to Batavia and Java.

Saturday, July 11, 1908.

And my skipper says Yes. He is enthusiastic over the idea, and Mr. Harding offers to pilot us to Bellona and Rennel when we are ready to go. The *Snark* adventure is only just beginning—indeed, to-morrow we do our first real exploring, a trip up the Balesuna in canoes, to a village where no white woman has been, and, a few miles beyond, a place

where no white man ever set foot. It was up a river farther
to the west that the ill-fated Austrian Expedition explored,
sent here on the Austrian man-o'-war *Albatross* only a few
years ago. They penetrated into the foothills, made apparent
friends with the natives, let them handle and grasp the significance of their firearms. The natives cunningly bided
their time until the white men grew careless and confident,
and then massacred all but two or three, who escaped to the
coast.

The village Saarli is in sight of the foothills, but we do
not plan to venture farther. And yet, the inhabitants of
Guadalcanal are considered "friendly" compared with the
Malaitans!

Harding has planned the trip for a long time, and is glad
to make this the occasion. He has some sort of friendship
with the chiefs of these two villages—based, of course, on
what they can get out of him in trade goods, and, for his
part, on the protection their favour means.

I could not help but scan anxiously for the returning
whaleboat yesterday, and had a clear day for watching—
once so clear that we could see the sun-flash on the Resident
Commissioner's house on Ngéla. We are delighted to find
that the Commissioner is none other than Mr. Woodford,
author of the book we so often refer to. Mr. Woodford
was unfortunately absent when Jack sailed into Gubutu, and
he had to deal with a deputy who very tersely demanded
the penalty of five pounds for our breach of quarantine.
Jack says it is cheap at the price when he considers the six
hundred extra miles he would have had to sail if he had entered properly in the first place, beat back to see Port Mary
and then covered the return trip to Pennduffryn. We are
going to frame the receipt for the fine.

I killed a little hawk at eighty yards this afternoon, with
my 22 Automatic rifle, greatly to Mr. Harding's surprise,
I think. He had been boasting of his lady wife's fine marks-

manship, and I said laughingly that being one-eighth Spanish myself, I should like to see what I could do. They wage war continually on these small hawks, which kill the pretty kingfishers that build about the place, and also another species that look like humming birds.

Jack made the whaleboat trip from Gubutu in two hours, arriving here at six. When I saw his scarlet sunburn, I was glad I had not gone.

Wednesday, July 15, 1908.

The day after Jack's return, he came down suddenly with an attack of the vicious malaria one must battle with in the Solomons. Promptly he went out of his head, and after raving a while, fell asleep in the violent sweat we induced with blankets and hot-water bottles. In three hours from the time he was stricken, he was on his feet, weak but cheerful, and enjoyed a hearty dinner. Mr. Bernays played doctor and dosed the patient thoroughly with quinine. I was inclined to be alarmed by the suddenness of the attack, and the raving of the unconscious man; but the matter-of-factness of Bernays and Harding pulled me together.

. . . There is such a glamour over the past three days that I hesitate to write about them. "Sun he come up!" was our pretty call from Vaia-Buri on Saturday morning early, and before sun he had got up more than a long way little bit, we were on the way up the cool green-arboured Balesuna in canoes paddled, or "washee'd," by kinky-haired servitors. Nakata was on his back with malaria, and could not go. Mr. Harding and I travelled in a canoe paddled by Ornféré and Forndoa, another house-boy, while Jack (reinforced with fifteen grains of quinine against a second bout of fever, and rather shaky with the medicine), along with Bernays and Martin, came next. A dinghy carried the outfit of tents, blankets and kai-kai.

The river is too beautiful for words, narrow and tortuous,

A Kingpost and a King (note Ear-lobes)

green as a bower, the banks all painted sliding scenery of
verdant jungle, trailed with vivid flame-red blossoms and
vari-coloured morning glories, and mangroves reaching
their fingered roots into the flowing green water with its
bank reflections.

We heard the light clatter of parroquets, and the sweet,
querulous calls of strange birds. Once, the astounding
resonant conch-boom of a hornbill broke the rippling stillness. We saw magnificent breadfruit trees with their
knobby, glossy fruit, and recognised our Hawaiian familiars,
the hau and lauhala. Sometimes, through a break in dense
woods we could glimpse the Lion's Head, "Tatuvi," reared
into the everlasting tropic clouds.

We sped fast against the slow current, and fought ex-
citingly up occasional riffles; and more than once we hung
on sandbars, where great black velvet butterflies, accompanied by flocks of little blue ones, floated out to see the fun.
The "boys" were certainly not lazy, and worked with a will
to free the boats. Bernays blasted fish in a green pool at
one side in a wide space, and, once, the fuse was too short
and the stick exploded almost immediately it left his hand.
His handsome sullen face went white under its deep tan.
"Every fellow that monkeys with the stuff gets his sooner
or later," he observed carelessly after a moment.

In a clearing on the right bank a group of wild women
came hurrying, clad in full short ballet-skirts of dried
grasses that bobbed and wabbled amorously at every movement. We were evidently a pure novelty to them, for their
faces were studies in startled wonder.

Finally arrived at Binu, late in the afternoon, we had a
good supply of fish, and wild pigeons which we had shot on
the way. There were few villagers about, and the men evidently expected us. They spoke the bêche de mer English,
and were friendly—in fact, most of them are familiar with
the plantation. It is the bush natives who seem to be un-
tameable; and the "salt water" peoples, who are not exactly
angels of mercy themselves, are more scared of their bush

relatives than are the white conquerors from England and Germany.

While our three tents and kitchen arrangements were being set up in a bosky grove, we looked about the village, which was notable principally for its inferiority. The dwellings lacked the imposingness of even those on Santa Anna and Ugi. There was one large house that we were barred from entering, and over the door a crocodile skull with all the teeth intact. I wanted the skull, and Harding broached the barter. There was considerable pow-wow, but the shillings won the day. The women were unapproachably shy, fleeing even from me, in a giggly panic and flurry of rustling ballet-skirts. The men whom Harding talked with shook their heads ominously when they learned we were bound for Saarli, and all but two or three resisted his prizes to join the trip.

Harding and Bernays were begged to look at a sick man in a filthy hut. I was not invited, on account of the nature of the ravaging disease. Jack said it was a horrible sight.

After our hearty supper of fish, pigeon, and roast sweet potatoes, we sat around a small but cheery white-man's campfire, and Jack and I listened to the outlandish experiences of our companions—narrow escapes from the natives on the Malaita coast, and narrow escapes on reefs in bad weather. In fact, the whole of life in this "neck of the woods" Harding summed up when he concluded: "No use in any man saying he's safe in the Solomons, because he isn't."

It was a weird place to spend the night. Every one slept but me, and I could hear the strange uneasy noises made by our native escort in their slumber. It was as if they never rested from fear, even in sleep. Then there were crawly things in the coarse damp grass outside, and queer sounds in the distance and in the trees and from the river, while, near at hand, the rasping song of fever mosquitoes made me glad of our net. But I did not lie conscious from nervousness— something had flown in my eye around the campfire, and it hurt all night; so that when we struck camp early in the morning, I travelled with a thumping headache.

The river was more shallow and riffly hence on, and the boys worked hard. The two or three who went on with us from Binu were augmented by a picturesque score at least, unable to resist the adventure. Some of them preceded us, and every little while we would be startled and interested over a handful of woolly savages ahead on a sandy spit, or suddenly appearing on the bank, only to find they were from Binu, and wanted to go along. They looked as if ready to fight any common foe, armed with bows and arrows, spears, and naked trade knives stuck through bark or leather belts about their hips. Bernays assured us, however, that they were just as likely to desert as stay, in event of trouble. Bernays retains no illusions about the "niggers," as he invariably calls them.

Some of these islanders are the biggest men we have seen since Samoa and Fiji—indeed, the people of Guadalcanal are said to be the best bodied in the Solomons. I saw some remarkable types of other peoples, particularly of the Semitic; and one old man with a lofty mien and a beard, might have been a king in Babylon.

It was a spiteful, squally day, and once we were driven to take refuge ashore under an umbrageous tree, where we ate a brief lunch of soggy scones and jam. When the rain eased, we climbed the steep bank, to learn what sort of country our eyes, first of all blue eyes, would see behind the fringe of river vegetation. And what we beheld made Bernays and Harding curse under their breath with the rich wonder and possibility of it—a boundless champaign of grassland, league upon league of it rippling in the wind, sloping almost imperceptibly to low foothills that flank the upthrusting-mountains about the Lion's Head. The grass was very long and rank, green beyond description, and in the eyes of the planters as we stood there, long, and silently, were dreams of the wealthy future when not they, but those to come after them, should see their cane harvested on these illimitable plains and the sugar transported to waiting steamships at great wharves on the coast.

We walked back quietly to the boats, Harding being especially overcome by what he had seen. "I knew it was there," he said; "—I knew it had to be there; but I didn't dream the immensity of the savannah."

By two in the afternoon we were scaling a muddy river bluff to Saarli, which was only an excuse for a village, the scant inhabitants of which had a way of fading away when scrutinised too closely. The men recovered themselves, but the women remained bashful. Only my interest in the babies would stay them for more than a few minutes.

My head was pounding so badly that I lay down most of the time. There was not much to see anyway—it was mainly the fact of being there, the first white faces, that constituted the novelty. We walked to where we could again view the grass-waving savannah, and the natives shook their heads and contorted their faces over their atrocious brothers of the bush, when we pointed to the foothills now not far away, and made motions as if we wanted them to take us there.

Harding's brain was in a buzz over what he was seeing. He studied those hilly approaches to the mountain strongholds of the head-hunters, and in the evening went so far as to suggest to Jack that they get up an expedition into the bush, some time during our stay at Pennduffryn. Jack said, "Sure!" in his easy way; and then I *was* frightened, for this would mean a man-trip, and I would have to face being left behind to await nameless horrors; for know that the wily man-eaters of the bush have their paths and runways full of pitfalls and poisoned traps—such as horrid contrivances where a man steps on something that lets loose a poisoned dart from a strung bow at the side, and various and crafty and deadly other manners of obtaining the heads of enemies or friends for the smoking. I said very little, only, "*Would* you go?" Women who would keep their men have learned in long ages gone not to stand in the way of heart's desire, even where it leads afield. Of Harding I learned more of the dangers than I had read in the books. He had burned himself out a little, perhaps, for presently, sensing my worry, he said:

"I'll tell you—I won't say anything more about it to Jack." I thought that very "decent" of him, as he would say, but turned it off with, "Oh, well, but if he wants to go . . ." However, aside from much interesting conversation about general conditions in the interior, Jack has not pursued the subject. Oh—it might be done, and safely; but it is a ticklish risk.

There was rain during the night, and we had a damp and soggy time of it, with broken sleep. I for one was glad of the morning sunshine and a dry place with Jack in the dinghy, which followed Bernays' canoe.

The Saarli natives were hugely pleased with the remainder of our kai-kai, and watched us from the bluff as we got under way. The morning was a bright Elysium, after the dank rain, the Lion's Head thrust through a cloud-wreath against a blue sky, and the abundant foliage on the river's brink shining and sparkling. We saw a hornbill on a high branch, and some one shot, but missed it.

There were some close calls from capsizing in the riffles and on snags in our swift water-flight, and we often profited by Bernays' disastrous haps on ahead. Harding's canoe hung up on a snag and came away with a hole in the bottom. From Harding's face and eloquent fists we judged he was using language and that the boys were having a warm time of it.

So fast did we travel, however, what of current and oars and paddles, that we were at the plantation in less than three hours. There we found George Darbishire, returned from Sydney by the Burns Philp steamer *Moresby*. Darbishire is a big blond Englishman, vastly tall, very pink, and so lovable a personality that to shake his long, kind, freckled hand is to find a friend.

Perhaps the utter dissimilarity of Darbishire and Harding,

physically and mentally, may account for the devoted friendship that evidently exists between them. They are very close, and, from certain signs, we fear they are in some trouble, concerning which "Darby," as every one calls him, took the trip to Sydney. He brought bad news of the *Eugénie*, too, having heard at Gubutu that she is on a reef on Malaita. Harding wears a very long face for so round a face, for the schooner is the idol of all his possessions. Jack has put the *Snark* at his disposal to take back to Malaita a bunch of "boys" who have finished their term on the plantation. Jack says I may go, but Harding strongly disapproves—has ideas about where "a woman" should go and not go—wouldn't let his wife travel to Malaita on the *Eugénie,* nor would he allow me to do so. (We had suggested going on one of her recruiting trips.) I wonder how he reconciles his censorship with my many months on the *Snark.*

Darbishire quotes Kipling voluminously, and is overjoyed that we love him also. We lounge in long chairs on the verandas, and watch through our eyelashes the occasional dim schooners and cutters plying the sparkling level of Indispensable Straits, and listen to our favourite poems as Darbishire recites them, no matter how long, from McAndrews' Hymn to the Recessional.

.   .   .   .

From July 15 to August 8, we spent at Pennduffryn, with the exception of an abortive start for Bellona and Rennel, on July 24. Jack beat me to the fever, coming down suddenly one day. The heat flared up in him, he went promptly out of his head and thus missed consciousness of the severer aches and pains, and in three hours was almost quite himself again—merely a little weak. A few days after I had a touch of it, but only a touch, which led me to hope I might escape any bad attacks. And I took the first quinine of my life!

Harding had implored the boon of piloting the *Snark* to Bellona and Rennel, and requested that we let him take a crew of his own boys, to which Jack consented, although he and I much preferred otherwise.

The *Snark* got under way at six A. M., after waiting all night for a ''land breeze'' Harding said never failed after sunset. We were simply cluttered with the black crew, who, whatever they might or might not be on the *Scorpion*, were perfect numbskulls on the *Snark*. Harding's temper was not improved by their stupidity before us under his orders, and their utter vacuity under Jack or Henry on their watches. I could hear exasperated inarticulate ''language'' of both the latter when they tried to accomplish anything with the stranger crew, especially in the fierce squalls we encountered. Although Jack had paid for the scraping of the *Snark's* copper by divers at Gubutu, she several times refused to come about, and he could only conclude that she was badly barnacled—which Darbishire later discovered to be the case when he sent his boys under to investigate.

We did not get far, what of light adverse airs and perverse currents, but beat our way around the first point, a few miles west of the plantation, where we went to anchor in the company of two other ketches that were in the same case. . The *Eugénie* (the report of her going ashore had been a joke of Darbishire's) bound with recruits for Malaita, sailed by, her larger sail plan enabling her to outsail the rest of us. But she suddenly turned around and ran back to Pennduffryn, much to Harding's discomfiture, for he had launched into praises of his pet. Later in the day we weighed anchor and went ahead a few miles, during which we encountered the squalls and had the trouble about tacking.   •

Harding had a severe sick headache, and was anything but a cheerful comrade. His squally watch from eight to twelve that black night, with his scared and inadequate ''niggers,'' was a rather pitifully ludicrous incident—for us. Everything was at sixes and sevens, and the general disgust resulted in a change of course that blew us back to Pennduffryn in the early dawn. I went on deck at seven, and could not believe my eyes when I saw Darbishire and Bernays manipulating signal flags in the most absurd messages to us, which did not in the least cheer up poor Harding.

We found the *Eugénie* at anchor, and on the veranda her mainsail was being mended of a bad rent. Wada was tottering around after an attack of fever that had kept him from the ill-fated Bellona and Rennel cruise, Nakata having taken his place as cook and acquitted himself splendidly. An observant stripling, Nakata.

Next day, Wada was pacing the deck of the *Snark* in a blue funk over the fever, and over a skin irritation called *ngari-ngari* that itches and burns like a thousand attacks of poison oak. The native name means *scratch-scratch*. I have a touch of it myself, so I can sympathise. It is a vegetable poisoning, and we have learned that the *Sophie Sutherland* (Jack's old sealing schooner) which came to the Solomons some years back, lost her crew from ngari-ngari. They went into the hills, were poisoned by the bush, scratched themselves without control and without antiseptics, and ended in a terrible fester that caused their deaths.

Nakata has suffered two severe attacks of fever, but continues inexhaustibly cheerful. Henry had a milder attack, and refused Jack's quinine capsules because they did not look like the tablets dispensed by the doctor at Tutuila. Martin was so downcast over his ulcers, that he was badly disaffected and almost ready to quit the *Snark* at the prospect of several months in the Archipelago; but he became so interested in the social life ashore, the billiards, and poker, and various mild gambling, that he changed his mind.

Ornféré's cooking lapsed to such an extent that Harding was glad for us to bring Wada ashore, until he went sick with fever and hypochondria. And the anxious, poetic-faced Ornféré's imitations of the Japanese's doughnuts, dumplings, bread, and cake, were something appalling.

Jack has finished a beautiful South Sea story entitled

The Heathen, based upon a noble and sublimated Tehei, and is now deep in a novel—*Adventure,* with the stage of action right here on Pennduffryn Plantation. He warns me that I need not be surprised if he runs away with his heroine, Joan Lackland, as he is quite falling in love with her. Besides our steady work these past three weeks and over, we have boxed, ridden horseback, and swam at sunset, sometimes in tropic showers when the palms lay against the stormy sky like green enamel on a slate background—with ever an eye for alligators. One was seen near the *Snark,* also a shark. Tehei has enthusiastically joined with Bernays in his trap-making and -setting, although with no better reward so far than sand-tracks and broken traps. Bernays seeks their destruction grimly and unceasingly, for "They killed the best dog I ever had," he says. Speaking of dogs, there is one here, a jet-black, large mongrel terrier of parts, who gaily answers to "Satan" whenever he is called to show off. Made of coiled springs, he can jump straight into the air to impossible heights for food or sticks, or unhusked cocoanuts which he incredibly strips with his teeth and claws in short order. He is the terror of the "niggers," and a word to him clears the compound of an unruly crowd in less time than the spoken command. Jack is putting him and certain tales of his valour into *Adventure.* Sometimes we visit the "quarters" after dark, armed, and escorted by Satan.

Bernays' devotion to the *Brindisi Drinking Song* has in no wise abated; only, he now protects himself and the playing record with a tomahawk in one hand and a New Guinea club in the other. "New Guinea" reminds me that aboard the *Makambo* one forenoon where we went out to breakfast, we met a Mrs. Donald McKay, whose husband is exploring in New Guinea. I felt sorry for the lady, for she is presumably as happy and peaceful in her mind as I would be if Jack were in the Guadalcanal bush.

We miss the pleasant fruits of Polynesia—the oranges, and bananas, mangoes, and limes. And we should thrive better if we had them. Jack seems headed for another spell of the sickness of before and during our ''discovery'' of the Solomons, and I am afraid of the dysentery for him, as it has broken loose among the boys, and several are in the pitiful shack dubbed ''hospital.'' Jack took a look at them the other day. One, lying in pain and dissolution, had a weeping, frightened brother at his feet, who could not be made to understand that his noisy grief was deleterious to the sick man. And the masters are not happy over the loss of their boys. Bernays, who works hard, says bitterly: ''They die on purpose, the brutes!'' These islanders have no more resistance than a mosquito, no hold on life, and succumb mentally as well as physically.

.   .   .   .

On August 8, 1908, the ketch *Minota* dropped in, and Captain Jansen renewed his invitation for the Malaita recruiting trip. We looked at each other, Jack and I, nodded, and packed our grips and the typewriter. Meanwhile, Jack arranged that the *Snark* be taken to Gubutu, at which place we would join her in a week or ten days and sail her to Ysabel Island, where we had learned we could safely careen and make a raid on her barnacles.

We rowed aboard the *Minota* after a gay and festive dinner, in a lovely night of stars with a pleasant light breeze ruffling the spangled water, and slipped out to a string of Darbishire's ridiculous code messages winking from the signal staff in the compound.

The *Minota* was originally a gentleman's yacht in Australia—a beautiful rakish thing of teak and bronze and lofty cedar, fin-keeled, very fast, and now owned by a wealthy planter of the Solomons, Captain Svenson, a man famed for the number and success of his ventures in the Solomons and elsewhere. She was not much larger than the *Snark*, but her interior consisted merely of a main cabin, and one stateroom for'ard. Captain Jansen and the mate would have it that we take their quarters, and themselves turned in on the long bunks in the cabin. The door to our room still bore the tomahawk marks where the Malaitans at Langa Langa several months before broke in for the trove of rifles and ammunition locked therein, after bloodily slaughtering Jansen's predecessor, Captain Mackenzie. The burning of the vessel was somehow prevented by the black crew, but this was so unprecedented that the owner feared some complicity between them and the attacking party. However, it could not be proved, and we sailed with the majority of this same crew. The present skipper smilingly warned us that the same tribe still required two more heads from the *Minota*, to square up for deaths on the Ysabel plantation.

Nakata and Wada accompanied us, the latter in a pale panic lest he lose his precious head, the former cannily alert; and, besides the four whites of us, the ship's complement was made up of a double-crew of fifteen and between thirty and forty recruits who had served their three years on Ysabel and were being returned to their tribespeople. And what was my surprise, when I explored the dimly-lighted cabin, to meet the shy, half-wild eyes of a kinky-headed "Mary" peering from a dark cubby under the deck, behind the companion steps. Captain Jansen explained that a Malaitan chief, in return for some favour, or to curry one, had honoured him with the gift of his daughter Teséma—a tidy morsel, should big fella marster belong white man choose to kai-kai the noble damsel—for thus are the poor females disposed of at the whim of their ruthless kin.

"She's a very embarrassing parcel," the captain said, with a grimace of distaste, "but I thought too much of my neck to refuse her." He called her out, and she came crawling obediently and stood before us, in a single calico chemise, the first garment she had ever known. "Look at her—she's got *bukua* from head to foot!" And even as he spoke, her hands were busy scratching the dandruffy, ringwormy skin. Captain Jansen was heading for a Mission as soon as he finished his recruiting. "It's all I can do," he said. "If I leave her anywhere else, ten to one she'd be kai-kai'd before I'm out of sight.—The fleshy parts of a woman's forearm and leg are the favourite feast-bits. . . . But they wouldn't get so much off her," he concluded, looking at the slim, scared being.

It was insufferably hot in our bunks, which were high, with the heated ceiling close. The deck was packed with blacks, who, when they were not sleeping in their brutish, restless, muttering way, chattered incessantly in staccato high eunuch-voices, a polyglot of native dialects and béche de mer, with frequent interpolations of "My word!" "Fella," "You gammon along me," "No fear!" that were comically startling. Jack laughed right out when one bush-boy, uncongenial to the sea, who had been moaning in incipient nausea, exclaimed: "Belly belong me walk about too much!" Whereupon another falsetto piped up in sympathy, "Belly belong *me* sing out!" Then would come sudden breaks into light, short child-laughter.

What could their meagre infantile brains find to talk about so interminably? A miserable black wild-dog puppy from the Ysabel bush, termed by Jansen "The Wandering Sausage," hunting for human kindness and nursing, wailed and yapped at the thoughtless pinches and pushes and slaps with which it was bandied about. Peggy, a blue-blooded Irish terrier of five tender but dauntless months, from Svenson's famous breed on Ysabel, and the pride of Jansen's hopes for a "nigger chaser," stirred up added ructions by bullying the weanling baby-dog. There was not a single minute of silence on the *Minota* that long, sweltering night. And yet it was wonderful to lie there, pistols and extra cartridges under our pillows, a rifle apiece alongside on the couch, realising the slashing riskiness of the situation, nothing between us and danger except our wardfulness and our lucky stars.

When I came on deck, the "boys" were making their toilettes with native combs and cheap new trade mirrors, to an intermittent accompaniment of short bells, which struck whenever certain small trade chests were opened or shut. The "bokkis (box) belong bell" (a trade-box with a bell that rings when the lid is raised or lowered) is the pride and ambition of the plantation hand, and I can imagine is one of the fruitful causes of the scant remains of wages at the final expenditure when the working term is up. They were gabbling and giggling like a lot of girls—and singing in their emasculated voices, monotonous, but not unmusical, intervals.

One person who affords great amusement is the mate of the *Minota*. He is a good-looking German, with large brown eyes, straight nose, and small mouth; but he has a loose-seated way of wearing his baggy trousers that gives him a ludicrously Dutch aspect.

Our clean, swift hull had made good time in the smooth water, helped by a favouring tide; and Malaita was clearer in the opal-misty morning than was Guadalcanal astern. Nakata, industrious and full of quinine, was a picture of intentional cheer, I think partly to offset his weak brother Wada who, cooking for us four in the tiny open deck-galley, was reduced to just simply a white-livered sea-cook. It was shocking to see a Japanese so go to pieces. There was no "buck up" in him. But then Wada, despite his manifold virtues theretofore, always was suggestive of an Indian in his appearance.

It commenced to look very much like business when the boat's crew went about rigging a significant double line fence of barbed wire above the yacht's six-inch rail, the only break being at the narrow gangway, which would be especially guarded in port.

Jack and I worked all morning in the stateroom. The captain, who had been led into a relation of certain tragic passages in his life (he had fled home and stepmother at eleven) threw himself down in the cabin and slept—"Just to forget, good folk—that's what I am always trying to do." He came from New York State, of Knickerbocker stock, and is unconsciously Rembrandtesque in every posture of his fine body and blond Dutch face, pale-blue dreaming eyes, and an invariable small felt hat over an ear.

Our first anchorage was to be at Su'u, on southwest Malaita.

The chart presented an unbroken line; but as we neared in the late afternoon, a small deep indentation pricked into the coast. The fifteen Su'u boys were eager children, scanning the dim land, never still a moment in their excitement, bodies or limbs or tongues, chattering like cockatoos and wildly gesticulating as they recognised landmarks at close range. And I know I shall never again hear the bell of a cash-register without being transported to the *Minota's* savage-cluttered deck, for every child-man incessantly hunted for the ghost of an excuse to keep opening his melodious bokkis belong bell.

The Rembrandt skipper awoke his own care-free, happy-go-lucky self, passing in turn into an alert navigator, his light-blue eyes roving keenly about as "Johnny," the pick of the boat crew, sounded along inshore. The bay might have been absolutely uninhabited for aught we could detect of man or evidence of man. Not even the whistle of a "watch-bird" broke the primeval stillness of jungle that grew to the water—a warning that often acquaints the visitor of prowlers ashore. "You wouldn't dream that a hundred pairs of eyes or so were looking right at us now, would you?" the captain said. "They're not missing an eye-winker—I know them," he finished grimly.

"If I had a kicker, we'd go in closer," he remarked when the anchor rumbled down. "But you can't get out quick enough without it, if you have to."

The landing of the fifteen Su'us on a clear stretch of beach opposite the jungly side of the harbour was accomplished before dark without event other than the appearance of two or three of their people to greet them. The mate went in the boat, armed with Snider rifle and a formidable six-shooter, Johnny at the steering sweep, and the boat's crew rowing each with a Snider or a Lee-Enfield beside him on the thwart. Captain Jansen, gun ready for prompt assistance, sensed our tense interest, and posted us on the manœuvre. When a recruiting boat nears shore, it is turned around and the landing effected stern-first, the crew resting on their oars, prepared to pull away at an instant's order if necessary. Thus, also, every man faces the enemy, and the blacks are more afraid of hostile tribes than are their white masters. Many a "pierhead" recruit, fleeing from his own village, is gathered in under fire. We saw the boys climb ashore, and the mate and Johnny talk with the strangers; then the boat rowed safely back, the mate reporting that we would get no recruits this trip, and that the men he talked with were ominous with trouble brewing ashore.

The *Minota's* boat works under small security, for the size of the yacht precludes carrying the otherwise invariable "covering-boat" that hovers, well armed, about the boat that lands and takes off recruits. "Captain Jansen certainly has his nerve with him," Jack commented admiringly to me, after that gentleman had explained the custom.

After supper, a merry repast in which we made shift with two knives ("knife-fees"), two spoons and one fork (the Langa-Langa loot had not yet been replaced from Australia), Jansen fished up a tiny Edison phonograph, and we lay around aft on deck, listening blissfully to cracked and much worn records of "Narcissus," "Pirates of Penzance," "Marching Through Georgia," and "Red Wing," over and over, meanwhile teasing and fondling by turns the ubiquitous yellow-velvet Peggy, who never rested night or day unless from sheer inability to keep going. She picked a scrap with as much abandon as she adorably and stormily apologised when brought to time for her sharp needles of teeth, and when nothing else was doing for the moment, went stalking her low-born victim, the wild-puppy. Wada lay at a distance, with drawn face and hopeless eyes, while Nakata rattled on affably with the blacks, doubtless going them one better in their outrageous English. Their shining black and white eyeballs, and the sweet face of the sick little Mary at the companionway in the lantern flicker, lent all the local glamour that one could ask. We felt the jab of our pistols at our belts when we turned on deck, and Jack whispered, "Quick, Mate! Where are you?" as "Red Wing" commenced again and the captain rolled over to peer between the barbed-wire strands toward a slight noise off-shore.   It was a small canoe, and it came alongside where Johnny stood with his rifle at the gangway.   A solitary naked youth brought word from the "friendly" chief Ishikola, that no white man must step ashore on the morrow.   Jansen pondered as to the friendliness of this warning—"Or is he cuddling some crafty scheme of his own?"   Suspicious lights could be seen all that night, blinking among the trees, trending toward Ishikola's village—for Jansen did not permit himself to sleep under such suspicious circumstances.   "That's what my nap was for this forenoon," he reminded us.

I slept heavily from sheer exhaustion, and opened my door just in time to see Peggy take a short-cut into the cabin from the deck—an unbroken fall of eight feet—and lie still where she landed on her tender spine.   Captain Jansen dropped his razor and sprang for her, gentle as any woman, and felt her over for a broken back.   It was five minutes before she showed signs of coming to, and we were all more affected than we cared to talk about until we made sure she was sound.

The lovely sun-dyed mists in wood and hill thickened into a drizzle.   A couple of handsome high-ended canoes paddled alongside from hidden places in the mangroves, and in one of them Johnny's sharp eyes discovered a rifle.   When the naked rascals fell to the fact that the captain was "on," they pushed quickly away from the yacht and did not return. Jansen said three of them were the bad "bush" people, down from the heights to take the least advantage that might open up.   They were strong-bodied, fit warriors, and their punctured and decorated crafty-sullen visages were the *beau ideal* of one's fondest dreams of howling cannibals.   "The paddlers are salt-water," Jansen called our attention, "—praise the Lord the bush boys can't swim.   A bunch of good swimmers can steal upon a vessel and board her quicker than you can drop them off.   A stick of dynamite is the only thing that will scatter them.   You don't have to light it, and even if you did, there wouldn't be a nigger in sight when it went off—they're that slick.''

A smudgy smoke rose from the beach, and our boat went over, this being a sign of recruits. With the glasses we could make out three naked men and a pickaninny, and a cluster of spears leaning against a tree. Our men were especially wary, for the very air breathed treachery. Instead of recruits, when they backed up to the beach, old chief Ishikola himself embarked, and paid us a visit. Glancing up the gangway, he spied me fella white Mary, and immediately shrank into himself until a fathom of white ''calico'' was passed down. Arrayed in this modest drapery, he limped aboard, and after greeting Captain Jansen, turned to us strangers:

''My word! you fella come long way too much big sea.''

Once a fine-bodied man, a downward deep thrust of spear in the left hip had rendered him badly crouched on that side. The dirt-encrusted old knave, squatting on deck and informing the captain that big fella too much bad business was brewing for us from the bushmen ashore if we gave the slightest loophole of carelessness, flirted brazenly with the white fella Mary he too good. He played deliberate peek-a-boo from behind the captain, leered like a good fella old devil, grimaced, and even winked in true white masher fashion. Captain Jansen, greatly diverted, and seeing the chief somewhat puzzled by my bloomers (he had seen duck-skirted missionaries), soberly assured him:

''This fella no fella Mary, Ishikola; he fella boy—my word!''

Ishikola's jaw fell, and he thrust a blank face far out to study the phenomenon. Never did woman receive a more searching look-over, up and down and back again. I had to remember who and what he was in order not to feel embarrassed. Slowly the wrinkle-cracked wooden face lighted up, and the jaw closed only to open in a grin that matched the laugh in his wicked smoky-black eyes, as he emphatically enunciated:

"No fe-ah!"

He joined in our laugh; but his dignity was wounded, and he paid little further attention to me.

Our skipper embraced the occasion to try out the firearms, and we made the tight little bight reverberate. After which, Captain Jansen coolly invited us to go close in to the mangroves and dynamite fish for supper. The sheer impudence of it appealed. The debonaire brass of this south-sea sailor-adventurer is an amaze.

We went. Bristling with rifles, every man of us (!) with a pistol in his belt, we approached to within less than thirty feet of a fallen tree outjutting from that soundless, moveless wall of mangroves, reversed the boat, and the charge was tossed into the water. And simultaneously with the explosion, like screen pictures on a prepared scene, there appeared a score of stark naked cannibals, armed to the eyebrows with every fighting device known to savage man, while one, who had leaped to the end of the fallen tree, held his rifle on us. And he and Johnny, who had as instantly sprung to position, stood muzzle toward muzzle. Absolute silence, absolute immobility, save for shifting eyeballs—but the eyeballs of the two with guns never wavered for a long minute. Then the savage on the fallen limb slowly, slowly lowered his barrel, and his eyes fell as he smiled sheepishly. The anti-climax, when the whole kit of warriors laid down their weapons and dived with our boys at Captain Jansen's invitation to help themselves to the white-bellied litter of floating fish, was positively painful. The snap of the string of curious intentness made me almost cry when I began to laugh at the comedy. And it was Captain Jansen's pure, insolent bravado, based on his knowledge of primitive psychology, that made the prank possible. He knew nothing would happen; and yet, one false move . . . he acknowledges this himself.

"I don't know a white man who has gone ashore in here of late years. Things have changed with the recruiting, and with the return of the blacks from 'All-white Australia,'" he told us. "Count Festetics and his American wife landed from their yacht, but that must have been ten or twelve years back. They walked some distance in, and the only living things they came across were three or four Marys, with their bones broken, staked to their necks in running water, being made tender for the roasting.''

... And all the time ''Just Because You Made Those Goo-goo Eyes'' and other equally apposite selections were bawling across the water from the *Minota,* where the pensive German mate, Snider beside him, handy if needful, beguiled the hour away.

The following morning,

August 11, 1908.

We got away from Su'u at nine in a warm drizzle. In lieu of either wind or ''kicker,'' the sweeps had to be employed, for, once the anchor is broken out, no chance must be taken of going aground in a hostile neighbourhood. I could see the crew, as well as the remaining return boys, hold their breaths while they measured the distance between the vessel and any possible entanglement. They all know what it means to be on the wrong side of fate in such misadventure.

Our course was northwest, along the coast to Langa Langa, where the *Minota* and her problematically faithful crew were to stop for the first time since Mackenzie's murder. The wind freshened and drove the rain away, the mate brought up a long cushion, and I lay, with a hot headache, watching through our barbed railing the slow unfolding of Malaita, hill and vale, and finally the green crown of Mt. Kolorat, over four thousand feet high. No sooner was the grand panorama fairly clear, than we began to notice wavering pillars of smoke that steadily increased in numbers scattered all through the bush region to the green summits.

Our blithe buccaneer of a skipper stood with legs apart, carelessly intent, infinitely graceful, and relishing grapples with danger as the food of life, I do believe.

''Signal fires,'' he indicated to us. ''Not a mother's son on this side Malaita but knows this ship and is watching every move toward Langa Langa. I'll bet they're laying wagers on whether she'll dare to go into Langa Langa after the Mackenzie fracas.''

The wind blew up a small tempest by noon, and we did not fancy lunching below; so we backed up against the skylight and managed our plates with one hand while we hung on with the other in the rolls. Johnny, at the wheel, more apprehensive than efficient, demonstrated himself no artist at easing over the big seas; and the biggest of three swept our dinner into the buried lee scuppers, along with my parasol and everything else portable on deck, and dipped several yards of the spanker canvas. The captain fetched up in a swashing entanglement of things against the barbed wire, and extricated himself with most picturesque language as the vessel righted, and a gallant apology to ''the Missis.''

''Another thing you can't teach the best nigger in the Solomons,'' he chuckled ruefully, after dodging a skating chest on the back wash, and contemplating his torn singlet, ''is how to steer. They go to pieces when the least strain is put on their judgment. I'd trust Johnny anywhere but at the wheel—and in a fight against his own people. You can't depend on any one of them for that—strange to say, not even when they've good reason not to fall into the hands of their own village.''

Here Peggy, who had been moping aimlessly all morning, appeared wearily at the lurching companionway, gazing appealingly out of flour-rimmed topaz eyes, her entire person a shapeless ruin of white flour.

''My word! She's been sleeping in the flour barrel!'' the mate cried, reaching for her. But the next lurch was too quick for him, and he and Peggy rolled down the steps together into an avalanche of sweet potatoes that had got loose below. The next time I descended, I found that the two big drawers under my bunk were opening and shutting with the rolls, and it was more funny than scary to discover that they were filled with dynamite, detonators, and ammunition.

We made a five hours' run from Su'u to Langa Langa, and

there saw our first reef villages. I had nearly forgotten what little I had read of them, and they impinged on my willing imagination with the charm and surprise of a dream come true. Who in God's white world ever heard of this great island of Mala, garlanded with palm-plumed little Venices, tiny sea cities builded upon outlying coral by the weaker brothers of the bush who long ago were driven beyond the beaches of their own land? Very curious and beautiful are these snug strongholds against man and nature, close-walled with firm masonry of coral blocks to resist the smashing sea, the straight lines of walls broken by thatched village roofs and the graceful bendings and sketchy angles of cocoanut palms. The openings for canoe landings are narrow and rough and steep, as if cannon had tumbled in a thick section of wall, the sides waving with ferns.

To such an outland citadel we were bound, Langa Langa. We made our way around a mess of reef into a passage the outer side of which was the reef village, and anchored between it and the near-by mainland. As we entered the passage, a canoe came out, and an excited salt-water native informed us of the not surprising coincidence that the *Cambrian* had just steamed out (Captain Lewes again!), and that her mission had been to locate the murderers of the *Minota's* master. We gathered that the officers with their men had marched into the bush a short distance, and, the criminals not being forthcoming, burned five suspected villages, and killed a few pigs, leaving with the ultimatum that if the men were not delivered up at the stated next visitation of the *Cambrian*, worse things would follow. Immediately the innocent burned villagers had pitched into battle with the guilty, and "hell he pop" was the order of the day up bush. Captain Jansen left no item of this intelligence dark to his crew, who, if they had had any notion of collusion with the shore, now could see that the *Minota* was fairly *tambo* for the time being.

Fairy shallops, with great cocoanut fronds for sails, came skimming from every direction across the lagoon, which was flat as a mosaic floor of lapis lazuli, turquoise, and jade.

They clustered about us a dozen deep, the natives, mostly salt-water, cackling subduedly about the *Minota,* and I could catch a bit of hastily concealed pantomime now and again, that showed they were recalling the tomahawking of her last big fella marster belong white man. Next to the ship, I seemed to be the attraction, and the paddlers stood up to get a look at me. Only one did Captain Jansen allow on board, a chief called "Billy," who was glibly effusive, and confidential about current affairs. When I say he was allowed on board, I must qualify. No sooner had he stepped on deck and started forward, than the captain halted him with a peremptory but kindly:

"Hey! You! Billy—you better drain overboard, my word!"

And then we saw that he had an enormous and very active ulcer on his buttock. He begged for medicines and applied them, over the edge of the rail, while he recounted all he knew of matters ashore.

Billy was much taken with the chance to talk with a white Mary, having met some of the missionary women, and was very gallant despite his disadvantageous posture for social amenities. Thus did he bid me to his village:

"You come along island belong me, to-morrow, Mary— Missis?"

"Yes, Billy, I come, sure."

"You no gammon along me?" he quizzed. And, being reassured, he smiled fatly. "My word! You bring me fella wife some tobacco?" in a wheedling tone.

"All right," I promised, "I bring tobacco wife belong you.—But what present you big fella chief bring me, Billy?"

Billy got around it nicely:

"Me fella no have present for Mary—Missis," he explained. "S'pose you fella man, me give him fella present one spear belong me."

And he made good, presenting Jack next day with a deadly poison-tipped spear that I could not bind up quick enough for fear we might abrade ourselves on it.

Fancy the German planters in the Archipelago, who have never learned English, essaying bêche de mer. It is said to be one of the funniest things imaginable.

It was a treat to watch Jansen. Apparently nonchalant and unobservant, he had an almost unbelievable awareness of everything going on. "Hi! Whiskers! Get away from that rail!" he would rap out, three quarters back toward the inquisitive climber. Aboard and ashore, he avoided risking his back near a "nigger," and cautioned us likewise. With the chiefs he was all easy affability, breaking off to give a command, or order some one off, in an unequivocal, even tone that even a raw savage, unless he were a born idiot, could not misunderstand.

A few fowls were offered, with the question: "You fella want kokoroko belong me?" and became ours for stick tobacco; also a garfish or two, long-nosed fish with teeth, that go human aristocracy one better, for their very bones are blue! And glad we were for this fresh addition to a very much tinned larder. Sometimes I hoped I'd never see a tin again.

The canoe people had magnificent brown muscled shoulders, round-sloping down the arms, and splendid torsos; but when they stood erect, their legs were comic, short and bandied, with warped and weazened calves. The reef dwellers have little walking to develop their underpinnings.

We rowed over to the elongated reef city and looked about, the older women, unsightly, dragged-out hags, skurrying the young girls into the houses as we approached. We saw two or three who were comely, but the clipped heads, as usual, robbed all but the exceptions of their looks. They were mostly naked, old and young, and the heads of the little tots of pickaninnies were shaved all but a bleached tuft atop, which might have been left to handle them with. All ages were nose-ringed and bead-necklaced, and wore an endless choice of unlikely objects in their tortured ears. We saw a squatting group of Marys shaping and drilling "money"— tiny pierced disks of shell both pink and white, which are strung on cocoanut fibre. A fathom of the pink brings a golden sovereign.

Of course it is not to be expected that these earth-edge mortals could raise any produce in such small and unfavourable spaces. They must depend upon fish as their main staple. The bush people, on the other hand, desiring fishy sustenance, an armed truce obtains at frequent intervals, wherein the Marys of both factions hold a market on the open beach, under guard of their respective lords, and trade vegetables, fruits, and fowls, for sea food. One large fish brings twenty taro, for example. Just now, with the conditions up bush, the salt water folk were hungry for fruit, and we saw grimy little pickaninnies whimpering for their "tucker." "What name altogether you cry along tucker?" Johnny demanded good-naturedly of one disconsolate kiddie.

A detached portion of the walled town was reached by a bridging tree-trunk; and here, as at Port Mary, Jack was able to crow, for even this white fella Mary was not allowed to profane it with her foot. Jack walked across with the other males, joking me as I was rowed by in the boat. As I stepped ashore blackness spread over everything. I commenced to shake uncontrollably, and called to the others. "Fever," Jansen pronounced laconically, and I was taken back to the *Minota*. Followed three hours of racking nerve breakdown in a raging fever, during which Jack turned to nobly with blankets and hot-water bottles and steaming drinks brought by a pitying Nakata, to induce the sweat that is the only relief.

> "By the shivering fits which chill us,
> By the feverish heats which grill us,
> By the pains acute which fill us,
> By the aches which maul and mill us—"

I thought I knew all of it by the time I had been sponged off—a heavenly process that marks an immortal bliss of easement. Jack allowed himself only one jibe—that the fever was precipitated by shock at being excluded from the bridge.

Ugi

In the evening, burned-out and weak, but happy, I was on deck, listening to "Narcissus" and "Red Wing," cuddling a convalescent Peggy, watching the ebb on the black reefs, where red fires glowed in the villages. Single silhouetted canoes with their gondola ends, glided across the lagoon where a golden moon dropped golden pools in the night-purple tide. The mountains melted in soft luminousness, their summits frosted with light clouds. Never in all my years shall I hear the dear, foolish

> ". . . moon's shining bright on pretty Red Wing,
> The breeze is dying, the night bird's crying,"

without a tightening of the heart.

Thursday, August 13, 1908.

Captain Jansen had by now accomplished several things that brought him here, such as recovering a spare sail from the village that had stolen it on the *Minota's* last visit, and collecting good gold from Chief Billy for two deserters of his tribal brothers from the plantation. As there was no chance of gathering any recruits from the troubled bush region, we set out for Malu, on the north side of the island, to land the last of the homing blacks and drum up a new supply.

Johnny, losing his head as we were getting under way, jammed the wheel in the wrong direction, and nearly crammed us on the inshore reef. It was an apprehensive moment, even Captain Jansen knitting his blond brows as he watched the inches finally widen between the boat and the milky-purple menace below the pale-green water. Even with the punitive *Cambrian* so shortly departed, for the *Minota*, of all vessels, to hang up at Langa Langa, might mean a concerted rush that would finish us all in smoke and blood.

We wove along the lagoon made by the outer and inner reefs, picking our way so swiftly among prismatic coral shallows in bright green water to the guidance of a man at the cross-trees, that the near coral islets and low lands of the mainland, belted with mangroves, produced the illusion of shifting in an opposite direction from the mountain behind. The low, continuous ivory-sanded reef to seaward showed the kind of "land" the natives have built upon, and now and again a tiny village broke the line. Beyond the narrow strip, across a white-crested indigo sea, to the west we could glimpse Ysabel Island, showing on the heaving horizon in a string of isolated hummocks.

Four miles of this exquisite traverse brought us to Auki, a beautiful walled double-village on the reef off a bight in the mainland. An enormous banyan had taken root in Auki, and overhung the wall. Close alongside, as in a moat, a shell-garish war canoe rocked. We almost touched the mossy coral wall as we went about to head-reach out a narrow passage to the open water. We could smell the salt deep-sea smell distinctly as we emerged from the lagoon. A little later, we spied a schooner anchored off shore, and Captain Jansen recognised it as the Melanesian Missionary Society's *Evangel*. They have a mission near by, and one at Malu; but not a trader has been able to stick on Malaita.

It was ten at night when we came to anchor at the extreme northwest end of Malaita, between Cape Astrolabe and the tiny island of Bassakanna. Here Captain Jansen told us he had once been becalmed for four days, the tide carrying him back and forth against his will. And here, on another occasion, he had picked up the survivors of the Sewall ship *Rappahannock*.

The *Eugénie* was a short distance ahead, and she, too, went to anchor for want of wind. Captain Keller rowed aboard for a "gam"—a good looking fellow of but twenty-two, of German descent, who seemed very young to be in command of a schooner in such waters. He volunteered that he had never learned navigation.

And all this day, Jack had been kind enough not to jeer at me, for, at last, I had a well-developed Solomon Island

sore just abaft my left outside ankle-bone. He saturated
it with corrosive sublimate, for I was too shattered with the
left-over of my fever to have the nerve to doctor the aching
thing myself. But I tied a raffish bow in the bandage, and
Jack said that even in my rags I was picturesque.

August 14, 1908.

With the aid of tide, and a mere zephyr, with steady working of the sweeps, we rounded Astrolabe, entered Malu Bay,
and landed the recruits—outdistancing the *Eugénie*, which
was too big to sweep. The missionary at Malu, Mr. J. St.
George Caulfeild, came out, rowed by his mission boys, and
told us the natives were in a subdued state, as the *Cambrian*
had lately paid an admonitory visit. We were in turn able
to give him the news of the *Cambrian's* actions at Langa
Langa. He congratulated us upon getting out safely from
both that port and Su'u, as the moral effect on the natives
is very salutary to the white man hereabout. Any new disaster to a white vessel makes them bold, he explained. Mr.
Caulfeild has stuck it out at Malu longer than any other missionary. If the bushmen didn't get him, the fever did.
He either died here, or fled to Australia. The first missionary, in the early nineties, lived only five months. And
Caulfeild goes about entirely unarmed, with the gentle belief
that his faith, combined with the superstitious awe of his
fearlessness that obtains among the people, will protect him.
He even dares to interfere with some of their practices, going
so far as to try to prevent contemplated bloody tragedies that
he gets wind of. He came here with a deep-seated prejudice
against taking quinine for fever, which he lived up to for
some time; but he confessed that he had come to it finally.
He is a slenderly built, sandy-haired man, one of the sweetest
and most unaffectedly righteous souls we ever knew. On
a high bluff, reached only by a slippery and difficult defile,
so narrow and so beset with rock and root that one man
could hold it against a thousand, we found the grass-plaited

mission church, and the good man's tiny abode on stilts, with a little cookshed near by.

It was not until the next day,

August 15, 1908.

A whistle was heard ashore that betokened recruits. We could see our boat, with the rowers resting on their oars, while Johnny talked from the stern to the beach. Every time a recruit stepped into the boat, a yell went up from the boys on the *Minota*. The new boys were innocent of covering, and a white breech-clout was handed to each, before he came overside, awkward and shy as a wild animal. The bewildered and scared but willing captive was then hurried into the cabin, where his picturesque name, be it Kapu, or Nati, or Gogoomy, or Mgava, was written in a book, and his hand guided to affix a cross thereto. The deck then became his quarters, where he was promptly assimilated by the inquisitive crew.

Never believe that the untutored heathen has good teeth. He hasn't. His teeth decay and ache and become unsightly, just as do our teeth, only we have the means of arresting disease. In addition to these ills, often brought about by lack of right nutriment, the islespeople's custom of blackening their teeth, before referred to, renders their mouths hideous. Only from Caulfeild at Malu did we learn the true inwardness—abundantly backed by Johnny, and Ugi, Manoumie, and Lalaperu, other stars of the *Minota's* crew—of the process. We had always been assured by the planters that the discolouration arose from lime-eating and chewing betel nut. It seems that a certain mineral found in landslides and erosions of the earth, is worked into powder, and put indelibly upon the teeth when young, the process taking an uncomfortable twenty-four hours during which the patient has no wink of sleep.

Jack and I absorbed many significant items of Solomon life. Jansen mentioned to Caulfeild the murder of a planter in the Group:

"Which murder do you mean?" mildly inquired the gentle disciple of peace. ". . . Oh, man, that was a month ago. I thought maybe you were referring to . . . or . . ." And then would follow the curdling details of one or more outrages that had been committed in the interim.

"They're careless—they get careless, and let the beggars get behind them," Jansen would complain. "Mackenzie, poor chap, had no manner of business to be alone on this boat that day, or any day. A Mary did the trick, I understand—a nice harmless female woman peaceably aboard with three or four men. Mackenzie'd no business to be fooled."

Caulfeild told with a shudder how a chief on one of the islands had stalked into a mission dining-room and tossed a white trader's freshly severed head down the long table—a head that had once talked and eaten at that very board. And there were sanguinary tales of the reeking bush, such as what happened at one place on Malaita, where two hundred men were cut up by their enemies, and the women forced to carry the decapitated heads down to the beach, where they were themselves beheaded. Jansen had already recounted to us how, five months previous, thirteen boys ran away in a stolen whaleboat from Ysabel plantation, and during their voyage to Malaita killed a Guadalcanal boy, and one other, who were with them, and kept the heads under the sternsheets. Jansen, who had followed in the *Minota*, recovered the boat, and saw the butchery mess, which, he assured us, was very "loud" by that time. All these months Chief Billy has been in possession of the mast, boom, and sail of this very boat, but Jansen has recovered them and they are snugly stowed below. It is nothing to find an arm or a leg, fresh or otherwise, hanging in a tree—ghastly warning or signal of one tribe or faction to another.

And in this atmosphere of merciless carnage, Jack and I performed our regular work, read books, played cards, and taught Nakata English. I embroidered on fine linen in odd moments, and nursed the drilling hole in my ankle, feeling still uncertain and rather vague from the fever. Nakata was our joy and luxury, helpful, interested, and appreciative of this rare opportunity to observe the fringe of the earth. He called my attention to the beauty of the woods ashore, where a river flowed across the pink-tan coral sand into the sea, and especially to the splendid depth of blue shadows among the enormous trees.

Sunday, August 16, 1908.

We were fortunate enough to witness a big "market" on the broad beach this forenoon. While I mingled with the women, at least two hundred of them, Jack guarded me from a little distance, and our whaleboat hovered just off shore for the same purpose. I could glimpse the bush men, with their Sniders, spears, and arrows, in the gloom at the edge of the forest, and the canoes of the beach people protected their Marys in like fashion. The majority of the women were not large, perfectly naked, except for a string of sennit, and went about their exchange of comestibles in business-like fashion, with a great hubbub of dialects. I was less than a nine minutes' marvel, so intent were they on trade. But before their little minds tired of me, they felt me over, examined my pongee, laughed at the bandage-bow on my ankle, and one old mother, all kindly pucker of wrinkles, looked at my hands, and rubbed her calloused ones against them, explaining, in unmistakable pantomime, that the softness of mine was because they had done no work.

There was noticeable lack of variety in the food stuffs. Dried fish of half a dozen kinds, a limited choice of vegetables and a few fowls, were all they offered. The missionary told us that there is sickness because the people have too little change.

The bush women are physically superior to the beach Marys, well up to their stalwart warriors in size, for mountain climbing has developed them to fine proportions. Some of them have really beautiful bodies, with long, strong legs such as artists paint on Greek girls playing ball. Their only imperfection seems to lie in the unlovely, shaven heads.

I had been conning over a fascinating plan to adopt some attractive pickaninny, and take her home with me. Visions of a perfectly trained treasure of a maid lured me on to inquire of Mr. Caulfeild if such a scheme would be possible. He thought it would be easy to get permission from the Resident Commissioner, and I was sure I had found exactly the right girl at the mission—a fine looking child of nine or so, with intelligent brown eyes, wide apart, pleasant mouth with good teeth, and a well-shaped head ringed with soft brown curls. Her euphonious cognomen was Fakamam, and I had busied my brain already with diminutives coined out of the unlikely material. However, everything was settled for me, when the little maid's cannibal aunties and uncles up-bush (her father was a convict in Fiji, and her mother's head had been smoked) took a hand, and refused to let her go, claiming that they had to be responsible to him for his daughter. Nakata, I think, was more relieved than was Jack at the outcome of my quest. Nakata was appalled into bold utterance:

"Why, Missis-n, where *could* we put her on *Snark?* Your room too pickaninny altogether, and oh! Missis-n, she *can't* sleep out in cabin—and you many times say would not have even little dog aboard *Snark* extra!"

. . . Later in the day we sailed out of Malu, following in an easterly direction the inward curve of the land, to a couple of reef villages, Sio and Suava, where the natives were so frank and friendly that Jack and I waxed reminiscent of Polynesia. Their gentleness must have been the weakness that led them to flee to the land's end, for they are farther out than most of the similar settlements. Quite an expanse of navigable shallow lies between them and the mainland.

We were promptly surrounded with a bevy of canoes, and, contrary to the other anchorages, young women and children flocked out, laughing and coquetting, chirping and twittering with excitement over me, all naked as the day they first saw the light, many of them very prettily formed. A score of yellow-headed kiddies swarmed over our sides, and were not repulsed, for Jansen knew his ground here. We saw some funny ornaments and clothing. A young chief, Eiraba, wore an exceedingly short coat patched variously as a crazy-quilt—and nothing else. And one older fellow, otherwise naked, was decked in a battered derby hat, with a broken saucer bumping on his unclean and matted chest.

In the morning,

August 17, 1908.

Sinulia, big fella marster belong Sio, whose grey head and rugged features were startlingly like those of the actor, Louis James, paid us a call and invited us to inspect his village. His daughter, Vavia, sat in a canoe alongside, making motions for me to come ashore—a tawny-skinned, beautifully formed girl, apparently about nineteen, with hazel eyes and light soft curling hair, bleached, of course. As we entered the village, up the mossy, ferny break in the deep masonry, the golden princess Vavia took possession of me, while Jack and the captain were entertained in her father's house, into which no female might trespass. In fact, while the old man had been most affable to me, and liked to talk with me, he had himself made clear that he was tambo from the touch of any Mary, and I was therefore deprived of the dubious boon of shaking his dirty old hand.

It had begun to drizzle, and Vavia hovered me in under the long eaves of a house, where, pressed from all sides by her nude maidens, I was subjected to the most searching examination I had yet encountered, Vavia putting up my sleeves to the shoulder, and caressing my flesh with her small hands, making little velvety cries and moans over the white surface and texture, and sniffing the length of arm as daintily as a child scenting the perfume of a flower. At this extremely close range I was shocked to find that the secret of her gold-tan hue was plain and simple bukua, which had ravaged the entire brown cuticle, and left her an even shade that matched her bleached hair and yellow eyes. Considering the tint of the latter, however, I judged she must originally have been one of the lighter tones of the countless variations of black and brown that the Solomon Island "blacks" sport. I was rather shy of her contiguity, this warm and sticky-wet day; but she seemed to have passed the dandruffy stage, and I was helpless anyway, unless I gave them all hurt by withdrawing. So I yielded myself to the experience of being adored by the little naked ladies of Melanesia, who were lavishly sweet in their attentions. And they bore such charming names—Mahua and Lurilna, Rarita, Ema, Masema, Heura, and Kassua, and a dozen others as musical. They had seen the missionary women, so I was not an unmitigated curiosity. Vavia finally, by patient reiteration of signs and sounds, got me to comprehend that she wanted me to *sing*. I hummed a familiar hymn, thinking that would most probably be what she had heard. She laid her face near mine, and, fluttering her small hands, followed me note for note, in a soft humming voice, an almost inappreciable interval behind, until I was sure she had heard the air before. Then I tried something that it was impossible she could know, and to my delight and astonishment, she repeated her achievement in a perfectly true voice. She reminded me of Bihaura, in her serious application. And she was so very, very winsome and pretty, was Vavia, with her round-breasted, round-limbed body and the infantile fair curls on her round head. She made me pensive and very wistful, for I am sure she was more than a half-soul—such as are the bulk of these evil, sub-human creatures who people her land. We were loath to let each other go, Vavia and I, lingering behind the rest at the end, with clinging fingers. How she wanted to learn, and how I should have loved to teach her.

Sio is an exquisite gem of the sea, perched on the coral, in two sections, with a tiny lagoon between, wherein float canoes inlaid with mother-of-pearl. Great banyans grow among the thatched houses and overhang the low battlements of the walls, and the cocoanut palms are heavy and fruitful. The lanes echo to voices of plump pickaninnies, and we saw never a half-caste—the grim reason being, so we were led to believe, that any child showing white blood is destroyed at birth.

Tuesday, August 18, 1908.

We returned to Malu for the purpose of picking up a bunch of promised recruits on our way to Gubutu and the *Snark*. But no arrangement of one's activities in the Solomons ever eventuates as mapped out. And here was where Jack and I went through an almost classic experience, viewed with the Melanesian twist.

Captain Jansen decided to lie at Malu over night, so we took advantage of the afternoon to see a little more of the shore. Mr. Caulfeild, who came out with generous offerings of fresh vegetables and bread, warned us that a bad lot were prowling about near the beach, led by a certain chief so notoriously pernicious and the author of so many murders that the government had been looking for him a long time. So we landed with eyes open and revolvers handy. My back had by now grown callous to the irk of the holster. Jack and I, in bathing suits, treated ourselves to a bath in the dark still river, overarched with lofty trees, some of them banyans that covered acres with their tentacles—vegetable octopuses. The pink strand and blue-green bay, with the sparkling sunlit reef, was a dazzling contrast to the dense green gloom where we stood shoulder-deep in the cool slow flood of the river. Men from the *Minota* stood guard, and we were careful to hide our guns at a little distance from our heaps of clothes, as, in case the latter were taken, the savages thinking the arms would be in them, we ourselves could rush to the guns. It sounds lurid and spectacular, I know, but was all necessary commonplace. It was not a case of the horse-play theatricals sometimes practised on "new chums."

After our dramatic ablutions, Captain Jansen took us for a walk through the mangroves alongshore, going ahead with pistol in hand. This was the first time we had ever tried to make our way among these remarkable roots. The earth was of a rich black, saturated, "squdgy, sludgy" quality, and where we turned uphill the bush trail reeked with dampness and mould. We felt very subdued in this atmosphere of dark-souled savagery, spoke low and stepped warily. But Captain Jansen did not lead far—even he, so unafraid, knew where special caution should enter in. If any human thing lurked in the jungle, we saw it not, and the silence was heavy and oppressive.

By the time we were once more on the sunny hot shingle of coral and shell, the bad high-bush chief with his gang had come into the open, or nearly so, keeping just inside the edge of the trees—a tall, lean, sneaking individual with cunning eyes set near together, and an unclean fringe of whisker. The smiling friendliness of our meeting with him was rather comic, as we all were patently pretending that we were not taking inventory of one another's weapons, and the mock armed equality was rather overborne when that engaging swashbuckler, Jansen, with the most ingratiating insouciance took the chief's old Snider and emptied the horrible, soft-nosed cartridges into my hand.

"Nice little barn-door that would make in one's carcass, no?" he commented, returning the loaded gun to its owner, and taking another from one of the blacks.

"Look at this old cartridge, all made over. This beggar is a returned Queenslander, and they're the worst of the lot, for they know firearms and teach the rest how to make this sort of thing. They smuggled guns back into the bush with them, and there's been the devil to pay ever since."

He also referred to what we had already learned, that these people know nothing of marksmanship, and for this reason, and also to conserve their scarce ammunition, they shoot only at close range, and *from the hip*—insuring the most awful abdominal damage to the victim.

At Jansen's sociable suggestion, as if for the special entertainment of the others, Jack emptied a few magazines from his Colt's Automatic, and the bushmen stared and emitted guttural sounds of astonishment and awe at the stream of lead the pickaninny fella gun belong white man could pour out. My modest Smith & Wesson, being in the hands of a mere Mary, impressed them to foot-shifting embarrassment. The fact that we can hit objects at a distance also acts as a check to undue mischievousness on their part. And in view of later happenings, our bombast was lucky for us.

Wednesday, August 19, 1908.

At nine-thirty, after a wade in the river, we of the *Minota* set sail in an ebb tide for the final lap of our "blackbirding" cruise, with some forty new recruits on deck, to say nothing of a half dozen Marys bound for another port beyond Gubutu. The wind was baffling, and the current setting strong upon the ugly point of reef. Just as we were about to clear it, the wind broke off several points. We tried to go about, but the *Minota* for once missed stays. Jansen never had got back two of three anchors lost at Langa Langa, and he now let go the one remaining one, giving plenty of chain that it might get a hold in the coral. The bronze fin keel ground on the reef, and the main topmast, which we knew to be risky from dry-rot (although only four years old) angled from the upright mast in a way that threatened our skulls. A huge comber raised and threw us farther on the reef just at the instant the vessel fetched up on the slack of the cable, and the chain parted—our only anchor gone. We swung around and plunged bow-first into the breakers, crunching deeper and deeper into the brittle surface of the adamant ledge.

The instant the *Minota* struck, the boat's crew had sprung to their rifles and stood facing shoreward. This seemed to us a touch showy and unnecessary; but in an incredibly few minutes the bay, which had been deserted except for a few desultory small fishing canoes, was thronged with boat-loads of eager headhunters, rifles and spears and clubs sticking out in all directions. The captain told us this springing of the crew to arms in such situation is drilled into them from the start.

While the whaleboat started off with a tow-line in an attempt to keep us from smashing farther on the coral, and Jansen and the fever-shaky mate rigged up a scrap anchor from out the ballast, a dead-line of a hundred feet was established, and the hungry-looking savages hung there in their gorgeous war canoes, willing to wait any length of time for the *Minota* to break up and yield her loot of tobacco and stores, not to mention other, rounder prizes.

The crew behaved splendidly, likely as not, in the main, more from deadly fear of the hostile bushmen than special sense of loyalty to their masters. Some of the recruits had sprung for the rigging and clung there frozen with fright; but the captain got most of them below deck, and presently had them hard at work passing the pig-iron ballast up on deck, where, as the tide fell and the vessel jammed down harder and harder on her keel and rolled over from side to side, the eighty-pound pigs hurtled dangerously back and forth. I came near losing a finger in one dizzy lurch.

The missionary, whose boys had run to him with the news that we were "lost," hastened out in his whaleboat, and then, Jack with him, approached the dead-line of black canoes, where the two eloquently tried with much tobacco to bribe some native to go with a message to the *Eugénie*, five miles away, near Sio, either to sail to our rescue, or bring anchors and cable. Our first kedge to the reef-shallow on the other side of the passage had parted the line, and our plight was increasing momentarily, with a heavy surf in the squalls.

At length, one old man, alone in a tiny canoe, despite murmurings from the others, fell to the bait of an entire half-case of tobacco—a prince's ransom—and forthwith started with Jack's note. He set out in a gusty squall, and it did not seem as if the frail shell could live in the smother.

In the meantime, while work went on aboard, and divers tried to raise the lost anchor, and the shivering sick mate went aloft to try to chop down the tottering topmast, that good man Caulfeild, unarmed himself, harangued the malevolent dead-line in true militant fashion, telling them in thrilling bêche de mer that they need not expect to get any tobacco from the *Minota;* that what they would get was *bullets,* close up too much, thick and fast, if they dared come any closer. So convincing was he, and so determined did we appear with our arsenal, and the advantage of the near *Eugénie* already being advised of our predicament, that the unpitying vultures finally dispersed their close formation, and lay around in the bay and off shore. ''They'll get even with Caulfeild for this, I fear,'' Jansen said.

Signal fires were sending up their bending smoke-pillars all over the steep mountains, and we could not fail to note the gathering of clans beachward; while the longest war canoes we ever saw were coming along the coast and entering the bay—some of them paddling near and showing the faces of returned recruits we had landed at Sio. One big canoe, propelled by women, dipped out after a while, and was allowed to take off our Marys. This relieved the boat of weight, and Captain Jansen considered the situation well enough in hand for the moment to send ashore spare sails and other heavy gear, which were stored in a little shack he kept there for such things. The returning boat reported a restless and augmenting mob; and the exodus from bush to beach was taken advantage of to hold a big market. The crew also brought back lengths of trees they had cut, to put under our keel for its protection from the coral, and our divers did some splendid work placing these logs. As the water lowered and wind increased in ugly squalls, the swelling breakers lifted our helpless hull repeatedly, crashing it down with terrific shocks, when it would roll the deck almost perpendicular only to duplicate the performance to the other side. Everything broke loose, above and below, and the blacks, certain the bottom would cave in, made frantic crushing rushes for the deck, only to return laughing foolishly. The wretched Peggy screeched honestly and shamelessly, as she swept across the floor in an avalanche of potatoes, limes, flour, and bilge-water; the men yelled, breakers crashed, and it was altogether a nerve-racking bedlam.

And yet, I wasn't afraid. When one is in the midst of such a situation, the interest is so breathless, so absorbing, and so much there is to do, that an element of keen joy of living enters in. Right in the thick of the first trouble, not wishing to be in the way, I called Nakata (Wada was useless with fear), and we fought our way through everything below to the stateroom, where, alongside the banging drawers of explosives, we packed our belongings in compactest form and order—manuscript, clothes, money, typewriter—ready for prompt transportation in case we had to take to the whaleboat. My helper was cheerful, even enthusiastic:

"Why, Missis-n, this more like old years with my father, in fish sampan in what-you-call Inland Sea—oh, Missis-n —*big* blowing, big trouble, many time!"

It was fully three hours before the *Eugénie's* whaleboat surged into sight across the white-whipped peaks of surf, the yellow-haired master standing at the steering-sweep—white man to the rescue of white man the world over. Jack and I were solemnly touched with the romance and beauty and *bloodedness* of it. Captain Keller with his men and ours worked for heartbreaking hours trying to kedge the *Minota* off with the new anchors. It was a stirring spectacle, the boys shining with sweat under the brassy midday sun, shouting and crying the invariable necessary accompaniment to their every endeavour.

But the scene we shall always remember above all others, was when the missionary, after striving steadily with the rest to help us out of peril, said smilingly:

"Well, we've tried and tried, one way; now I'm going to try the other way."

He forthwith gathered about him his boys, who had been put in charge of certain of our rifles (the captain thought wiser to disarm several of the crew who hailed from Malu), and they descended into the wrecked cabin, finding foothold where they could, for the floor had been ripped up to get at the ballast. And down there in the dim light, with the vessel heaving, falling, crashing, the blue-eyed man of Christ uncovered his fair head and prayed aloud in the shouting din where above men toiled with fervent profanity, his meek disciples bending their brown faces on their hands folded on the muzzles of the guns. Ensued a moment of silent prayer, and then the child-men's voices, led by the white man's baritone, rose and fell in "Nearer, My God to Thee."

And when it was ended, they returned soberly on deck to work with the heathen.

Jack finally consented to let Mr. Caulfeild take ashore the typewriter and one suitcase of manuscript and notes, for fear of salt water below. Care was observed in not sending a noticeable amount of luggage, lest our enemies get an idea we were abandoning the ship. Nakata went along to carry the machine up the steep ridge; and when he came back, with the missionary, Jack had decided after all to make safe the remainder of our things, and I heard him say, "And Mrs. London will go ashore also." I was glad of this, for nine hours of the keen excitement, to say nothing of the violent pounding, had nearly exhausted me. Caulfeild assured us I would be certainly as secure in the tambo of his precinct as on the *Minota*; so I dropped into the whaleboat on a big swell, Peggy in my arms, and was rowed to a point on the beach nearest the trail. Jack sent Nakata and Wada with me, and we carried the ship's money and the mail. Willing hands of Christian boys helped us up, and Nakata bustled about making me comfortable in Mr. Caulfeild's one-room shack, with a mere closet adjoining which contained his bed. Wada, with his spine of jelly, was of little assistance; but his countryman foraged in the vegetable garden and rustling cornfield in a little meadow, and served me a delicious and welcome supper. He is possessed by the very spirit of loving service, that brown cherub.

A letter home, written during that grave night, tells freshly how I spent the hours:

"And here I am, at eight-thirty, alone on the windy ridge but for the two Japanese boys, and a small black Christian who is patrolling the premises on his own account in defence of the 'white Mary,' with a long strong bow and a quiver of arrows. He just now, on one of my scouting essays, told me quaintly in stage whisper that Malu beach is full of 'wicked men'—which means that the murderous bushmen are gathering in greater numbers, reinforced by neighbouring salt-water men of the worse sort. No man or woman ever knows what freaks of fancy may actuate the cannibal brain, so I think I shall not go to bed in the tempting nest Nakata has laid for my broken back and aching limbs and head, although I am dead tired from the long day of buffeting down there on the crashing reef.

"I am writing at a little green-topped table on which lie my five-shooter and a Winchester automatic rifle containing eleven cartridges. Outside is an intermittent gale of wind, thrashing the banyans and palms, whipping the breakers into hoarse, coarse roaring, varied by blasts of thunder, and lightning of all descriptions; and through the clamour I can just catch the pulling-calls of desperately hauling men on yacht and reef, as they work to clear the vessel at high water —and I hope and strain hope until it hurts, that she is even now leaving the bed she made for herself in the coral, to float in the merciful deep water of the bay. I cannot see, I do not know; when I go out, every quarter hour, I can only glimpse a light far below on the reef, which is blotted out by the wet veil of a squall. I hear no shots, and am fairly certain our crowd is not being annoyed by the scoundrelly man-eaters ashore. I am not exactly happy, with my man out there, tired and anxious and supperless; and the yacht, in spite of almost unbelievable staunchness, *may* break up in the night. They could get away in the whaleboats, but what would they meet if they tried to land on the beach—the savages knowing the ship had been deserted!

"My house reels and whirls, 'lifts and 'scends,' all but bumps. I came ashore for rest, and rest there is none, for the terrible swaying and pounding and grounding of many hours is in my brain, and I swirl and sway on solid ground.

"How good Jack's face would look in the doorway.

"My two boys are sleeping on the floor near by, Wada moaning and twitching in a light attack of fever, and Nakata dead-o, with a tired face.

"9:05. Just now I went out reconnoitring, to the cautious edge of the bluff, but could detect through the glasses no change in position of the distressed ketch's light. Nor did I see the redeemed James on guard. I stepped quietly about in the dense blackness twinkling with fireflies, and saw glow-worms softly luminous in the damp wold. In a long silken thrall of lightning my staring eyes saw that one of the piles under the high cottage was of a peculiar bungling shape; and I walked toward it with gun poised, 'singing out' sharply in the vernacular: 'What name stop you fella?—What name belong you?'

"'Jam-ees,' meekly responded the uncouth post, and in the utter blackness my faithful policeman added: 'I walkabout look my eye belong me.'

"Fortunately I never was timid about being alone in a house, or I should be 'properly,' as they say here, scared out of my wits to-night, in spite of the missionary's assurances, for it comes to mind that I heard him say, before the *Minota* hung up, that last night he found footprints in a freshly made vegetable plot, where his own boys know better than to tread, and other signs of prowlers.

"10:45. If only the earth would not seem to heave and plunge so! I am tired, tired, tired, and have been awake since three this morning, when, on board the *Minota*, the recruits began cooking their breakfast of sweet potatoes. The native cook, Bichu, had deserted at Sio.

"—Wouldn't it be funny if I actually should have to fire on some one? Well, if it is necessary, I'll call up a firm New England jaw, and go to it; and if I fire, I'll not miss, I promise!

"Thursday, August 20.

"The missionary returned last night about 11:30, just as I was falling into a doze in spite of myself. I must have heard Nakata start for the door, for before I knew it, I was there ahead of him, and met that gentle soul, Caulfeild, revolver in my hand, albeit with the muzzle pointed downward. He reported that they had failed to move the yacht at high water, because every line bent had parted at strain. (In twenty-four hours she had parted two anchor-chains and eight sturdy hawsers.) She still stuck fast, and was striking hard, although there was no break yet in the bottom; and he said he had left Jack asleep for the moment. He also said the beach was covered with armed bushmen.

"I went to bed, first being sure that Nakata was making our good friend comfortable, and when I opened my eyes at 6:30, found I had not moved from where I fell asleep. The weather was still blustery, and the sky soiled with thunder clouds, but the sea had abated. Captain Keller had returned to the *Eugénie* during the night, and his whaleboat was washed on the rocks twice in squalls; but he made the schooner, and brought her to Malu in the forenoon—her arrival was a beautiful sight that brought tears to our eyes. Her presence, coupled with the stubborn refusal of the *Minota* to become flotsam and jetsam, had a pacifying effect on the cannibal horde.

"Last evening, Mr. Caulfeild carried a warning to the *Minota* that one of the new recruits aboard had a price on his head of fifty fathoms of shell-money and forty pigs; and the modified desire of the baffled headhunters was to capture this valuable cranium. Jansen decided to take the offensive, and went in the whaleboat to the beach, where, interpreted by Ugi (the Red Jew we called him, from his fairness and a ruddy tone in his wool), he had told the sullen, uneasy pack a few things—the essential one being that any canoe sighted that night within range, would be 'pumped full of lead.' Ugi warmed to a fine frenzy, and finally jumped up and down in the sternsheets, waving his arms and screaming shrilly that if they harmed a hair of his captain's head, he would drink his blood and die with him! It was an amazing performance, proving the spark in the clay that will out.

"Jack came ashore this morning. I met him on the trail in a shower of sunshine and rainbow from a breaking sky. He was very, very weary, but full of enthusiasm over indomitable mankind that can fashion such a boat as the *Minota,* and fight so unwaveringly and cheerfully for endless, unsleeping hours. The mate, by the way, had been thrown into a fearful attack of fever, and had lain in the cabin, senseless and raving by turns, but had risen later on, weak and shattered, determined to go on working.

"Captain Jansen kept some of his crew on guard at the storehouse all night. When Mr. Caulfeild came ashore near midnight, a bolder chief was trying to break through the guard. Caulfeild took him by the shoulders and threw him backward. And he and the muttering, scowling spawn did not dare touch the white man who blazed at them with his straight blue eyes—not yet; but I fear, I fear.—A shack on the beach under the bluff, belonging to one of the mission boys, was burned during the night, in retaliation for his helping the white men.

"Small Nakata, with a parental arm half around Jack's husky shoulders, fathered him into the house, brought him every convenience of toilette that he could muster, the while setting the wan Wada at the preparation of a hot breakfast of rolls, eggs, and coffee—and a steaming tender ear of sweet corn. How could one help loving such a creature, and being willing to live and die with him—die for him, if need came?

"This evening we packed our things back down the dripping trail, and were taken aboard the *Eugénie.* I was to voyage on Harding's tambo idol in spite of him, and beyond choice in the matter."

. . . .

The *Minota* was not pulled free until the afternoon of the

21st—two nights and three days she withstood the punishment of sea and coral. Three whaleboats towed the gallant shell of her to an anchorage, and a great cheering went up from us in the schooner, with a "Hurrah for the Dutch!" —our black boys dancing, and yelling "Hita! Hita!" in shrill falsetto. The *Eugénie* was to take us to Gubutu, land her raw recruits at Pennduffryn, and return as quickly as possible to Malu. Captain Jansen came aboard to shake hands good-bye, Jack said a few warm words for the wonderful time he had made possible for us, and Jansen reddened pleasedly, but only said, as they wrung hands:

"That's all right, old man—leave the change on the plate. —And you, Mrs. London, won't you please leave Peggy for me at Meringe, and tell Schroeder to bite her tail off good and short, and I'll pick her up when I land the boys. She already hates a nigger—the very spit of her mother! and I want her ready to train."

Then, not wasting a minute of precious time in getting to work reballasting and patching up his raffle of rigging, he swung overside into his boat with a "Right O—so long, good people.—'See y' in Liverpool!'"

. . . .

The *Eugénie* sailed in the afternoon of the 22d, and, to make assurance doubly sure (she had already made one unsuccessful unaided attempt to get out), had three whaleboats tow her past the bursting surf. Then, a boisterous trade-wind and -sea favouring, we swept around the uttermost capes of black-hearted Malaita, and down to Florida (Ngéla), sailing past the trading station at Gubutu, into the Tulagi anchorage near by, where is the government seat. An æon of time might have passed over our heads in the race of man, for from primordial red savagery we crossed smoothly into the machine age. The harbour of Tulagi presented a most populous twentieth-century picture—the *Makambo*, in from Sydney, the *Cambrian*, from anywhere and everywhere, and we dropped hook just astern of the *Evangel;* while a little distance off, we saw our own *Snark*, and the planters of

Pennduffryn putting off in surprised haste at sight of Jack and me aboard their schooner. Harding's face was a study when I grinned at him over the rail.

We were lunched on the *Makambo* and the *Cambrian,* at last meeting up with Captain Lewes, who was the soul of kindness, sending his electricians aboard the *Snark,* and placing any and all things at our disposal. And we were invited aboard the *Evangel,* where we met the women and men who spend the best part of their lives going about these soul-slumbering islands. Miss Florence S. H. Young, the head of the South Sea Evangelical Society, twenty years ago became interested in the work through trying to civilise the Solomon men working on her father's sugar plantations in Queensland; and, when Australia voted "all white," she followed the expelled labourers and continued and enlarged her activities.

We were bidden to the Residency on the shining, gardened bluff, by our Naturalist Among the Head Hunters, Mr. C. M. Woodford, and his good wife, who was over the water from England to see him. And he was no disappointment, this clear-eyed man who has served and studied the most of his life in "the terrible Solomons"—a man of learning and of great personal charm, with valuable tomes to his credit on the subject of the flora and the insect life of the Archipelago.

Jack had by now definitely concluded to lay up the *Snark* at Marau Sound, near Pennduffryn, with her crew, take a run to Sydney on the next following trip of the *Makambo,* and go into hospital for an operation. So we engaged passage ahead, with Captain Mortimer, and went aboard our blessed boat for the short cruise to Meringe Lagoon on Ysabel, with a run north to Lua-Nua (Lord Howe,—the Ongtong-Java of the discoverer), and Tasman, for a few days. This would partially compensate for the failure of the Bellona and Rennel adventure, for Harding had backed and filled until Jack was possessed with one of his deep disgusts, and I knew that that particular picnic would never come off. On

Wednesday, August 26, 1908.

We left Tulagi, watered at Gubutu, and, with Tehei aloft to watch for coral patches, had just cleared the wharf and got well under way, when an unmistakable American voice shouted from an anchored ketch:

"Long time since I've seen that flag here!"

"How long?" Jack demanded genially.

"Oh, several years," the man replied. "—I guess you knew the schooner, *Sophie Sutherland*—Alec McLean!—eh? How about that *Sea Wolf!*"

And in the brief passing, we learned that he was a Pennsylvanian, and that he wished there was room for him on the *Snark*. How many wished that! We did not blame them —we were so glad to be there ourselves. And the happenings of our wonderful nine days on the *Minota* seemed very remote—like the fulfilment of a long ago dream.

We had an inspiriting brush with a big recruiting schooner, the *Malekula*, whose men we knew at Pennduffryn, until our engine, ever faithful in failure, broke down. After a night of brisk but steady wind and sea, in which Jack kept unbroken vigil (for there were coral shoals to dodge), in the morning,

August 27, 1908.

We found ourselves rocking along the northern coast of Ysabel, her mountains all lovely colours in the dewy waking day. Meringe Lagoon is a passage formed by a garland of coral and islets off the mainland, the waves of which lap the roots of mangroves where, above the water, cluster very edible rough-shelled oysters. "Wait till we tell 'em at home that we have picked oysters off trees," Jack grinned, as the first one slipped down his throat. "—Say, that tastes like another!" And a round dozen followed after.

We came to rest in five fathoms, and were first greeted from the beach by a brace of enormous terriers, one red and rough and the other smooth as a sorrel horse. The pair trotted like a span of ponies, and barked with throats like bells.

"Oh, they're Prince and Biddy," Jack cried, and Peggy set up a hysterical howl, overbalanced, and *plopped* over the rail. Once in the water—for the first time in her life—instead of trying to get back, she made valiantly for the maternal bosom, where Biddy, beautiful with motherhood, raising and setting her narrow feet alternately in the edge of the tide, received her lost daughter with a thorough going over of tongue and paw, to see if she were clean and sound, while the interested but more dignified sire stood a little apart, occasionally wagging his shaggy stub-tail. I have forgotten to mention that Peggy, most human of four-footed beings, had contracted at Tulagi a perfectly human and very painful malady—urticaria. Pitiable as were her deep eyes of suffering, she was a mirth-provoking figure, for her poor little face, broad puppy-paws, and lank and as yet untrimmed tail, were all shapeless with knobs. She tried to hide herself under canvas, anything—but any contact, however slight, made her shriek with sensitive agony. "I'm not surprised a bit at Peggy contracting a human disease," Jack had commented. He had had urticaria himself, and was in full sympathy despite his laughter at the asymetrical, unfinished form of her, like a partially thumbed dog of clay.

Next arrived John Schroeder, and his assistant Mr. Meredith. Mr. Schroeder is brother-in-law to Captain Svenson, and manager of the plantation. He placed his house at our disposal, and regretted that he was minus a cook, so he could not ask us to lunch. We had both men eat with us, of course, and listened to advice about careening the *Snark*. At high tide we ran her aground on a steep-to part of the beach indicated, and strange enough it was to feel her forefoot stop on the firm sand—touching for the first time in her tale of many thousands of miles of sea-faring. As the tide went out, and the hull lay over, all hands and the cook

went about removing the astounding accumulation of barnacles, working until ten at night. It was a wonder she had
handled as well as she had. "Gee! They're like *oysters,*"
Jack delivered himself, trying to pry a large shell loose from
the man-o'-war copper that we hadn't laid eyes on since the
boat was launched from the ways in South San Francisco.

Mr. Schroeder strongly advised that I sleep ashore, as
the yacht would assume all sorts of unrestful angles. Jack
begged me to comply, although he felt that he must stay
aboard, as there was more or less risk to the boat in careening on so sharp an incline. He sent Nakata along with me,
and

August 28, 1908.

When I arose at six, to the resonant boom of a wooden
drum in the quarters of the Malaita boys, after eight untroubled hours, I found the little man curled fast asleep
before my door, where he had lain all night. He sat up,
wide awake on the instant, rubbing his cheerful eyes. Always he knows exactly where he is at the moment of awakening—no slow Oriental drowse in *his* return to consciousness.

Wada, who had perked up considerably when he sailed out
of Malu on the *Eugénie,* had lapsed when the *Snark* touched
Ysabel. We explained—what he could see with his own
eyes—that the Ysabel natives are of a better grade (they
have a very slight infusion of Polynesian), that there are no
bad bushmen. All to no avail; he knew the plantation was
worked by Malaitans, and his terror augmented, throwing
him into fever again.

When Mendaña, nearly four hundred years ago, discovered "Santa Ysabel de la Estrella," he found the natives
lived principally on cocoanuts and roots, and was beginning
to think they lacked animal food, when a chief sent him a
lordly present, a quarter of a boy, with the hand and arm attached, and was deeply offended when it was promptly
buried. We trusted Wada had not heard this scrap of his-

tory. As soon as he went down with fever, Nakata, to our surprise and pleasure, stepped gaily into the galley, and prepared a meal of which oysters fried in batter was but the appetizer. "Oh," he grinned, "I 'look 'm eye belong me' one year now, and I t'ink I can cook good 'kai-kai.'" And "Perhaps," he added musingly, "I shall be with you always; and I like to learn all kinds of work."

To my delight—and sorrow, when I thought of parting— Peggy established herself my shadow, as if she considered herself my particular property and devoted slave. Mr. Schroeder had done his worst—and best—to her, as was eloquently attested by a gory bandage at one end and a plaintive voice at the other. Never was there such a puppy. Her brother, Possum, himself an adorable armful, appeared a mongrel beside this fine, super-soul of a dog, Peggy—"Peg-tail" for the nonce. Martin earned indignant protest from Jack and me when he said, honestly:

"She's a nice enough dog, I'll admit; but I *can't* see she's any different from any ordinary yellow cur."

The only criticism of Peggy ever wrung from Jack was when, having wallowed instinctively and luxuriously and thoroughly in a rotting carcass on the beach, she tempestuously flung herself to cuddle in his neck, where he lay against a rock on the beach:

"You brute—you filthy imp—Peggy, Peggy, I thought you were a *white* woman!" he concluded accusingly to the abject heap that cowered where he had involuntarily flung her.

Well it was that Jack stayed by the yacht, for, having worked a little farther up the slope at high water, she nearly capsized outward at low. Jack went through a terribly anxious period as he observed that she did not right in the rising tide, and the water crept and crept over the rail, up the vertical deck, until it lapped the edge of the skylight. Then he acted, and things popped for a while as additional lines were carried ashore from the mastheads. It was nip and tuck for a time, but at last the heavy hull slowly began righting. Every one looked strained after the close call.

. . . .

For me, the two weeks at Meringe Lagoon were a stretch of almost unmitigated repose and beauty—long nights of sleep, rainbow mornings on the curving pink north beach, on the way to the *Snark*, Prince and Biddy, those wedded comrades, racing and frisking along to a swim aboard, where they knew awaited them a bite or two of delicious fried pigeon, or broiled goat (Martin went hunting on a tiny reef island), or succulent, coloured fishes; happy hours of work aboard or ashore, romps with the pups, and an occasional swim—always a risky amusement, what of sharks and crocodiles, both of which we saw from the yacht. Our stay was delayed beyond the few days we expected, waiting for bigger tides to careen the hull properly.

I had been looking forward for months to finding turtle shell, and here the natives brought a "scale" or so aboard, the armour of the huge Hawksbill turtle, some of the pieces eighteen and twenty inches long, and broad in proportion. But Mr. Schroeder, learning my desire, opened up a box of specially selected pieces, already sealed for shipment, and told me to select the best of his best. Of course, Jack would not listen to a gift of such value, for the choice shell brings a large price in Sydney, and our friend at length, overborne, consented to talk business. It was the thickest and most beautifully marked shell we ever saw, and Jack revelled with me in picking out a goodly pile. Already I was sketching designs for combs and pins, and dressing-table boxes, while Nakata, fired with enthusiasm, could hardly wait to get where he might buy tools and learn to work the enticing material.

Martin tramped to a hill village, but we did not go into the interior. Only one trip we made from the Lagoon, and that was to a dot of uninhabited islet, Kiaba, a few miles directly north, to shoot the pigeons that home there afternoons from their mainland feeding. Mr. Schroeder took us across the indigo summer sea in a nineteen-foot open cutter with a large sail. Kiaba is nothing more or less than a round miniature sea-girt garden of Eden, a dozen feet high and a third of a mile across its sanded floor, ringed with a gleaming beach of disintegrated coral, a handful of which looks like ground colours. The woods are a breathless Paradise of big white-shafted trees and lightsome foliage of banyan and bamboo, tendrilled with lacy creepers. The stillness was broken only, by the coo and rustle of pigeons and the stir of strange forms that clung to trunk and limb. It seemed a shame to discharge a gun in such environment—until we had a good look at our first iguana, three and a half feet in length. "Gee! look at the alligator up a tree!" Martin gasped; and I wondered if this could be one of Woodford's "lizards several feet long." At any rate, so utterly evil is the appearance of an iguana, so absolutely is it a conventional devil in shape and style, that it invites destruction. We played it was the Serpent, and blew off its horny head. Yet it is as harmless as it is horrible, the poor iguana.

Martin and I, with much yelling and laughter, chased a frightened shark in the reefy shallows off shore, trying to hit it with our pistols. On the jewelled beach, where our every step flushed a clatter of tiny hermit-crabs, Schroeder found a turtle's nest, from which we gathered a hundred eggs like ping-pong balls, buried eighteen inches in the sand. I never ate anything better, in way of an omelette, than those Nakata made from the tiny soft-shelled eggs. The consistency was as if they had been mixed with a pinch of fine corn-meal, and the flavour was excellent.

There must have been too much excitement for me, or it might have been the extra coolness of the day, for I was stricken suddenly with fever, and went through a novel sweating—swathed in the boat's canvas, and laid on the beach in the sun, with my head shaded. How touchingly kind and tender men can be! They carried me back to Ysabel in the bottom of the cutter, weak and with a racing pulse, but noisy and optimistic. Fever grows to be all in the day's work here—Wada to the contrary; and Henry is not as yet re-signed to its recurrences.

Seventeen pigeons were all we bagged, and Jack had been hugely put out at finding that the smokeless cartridges he had ordered were black powder. But it was a red letter day anyway.

The Southern Cross dipped behind a towering height of Ysabel as we ran homeward, and a silver moon two days old sank into the fainting rose of the west. Soon the bright sky clouded over, and our placid day of sun and smooth sea was followed by a night of rain and squalls—the "dusty" weather that comes with the moon's first quarter. But be-fore the wind blew up, we gave the shore and ourselves a treat with the searchlight, fish leaping by thousands out of the illuminated water, where the reflections of our mooring cables wrinkled like black snakes.

The upshot of the outing to Kiaba, in spite of caution, was bush-poisoning for us all—the excruciating "scratch-scratch," ngari-ngari, that did for the *Sophie Sutherland's* doomed crew. Jack had it the worst, Martin and I ruefully admitted while we vainly tried to keep our hands quiet. Nakata had caught it on Guadalcanal, and to our great sym-pathy confessed that he had not sat down for a month, and that he was now obliged to tie his hands at night. We all pitched into the lysol, and added another kind of doctoring to our list, alternately dosing Solomon sores with peroxide of hydrogen and other things—our bottle of corrosive subli-mate solution having been finished on the *Minota,* and our main supply of tablets left at Pennduffryn. Jack, who had now completed his article "Cruising in the Solomons," set to work on another, "The Amateur M.D.," wherein he ex-ploited his medical experience from pulling teeth on Nuka-Hiva to abating "scratch-scratch" on Ysabel.

On September 7, Wada, terrified by light recurrent attacks of fever, parted with his last vestige of common sense, and with the *Snark.* I was not on board when he announced his intention to quit. It followed the serving of a very much overripe goat-stew with a cup of inexcusably weak and dish-watery tea, all of which Jack pushed aside. Wada was some-what taken aback by the way Jack accepted and accelerated his resignation. "Very well, Wada—pack up your things quick, while I get your money; and, Henry, you have the boat ready."

Months of wages were due, and an extra regular allow-ance or present Jack had credited him ever since the beating up Warren had meted him—altogether an unwise sum for a lone Japanese to carry about on his person should the natives get wind of it. Poor muddled mortal—he had a notion he could walk right into the plantation kitchen, as he had heard Mr. Schroeder say they were distressed for want of a cook; but direly as that true gentleman needed one, he met Wada's shameless proposal with cool refusal.

Nakata helped his friend pack and land, then came imme-diately back to the *Snark*, stepped into the galley and said he would be glad to cook for us any length of time it might take to get another cook. But he made it plain that no salary could tempt him to cook permanently. "I t'ink sea-cook all get crazy in head!" he smiled his reason. In return for his help in the difficulty, Jack promised him the steamer trip to Australia, a new suit of clothes, and other emoluments. There was more than a touch of pathos in the boy's sturdy attempt throughout to be loyal both to us and to his coun-tryman.

After Schroeder's turn-down, Wada declared he would go a-tramping in the bush, albeit he was scared of his very life. But it was discovered that he was hiding in a near-by native hut, in hope that Schroeder's mind might change when we were safe out of ken.

A conviction had been growing in my brain that it would not be good for Peggy and myself to part. The little super-animal clung to me night and day, and, when not in actual contact, sat and regarded me with fathomless great eyes of love and speculation that made me almost apprehensive. So, when the day of sailing came round, I left a letter for Cap-

The Impact of Civilisation

Crew of *Snark* at Penndulfryn

tain Jansen, stating the case clearly—that I could not yet bring myself to separate from Peggy, and would deliver her over to him when we returned to Pennduffryn. . . . Jack watched me curiously—I had merely stated my intention and asked no advice. I suppose he concluded that, doing such an unusual thing—for me—as to steal another person's property, I must be acting in the only way I *could* act.

Thursday, September 10, 1908.

Jack says he never shall know just what did happen when we attempted to get away from Meringe Lagoon—or, at least, the cause of what happened. The yacht was floated at 3 A. M., and lay at her largest anchor, which was properly provided with a tripping-line to make sure it could not foul. At eight, when we began heaving, the thing would not hoist, and, at the same time, seemed to be dragging, as if it had got caught under a cable. The boat with her skating hook was drifting fast toward a ledge of inshore reef, and our friends on the beach began to look anxious. The anchor still failing to break out, still dragging, we hove until we parted the big main hawser and the tripping line.

"Find it, and you can have it!" Jack shouted shoreward, once he was clear of entanglement. Fortunately we were not really crippled by the loss, as it was an emergency anchor, say for on a lee shore in a blow; but we were sorry to let it go.

There was a heavy cross-sea outside, which, with the brisk easterly wind, made every soul of us sick except Henry, who, like Herrmann of old, is blessedly immune. We have logged no less than a steady seven knots all day in the adverse sea, and figure, at this clip, to see Lua-Nua (Lord Howe) early to-morrow forenoon—one hundred and fifty miles north of Meringe.

We parted with some of our stores to Mr. Schroeder, as the non-arrival of the *Minota*, by way of Gubutu, has left him short; and to-day Nakata, creeping about after a tussle with fever, announced with concerned and puckered visage that we had kept no flour for ourselves. Martin exploded "Impossible!" But his search of the snug forepeak was fruitless—or flourless. However, toward night, when we all began to sit up and feel hollow, our stout pilot bread was as satisfying, we thought, as Nakata's hot soda-biscuits that we didn't get.

The weather is very smoky, and we are wondering if it betokens a trade gale.

September 11, 1908.

Wind dropped, and, to make sure of port to-day, the engine went to work at nine and a half knots, acting the best it ever has yet. Jack roughly calculated our distance from Lua-Nua at 6 A. M. to be twenty miles. Everybody felt better, and Nakata's fever had burned out. He was even chirpy enough mildly to criticise some of Wada's galley practices, the while he whipped batter for shrimp fritters.

The island failed to show at the anticipated time, but the sky was clear enough for Jack to take a morning sight. Then, alas, when he came to work it out, he found he had left at Pennduffryn the corrected tables he had so laboriously made up. Hence, also out of practice these many weeks, he was forced to dig his results the hardest way. And such results! According to them we have sailed right over Lord Howe, and no explanation can be deduced for being so out of our course.

We beguiled ourselves with Peggy, who was very dull yesterday—probably seasick. In spite of our declaration never to risk pets on so small a boat, we now find ourselves with this fragile-boned creature, and a still more fragile feathered one, a white cockatoo with strawberry-pink crest and round dilating yellow-and-black eyes, which Martin mutinously brought from Tulagi. As its wings have been abbreviated, it is in as much peril about the ship as is Peggy—more, for it cannot get out of the way so quickly with its two legs. Peggy is jealous of the cockatoo, and droops dispiritedly when she hears our gales of laughter at the canny bird's pranks. When he cannot get what he wants, after storming up and down the deck and ruffling his indignant feathers he changes tactics, climbs up our wincing arms, lays his flattening crest against our ears, and caresses and wheedles in the most ingratiating upward inflection:

"Hello! Cock-*ee!* Cock-*ee!*"

Something seems to tell Peggy that she will be hurt if she tampers with the sharp-nosed beak or prickly toes; and something also warns her that any annihilating rush at the despised biped would be an infringement of our property rights. Peggy is taught more from within than without.—Which reminds me that to-day, in five minutes, she learned to "speak," and in the same five minutes grasped that she must speak like a lady, "ever gentle, soft, and low," and not like wild-dog puppies from the unregenerate and vulgar bush. To carry chicken bones to the painted covering-board, whence they must not be worried off to the white-scoured deck planking, will require two lessons—not because she fails to compass the idea, but because, with a ravenous growing-appetite, she forgets in her eagerness. And she does apologise so generously with her snuggling black velvet muzzle and great speaking eyes, the while she wags the unlovely rag on her violated tail.

It was a strange sweet evening we spent on deck, in our puzzling frame of mind, the softly piled clouds, lighted by a drifting moon, casting white reflections in the dark grey sea. Jack hove the yacht to (she handles "like a witch" with her clean hull), and lay on his side on a cot, with the blissful puppy curled in the hollow of his arm; and Martin, tired from hours in the engine room, and feverish in addition, flattened out on a deck mattress, with the cockatoo, head-under-wing, on his chest. I nestled under the light covers of a cot beneath the awning, and hummed Hawaiian airs to my thrumming ukulélé, until the men all were breathing deep, except Tehei who had taken Martin's watch.

September 12, 1908.

Did ever a yacht's company spend such a day? Land there should have been, and land there was none. It is the season of especially unsettled weather, even for the Solomons, wherein the southeast trade changes to the northwest monsoon, and everything is topsy-turvy. Jack got a most unsatisfactory observation, which again attested that we had fabulously sailed over the dry land and shallow waters of an enormous atoll. Our patent log seems to be in perfect condition, and we can only wonder if the chronometer is out of order. Martin, who has been with the *Snark* continuously since we left Penndufryn on the *Minota,* swears by his budding beard that he has never neglected the daily winding. Can the equatorial current be setting us off our course? With the worry of this unaccountable situation, with fever threatening, and a new crop of small sores eating into his nerves, I don't see how my husband can be so merry—except that he relishes a set-to with adventure and the unknown. On top of everything, he inadvertently got a bad sunburning on his back, while reading at the wheel in a net singlet, and I have been soaping it at intervals, which has drawn the heat and brought great relief.

Martin tried to run the engine, collapsed, and had to lay up. Peggy sustained a fall which would have been a header if she hadn't curved and landed on the end of her outraged appendage, to an accompaniment of piercing shrieks which Cockee accurately duplicated. As if the general atmosphere were too surcharged for any thinking bird, the cockatoo has muttered and stuttered and nearly burst himself the livelong day, trying to say something besides "Hello, Cock-ee!" Once, when Jack had persistently replaced the spoon in his tea (of which Cockee is inordinately fond), after the bird had removed it repeatedly with great pains and was ever about to sip, there was no mistaking the fervid swear-tone that filled his throat, although no words could he muster.

I took the second dog-watch for Martin, and enjoyed once again the two hours of solitude in a black and unstable world.

It was squally, with a rough sea. Full many a month it is since I have stood a watch, and my only steering has been when making entrances and departures.

September 13, 1908.

There has been very little of the conventionally enjoyable in to-day's programme. As if there weren't novelty enough, we three white ones have been deathly sick the forepart of the day, undoubtedly poisoned from tinned cabbage, although we had hardly swallowed any of it before deciding it was "off."

Weather variable, with a mean, seasicky swell. Jack secured three sights, seven o'clock, nine, and ten, but no noon observation to follow; nor could he obtain any latitude yesterday. He is trying to hold his weatherly position—to the east—beating to wind'ard under short canvas and heaving to at night, until such time as he can secure a good sun- or star-observation in order to find his latitude. This determined, he will head by log to the latitude of Lord Howe, and run both that latitude and the island down together to the westward. We humorously think of ourselves as in one of "the outermost pits of the sea," where sun and stars and all stabilities have deserted us. Once, to-day, we saw an ominous black cloud, while under it a waterspout formed and spiralled —the first I ever witnessed.

. . . 'Tis the twitching hour of midnight, when tired wives yawn; and I have just watched Jack fall uneasily asleep in a copious sweat, after a raving period of intolerable fever-burning. The blast of fever struck him after supper, just as we vociferously won to victory over Martin in a rubber of dummy whist. Our vanquished opponent, who was suffering the tortures of the unredeemed with corroding bluestone on his shin-sores, and had preceded the playing by wiping up the cabin floor with his writhing person in the first agonies of the fearful application, lost his temper at our noisy victory.

This being the only time since the *Snark's* keel was laid that we had ever seen our blond friend's temper disturbed, I think it must have been the shock that overthrew Jack's equilibrium!

With the exception of the man on watch, I am the only one awake, and I am very much awake. This is a commonplace of my life—to be in a state of luminous consciousness in the dark hours, while all else is normally reposing. But everything becomes commonplace where there is no standard of commonplaceness. Consider us here, aimlessly adrift in a black and starless world of water above and below, the land of our objective sunk beneath the sea for aught we can disprove, calmly going about our work-a-day business quite as if we weren't lost.

. . . Jack is sleeping with one eye half open, and I wish he would either close it or wake up, he looks so ghastly. The past two weeks have been very wearing on him—the responsibility of the ship careened on that risky incline, the loss of rest, and the shocks of fever. But he takes his attacks easier than do I, for at their height his mind wanders, and in the easement of temperature he falls asleep, and so misses the conscious nerve-suffering that I endure because I cannot go out of my head.

September 14, 1908.

The first I heard through the skylight (it had been too wet to sleep on deck) was an inexcusable punning exclamation from Martin:

"Lord! Howe did we miss that island!"

And that was but the forerunner of similar combinations, which I leave to any imagination foolish enough to dwell upon their possibilities. Even poor little Nakata, moaning and turning in violent malaria, while we steamed and grilled him in the hot cabin, gave forth little cackles in his conscious moments at our brilliant competition (American humour is an open book to Nakata), and finally poked a scarlet face from a blanket scarce as red, and finished us all with a trembly:

"Lord! Howe I wish there was no fever in the Solomon Islands—don't I?" and then wept at his own quip, from sheer nerve-rack and weakness.

Yes—and what a pity that so wonderful a space of great islands, so rich in promise, should be so variously unhealthful. But never mind—such things are beaten out slowly—the day will come when, along with the wondrous savannahs on Guadalcanal, all these lands will be brought under scientific cultivation and control, the stripèd mosquito that is the author of so much suffering and disability shall be destroyed, there shall be no devastating ulcer-poisoning and filthy flies to carry it to flesh that is no longer unantisepticised—a time when the islands will lie blossoming under the light of applied knowledge, and disease and unnecessary death shall be no more. As we of to-day cannot gaze upon this certain reality of the future, it is good to see it in the mind's eye.

Rain, rain, rain; and the barometer rises and falls as if indicating the insanity of the universe. There is no sun to dry out above and below, and we must endure, with what fortitude we may, the encroaching mouldiness and staleness and stuffiness of our quarters. I peer into lockers, fingering the wax-paper wrappings of my perishable clothing to see if they are intact, for these are disastrous conditions for silk-stuffs and gold threads, and the very atmosphere implants indelible rust-spots in linen and cotton.

Tehei cooked to-day, and Martin was barely able to help with the dishes; while Jack, in his stateroom, hot and sealed against the torrential downpour, added new items to his "Amateur M.D." There was no chance for a noon sight, and a late partial observation proved of little value. Coming below to put away his sextant, he smiled brightly at me and said:

"The most remarkable thing about our whole remarkable situation, Mate Woman, is the way you, most sensitive of women, nearly transparent from lack of sleep, go about doing anything and everything, and actually *enjoying* it all. The more I see of you, the more I marvel at you."

I was really taken aback, with surprise as well as pleasure, for it hadn't occurred to me that I might be otherwise than happy-hearted, despite tiredness and the unresting gnaw of two small sores that have taken hold on my instep. I *am* happy; I *am* having a good time—the time of times; for I am doing what I want to do, in the company I crave, with "life and love to spare," and too absorbed in the potentialities of being to be more than superficially arrested by the flip of little irks or fears. Believe me—there's been more vital snap of interest in the few hours of waging war with Jack's fever yesterday and Nakata's to-day, than in a month of placid existence in well regulated conditions. And then, think of coming up for a breath of squally air, and taking a turn barefoot along the streaming deck, wondering the while if it has settled down for weeks of rain, or how near we can come to missing Roncador Reef to the south (called The Snorer, and 18 miles in circumference), or if we may drift far enough south and east to encounter Bradley Reef—both deep-sea banes of mariners—or how many other reefs there may be that are uncharted.

Happy? I never was so happy in my life, take it all round, nor with more reason. Jack says we are

> ". . . those fools who could not rest
> In the dull earth we left behind,
> But burned with passion for the West
> And drank strange frenzy from its wind."

September 15, 1908.

Driven out at six by the insufferable stickiness, I found Jack at the wheel all glowing in a deep red sunrise, with Martin and Nakata laid out completely, while Tehei puffed and perspired in the suffocating galley, and went about the cabin work.

"My Lord, Howe bluff you look in that good sun!" I ventured to Jack, who came back at me gaily, nodding to the tragic spectacle on deck:

> "With our sick beneath the awnings
> On the road to . . . where?"

"Don't know, and don't care," expressed my feelings, for I had slept well, if briefly, and the sun was drying and cheerful, if hot. Jack was able to get morning sights, but noon was cloudy and he failed of his latitude.

Martin's illnesses are of an exclusive sort—unlike the common fever. I can't make it out. He absolutely declines to admit that he has fever, and will take no quinine, and as a matter of fact, I cannot see that he is especially feverish. He is up and down, supine for hours, then recuperates and sails into a whist-game with dash and ambition. It may be that he is subtly poisoned by the chain of bandaged ulcers on the lean blades of his shins.

When other interests flag, there are always the cockroaches. I go on still hunts for them, whopping the daring ones that scout from the overhead sliding boxes in the cabin, and occasionally taking down those same boxes and raiding the shell-backed pests that have grown too large to scout, and which finally die imprisoned. But no cockroaches on the *Snark* approach in size the enormous night-frights we had on the *Minota,* when they debouched in myriads in the dark and spread wings at being disturbed. Ours do not seem to have developed wings; but they have teeth, and steal nibbles at our toes while we sleep.

. . . There is more than a vague depression among us this evening, in spite of Tehei's nice supper, an exciting rubber of whist and my efforts on the "baby guitar" to 'liven things up.

"The hospital ship *Snark,*" Jack summed it up, and there was a little catch in his voice, for on my bunk lay Peggy the Beloved, pulling at our heartstrings in her pain, one leg apparently useless from a fall through the skylight into my room—the eager child could not wait to go around; and on a cushion in Martin's bed a limp cockatoo that has grown strangely dear, with his affection and intelligence and his sense of humour, breathes with difficulty and half-closed, filmy eyes. Tehei, with a dozen things to do at dinner time, rushed to drop the skylight in a sharp rainsquall, and shut it on the napping bird roosting under· the edge. The frail frame of him seems to be crushed, but we want to give him every chance. Just now we feel guilty that we ever broke our rule about pets on the voyage.

Tehei has been touched by the over-animal consciousness displayed by Peggy and the bird, and shakes his head again and again, with his sweet Polynesian smile:

"No dog—no fowl—I no can say. They got somet'ing in here, and here, like you, like me," tapping his breast and forehead. These two denizens of earth and air have met with and grown to us with all there is in them of common likeness of entity.

We are hove to "under a bright and starry sky," but there is no sight nor sound of land.

Wednesday, September 16, 1908.

This is *my* day to feel dumpy and dull, with neuralgia in the head to enliven the dulness. But Martin, Nakata, Peggy and Cockee have brightened, and Tehei is glad to return to deck duty. Henry replenished the board with a baby shark and a fine bonita. The heat of the clear day calls to mind that we are nearer the Equator by a presumable two degrees or so—although Jack declared in the morning that he might be several degrees north of the Line for all he knew! But he was able to take a perfect noon observation, and steered for the latitude of Lord Howe. At six in the afternoon, he told us he figured we were about seventeen miles from the island.

September 17, 1908.

This afternoon the engine was set going, and, with perfect trade-wind weather assisting, we surged due south. The sea was like dark-blue crinkled satin, and sun and wind freshened the boat and all on it with new life. I climbed up on a shroud and let the flowing liquid breeze blow through me as it seemed, and was possessed with an enchanted sense of detachment and the illimitability of the cloud-land and the world of water. Solid land does not exist in such exaltations.

Henry and Tehei, as the sunset wore, kept insisting that we were near land—perhaps they smelled it unconsciously; and we were taking one last sweep of the waving purple horizon, when Tehei, who had gone aloft, screamed like a child:

"Lan' ho!"

We could not see it from the deck, but Henry climbed up and verified the glorious find, while Jack noted the bearings, west by south, one-half south. The grand little *Snark* hove to beautifully, even working to wind'ard a little under staysail, jib, and mizzen. Jack glowed at the excellent performance—"The old girl—eh?"

Our immediate joy was short-lived, and a small but real grief fell upon us all. The lovable cockatoo, who had rallied in the forenoon, had been wilting perceptibly, and it was plain that the only kindness would be to end his misery. But who was to do it? Martin, whose bird he was, backed down with a sick face; Tehei begged off, with tears; Nakata said, "I'd rather not," and Jack, with misty eyes looking at the poor thing caressing his hand with its gentle crest, said to Henry:

"I'll do it, Henry, if no one else will, because it must be done; but how do you feel about it?"

Henry, grave and concerned, came up nobly:

"I no like, Mr. London. . . . But I do for you. Give here."

The last sound our pretty white pet ever uttered was when I took his broken body for a moment and laid it against my neck.

"Cock-*ee*," he said in the shadow of his sweet and wheedling tone that ended in a little rasp.—Just a wisp of sentient down, he was, with a modicum of plucky spirit; but he left his mark on us all, and we separated very quietly and mournfully for the night.

Lua-Nua (Lord Howe, or Ongtong Java Atoll),
Friday, September 18, 1908.

Not only are we rocking at anchor after eight days in an apparently chartless void, but we are encompassed by our first atoll, albeit this rosy coral ring is so big we cannot see the far low side of it. A one hundred and fifty mile hoop gives a brave diameter.

Hove to, we drifted S.S.W. during the night, at five o'clock set sail north, and shortly sighted land again, three miles to west'ard. But just when a good position had been attained for the reef opening, a succession of squalls overtook us, and we dared not risk an entrance that could not be seen; so Jack hove to the obedient little ship until the watery swift tempest abated, when he put me at the wheel, Martin at the engine, and Henry aloft, and we raced through the swirling passage into the choppy sea of a fresh squall. From outside we had glimpsed two white cutters across the line of reef, but the first craft to reach us was a welcome outrigger canoe, the sight of which filled our cannibal-cautious souls with sense of rest and security; while Henry and Tehei gurgled and glowed with delight and anticipation, eager from their hearts to find if they and the gentle-faced, tattooed strangers (who, by the way, were of much smaller stature) could speak a common tongue. They could, although with various garnishments borrowed from their own slight strain from the southerly; and we white ones met them with bêche de mer and our mild mixture of Polynesian patois —while Nakata's language, all his own combination, was entirely adequate. As soon as we looked into the inquisitive but friendly faces of the three paddlers, came the realisation how little affection we had learned for the western breeds— our feeling for the people of Melanesia was one of fascinated interest, but developed no ties such as now pulled when these dusky men of Lua-Nua clambered over-rail. One, a benevolent middle-aged fellow with a tuft of curly hair over each ear and a straggling beard touched with grey, seemed to be a personage.

"How do?—Me fella Bob.   I pilot—I take you Lua-Nua—right O.   I like you—any amount."

"Any amount" is a favourite expression of old Bob's, and it is infinitely entertaining to hear his musical husky voice saying, "My word!" "Right O!" and other exclamations gleaned from English and Australian traders.

Old Bob's two companions took our breath away with their beauty—princes of youth, heads a-toss with sun-touched ringlets, eyes sweet and long-lashed, and mouths fine and small, curling lovably over white small teeth.

Bob, after the exchange of greetings, became very important in his rôle of pilot, and, with austere face and solemn arm-weavings in the mist, warded off the rain; the young princes the while reciting measures of warning incantation to the gods of ill weather.   We were thus poetically guided to an anchorage near the village, which lies snug under beautiful tufted palms.

These people are in one respect like the bird family.   Their beauty is mostly vested in the males.   When we came to observe the girls and women, there was no comparison, and they were still further set at disadvantage by cropped skulls, one of several un-pretty Melanesian customs that have crept in.

Harold Markham, trader for the Company, a husky sailor-built blond Australian, had started out in his cutter through a smaller passage, but lost us in the wet gusts that blotted out everything.   He now followed in the way we had come, and, among other things, recounted how the big schooner *Malakula*, on her last trip, entirely missed the opening and had to enter forty miles away, at the next entrance. Markham took us ashore, where, in his neat high-pillared house, the first notable incident was the meeting of Peggy with a good-humoured, lumbering, white bull-pup.   Our patently inadequate terrier advanced stalkingly on thin, stiff-stilted legs, her back ruffed like a wild boar's, and when the unsuspecting bull tipped her over at the first friendly on-slaught, she came up in a still frenzy of outraged dignity, lips tight-snarled, and stood over the abject flattened white-jelly puppy with blood-curdling growls of menace.

"The big bull has no chance altogether," chuckled Markham.

Next, we met the lady of his choice of Lua-Nuans, a healthy, beaming bronze girl of seventeen or so, of whom he is unaffectedly proud and fond. He explained frankly the unfaceable loneliness of a life like his, at the ends of the earth, and how happy "I and my wife" are together; planned trips with her to other islands in leaves of absence; and, dropping into her vernacular for a moment, accompanying his words with free pantomime, he laughingly translated her pleased exclamations over the pretties he was promising. It did give me a queer little start, though, when, with the most unembarrassed air in the world, he told how he had paid ten gold sovereigns to the parents for their daughter, who, he added with utmost childlike pride, was of high degree.

"An' she's a sight better off with me—right as rain," he confided. "You'll soon notice she's entirely deaf in one ear, an' the other side nearly so. The vahines would plague her, but as my wife she's protected from all that—my word! I should say so.—Also, a woman that can't hear don't talk one to death, and she can't squabble with the other vahines, either.—An' she don't take to clothes at all," he went on, with charming naïveté. "All she wants is a new fathom of gay calico an' a change of beads . . . an' soap: she's daffy over soap. Whenever I don't see her around, I only need look under the shower I fixed outside there on the veranda, an' she's there latherin' herself from head to foot."

The modest young matron, with not a stitch above the waist and only a scarlet-patterned paréu below, smiled contentedly and affectionately at her lord, as his gestures told her the matter of his monologue.

The whole spirit of the situation was so clean, orderly, and natural, that I decided I was having the oddest, maddest, merriest time of all our "Snarking" in the unswept corners of earth, and planned no end of good fun with the girl when

I could get her aboard to surprise her bright eyes with garments such as she had never seen, and, perhaps, dress her up
as one would a new doll.   There is no danger of bankrupting
Markham by my foolishness, because I find these primitive
minds grasp but a bit at a time, and are shocked into only
the briefest interest in things complicated.   I would back
the speed of Peggy's reasoning against that of a large per-
centage of these natives.   And, if a dog's logic reaches its
limit at a given period, so does the savage's.   One thing more
than reconciles me to my inability to adopt Fakamam—they
tell me that the average maid of Melanesia reaches her apogee
of mental development somewhere along in her mid-teens,
and is a burden thereafter.

The third and last member of Markham's household is a
mild-faced Solomon Island cook, who, despite his deceptive
weak prettiness, is deservedly serving an aggregation of sentences that cover eight years, for murders, escapes in handcuffs, thefts of whaleboats—a history of bloodcurdling
crimes and reprisals too long to go in here, but which so
tickles Jack's fancy that he intends making a short story of
it, to be called "Mauki," and including it in his collection
South Sea Tales.

There was quite a gathering around the tiny compound
when we came out for a walk, gracefully formed, gracefully
moving men and women, and a tumble of cherubic kiddies.
Among them we saw two or three albinos.   They were rather
weird and ghastly—white human beings on the face of it,
and yet not white.   Their eyes were not pink, but very faded,
and their pinky-white skins blotched with light freckles.
The hair was almost white.

We found there were two villages instead of one, at some
little distance apart.   No maiden may cross from her village
to the other, except to marry; and it is compulsory to wed
men of the opposite community.   Even with this precaution
fairly close inbreeding must obtain, for there are but five
thousand inhabitants on the entire coral circle.

It was sheer bliss to pad along the soft pathways under

thick palms, all in a green-golden atmosphere, and be accosted
courteously and unaffectedly by a beautiful race with whom
smiles are currency and love the password. Into the lofty
gloom of the king's house we were ushered, and there presented with grave pomp to a man who lost none of his magnif-
icence because he was not great of stature. Henry and
Tehei, six feet in bare soles, seemed gentle giants looming in the cocoanut-scented twilit spaces. A small fire
burned in the centre, sending up an aromatic smoke. The
rest of the large floor was covered with coarse, clean mats,
while finer ones were laid for us by the hands of the king's
two wives. Children flitted about, lovely curly-pated cupids.
We duly submitted our offering of tobacco, with bead neck-
lets and bracelets for the "queens," and in true Polynesian
spirit a return was ready to hand—a shark's jaws, with row
upon row of jagged teeth.

As our eyes grew accustomed to the half-light, the beauty
of the king shone out more and more; and in the corners and
mid-distances of the interior, groups were disposed, leaning,
crouching, sitting, standing, in lovely unconscious composi-
tions, while the doorways framed sweet faces with tumbled
curls that were touched with the gilt of afternoon sunlight.
The forms seemed perfect, with skins of satin, unhidden save
for small loincloths, and the men moved like actors, deliberately, unhurriedly, with calm, sure eyes in which there was
no boldness. The colour of their tattooed skins is variously
bronze and copper, but many rub in a yellow oil with a certain
leaf that turns them a greenish hue which is less unpleasant
than curious—like the mellow greening that copper and
bronze attain.

On returning to the yacht, we found Bob had already
drummed up trade for us, and before the blue and silver
sunset I had filled a large fine-woven basket-bag, the gift of
Mr. Caulfeild, with turtle ornaments, string upon string of
"money," and wide girdles made of "money," both shell and
cocoanut wood, and an assortment of shells, the most important ones being two "orange-cowries" of splendid colour,

rare and much coveted by collectors, who pay for them in Sydney five pounds a pair. There were little tiaras of shark-teeth, with tie-strings of sennit, and, to Jack's delight, some fine specimens of whale-teeth. The fans submitted were exactly like those in Samoa.

"Man-fowl and woman-fowl he stop," Bob introduced the chickens, a man-fowl bringing about eight and a half cents to its owner, and the woman-fowl a little more, what of her capacity for "pickaninny he stop along woman-fowl too much."

September 19, 1908.

Jack says "Lucky we were not at sea last night," for it blew worse than any time in the *Snark's* history. It was quite rough enough inside, and one of the blackest nights in our experience. The sky seemed to press down. But it was not so black in the early evening as Martin adjudged. He came up from the lighted cabin and gazed overside. "My! I never saw it so black!" he said. Jack and I, who were already on deck and our eyes better focused, began to laugh, for within six inches of Martin's face hung a pair of heavy blue-flannel bloomers of mine, winter wear put out to air.

Our men-fowl crowed me awake before five, and a rainy forenoon was not specially inspiriting. But the pleasant, eager traders 'livened things, and I became possessed of three new clam-pearls. Jack turned some small iron puzzles over to the visitors, who were like a lot of holiday children, bobbing their ringlets and crying over and over: "Ah *hé* hé! Ah *hé* hé! Ah *hé* hé!" "Wow-*ow-ow!* Wow-*ow-ow!*" and laughing heartily with me at my amusement.

The Tongan Wesleyan missionary, Mr. Nau, with his wife and daughter, and his Tongan associate, Mr. Bolgar, paid us a call—big, gracious Polynesian love people, all of them, with whom Henry and Tehei were overjoyed to talk. Tehei has been under the weather all day with headache, but we cannot discover any fever.

Peggy, still uncertain on her off hind-leg, took another fall, and lamed the nigh fore-leg, so that she is neither seaman-like nor silent in her meanderings. But meander she will, as long as any brown-skinned human stranger is aboard her ship, although she seems to divine the difference, undoubtedly from her association with our two Polynesians, between the Lua-Nuans and the burly, Semitic-faced Solomons.

Jack is a bit shaky with fever, and a peculiar swelling has appeared in his hands, the sensation being similar to chilblains. It hurts him to close them, and the skin peels off in patches, with other skins readily forming and peeling underneath. I do not believe his nervous system was ever made to thrive in the tropics.

. . . Just now, as I write in bed, there came a fluttering of wings, distinct through the ripping of thunder, against the ventilator, and Jack, roused out of his first drowse, dropped from his bunk and went up in the rain expecting to find a bat. Instead, his hands encountered a white bird that had stunned itself on the rigging. He straightened it out, and it presently flew away. When Jack came down again, he put a damp and towelled head through our tiny doorway and blinked smiling at me:

"It's a royal life we lead, isn't it? There's nothing in the world to equal it!"

September 20, 1908.

Tehei has fever at last, and is very languidly and pallidly interested in himself and his symptoms, with a sweet smile watching Nakata pull together and return to the galley. It is now three weeks since my last attack; and Jack's threatening state yesterday proved only a slight cold.

Markham brought his lady-love aboard, and I dressed her up in stays and lingerie and an evening gown and sent her on deck, to the huge entertainment of the men. But it was as I thought—beyond the gift of some scented toilet soap, a string of beads, and a gay paréu, she was not at all covetous—although I have a suspicion that steady association with a certain huge powder-puff would tempt her.

Ashore in the afternoon, we were treated to a big dance, called "sing-sing." The women hula'd in dresses of grass and leaves and gay calico, and a bevy of naked girl-babies mingled, dancing amorously with unwitting faces, tiny point-fingered hands on swaying hips, while King Kepéa and his councillors watched us to see how we took it; for they seem to have gathered a notion, probably from the enlightened Tongans, that the hula is not a white man's dance. One cross-eyed infant, girdled in flowers, danced herself into a frenzy of contortions of body and plump limbs, until her mother caught her up amidst shrieks of laughter from everybody, and held her kicking on high.

The incongruity of actions among these simple folk (who are far more comely and gracious than the general run of one's white acquaintances), when they become absorbed in trivial and childish affairs, is rather rude on one's imagination. We had brought a half sack of sweet potatoes for His Majesty, and a big square tin of assorted "lollies," and the handsome chief kept a keen and frequent-dropping eye and hand on these treasures—as did some of his court who sat around on hand-wrought four-legged stools of hard wood. And *I* had *my* eye on the king's seat, which was the best of the lot, and which I intended to possess sooner or later. The dignified and graceful acceptance by the lofty-miened prime ministers (Bob among them), of a single potato or a sticky handful of lollies, sorely tried our gravity. Some inimitable young prince, flaunting his love-locks in the sun, made bashful eyes at us behind a slanting palm, until he was beckoned to come up and receive a fistful of the garish-coloured dainties —at which a coquettish hoyden swayed close to him from a dance figure, snatched his prize and broke into a run, he after her, and both laughing shrilly. There were practically no dances new to us, even the "jumping widows" of Taiohae being represented by various vahines who bumped stiffly up and down in the midst of a weaving circle.

Old Bob was general of affairs, and fearfully important. When the entertainment waned, he called our attention to a half dozen fowls lying bound beside the king, who looked uneasy, as if he were afraid we might depart before he could get something off his mind. And then his high Majesty majestically suggested that we buy his six "woman-fowl"! The descent from sublime to ridiculous was so abrupt that Jack and I stood open-mouthed for an instant, and Martin made an actual *shy* away from the august presence. "Well, what do you know about that!" he breathed—"well—I'm a son of a seacook!" (Martin's words often contain the spirit if not the sound of his emotions.)

Oh, we bought the chickens, never fear; and as the elegancies of our language are not understood here, Jack's genial and respectful "Good-bye, you old robber!" and my "Farewell, you magnificent skinflint!" carried nothing but pleasure and sense of well-being to the soul of the sovereign. Henry looked aghast at our temerity; but as nothing fell from heaven, and as not even the astute Bob suspicioned the mock homage, our big Rapa Islander smiled his whimsical three-cornered smile and chuckled all the way to the beach. Henry hasn't spent most of his years on white men's boats without learning a bit of their humour. He was about to toss me over his great shoulder (he has relegated to himself the duty of passing "Missis" high and dry from beach to boat and vice versa), when a hubbub arose ashore, and there was an exodus of the crowd across the belt of land. Something was up, and we joined the rush, praying against hope that we might be about to witness the drawing ashore of a lost canoe drifted from some far palmy isle. This drift peopled Lord Howe and Tasman, Bellona and Rennel, and at long intervals, still other canoes are cast up. Sometimes the voyagers are all dead—we are possessed of several spears from such a funeral canoe that was once washed on the reef. But think of the meeting when the strays from fabled lands are still breathing, and are welcomed and resuscitated by their saviours! It was not to be that we should gaze upon such a scene; far from it, what we saw was a steamer plying slowly outside the reef toward an opening farther west, and Markham told us it was the *Sumatra*—smallest of the North German Lloyd fleet, which makes more or less regular trips among the German islands for copra and to bring stores; and he said we would take a run down to her in the cutter to-morrow, with our mail, as she does not like to come to the shallower waters at this end.

On our walk to-day, we found the breadth of this coral band to be not more than three hundred yards at the widest, and could realise how easy it must have been for the first white men who came here to subjugate the natives. Although in the main descendants of a purely Polynesian drift from the eastward, they had a leaven from an occasional Melanesian contribution in the season of the northwest monsoon, and were hostile to white invaders. They fought well and bravely, but learned their bloody and heartbreaking lesson, and the entire population of the atoll is as peaceable as we see them here. The story of their trimming by the "inevitable white man" is so stirring that Jack will add it also to his collection, calling it "Yah! Yah! Yah!" which was the gleeful slogan of one of the reckless white mariners who took an important hand in the trimming.

Owing to bad weather, we had not been tempted much inshore since our arrival, and now took occasion to examine the Lua-Nua cemetery—the most remarkable thing in its way that we have ever come across—itself worth a voyage to this great atoll, which, in spite of contiguity and control, belongs to the Solomons neither geographically nor ethnologically.

This burial ground, wandering along for some distance, is really very beautiful, although it is hard to say exactly why, for it is comparable to nothing in the world. Through the emerald-green forest of luxuriant palms, you come upon what most nearly resembles a miniature ruined city all in white coral, tipped and decorated with rose-red pigment—a little Pompeii with painted walls and silent streets. The buildings are rows of tombstones, the graves are covered with fine white coral sand, and widows and widowers sweep these graves regularly every day for hours, over periods that endure according to the devotion of the bereft. Once I accidentally stepped on a square of wood lying in the way. Markham's girl drew me aside quickly. *"Maké,"* she whispered—the Hawaiian word for "dead."

The "widowers' (and widows') houses" stand at intervals on the other side of a sort of avenue running parallel with the city of the dead, and we saw the mourners (more women than men) wrapped to the eyes in what looked to be literally sackcloth, of an ashen and dusty dunness. They answered our "alohas" with most unbecoming cheer and merriment.

We passed several turtle-pools—small dark holes crisscrossed with logs, in which the captives slowly grow new houses for their backs after the harvest of shell has been cruelly ripped off.

In some of the homes we visited, sweet-faced vahines gave me presents—bead-necklaces and bracelets, and fans. I had my own pockets and Jack's full of pretty trade articles, and made them happy in return.

During the latter part of our stroll, Peggy disappeared, and I reached Markham's house in a panic. Markham sent several natives to look for her, and they met a curly-headed youth hastening beachward with the puppy, who, when her eyes lighted on us, went into a perfectly feminine hysteria. A ship's dog, unused to regular exercise, is very likely to run amuck when it discovers endless pathways for the chasing.

September 22, 1908.

At nine yesterday we started with Markham in his cutter with the impossibly huge sail and absurdly short tiller, and two leaf-chapleted sons of high men in Lua-Nua, Matukea and Tunaka—beauties, both of them, in face and form, and as stupid of wit as they were beautiful. They appeared to have no judgment whatever in handling the cutter, and Markham was obliged to watch them every minute of the thrilling traverse. No use scolding them—they only look puzzled and grieved, then smile irresistibly with a flash of teeth and dimples, and return to their singing and declaiming for fair weather.

We were bound for the station Nuareber, miles away, where the *Sumatra* was anchored, and the cutter raced along like an ice-boat with her enormous canvas spread to the squalls. Time and again it seemed we must capsize, and Markham's cheering assurance that there were only fish sharks in the lagoon did not make me any less desirous of keeping up on the windward rail. As we had started in the rain, I had not changed from bloomers, and merely added an oilskin and a pongee parasol for sun or rain, packing a skirt with Jack's inevitable book and magazines. There was quite a swell as we ranged alongside the black side of the steamer, and I entertained visions of courteous Teutonic officers reaching to help the white lady aboard. A couple of Black Papuan sailors looked lazily down upon us, and made no offer to assist. Jack prepared to board the ship in order to give me a hand up, when a door opened and two immaculate plump pink Germans looked frowningly out, then, to our amazement, closed the door again. "What are we to them?" Jack laughed, landing on the deck at the next rise of the cutter. "Up with you!—they took you for a boy."

Markham found Captain Müleitner, and soon everything was ours, the two officers profuse with apologies, saying they had seen only the native boys in the cutter. We gave our mail to them, for the *Sumatra* expected to connect with an Australian steamer shortly. Of course, with our delay in reaching Lord Howe, we knew we should miss the *Makambo*, and now planned to take her next following trip, six weeks later.

We had a capital lunch with our hosts, the captain explaining in his broken English (not bêche de mer, alas!) the various German delicacies. But the sauerkraut and noodles and Pilsener and Rhine wine needed no interpretation, and the ship was able to spare us an assortment of things for the *Snark*—sausages, Camembert cheeses, sauerkraut, fruits, cakes, and toothsome potpourris of German tidbits in gay tins. We were served by slender young Chinese with refined faces and soft manners, and beautiful hands. The sailors, Black Papuan from New Britain, were blacker than any Solomon Islanders, and we could not but compare their lean, asymetrical bodies and round, knobby, sloping shoulders with our shapely cupids on the cutter.

After lunch, the weather being fine, with an untroubled lagoon, Captain Müleitner announced that he wanted to see the *Snark* and would take us back. Jack was glad of this, especially as he was very anxious to rate our chronometer. But our scheme failed early, all because of the inability of those love-children in the towing cutter to steer after the *Sumatra's* stern. The cutter capsized, and was dragged under, coming up and submerging repeatedly before the steamer could be stopped. One of the Lua-Nuans went free after the first immersion; but the other, as if from sheer inability to let go, hung on to the stern and came up blowing prodigiously each time. Fortunately he did release his hold before a final twist drew the dismasted cutter clear under the *Sumatra's* propeller. We saw everything in the clear water —the pretty hull sink and twist beneath and then float to the surface on the other side, bottom up. The boy was now astride a trade chest, with other litter around him, including my parasol, his eyes bulging with fright, while his companion swam frantically to join him. And presently, hearing our chorus of mirth at their panic, the pair were laughing with us between panting breaths.

The loss of time occasioned by the accident was so considerable that the captain said he would entertain us over night instead of putting us aboard the *Snark*, while the *Sumatra* went on with her business and Markham got the cutter, whose hull was intact, in shape at Nuareber. We spent a luxurious evening lounging in hammocks and big rattan chairs on the long, canopied after deck, listening to a variety of splendid operatic records on a big phonograph. Jack slept here, along with the others; but the captain insisted, with elaborate bows,

Guadalcanal

The Squall off Lord Howe

A Cannibal Venice

that "Frau London" occupy his stateroom, a large and handsome apartment, well stocked with firearms. Mr. Timm, chief engineer, sold us some New Britain and New Guinea curios. One was a long spear, jagged with rows of sharks'-teeth, encased in a woven sennit sheath—a very choice acquisition. He told us stories of these wild countries that sent our thoughts far beyond the trip to Sydney, when we should return to join the *Snark* and fare westward again.

At nine this morning, we set sail for the *Snark,* and it took six long hours beating to windward to cover the distance we had sped in an hour the day before in the running cutter.

Monday, September 28, 1908.

For a week we have lain here, just pleasuring in the life, and because we have ample time on our hands. Also, and most important, Jack has been lying in wait for observations, so that he could settle the little matter of the chronometer. He has tested it by longitude sights, and discovered it to be something like three minutes out—a very grave total error, when it is considered that each minute is equivalent to fifteen miles. By repeated observations, he rated the chronometer, finding that it had a daily losing error of seven-tenths of a second. Nearly a year ago, when we left Hawaii, the thing had the same losing error. That error was always added each day, and has not changed, according to these Lord Howe observations. So what in the name of all watch-makers made our chronometer put on speed and catch up with itself three minutes? There is no explanation, unless it was allowed to run down in our absence, and was wound and corrected by some chronometer at Tulagi. But Martin stoutly avers that nothing of the kind took place. It is very curious.

Tehei, frightened by his fever, begged leave to spend a couple of days ashore to visit and pray with the Tongan missionaries. He came back more optimistic, but is very self-centred in the observation of symptoms. I once had a male relative-by-marriage who eternally searched for symptoms—and found them—so that he was always ill or on the verge of becoming so. Tehei reminds me of him.

Jack's hands have not improved—in fact, he is sorely bothered by them—even holding a pen is uncomfortable, and a pull on a rope is positively painful.

Nakata, flouting all symptoms, although he has not been entirely free from fever for some time, goes about the cooking without complaint, and many's the delicious odour that floats out from his galley—steaming clam-meat from fluted marble shells, sizzling small-fry brought by the natives, wholesome boiling or frying taro. The people here and in the Solomons are largely tambo in respect to clam-meat, as a devil-devil resides therein. So we, who are especially fond of it, raw or cooked, have difficulty in obtaining all we want. Henry has come nobly to the rescue, with indulgent amusement at the superstition of the lesser breeds, and dives overside when, in the clear brine, we locate on the white bottom, sixty feet below, a desirable shell. Slowly filling his deep lungs, he leaves the rail feet-first, then, well under, turns over and swims down leisurely, as leisurely picks up the shell, and rises very slowly, in order not to change the atmospheric pressure too abruptly, which is the cause of the terrible "bends." He is quietly pleased over our praise, although he knows we know he has only done half the depth of his old-time record. Henry hasn't that slightly depressed chest for nothing.

Jack and I have done a little swimming around the yacht, and the other day, while he was resting on the rail with a dripping and solicitous Peggy beside him, both watching me under water, he saw not fifteen feet below me a long shape. Then I saw it, too—only a fish-shark warranted not to bite . . . but I made my record climb up the gangway ladder.

I do not feel well any of the time—am tired and listless; but a strange elation of happiness possesses me, and all's well.

Every day Bob, who affectionately calls me "Mamma,"

and assures me I am the first white Mary who has visited this end of the island, comes out with something we want, whether tattoo-sticks pointed with sharks'-teeth, or strings of little carved-wood cups, wooden or stone poi-pounders—fine specimens from the Stone Age brought here by the canoe-drift from the high islands—or broad bead girdles of gorgeous hues. And I lie on a cot under the awning and listen dreamily to the musical-husky voices and the soft lapping of little waves against our tumble-home sides, and look out across the warm blues of the lagoon to the isle-dotted pink reef, and am just . . . happy.

Or at night, on deck, we watch the searchlight on shore and water, fish leaping to the illumination, screaming terrified white birds fretting the brilliant green foliage, while weird cries and shouts rise from the villagers, and groups of naked brown forms dance singing on the gleaming sand.

One evening we went fishing with Markham and his girl on the inside reef by lantern light. There had been an astounding sunset, crude blue-and-pink fanrays out of a brazen green-orange horizon band, the reef islets picked out in dead black. The swift passing of all the riot of rude colour was succeeded by a purple night-sky spangled with enormous electric stars, low-hung; and as we glided across the warm water, down out of a sudden blot of cloud shot crackling a round red ball that died through red and rose to pale nothingness ere it reached the sea. A ferine chorus of panic yells went up from the beach at the meteorite, and two scarlet-cinctured, curl-crowned amphibians in our canoe emitted queer little guttural cries and with their arms wove magic spells against devil-devils.

It was a wonderful night. Great stars, reflected in the lagoon, made a strange blue light, softened by fleecy vagrant clouds that also met their reflections in the waveless water. The girl beside me caressed my tired body and limbs with the everlasting blessing of lomi-lomi, and the brown prince-things sang and laughed in undertones at their fishing. The water was so quiet that we could see by the starlight the moony gleam of the sandy bottom, broken with grey fanciful shapes of branching coral. A low groan and growl from the outer surf came across the palmy strand, but we hung motionless in a magic still circle swept softly by perfumed airs.

. . . And to-morrow we hoist anchor for Pelau, at the other end of the atoll, thence straight north for indefinite two-score miles to a ring of reef not a seventh the size of this—Tasman, or Niumano Atoll.

At sea, Lord Howe to Tasman,
Friday, October 2, 1908.

To the south Lord Howe has sunk beneath a waving horizon of cobalt blue, and the dear old bowsprit is questing northward where Tasman lies but a fraction over four degrees below the fervid Line. And fervid enough it is aboard, despite a flowing breeze.

On the morning of Tuesday, the 29th, we sailed for Pelau accompanied by two natives, Kelango, a nephew of Bob's, and Boonaa, the very picture of an Abyssinian. The two put in their time on the bowsprit, guiding us among the brilliant coral patches in the rippling lagoon.

King Kepéa rendered a farewell largess of one hundred young drinking-cocoanuts, and that coveted four-legged "throne," which shall be my pet footstool some day in our Wolf House on Sonoma Mountain. He also sent a score of fowls, these, as we had come to learn, to be paid for.

Mr. Markham came out, and the girl was a sumptuous vision, swathed in sky-blue paréu held by a wide blue-beaded band close around her bronze body under the breasts. But she was entirely put in the shade when there hove over-rail our friend Bob, who had spent good money at the store on a coarse white cotton chemise (surmounted by an embroidered frill), that reached below his lean knees. Imagine the bewhiskered, fuzz-tufted, benevolent old fellow in this outrageous rig, stiff with pride in his unimpeachable correctness—and our struggle not to shout with laughter. And at the last, tarrying with us until he became separated from his canoe, he dived overside and rose waving a lean brown arm out of its embroidered puff-sleeve, before he struck for shore with a "Good-bye, my mamma! Good-bye, my friend!"

Jack trusted Henry with the wheel and went below to start his story "Mauki," which has greatly stirred his imagination. I spent most of the day fitting up our tiny state-rooms with yielding depths of fine mats on the floors, others soft-folded on the bunks, and rearranging things generally. They are such clean comfort, these native weaves, in this melting temperature.

At 5:30, with an hour of the engine, we came to rest in sixty feet of green-crystal water, and our eyes could follow the chain link by link to where the anchor hid under a dull-blue coral-hummock. Rosy rock-cod and dun fish-sharks could be clearly seen hovering in the shadows cast by sea gardens or gliding from tree to tree out of the violet glooms into opalescent sungleams and back again, and large bêche de mer slugs lay like blots on the wavy white bottom.

Before the natives commenced to swarm out, Mr. Bolgar (Mr. Nau and he had preceded us to Pelau) paid us a call, and more to our amusement than surprise at first, warned us against the natives, whose breeding includes a streak of Malayan as well as Melanesian. "S'pose you frien's look out along Queenslander fella," he explained. This we perfectly understood, as the presence of a "returned Queenslander" would make us keep an eye out for at least small failings, although nothing worse in this safe environment.

There is not a white face in Pelau, and we quickly comprehended the variance of the people from those at the other end. No lovely youths here—these were very like Solomon Islanders in shape and feature, although as elaborately if not as finely tattooed as any Samoan. All over their faces the patterns stray, and it makes one's flesh creep to look at heavy designs on the tender skin under their eyes, so

exquisite must have been the torture of the artist's handi-
work. The children are well sketched on their little chests,
and childless wives and the men wear irregular knicker-
bockers of intricate drawing. Some of them had "fella
muskets" limned on their satiny torsos.

Early next morning the roar of surf outside roused me,
and I dived for a cool swim with Jack before breakfast, as
the sharks really seemed to stay on bottom near the fish.
Imagine lying face-downward on the tepid beryl floor of
water, eyes open to the coral groves and lazy-shifting life of
the lagoon, and trying to spy a hide-and-seek anchor at the
end of a chain that partly lies in irregular lines and loose
coils in the slack of the tide; or, coming up for a lung of
fresh air, leisurely swimming under the beloved copper hull
of your boat, and turning face-up to look at her iron keel
before rising on the other side. It is all so indolent-easy.
If Jack and I did everything in the tropics as moderately
as we live in the water, I am beginning to believe there would
be little sickness for us.

A strange canoe with upright carved ends ranged alongside while we were having our fresh-laid breakfast-eggs on
deck, her paddlers equally strange—two Mongolian-faced
men under broad Chinese hats. One of them submitted a
large, perfectly round clam pearl, at which I tried not to
look too possessively, for he held it at a price that would
have commanded a true oyster pearl. Jack advised: "Let
him wait a day or two—he'll find his mistake and come
down." But he never could be convinced that it was not a
proper "poë" (Tahitian for pearl), and we sailed without
it, as I preferred to hoard the price against our pearl-junket-
ing in Torres Straits.

Mr. Nau and Mr. Bolgar sent out an invitation to visit
them, and under their commodious oblong roof, as we rested
on thick mats, we met the royalty, King Pongavali of Pelau,
and drank the good health of His Majesty and his wives and
prime ministers in endless libations of tender cocoanuts.
Many of the types were curious—not like the Solomons, not

like anything we knew—stern visages set around with Faun-
tleroy locks, faces slow to smile, their watchful black eyes
lid-dropping when too closely scrutinised.

Mr. Nau's sweet vahine piled in my lap several fine Samoan
mats, one of them thickly fringed with vari-coloured wor-
sted, an especial treasure in her eyes. While we were under
shelter a heavy shower cleared the oppressive air, and we
walked about the green island, where I was allowed to go and
come unchallenged in rickety devil-devil houses such as
Jack and Martin had never seen, nor even Henry and poor
weak Tehei, who could not resist coming ashore.

The Pelauans are not so fastidious as the Lua-Nuans, and
these devil-devil houses are noisome with a clutter of offerings of dirt-encrusted turtle shell, native kai-kai spoons of
the same shell and of mother-of-pearl, malodorous ragged
garments—I saw a grimy plaid shawl—dog-skulls, sharks'-
jaws, repulsive strings of fish-tails, and, under one conse-
crated thatch, a week-dead black cat swayed and swung and
perfumed the breeze. At all times watchers squat or lie in
these twilight temples—unpleasant creatures, some of them
with loathly skin diseases.

We picked up a few fine curios—Jack was especially
elated over several adzes of petrified shell that were routed
from obscurity by the ancient fathers of the tribe, wrought
years before white men introduced the first iron.

When we returned aboard, a large crowd saw us off, and
then dispersed to sleep away the heat. Just before sunset, in
what I suppose one might call the cool of the afternoon, we
roused from our deck-mats and brought to light some foolish
miracles to astound the gathering that paddled out to see
what it could see. Some were absorbed in "tuppenny" wire
puzzles until the marvelling murmurs of others called them
to where stupid paper wafers spread into coloured lilies in
pans of water, or Japanese flowers burst into swift blossoming in little pots, or harmless grey lumps of clay turned into
writhing snakes of fire at the touch of a match. Next day
the King, being indisposed and bored, despatched a courier

with request that we bring or send similar wonders for his amusement. It was too hot to leave the awnings, so we sent the things. We noticed that no reciprocal gift was forthcoming. How radically different peoples in the same part of the world can be! The missionary's wife was ill, so the household did not come to dinner as arranged. Very few canoes paddled out—either we must have gleaned all the curios, or else we had nothing the population wanted.

By the time we were ready to depart, our anchor chain, to say nothing of the anchor, had become so involved in the coral groves that we had to send native divers down to disentangle them, and could watch their every movement. I steered out the narrow reef entrance under power, snapping breakers close on each hand.

Jack, in addition to writing and navigating and general captaining, is studying up everything on the medical shelf relating to Tehei's sickness, and is treating him very carefully; for blackwater fever undoubtedly it is, and blackwater is no joke. What a terrible thing a death on the happy *Snark* would be! But we are not dwelling upon death, but life and recovery. Unfortunately, Tehei's mind, whether conscious or wandering, works directly against our efforts. He seems sweetly determined to become an angel, and meets all cheer-provoking suggestion with patient smiles; while all his childish-lisping talk is in the missionary nomenclature. His worship leads curiously into the channel of *aitu* observance. To-day I overheard him whispering; "O God, don't kill me! O God, don't kill me!" But we have simply *got* to pull him through.

Saturday, October 3, 1908.
Except for making safely out of Lord Howe at three yesterday, we did not employ the engine, but sailed on in the warm-blowing afternoon, through a glorious equatorial sunset, and into a scintillating night of electric moon and stars and phosphorescent water, until, at half past ten, Martin

sighted Tasman low-lying not far off. Jack hove to, but was up and down all night to be sure of holding his weather position. He looked very tired-eyed this morning, and I could see his burning, stinging hands gave him no respite. Happily, his natural curiosity is such that the study and working through even his own physical misfortunes (let alone others') nearly offset the personal pain and irk. Hence, his temper is equable, and no one else is forced to suffer unduly on his account.

Under power, once near Tasman, we skirted her purling reef, all strung with deep-green wooded islets, Henry at masthead, bald and hatless under the roasting noonday sky. Martin was triumphant above all Solomon sores at the way his smooth-running masheen was "sewing" on distillate; and Tehei, deciding to live until he beheld one more fragment of this mundane sphere, crept on deck and eased himself on to a mattress. Peggy, gallant soul, sat beside me, golden ears pricked, restless of paw, while I turned for the southeast entrance. A dun squall-curtain that had been swinging toward the opening swerved away and left fair going.

"The dear old tub—I love every plank and sheet and pulley!" Jack laughed to me from the bow where he was directing my course.

"This is an atoll what *is*," was his next call, for at last we were gliding into the fairy ring of our dreams, restricted enough for one to realise its bounds at a circling glance. Here the water is deep, and no coral patches could we see.

Out came Mr. McNicoll, a small, hard-bitten Scotsman, who holds power of life and death over the rapidly diminishing handful of almost pure Polynesians on this privately-owned island. He is here only temporarily, having come to help the manager, Mr. Oberg, to suppress an uprising of the natives consequent upon a scourge of dysentery introduced by Oberg's Black Papuan boat crew. So autocratic has Mr. McNicoll become in his long years of lording it over the dark races, and doing the thinking for their dull wits, that it never occurs to him that he cannot exercise unquestioned authority with other persons' brown boys. Hence, there were at least surprised looks on the faces of Henry and Nakata when our caller ordered them around quite as a matter of course. Henry's triangular smile took on a twist of resentment, but Nakata saw the humour, and was all polite respect and obedience to the quondam "bossing." I thought it was exceedingly funny, until the interesting character squarely kicked Peggy, merely because she happened to be standing between him and the mongrel he desired to kick. Peggy's tear-dimmed eyes wrung a protest from me, whereupon McNicoll was all apology for his thoughtlessness, and jokingly remarked that he fancied Peggy's tail had been bobbed "so's to make room for her on the schooner." Then he relieved his embarrassment by kicking the right dog with the threat that he'd throw a leg o' Moses at him if he didn't keep out o' way.

But McNicoll was solid at heart, and displayed every consideration, sending out fruit and vegetables to "Captain London and the Mate," bringing his sturdy, lawful native wife to see us—a stolid New Ireland woman in decent muslin wrapper—and their three-year-old son, the most beautiful child I ever saw. Other and older sons and daughters are being educated elsewhere. McNicoll is evidently a man keen to his responsibilities as a parent. He is full of story and anecdote, and will ever stand out in my memory, if for no other reason than that he is the first white man I ever talked with who has eaten human flesh, or, rather, admitted the same—albeit this one swears he did not know it was human flesh until afterward. "Man, man, I was fair blowed, I was, any amount, I tell you, by Jove!" he declaimed; then, to my question: "It was nigger meat, anyways, and . . . well, you might say it's more like pig-flesh than anything else, fine-grained, y'know . . ." and he trailed off into hair-lifting tales of his years in New Guinea, New Britain, New Ireland—where the natives are blacker in body, and soul, if that be possible, than the Malaitans. A missing thumb on his left hand was torn out by a winch when he, alone, hoisted overboard sling-loads of five hundred coolies dead from cholera, somewhere on the China coast.

McNicoll has lately buried twenty-three of the inhabitants here, dead from dysentery. There remain but ninety-three natives, thirty-six of whom are women, and there are only two children in the whole community.

This man verified Jack's diagnosis of Tehei's condition, and told dreadful instances of the mortality from black-water. As to Jack's hands, he examined the peeling upon peeling that was visible, and the painful, dry, hot swelling, and said he had once had something like it, but had got over it; didn't know what it was—maybe the salt, maybe the sun, and that Jack's and his own were the only cases he had ever seen.

Niumanu, Tasman,
Sunday, October 4, 1908.

The rain pelted all night, and the men were driven from their deck mattresses; but I, under a flap of canvas, stuck it out, with Peggy, who had been rudely detached from Jack's side when he was washed out, curled beside me. Peggy loves me more and more, but when night falls she hunts the shelter of Jack's arms, and, if he has to desert her, she goes to Martin, whom she has won to her in spite of himself, and who now considers her "a pretty good little yellow dog."

This forenoon McNicoll placed his whaleboat, manned by magnificent Black Papuans, at our disposal for the day. He also ordered a dance, in a space among tall dense trees—the most ideally primitive and savage dance we ever watched. Men and women were clad in bushy ballet-skirts of grass and leaves and feathers, dancing angularly with quick jerks and flirts of the undulating fringes. One man was a small satyr among his wood-fellows, and as they all moved hither and thither into the twilight, fireflies wove like shuttles among them and shot in and out the dark pillars of the forest.

A small, sweet, listless people are these Niumanus, soft-voiced, soft-mannered, without ambition enough to persist as a race. A wonder it is they gathered sufficient impetus to protest against the dysentery; but it was little more than an hysterical protest against fate.

The village is very picturesque, smothered in tufted, laden palms full of birds, and we saw only one devil-devil house, from the door of which a coffee-coloured little Mephisto peered. The rapidly dwindling female members of the population are the most comely we have seen in this part of the South Seas, despite their cropped skulls. What hair they have lies in tender, tawny-tipped ringlets. We did not see the pitiful remnant of Niumanu's childhood.

And the burying-place—that is even more curious than Lua-Nua's, although quite different. The import of the relics that decorate the rickety graves was very stimulating to our white imaginations. One tomb, plastered with pink lime, bore the rusted wraith of an old musket; another, a bronze rudder-pintle, green-crusted; a group of graves bristled with bayonets corroded to mere uneven toothpicks, while rust-splintered marlinspikes and crowbars stuck up at intervals, and one lone mound boasted an almost unrecognisable sauce-pan—indeed, here were all the copper and hardware that had been taken from two New England whaleships that the once adventuresome people of Tasman had "cut out" more than a century ago. One of these ships, the *Sailing Directions* says, they captured inside the lagoon, but the other they went out after in their canoes.

McNicoll happened to remark that some of the older graves near the reef had been washed open by the surf. Martin departed forthwith to see if he could find a skull. He was not allowed to get away with it for nothing, however, the natives, first shocked, then covetous, considering it worth three sticks of tobacco. "Some cheap head!" Martin commented, turning the ghastly trophy in his hands.

Monday, October 5, 1908.

This would have been one of our loveliest days in the tropics except for the heat that boiled our white blood. I have been frantic with prickly heat that rose in a rash, and Jack suffered greatly with his turgid hands. And I do not think our breakfast of tinned sauerkraut and frankfurters was the most approved diet for the climate! At any rate, we enjoyed an inactive day, indolently discussing the possibility of missing the next steamer to Sydney. Fancy being so moderate that one misses sailings five weeks apart!

Nakata seemed possessed with good spirits, and his vibrant Japanese lilts soared out and upward from the galley to a low accompaniment of self-pitying groans from Tehei, one of whose aberrations is that we over-persuaded him to come on the *Snark*. Martin was indignant, and reminded him sharply of the five different refusals Jack had given when Tehei began first to hint and then to beg to be allowed to sail with us. Jack gave the demented child a good talking-to, in the hope of bracing him up, but such result is not apparent. He turns an obstinate face to the wall and says no word. Meanwhile his fever is well in hand under Jack's unremitting treatment; but Tehei has long since decided that the only way to abate his homesickness is by way of steamer from Sydney, since there are no connections to be made from the Solomons; and gloom has settled upon his soul. This evening, to my ukulélé, Nakata and Henry danced a merry figure or two on deck in the moonlight; but Tehei stuck it out in the hot cabin and would not be beguiled.

Tuesday, October 6, 1908.

Early in our first sleep last night we were aroused by a low warning rumble from Peggy, and almost before we could locate the canoe, three womanish, ringleted men, with great soft eyes, were perched upon our rail, explaining that they wanted to ship on the *Snark*. It was all part of the recent panic—the poor things want to get away.

This morning we were under way about nine, Mr. Oberg and his crew helping us break out the anchor and hoist the canvas. Jack says these blacks, although willing enough, are very awkward sailors compared with the Polynesians. There was a certain relief in getting away from this anchorage, as the reef to the west was a trifle too close for mental repose.

And so we have left our first atolls—rosy garlands flung upon the sapphire sea—and are pointed for the Solomons again, which, while we do not love them, are more like home and headquarters than any other place in this wild region.

Tehei is almost laughable. Without deigning to notice Jack and me, or even Henry, he languidly ordered breakfast of Nakata, who offered us something very like a wink as he humoured the sick man. I think Tehei would have liked the last hen (the rest have flown overboard), but he did not have quite the courage to suggest it. The hen, by the way, a small brown person, is conducting a most scandalous flirtation with a sleek drake that McNicoll gave us.

This evening I took my watch. We are short-handed, with Tehei laid up and Wada gone. After I had turned in on my deck-cot, the squalls set in. Such rain! Such blasts of wind! Such sudden going-over of the hull, until the lee rail and half the launch were buried! And such rushes to the main-sheet! Henry handles the boat well, without orders, bringing her up into the wind and keeping the head-sails shaking just enough. He has a fine *feel* of a boat.

Wednesday, October 7, 1908.

It is one year to-day since we picked our way out among the floating islets of lilies in Hilo Harbor. I spent this forenoon on my cot, in a dead calm, trying to make up sleep. We are a little less than one hundred and fifty miles from Manning Straits. After the calm, came light airs, but only just enough for steerage-way.

Martin went at the forepeak, and gave it a "turning out,"

aired our precious saddlery, and discovered three tins of flour, along with two dozen tins of oysters and some fine dried apples, peaches and apricots.

And we saw two big dolphin—the first since before Nuka-Hiva.

Thursday, October 8, 1908.

So tired, so tired . . . spent forenoon in bed. But my passive illness is nothing beside the active stress of Jack's lamentable hands. Sydney is becoming very desirable, with its advice and help.

Last evening I took my watch—although Jack had arranged otherwise. Had good weather, but the next watch was fierce with squalls from black curtains on the horizon, and the mizzen had to be lowered. The awning was taken in, and the *Snark* looked bared for action. We ran fast, wary of the big mainsail jibing over in the "hummers." The worst squall came from two directions almost simultaneously. There was no sleep until nearly four. We were glad to be no nearer Manning Straits, which are imperfectly charted, and treacherous with reefs and warring currents.

Tehei went quite "luny," in a calm before dawn, took his best suit of clothes on deck, threw it overboard, and was preparing to follow, when Martin caught him. He evidently desired to enter the isles of the blest in pleasant raiment.

Friday, October 9, 1908.

I have heard Jack tell of the sun-dogs in the Arctic, and I surely never expected to see my first sun-dogs on a hot day under the Equator! But that is just the novelty which greeted us from this forenoon's sky—two soft blobby false suns, one on either side the true luminary. Another unusual occurrence was Henry's taking the chronometer time for Jack's morning sight. Henry has been working very faithfully of late at his navigation.

Later in the day we could see the dim blue tops of Ysabel rising from the horizon to the southeast, and a tangle of islands ahead that made our senses prick with caution once more.

This being Martin's birthday, we made Cupid stew (see Jack's play, *Scorn of Women*, for recipe) of the flirtatious brown hen, and opened a bottle òf the *Sumatra's* Rhine wine. The *Snark* logged along slowly and evenly, into a lovely sunset of lavender and rose and gold, with glorious piled clouds on Ysabel's peaks, and woolly puffs dotting the horizon. Before the huge crimson sun had touched the western waves, like a pale reflection the full moon had grown in the low sky opposite, so silvery delicate that it seemed a transparent gossamer hoop through which the ineffable colours drifted and filtered.

Jack hove to for the night, and while we drank in the restful beauty, and cooled in the evening air, the anthropomorphic Tehei, below, called upon his concept of the Deity not to kill him. Henry, his sneer almost a triangle, called down in his husky staccato:

"Hey! Tehei! You killing you'self! God, he no Solomon to kill you—you kill you'self, I tell you!"

I cannot reconcile this futile, febrile thing with the old Tehei. He is behaving according to his lights—of course; but methinks they are rushlights, and burn but dimly.

. . . *Midnight:* I feel quite weak from relief. Nakata, a little less careful than usual, had eaten some salmon that was past virtue. Shortly before nine, when all were asleep, the little man became violently ill with ptomaine poisoning, and for three hours Jack and I wrestled for his life with every means at our command—and won. He is sleeping now like a tired baby. It was terrible, fighting one rigid convulsion after another, conquering, and watching the attacks grow less frequent. Nakata's last observation before he drifted into sleep, was: "Never I want to taste mustard again!"

Saturday, Oct. 10, 1908.

Blue sky, blue water, snowy surf, low woolpacks on the blue rim of the world, light breeze, mountains of Ysabel to port, and the blue velvet hills of Choiseul to starboard—and you think you have it all, a picture of peace and security. But the two hours I steered this morning, nine to eleven, through torrential currents and tide-rips that brimmed and followed and seemed ever about to roll over our stern, was one of my most exciting experiences.

We saw our way largely through the eyes of Henry, aloft, who called down to Jack, forward, who in turn shouted instructions to me above the racket of engine and rushing water and impact of wind. The steering gear was stiff, and Jack told off Nakata to help me at the wheel if I found it too much for my strength. But I managed it unaided from start to finish. There is a wicked reef off Ysabel, in Manning Straits, and the tide-rips look like surf on reef, so that I needed quite desperate nerve at times to obey orders and steer unswervingly straight for a toothed line of white water. Some day I shall learn never to question Jack's judgment, no matter how secretly, in matters of the sea. In spite of two charts, which, in addition to being frankly inadequate and unreliable, flatly contradicted each other,—in spite of phenomena that to the rest of us, even Henry, appeared convincingly disastrous, my blue-eyed sailor exercised his everlasting unerring judgment in this intricate maze of rock and coral, shoal and crazy current. ''Oh—just my luck!'' he will say; but I know better. We who sail with him are not born to be drowned! I have observed him too much to have any doubts.

My happy heart! My brave boat! The tonic of exploring in uncharted places, wondering each moment if the keel will not bump on a hummock of coral in the watery, swirling plain of shallows! A few remembered words of advice and reminiscence from men who have been here, or know others who have been, is all we have to go by; the rest is guesswork and judgment.

"Watch out lively! We're going into another rip!"

And I watch—meeting with all my weight on the brassy teak wheel the shock of the combing, fighting water; and then—

"Mate Woman!"

"Yes!"

"Keep her off—keep her off!"

And keep her off I do, noting Henry's warning wave as well, as he sees a coral peril near at hand.

With the engine working full power, and every stitch of canvas drawing in a bright gale, we sail like mad; but the adverse current pulls so strong that, looking overside into the blue-green water, we see coral patches standing still so far as our progress is concerned. Nakata, peering over, sees, looks up at the marble-hard sails, and down again, incredulously:

"*Snark* stand still!"

But slowly, slowly, almost inch by inch, we win through, and are slashing along in gentler water, the contrary currents left behind, all sense of danger sloughed off in the whirling background. Henry descends and stretches himself, and recounts a tale of ripping tides where two strong men were needed at the wheel; then, three, and the vessel swung around in spite of their combined effort. Henry's imagination makes his broken English very dramatic; then he trails off with liquid chucklings in his veiled voice, while his black eyes shine with old Paumotan memories.

And through all the tumble and activity of the Straits, I am conscious of the pleasure of the keen whip of wind on bare calves and feet and the sting of spindrift on my cheeks, and, greatest of all satisfactions, the sense of doing my part, of being needed and making good in my station at the helm.

"Can you beat it!" would come the laughing shout of my skipper, who waves both arms in entire forgetfulness of his painful hands. Fine mental healing, this!

We had hooked a long, slender fish on our troll line as we

were negotiating a succession of rips, and the silver-blue sword was dragged from crest to crest of the creaming rollers by the combined speed of the yacht and the warring current. Not a moment before, Nakata, who was quite himself after his sickness, had broached the puzzling problem of dinner; and now, out of the chaotic passage, the little man served a delicious platter of that fish, dressed over with tomatoes and onions, and accompanied by German beer.

New Georgia is visible dead ahead, and all is plain sailing. Jack has fallen into a doze, and I yearn over his face, gone tired and sick as he relaxes. And I love the gear about him, the gear of his sea avocation—the spread chart, held flat with the dividers and parallel rulers; the binoculars, the sextant in its case, and the perpetually low-ticking chronometer.

Sunday, October 11, 1908.

A bad squall took us aback last night. Henry, alone at the helm, rang the bell to the engine room; I yelled to Jack, who landed on his feet at one bound, and started through the cabin. He stumbled over Martin, who had struck the floor on all fours, while Nakata, falling upon Martin from the upper berth, was saying "Excuse me!" in mid-air. The squall nearly buried the launch on the port rail, and the wind came from every quarter, accompanied by a deafening and blinding electrical display. The main sheet and main peak halyards carried away, and things were very tense for a while. During the night the mizzen was taken in twice, and hoisted as many times.—Just a sample of night sailing in the Solomon Archipelago.

Monday, October 12, 1908.

Last evening, during my watch, I had the one, grisly, hair-raising scare of the *Snark* voyage. It was an eerie night to be alone on deck. The lightning was almost continuous, and in rocking calms between windy puffs, the intermittent rattle and patter of loose blocks, and the whine of boom-jaws against tortured masts, were extremely uncanny.. Then would burst the squalls, with the clouds spitting flame, and the sharp rat-tat of reef-points and the taut hum of the rigging, and the unearthly swish of unseen waves, were no more soothing to my strung nerves. I am not overly timid, but for once I was not in tune with the responsibility of my post. Jack, coming up for a look around before turning in, must have sensed my distress, for he said:

"This is a nasty night. I'll stay up with you."

With him, I found the night very wonderful, and we amused ourselves counting the seconds between lightning flash and crack of thunder. Sometimes they were almost simultaneous, so close were the bolts. Then again, we counted several seconds. It was in a particularly long period that I received my terrifying experience. There was no breath of wind. Jack sat beside the rudder box, while I stood before him, facing aft, and rubbing his hot hands. There had been a blinding blue flash, an awful illumination, right in my face, and the moon at my back, veiled in a blue cloud, shed a ghostly gleam on Jack's upturned face. Then something seemed to be happening to us. Jack was staring horribly, and I leaned nearer, myself staring, fascinated by what I saw. It seemed that some spell was laid upon us, separating us as if all space intervened, and that we knew it, each to each, and were powerless to help ourselves. He seemed striving vainly to speak, his mouth open, and my horror-stricken eyes saw his jaw fall. I thought all the thoughts of my life, quickly, distinctly. I felt the voiceless tragedy of this ending to our exceptional life and of our existence on the *Snark*. I thought we were both dying, that some unlearned manifestation of electricity had taken possession of us and the end had come. Then, as I gazed and strove to hold our ebbing lives together, consciousness began to wane, and with a great effort I tried to let go Jack's hand from my two, saying: "Let go! Let go!" In my half-trance, the idea persisted that we had established some sort of "circle" that was paralysing our faculties. Also, I consciously stood clear of the iron wheel and other metal in the cockpit. Then Jack spoke:

"What is the matter?"

I came to myself and found, with relief that was a pang, that he had merely been counting the seconds, with his mouth and eyes open, and the whole million years I had suffered were encompassed in the space of eight seconds. I was shaking all over, but my ego succeeded in gasping:

"But I *did* behave with presence of mind, according to my lights, when I let go of your hands!"

"You behaved with judgment enough, I'll admit," he joked; "but your physics were darned bad!"

I agreed with him; but the freezing horror was still in my blood, and it was some time before it seemed to flow warmly again. The remainder of the night was fine, and we slept soundly.

The engine has been chugging away all this day, but we have made few knots, what of head-sea and -wind. Every one seems fit; even Tehei, evidently deciding, as Jack put it, that his tactics were "buying him nothing," greeted me with a smiling: "Good morning, Bihaura," and "Good morning, Tehei," to Jack. After which Jack haled him, gently enough, to the wheel, despite protest, and made him steer. The *Snark's* course was erratic in the extreme, for Tehei was weak as a cat, and wabbled badly. But the method worked— the man was stung to interest in life and to appetite, and ate a hearty dinner. Jack let him rest well, then helped him to the wheel again. "I'll make a man of him yet," he bragged to me.

It is high time we connected with Pennduffryn. Our kerosene is getting low; we have bread for but one more day; yeast and flour are gone; our last rice was consumed three days ago. We are pretty well down to our German tins, with their enormous duty.

Pepesala, Cape Marsh,
Pavuvu or Russell Group,
Tuesday, October 13, 1908.

Not much headway in the night, with light wind and north current. This morning Nakata came down with fever, and, in one of his lucid moments, made all of us, except Tehei, laugh when he chattered whimsically:

"Please, Lord, don't kill me!"

To assist Henry, I peeled the onions (our last vegetable) while I steered, under power, with my feet, and I smiled to hear the Rapa Islander's picturesque language as he struggled with can-openers on cans that had been intended to yield to their "keys," which had futilely broken off.

Into West Bay, or, more poetically, "The Bay of a Thousand Ships," the *Snark* glided before noon; and out to us came George Washington, or some one very like—Mr. Kissling, trader here at Cape Marsh. We had him to our midday meal, and found him a mine of interest. Twenty-three years in the South Seas, he bears many a mark of his prolonged tussle with nature and with man's devices. His great chest is coral-scarred, deep, to the bone, from some battle with the breakers. One leg was dynamited, and, while he can walk on it, the rended tissues have developed into a chronic sore. Mr. Kissling knew Stevenson, and loved him for his cheer against odds; and he remembers Lord Pembroke, who, although his income was half a million a year, preferred to roam rather than spend conventionally, and lost his yacht *Albatross* in the Ringgold Group—not far from the scene of our close call.

We had tea and dinner ashore, and I found a little organ in the trader's living room. Amongst other things he had once been a church organist!

Peggy had us in tears of laughter over her pompous approach to a monster mastiff, a good natured, indulgent soul who was awkwardly nonplussed by this intrepid insect that braced up so menacingly to him. Her superiority once established, she made friends with him and with a fat terrier of her own persuasion that was playing with an enormous Maltese tomcat grown lean with lizards. A family of guinea pigs caused Peggy to bark her head nearly off; and the sheep . . . But she respected the two big white cows, and we had already taught her that ducks and hens are taboo. She doesn't even see them as she stalks by, although I think I can detect a slight lop to one ear.

A walk about Levers Pacific Plantation showed us a very beautiful as well as unique island, for a slanting up-thrust of coral formation has created a basin that forms a lovely lake of fresh water. Looking seaward through the oblique pillars of feathered palms, in the blue lagoon with its purple coral-shadows, and in the waters beyond, we could see innumerable green islets, each a "fragment of Paradise."

In company with Mr. Kissling, and Messrs. Hickie and Birley, two young Englishmen in charge of the estates here, we saw the plantations, and were greatly struck with the deforesting that had been accomplished—a large area cleared of all but the grotesque stumps of colossal "board-trees," like those of Upolu. The great bases still stand, flanked by their satin-grey bastions.

We are now looking forward almost eagerly to Penn-duffryn, to get our mail and make ready for the steamer to Sydney, which leaves Aola, a station to the east of Pennduffryn, on November 5. We have sojourned in these Solomon Islands long enough for the present—too long for our good. Glorious earth monuments of verdure that they are, yet, in their existent state, they are no place for white men and women. Indeed, their own aborigines do not thrive; what with fever, ulcers, skin diseases and worse, bad teeth, and innutrition, they are a sorry lot in the main. And a Polynesian fares little better here than a white man. When we return from Australia, all mended and fresh for a new start, we shall go aboard the *Snark* and immediately fill away to the west—always west, and north of west, and south of west, the round world 'round until we are bound at last around Cape Horn and north to San Francisco Bay.

Thursday, October 15, 1908.

On a "windless, glassy floor," engine purring faultlessly, we slipped out of the Bay of a Thousand Ships and
by the fantastic green litter of the Pavuvu islets, like leaves
strewn on a peacock-blue mantle; on, hour after hour, past
Savo, the volcano island, where the water appeared dusty,
as if from volcanic ash; along beautiful Guadalcanal, her
mountain-laps cradling the mist; flying-fish scudding from
our sleek forefoot and tripping over the top of the absinthe
water. Tehei, contentedly munching a ripe guava, steered
for an hour or so. Jack was in great fettle—undoubtedly
with sense of safe ending to a voyage in such adverse environment. Coming toward me with his merry walk, he
stopped to listen to the regular throb of the engine, and said
very quietly, stating the mere fact: "I have figured that,
counting repairs, Martin's salary, and so forth, that that
engine has cost me one hundred dollars for every mile she
has run.—But what of it?" he added brightly. "We're
here, aren't we?" Which same is his invariable cheery
conclusion to all irking propositions.

"Look at Peg," Jack remarked softly just now; and I
raised my gaze to see the little slender golden thing sitting
before me on the deck, very upright on her thin, aristocratic
toes, regarding my face in the same searching, boding
manner as when we neared the end of our stay at Meringe.
There has been nothing unusual going on aboard, save that I
got out a box of handsome ribbons and made wide girdles for
summer gowns in Sydney. How does she fore-sense change?
Even if she could understand our speech, there has been no
speech—how can I talk about the possibility of relinquishing
her? By all right of sentiment, she is my dog. Her eyes
... here they are before me, and I cannot describe them
... up-cast, large beyond all eyes of dogs—stirless, stead-
fast, so deep, so deep ... there is no plumbing the warm
brown of the pure pools, where little golden lights play up
like live things; not little devils—though they could be such

—but glints of feeling made visible, love-lights from heart and brain. For Peggy loves with all of her, profoundly. How did the Creator come to house such great capacity of lovingness in so lowly a frame?

. . . Safe at anchor once more off Pennduffryn, and as there is a crowd of guests ashore, we shall sleep aboard to-night, and sail early for Tulagi, for our mail is being held there for us.

The cruise came near a disastrous ending. After dark, and before the moon rose, we headed in for what tallied with the signal lights we knew so well, and in relation to which we knew our anchorage perfectly. We discovered, and none too quickly, that we were at Boucher's Plantation, some miles to the west, and that he had adopted the same system of lanterns—rather a disturbing factor on this perilous coast, where the Pennduffryn lights are the only ones described in the Admiralty Directory. The warm night seemed suddenly to chill when we found our position, but, all working in unison, we swung around just in the nick of time, and soon afterward rumbled down the anchor in its old place off the tiny quay at Pennduffryn. A ghostly schooner, the *Lily*, rustled by under sweeps in the misty moonlight, and passed the word o' night.

THE ENDING

THERE is little more to tell. We did not dream that these were our last hours of travel on the *Snark*. The three weeks at Pennduffryn we put in busily despite illness. Days were spent in the shady grove of piles under the buildings, sorting, labelling and packing in great cases our vast accumulation of Melanesian curios for shipment. Jack wrote daily, except when the violence of fever attacks laid him low. His various ailments grew steadily worse. His hands alone were enough to drive a man wild—eleven skins peeling off simultaneously, one above another. Out of my own fever, and the anæmic and neurasthenic condition I had fallen into, augmented by worry over Jack, came moods of despondency, most unlike my happy-go-lucky wont. And instead of inviting repose, I foolishly worked harder than ever, and developed a siege of insomnia.

The life of the plantation at this stage in its downfall would make a romantic story in itself. The little Spanish Baroness Eugénie, Mrs. Harding, who had returned from Sydney, hid under forced gaiety, innate charm and loveableness, and the most enchanting of wardrobes, the tragedy of the disappearance of her own fortune as well as her husband's and Darbishire's. When she married Harding, in South America, she forfeited all but her title, the baronial jewels, and a mere modicum of her rightful fortune; and the latter had melted away in the failing plantation.

"I will show you my coronet and jewels some day," she mused, in a confidential moment, her incredibly large black eyes very wide. "They are in the Bank—and I cannot sell them, alas!"

The entertainment was lavish—perhaps this sort of thing was at the bottom of the failure to make things go; but they

480

Snark Careened at Meringe

The *Rembrandt* Skipper

A Polynesian Prince

died game and gay, all of them. Two dining-rooms ran full blast. The house was packed, among the guests being three men of different nationalities, taking moving pictures for Pathé Frères, and at many a meal eight languages were spoken—all of which Mrs. Harding understood, even to Swedish, and nothing could be passed about and escape her quick ear and brain. There were fancy dress and masquerade evenings, horseback rides, musicales, all night poker, billiards —anything and everything that two women and a dozen men could devise to enliven a house party, and make every one forget that the establishment was in its last days. It was admirable, and very pathetic. And splendidly English.

The schooner *Eugénie* had been chartered for Bellona and Rennel by some nitrate people, and had never returned to the *Minota* at Malu. The mate of the *Minota*, who had now left her, told us the ketch had got safely away for Tulagi for stores, thence to Meringe; and he further reported that Captain Jansen had been "wild" when he discovered Peggy's loss, but had been pacified when he read my letter. When he came to Pennduffryn, before we sailed for Sydney, he formally presented me with what he could see was entirely mine own, saying, with a twinkle in his Dutch blue eyes:

"She's spoiled for a nigger chaser anyway, now. My word! I couldn't make anything out of such a lady's-dog!"

Peggy helped me wondrously through all those feverish, sick days in the hot northwest season. Never a night, no matter how late, did I leave the drawing-room, but the little velvet form, outside on the porch, was pressing against me, seeing me to my netted cot in the grass bathroom on stilts. No awkward age was ever hers; she was a thing with the grace of God in her, mentally and materially. And she gave all her big and gallant soul in love.

With Captain Jansen, on the *Minota*, came Wada, landed back upon us despite his wishes or ours, by the very law of the land. He could not stay in the islands because no one would be responsible for him; he could not leave, because there was no one to put up the hundred pounds bond required in Australia on any dark skin. Mr. Schroeder, to save the boy's life when he was very low with fever in a native hut, took him in, and when he was better, had him cook, without wages, until the first chance to get him away from Ysabel, which was on the *Minota*, where in the galley he worked his passage. Meekly he came aboard the *Snark* to cook without wages until such time as we should return from Sydney, and sail to some port where he could take leave freely.

How blindly we plan. How little we thought, that starry, musky night under the Southern Cross, when we paid our farewell call on the *Snark*—now in charge of the *Minota's* mate—that this would be the last time we should ever descend her teak gangway ladder in these waters.

Martin as well as Nakata took steamer for Sydney, as there was purchasing for him to attend to, and he wanted to see doctors himself. Jack and I, in Captain Mortimer's roomy quarters, actually loafed on the twelve days of the *Makambo's* stormy voyage to Sydney, both of us suffering greatly and additionally from a prickly heat that boiled up in a fiery rash which in turn burst into water.

During the five weeks when Jack lay in a private hospital in North Sydney after an operation for, not one fistula, but two, his surgeon, Dr. Clarence Read, flanked by several skin specialists, puzzled and studied and theorised over his pitiful hands, the like of which they had never seen nor even heard. All agreed that the trouble was non-parasitic, and therefore concluded that it was entirely of nervous origin. And a different skin malady showed on his elbows, which they recognised as psoriasis, truly and actually the leprosy of the Bible, the "silvery skin," cures of which occur spontaneously, but of which no other cure is known.

One day, during my reading aloud to the convalescent, I said tentatively—and it had taken much thought and self-abnegation to come to it:

"If you think we'd better give up the *Snark* voyage . . ."

"Oh, nothing like that," Jack answered brightly. "We're going around the world in the *Snark*, you know."

But the unhealing weeks went by, and one day Jack gave me the result of his consideration of his case: that the one thing that would set him straight would be to return once more to his own habitat, to California, where his nerve equilibrium had always been stable. This, of course, meant the ending of our voyage. Although I had not ceased from thinking along these lines, the actual facing of the issue was too much in the low state of my nerves, and I broke down and sobbed unrestrainedly. This precipitated fever, and for days I lay in a little bed in the same room with Jack.

In short, Martin was sent back to the Solomons, accompanied by an old skipper, Captain Reed, to bring the yacht to Sydney, where she would be put up for sale.

In the meantime, we rented an apartment in Sydney, and worked and played as best we might, among other trips taking in the wonderful Jenolan Caves. But it was not all pleasure, for Jack's hands did not improve, but went on swelling and peeling prodigiously. The only relief was in massage, which caused them to break into wringing perspiration. His toenails became affected, growing as thick as their length in twenty-four hours, when he would file them down, only to have a recurrence.

We tried Tasmania, visited Hobart Town, and spent a month in a cool hotel resort at Brown's River, where the country was very like California, and our general tone was better for the time being.

We had been back in Sydney for some time when the *Snark* arrived, all hands alive and well, except . . .

Neither Martin nor Captain Reed had the courage or heart to bring the tidings, so the little old skipper wrote:

"I am very sorry to report that your little dog Peggy died off Bellona and Rennel, three days out from the Solomons."

I do not think Jack is ashamed of the tears he shed with me that night. She was too good to be true, Peggy, dear heart, dear heart. I cannot, must not say much . . . only

. . . the day before she died, wan and weak she came and sat before Martin, as she had sat before me that last day going back to Pennduffryn, and looked long and questioningly into his face with her dolorous eyes. I know, Jack knows . . . she was asking for him, for me, some word, some message, trying, at the end of her blameless days, to pass across all space and difference of kind, her deathless faith. I have claimed much for Peggy . . . not too much, I swear, for those few who have known such a creature—if there could be another—and who will understand, quite.

. . . .

It was a terrible strain, going daily to the *Snark* on a little ferry boat, to oversee the packing of gear that we were sending home. I know I shed tears during each return trip. I blush to think how little of help I was to Jack in the matter of cheer; but he says that out of it all he gathered the greatest proof of the success of the *Snark* adventure, that the one small woman, frail out of all proportion to the husky men, should be so broken at the abandonment of the voyage.

Martin continued on around the world by devious ways. Wada sailed as cook on some outgoing steamer. Henry and Tehei returned to the Society Islands; but Nakata went with Jack and me from Newcastle, N.S.W., one fine day, on an English tramp, the *Tymeric*, Captain MacIlwaine, bound with "coals from Newcastle" to Guayaquil, Ecuador. We were glad her orders were changed at the last moment and that we were to have a final flare of adventure in a new country before reaching home. Jack's general health benefited by the voyage, and he was able to box lustily with the three sturdy young English officers. But I fell from one fever fit into another, during a many days' gale early in the passage, and this weakened me sadly. However, the forty-three days in the tramp were an experience worth having.

One last link of our South Sea chain we picked up one morning at sunrise, when a squall-curtain lifted and parted over Pitcairn Island, high and sheer, green and gold and unreal in the rainbow shimmer. I looked out of my porthole with sick eyes of disappointment as my fancy wandered north-west over a thousand miles of the Paumotus, of which Pit-cairn is the one high, last, southern sentinel. Then in the fever I slept and dreamed we put out in a boat from the *Tymeric* and found a bay (that does not exist) inside the breakers, and went in and landed. Awakening with a start, I turned quickly to the porthole. It was still there—I had dozed but a moment—a sun-shot emerald, with the grey velvet pall of mist falling, falling, until it was blotted out. Isle of my dreams, waking and sleeping—when shall I see you, or any one of you, again!

   .   .   .   .

We crossed the Andes, on the side of old Chimborazo itself, at an altitude of 12,000 feet, the summit white and stark 10,000 feet above, to Quito, 10,000 feet in the air. After a month altogether in Ecuador, in which we escaped the rampant yellow fever, malaria, pneumonia, smallpox, bubonic plague, bacillary dysentery, and several other perils (not the least of which was an accident on the wonderful railway, of which we saw two frightful examples), we sailed for New Orleans, per Canal Zone, celebrating the Fourth of July, 1909, in true American fashion at Panama.

Nakata, our little rock of ages in all sickness and stress, was in due time safely entered into the United States, with less pow-wow than we had expected, to our mutual rejoicing.

Steadily, rapidly, Jack won back to health in his California environment. In a very few months not a trace of any of his curious maladies remained, glory be. But to his analytical mind the greatest cause for congratulation is that he found out what was the matter with his hands. He came across a book by Lieutenant Colonel Charles E. Woodruff of the United States Army, entitled *Effects of Tropical Light on White Men.* We later met Colonel Woodruff in San Francisco, and he told us he had been similarly afflicted, and had had the same experience with physicians. They sat on his case, and could come to no conclusion. It is very simple. Both he and Jack, and there must be many others whom we have not met, have a strong predisposition toward the tissue-destructiveness of tropical light.   The ultra-violet rays tear them to pieces, just as so many experimenters with the X-ray were torn to pieces before they learned to protect themselves.

I continued to suffer severe but lessening attacks of fever for nearly a year, and it took almost as long to recover my balance of nerves.   The last touch of fever I ever felt was when, in June, 1910, after fulfilling the godspeed of the sweet vahines of Polynesia, I lost my girl baby, Joy.

The *Snark* was sold long afterward, for a mere fraction of her cost, to an English syndicate which operated her, trading and recruiting, in the New Hebrides.   The next we heard, she was sealing in Bering Sea, and later on we met several persons who had been aboard of her at Kodiak, Alaska, in 1911, while one told us he had subsequently seen her at Seattle, in August, 1912—painted green!   Jack and I, landing in Seattle the month previous, from a five-months' wind-jamming voyage from Baltimore around Cape Horn on the Sewall ship *Dirigo,* thus narrowly missed meeting up with our little old boat of dreams.   I dare not think how it would have affected me.

It was not until we had returned to California, after the voyage of the *Snark* was over, that we learned that the much sinned-against craft had been built two feet shorter than her specifications called for—this in addition to the extra two feet draft.   The marvel is that she sailed as well as she did.

Now, one word: Jack has been severely and ignorantly criticised by untravelled book reviewers for the unreality and unveracity of his tales of the cannibal countries we visited, such as his novel *Adventure.*   And yet, in this Year of Our Lord, 1915, quite fresh in our minds is the report lately come to hand that Captain Keller of the *Eugénie,* who came to our rescue on the Malaita coast, and Claude Bernays of Pennduffryn Plantation, both lost their bonnie handsome heads in the Solomons, the former aboard his vessel, the second on his own plantation.   Poor Darbishire died of dysentery in the Gilbert Group only last year, leaving a young English wife and a fine boy.

It is all a sweet memory to Jack and me, our life on the *Snark*, and Martin and Nakata swear allegiance to any new venture we may pursue. There is now a little Mrs. Martin who also wishes to be counted in.

And, believe it or not, ye of little faith in the joy that was ours on the voyage, our one ultimate hope of earthly bliss is to fit out another and larger boat, and do it all over again, and more—and do it more leisurely, more wisely under the tropic sun.

THE END

Printed in the United States of America

THE following pages contain advertisements of a few
of the Macmillan books on kindred subjects

Highways and Byways of New England

By Clifton Johnson

Author of " Highways and Byways of the South," " The Picturesque
Hudson," etc.

Illustrated, decorated cloth, 12mo

This volume describes the characteristic, picturesque and his-
torically attractive regions in the states of Maine, New Hamp-
shire, Vermont, Massachusetts, Connecticut and Rhode Island.
Among the interesting chapter titles are : *In the Maine Woods,
Artemus Ward's Town, June in the White Mountains, August in
the Berkshire Hills, The Land of the Minute Men, Autumn on
Cape Cod* and *Shad Time on the Connecticut,* concluding with
Glimpses of Life. The illustrations, of which there are many and
which are reproduced from photographs taken by the author, main-
tain the standard established by the pictures in his previous works.

Through the Grand Canyon from Wyoming to Mexico.

By Ellsworth L. Kolb

With a preface by Owen Wister. New edition, with additional
illustrations.

Cloth, 8vo

Mr. Kolb's absorbing narrative of the trip which he made
through the Grand Canyon in a rowboat with photographic apparatus has, since its publication about a year ago, met with very
general commendation. It has been described as the most fascinating adventure story ever written. It is here re-issued with
minor changes in the text and with twenty-four new half-tone
plates, bringing the total number of insets up to seventy-two.

THE MACMILLAN COMPANY

Publishers   64–66 Fifth Avenue   New York

The Star Rover

By JACK LONDON

Author of "The Call of the Wild," "The Sea Wolf," "The Mutiny of the Elsinore," etc. With frontispiece in colors by Jay Hambidge.

Cloth, 12mo

Daring in its theme and vivid in execution, this is one of the most original and gripping stories Mr. London has ever written. The fundamental idea upon which the plot rests — the supremacy of mind over body — has served to inspire writers before, but rarely, if indeed ever, has it been employed as strikingly or with as much success as in this book. With a wealth of coloring and detail the author tells of what came of an attempt on the part of the hero to free his spirit from his body, of the wonderful adventures this "star rover" had, adventures covering long lapses of years and introducing strange people in stranger lands. It is a work that will make as lasting an impression upon the reader as did *The Sea Wolf* and *The Call of the Wild*.

Heart's Kindred

By ZONA GALE

Author of "Christmas," "The Loves of Pelleas and Etarre," etc.

Cloth, 12mo

There is much of timely significance in Miss Gale's new book. For example, one of the most interesting and powerful of its scenes takes place at a meeting of the Women's Peace Congress and in the course of the action there are introduced bits of the actual speeches delivered at the most recent session of this congress. But *Heart's Kindred* is not merely a plea for peace; it is rather the story of the making of a man — and of the rounding out of a woman's character, too. In the rough, unpolished, but thoroughly sincere Westerner and the attractive young woman who brings out the good in the man's nature, Miss Gale has two as absorbing people as she has ever created. In *Heart's Kindred* is reflected that humanness and breadth of vision which was first found in *Friendship Village* and *The Loves of Pelleas and Etarre* and made Miss Gale loved far and wide.

THE MACMILLAN COMPANY

Publishers   **64-66 Fifth Avenue**   **New York**

Old Delabole

By EDEN PHILLPOTTS

Author of " Brunel's Tower," etc.

Cloth, 12mo

A critic in reviewing *Brunel's Tower* remarked that it would seem that Eden Phillpotts was now doing the best work of his career. There was sufficient argument for this contention in the novel then under consideration and further demonstration of its truth is found in *Old Delabole*, which, because of its cheerful and wise philosophy and its splendid feeling for nature and man's relation to it, will perhaps ultimately take its place as its author's best. The scene is laid in Cornwall. Delabole is a slate mining town and the tale which Mr. Phillpotts tells against it as a background, one in which a matter of honor or of conscience is the pivot, is dramatic in situation and doubly interesting because of the moral problem which it presents. Mr. Phillpotts's artistry and keen perception of those motives which actuate conduct have never been better exhibited.

God's Puppets

By WILLIAM ALLEN WHITE

Author of " A Certain Rich Man."

Cloth, 12mo

Here are brought together a number of the more notable short stories by one whose reputation in this field is as great as in the novel form — for has Mr. White not delighted thousands of readers with *The Court of Boyville* and *In Our Town*, short intimate studies of life at first hand which, while quite different from the material in the new volume, nevertheless show mastery of the art? Mr. White is a slow and careful writer, a fact to which the long intervals between his books bear witness, but each work has proved itself worth waiting for, and *God's Puppets* will be found no exception. It gives us of the best of his creative genius.

THE MACMILLAN COMPANY

Publishers   64-66 Fifth Avenue   New York

RETURN TO ➡ CIRCULATION DEPARTMENT
202 Main Library

0471

LOAN PERIOD 1	2	3
HOME USE		
4	5	6

ALL BOOKS MAY BE RECALLED AFTER 7 DAYS

Renewals and Recharges may be made 4 days prior to the due date.

Books may be Renewed by calling 642-3405.

DUE AS STAMPED BELOW

MAY 25 1989		
MAY 2 6 1989		

FORM NO. DD6

UNIVERSITY OF CALIFORNIA, BERKELEY
BERKELEY, CA 94720

ImTheStory.com

Lightning Source UK Ltd.
Milton Keynes UK
UKOW06f2018131017

310925UK00024B/1918/P

9 781314 450408